Dangerous to Man

Some Other Books by Roger Caras

Antarctica: Land of Frozen Time
The Custer Wolf
Last Chance on Earth
North American Mammals
Sarang
Monarch of Deadman Bay
Source of the Thunder
Panther!
Death as a Way of Life
Venomous Animals of the World
The Private Lives of Animals
Sockeye

ROGER A. CARAS

Dangerous to Man

The Definitive Story of Wildlife's Reputed Dangers

REVISED EDITION

BARRIE & JENKINS
COMMUNICA-EUROPA

ISBN 0 214 20229 1

Printed in the United States of America

*To whom else could an author dedicate a book
entitled* Dangerous to Man, *but to his wife?*

For Jill . . .

Contents

Introduction   1

Part I   The Mammals

  1. The Great Cats   7
  2. Wolves   32
  3. Bears   42
  4. The Leopard Seal and the Walrus   54
  5. The Killer Whale   59
  6. The Elephants   73
  7. Venomous Mammals   86
  8. Other Mammals   91

Part II   The Birds

  9. Birds—Are Any Dangerous?   115

Part III   The Reptiles

 10. Venomous Lizards   123
 11. Giant Snakes   129
 12. Venomous Snakes: The Rattlers   139
 13. Venomous Snakes: The Other Crotalids and   151
     the Old World Vipers
 14. Venomous Snakes: The Sea Snakes, Elapids, and   168
     Poisonous Colubrines

15. Snakes: How Dangerous Are They?   183
16. Crocodilians   195

Part IV   Amphibians and Fish

17. Frogs, Toads, and Salamanders   209
18. Sharks   214
19. Skates and Rays   233
20. Venomous Fish   238
21. Some Other Fish   251

Part V   The Invertebrates

22. Insects   269
23. Spiders and Scorpions   279
24. Venomous Cones   291
25. The Giant Clam   297
26. Octopus and Squid   303
27. Jellyfish   313

Part VI   Epilogue

28. Other Potential Dangers   321

Part VII   Appendixes

Appendix A   Treatment of Injuries Caused by Wild Animals   327
Appendix B   Rabies   333
Appendix C   The Rattlesnakes   338
Appendix D   The Reptile "Hall of Infamy"   344
Appendix E   Snakebite Case Histories   348
Appendix F   Ciguatera—"Fish Poisoning"   355

Bibliography   363

Index   403

Introduction

Work began on the original edition of *Dangerous to Man* shortly after my return from the South Pole—that would have been in early 1962. Conservation wasn't a new idea then, not by any means, for those of us who cared had the words of Hornaday, Muir, Roosevelt, Osborne, and others burned into our conscience. But, who would have guessed? Who could have imagined what we have learned since 1962?

It has exploded like a bomb, with the same stunning effect. The fact is out, there is no denying it, most of the world's wildlife is in grave danger. It is going so fast we can't keep score. Over 1,000 species or subspecies of vertebrate wildlife are in danger at this moment (as is 10 percent of the world's flowering plants). Each year sees more and more wildlife approach extinction while man, for the most part, remains oblivious to what is not only the fate of wild animals but what must eventually be his fate, too.

The fight for wildlife is the fight against ignorance, and although I do not say the subject treated at length in this book is the answer for an end to ignorance, at least it can help interested people better understand what wildlife is all about. Wildlife is not our enemy, although we certainly are foe to it. All of the things some people would like to have us believe wildlife does to us, we do to it. They say it takes our land. It doesn't, we take its land. They say it threatens us. It doesn't, we threaten it. And so it goes, the sins are ours, not the tigers' nor the wolves'.

More often than not, absurd claims made against wildlife are cover-ups or excuses for our own idiotic behavior. A hunter tells you he must kill wolves because they kill his deer and ruin his sport. Then he tells you he must kill deer because there are too many of them and they will starve. When you suggest reintroducing wolves he looks at you as if you were mad and tells you that the wolves would kill his deer and ruin his sport. It is a little like being Alice in a more bizarre Wonderland yet.

We have come to the make-or-break point in the history of animal life on earth. It will survive or perish in wholesale lots entirely depending on our sense and sensitivity during the next quarter-century. After that it may not matter, or we may find a planet on the way back, life knitting together again into natural relationships after a few millennia of insanity. It is one hell of a choice, when you stop to think about it.

Anyway, that was the idea behind the first edition of this book when it was started in 1962; it is still the idea. Truth, that's all, just some of the incredible truth about wildlife, for its sake and our own.

Of course much has been done and much has come to light since 1962, and this is especially true of venomology. Whatever is new has been incorporated, and some more old things have also been included. Ultimately, *Dangerous to Man* is as old and as new as man and animal together.

Much of the research for this book, for both original and present editions, consisted of a search for statistics that simply do not exist. It can take as long to find out that something isn't there as it can to find that it is. And it can take as long to find nonsense, as sense.

No one *knows* how many people have been killed or injured by sharks in any one year, for reasons that should be obvious. The statistics available on snakebite, scorpion sting, and other venomous injuries are largely conjecture on the part of government agencies issuing them. Medical literature has been found to be as much as 200 percent off on some estimates of incidence and mortality. For years medical literature has carried death reports where the identity of the offending organism was totally mistaken (as has been true of death certificates as well).

Out of what has been available, we have given those statistics we felt were revealing, cross-checking whenever possible. Very often such statistics may appear dated; they were included because nothing had been done since they were compiled, or because they were the most reliable ones available. And sometimes guesses—not always very well educated guesses—were offered as statistical corroboration. Generally, we have picked and chosen and tried to avoid the obviously unsupported figures, and selected what seemed honest or at least representative whenever it was published, whatever the period covered.

When the first edition of this book was researched in 1962 and 1963 over two thousand letters were exchanged with field workers, laboratory research personnel, friends, and, very often, strangers. The amount of help that was received cannot be reckoned.

In the intervening years, between approximately 1964 and 1974 when this revision was undertaken, there were five trips to Asia, five African safaris, trips to the Yucatán Peninsula and many hitherto unvisited parts of the United States and Canada—unvisited by the author, that is. Always there were people who helped—people to share, to explain, to show and lead and assist in every way imaginable.

During the actual revision, scores of new people have been contacted, hundreds of new references drawn upon, and once again there is really no way of estimating the help received. Even the briefest check of the bibliography will give some idea of the debt owed.

Some of the people who helped with the first edition are no longer alive: Carl Kauffeld, Christopher Coates, Laurence Klauber, Clifford Pope, J. L. B. Smith, and I am sure others as well.

There is no way of listing all the people whose work, experience, and thinking are represented in these pages. But, to all of them my profound gratitude. In this edition, no less than in the one over a decade ago, they are gratefully acknowledged.

ROGER CARAS
East Hampton, New York
January 1975

Part I The Mammals

1 The Great Cats

There are about forty distinct kinds of wild cats known to inhabit the earth today. They range in size from the mighty Siberian tiger (up to twelve feet in length from nose tip to tail tip) to several little spotted species about the size of the average domestic cat. The cats (Felidae) are the most efficient land predators left on earth. They combine power, speed, "intelligence,"* patience, camouflage, and considerable individual skill, all assets of a true hunter. All swim well, most climb with great agility, and, at least for short bursts, most can move with amazing swiftness. The African lion can reach almost forty miles per hour when it charges.

Most cats are nocturnal and can make nighttime travel on foot within their range a hazardous practice. The surprising thing about cats is that relatively few become man-eaters. There is really no reason why the great cats should not hunt man. The number that have taken to man-eating demonstrates that human flesh is palatable to them. They are better able to take man than their normal fleet prey, and, in many parts of their range, man is in good supply. Fortunately, however, though man-eating is not as rare as is generally believed, most great cats avoid man whenever possible. Man, in fact, is usually the aggressor, for cats have long been major trophies for the hunter. It may very well be that

*Here, "intelligence" is not to be related to or compared with human faculties. The cats' strictly "animal intelligence," compared to that of other animals, *is* very high. In this sense it can be measured as the capacity to make choice as opposed to responding strictly to instinctive patterns. It also refers, of course, to the ability to learn.

the great cats were natural man-eaters before man developed his skill with weapons. The cases of man-eating that occur each year arise from a number of factors, and may provide insight into what may have once been normal behavior.

So distinct are the several kinds of great cats that they warrant individual attention. What is true of one is quite likely not true of the others. The great cats cannot be discussed as a group to any great purpose.

The Leopard (Panthera pardus) is, in the author's opinion, one of the most beautiful of cats. In the opinion of most hunters, it is the most lethal. Small by comparison to other felids—it rarely exceeds 175 pounds—it is, nonetheless, pound for pound, one of the strongest of the big predators. It can negotiate rocky ledges that most other cats would avoid and climbs with great speed and skill. It is capable of forty-foot leaps, and can climb a tree carrying a load twice its own weight. Its gray to gold coat, with its dark spots and rings, varies markedly from place to place, but always provides near-perfect camouflage. Its ability to freeze on the ground, or on a tree limb overhanging a trail, contributes to its success as a hunter, and to the legends of the ghostlike quality that surround its stealth. It is a silent, nocturnal hunter, as "clever" as any animal we know, and as potentially dangerous a man-killer as there is on land.

The names "panther" and "leopard" have caused endless confusion. No matter how often the explanation has been given, writers still confuse the issue in their efforts to differentiate between the two. Quite simply, panther and leopard are interchangeable names for one animal throughout the Old World. In the New World the mountain lion, or puma, is sometimes misleadingly called "panther" or "painter." The leopard is very prone to melanism (i.e., having a black pelt),* especially in some areas, and further mistaken notions about this have arisen. For instance, many people believe the name "panther" is reserved for these specimens; but this is not so. The words "leopard" and "panther" are interchangeable for both the spotted and black forms. The two color phases can be represented in the same litter and can reproduce each other. If you look at a black leopard in slanting sun rays, you will see its spots. Why so many people have fought this demonstrable fact is as confusing as why the leopard or panther so readily tends to melanism. The jaguar of South and Central America is

*This occurs in Asia, but very, very rarely in Africa. Black panthers (leopards) are common on the Malay Peninsula but may not occur on the African continent more than once every fifty to seventy-five years. The Asian and African leopard are the same species.

similarly inclined. In both the jaguar and leopard albinism is very much more rare. Indeed, in the leopard it may hardly ever occur at all.

Leopards are not only skillful hunters, whether stalking monkeys, peacocks, hoofed prey, dogs, or men, but they also tend to be scavengers. It is believed that this characteristic has led to some particularly devastating waves of man-eating in India. Raging epidemics have swept whole districts, leaving the dead numbered in the thousands for the leopard to feast upon. Smallpox and cholera, particularly, have been great scourges. Very often, these brush-fire epidemics have been followed by months of terror as leopards indulged their new taste for human flesh and started killing.

Not all cases of man-eating by leopards result from epidemics. Leopards become excited with little provocation, and it is almost certain that many initial attacks are made when the animal is in this state and not in an attempt to get food. Once a leopard has killed, however, and tastes or smells fresh blood, it is likely to eat unless it is well fed at the time of the incident. Even a medium-sized leopard can carry an adult man off into the bushes, or even up a tree.

The following is the text in full of a clipping from the Madras *Mail* of May 24, 1962:

LEOPARD MENACE
IN BHAGALPUR
350 Persons Killed
in 3 Years

Bhagalpur, May 23: The district authorities of Bhagalpur have launched an all-out drive to rid Banka sub-division of the menace of man-eating leopards which, according to local estimates, have claimed about 350 human lives in the last three years.

The District Magistrate, Mr. Srivatsava, told pressmen on Saturday that 82 persons were officially known to have been killed by leopards since 1959 in Karoria, Belhar, Bankan and Chanda in Banka sub-division. He said the number of victims might be higher.

He said eight batches of shikaris and hundreds of beaters had been deployed in a 20-square-mile area to liquidate the leopards. Provision had been made to use tear gas and also to dynamite caves, which were suspected to be the lairs of the man-eaters. A Deputy Magistrate was camping in the jungles of Banka, supervising the drive.

The late Col. Jim Corbett became world-famous for his one-man war on man-eating tigers and leopards. His book *The Man-Eating Leopard of Rudraprayag* is a treasure store of leopard data and his impressions. According to Corbett, leopards have a poor sense of smell and are the most easily stalked of all jungle animals in India. Once turned man-eater, however, they become wary to an incredible degree, and often require months of hazardous effort to exterminate. For one wave of man-eating, 1918–1926, Corbett lists 125 victims. Only one victim was claimed in the first year, three in the second, and six in the third. But in the sixth year, twenty-six known victims were claimed. Corbett felt that man-eating leopards are rare, but extremely difficult to deal with. Opinions vary as to how often they do occur, and there doesn't seem to be any way to establish what percentage of these cats do take to man-eating. Problems occur because leopards favor dog flesh. They will often enter villages at night to take dogs, and more than one rural villager in Africa and India has stumbled across a leopard in the middle of the night and been badly mauled.

The range of the leopard, although still vast, is but a fraction of what it formerly was. Known once from the British Isles to Japan, south to Indonesia and Ceylon, and through all of Africa, leopards are now restricted; in Africa, to below the Sahara. They are no longer found in Europe proper, although they still occur in the Caucasus, northern Iran, Israel, and along the Himalayas and the Chinese western escarpment to Manchuria. The Indochinese and Malayan regions, and India, still have fair populations. Leopards adapt well, and remain in agricultural, and even industrial, areas long after the other large predators are gone. Their great stealth leads people to believe they are rare or absent when, in fact, they are still present. Their predisposition to man-eating does not appear to be geographically delimited, although reports from India are better known.

The author has tracked and "ambushed" leopards with his cameras in many parts of Africa as well as in Asia, particularly on Ceylon or, as it is known today, Sri Lanka. On every occasion but one he found them to be extremely shy and retiring, and although able once to approach to within twenty-five feet of a leopard on its kill (a peacock, only a few hundred yards from the beach in southern Sri Lanka), there never appeared to be any suggestion of real danger. The one possible near exception was in Mozambique in 1973. While following a leopard, the author and his party found that the animal was lying in deep grass in a position to intercept the interlopers. With only a gruff cough and a snarl as preliminary warnings, the leopard "attacked." He came straight at the author for about twenty yards, then swerved away and vanished into deeper grass. He either changed his mind or was bluffing all along. It was a spectacular few seconds but nothing more. Had the author been a hunter, of course, he would have stopped the "charge" with a bullet. How many such phony charges have been stopped that way can well be imagined.

The breathtakingly beautiful Snow Leopard (Panthera uncia), an

Asian mountain animal, is quite distinct. It is a rare and intriguing animal. The author does not know of cases of man-eating by this animal, but its reaches are so remote that reports would be unlikely at best. The snow leopard, it should be noted in passing, does move down into inhabited valleys and is not restricted to the mountains all year round.

Strangely, the great cat of India, the Tiger (Panthera tigris), almost certainly began its career in the far north, possibly even in the sub-Arctic. Its migrations carried it to the southern tip of Asia and west to the Elburz Mountains of northern Iran where it reportedly still lives. In southern Asia it never reached Sri Lanka. Today, it still ranges from eastern Siberia, through Amuria and Manchuria, Korea, and China to Burma and India, Indochina, Malaya, Sumatra, Java, and Bali, although it is everywhere endangered and nowhere is there anything but a fragment population. It is in Siberia that the great, heavy-coated tigers are found. Like the snow leopard, the Siberian tiger is very handsome and rare. The total wild population is probably under a hundred.

The tiger's ground color varies from bright reddish orange to white. Blue-gray specimens of great rarity are said to be known in parts of China. The black stripes are characteristically different on the two sides of the animal. It is interesting that tigers tend to albinism, leopards and jaguars to melanism, and lions to neither.

Tigers grow to lengths of ten feet or more and can be bigger than the largest lion. They have immense strength. They clutch their prey to them, holding on with their claws, and depend on the crushing bite of their powerful jaws to end the struggle. They swim very well and are seen splashing about in water on very hot days, since they apparently suffer from the heat. When the air is chill, however, they avoid wet or damp vegetation. They can climb, but do not approach the leopard's ability in this. They can negotiate treacherous rocky areas but generally prefer to stay on level ground. They are not as well equipped with senses as one might expect. They apparently depend on their hearing while hunting. Their eyesight is not particularly good, and they seem unable to spot prey until it moves. Their sense of smell is reportedly no better than that of the leopard. They can consume an amazing quantity of food and will stay with a kill for days until it has been consumed. They will eat flesh even when it is very "high." They tend to be nocturnal and generally lie up during the heat of day. Hunting during the daylight hours is not unknown, however.

Tigers are generally thought of as the grand gentlemen of the forest. Indeed, there is a quiet dignity to their retiring habits, and a normal tiger is a sight of beauty rather than a menace. They avoid man as much as possible, and the fact that they still exist at all, after being hunted mercilessly for so long, gives testimony to their adaptability. They can raise absolute havoc with domestic stock once they develop a taste for this easy prey, and every effort is made to chase them out of an area once they are spotted. Hunting them on foot or on elephant back was considered fine sport until quite recently. Great beats, utilizing whole villages, were organized by wealthy sportsmen and the Indian government.

Occasionally, tigers that have been molested will attack an elephant, wild or tame, but they generally give the great beasts a wide berth. It is all but impossible for a tiger to kill a full-grown elephant, but an elephant has no trouble dispatching a tiger once contact is made. If a tiger gets onto an elephant's back, the latter can always roll and bring its greatest weapon, weight, to bear. Many elephant calves, however, are reportedly taken by tigers. Water Buffaloes (Bubalus) have been known to best a tiger in open combat. Generally, though, a large tiger can prevail in most battles into which it willingly enters. Occasionally, motion picture footage crops up of a tiger, or a leopard, having it out with a large python. The contest usually is depicted as ending in a two-sided retreat. Whether such encounters ever really occur in nature is not easy to determine. As recorded, they have all the earmarks of something that was rigged for the camera by Frank Buck.

Tigers live at peace when they are not hunting. They are quiet, solitary animals when well fed, and they are assiduously avoided by most jungle creatures. When one enters an area, birds twitter and the alarm spreads. Wherever the great cat goes, the alarm spreads before it. Finally, the kill is made and all is quiet for days until the tiger is hungry again and starts to move. A great traveler, it may cover twenty miles or more before feeding again. This pattern, or any other, may not hold, however, when the great striped cat turns man-eater.

A man-eating tiger can disrupt dozens and sometimes hundreds of square miles of countryside. The whole normal parade of life changes to adjust unwillingly to the appetite of one cat. Religious festivals are canceled to keep pilgrims from traveling the roads and making camp in forest clearings. Markets are closed, and harvests rot on the vine. Cattle are not taken to pasture, firewood is not collected, and, in the extreme, villages isolated from the main roads are abandoned. Doctors refuse to travel at night to treat the sick and injured, and people who fail to turn up before dusk are not searched for. One single great cat, wandering silently through the forest, can turn whole vast areas into ghost regions. A human being, unless armed and well qualified, is helpless against attack. Tigers, once turned man-eater, become even more wary and alert, and frequently abandon a kill after one meal. The result is more kills than normal. Victims often are taken a dozen or more miles apart, and there is no way of knowing where the next strike will be made. The most highly skilled of hunters can spend months, even years, in tracking down a man-eater. Bridges across wide and fast-flowing rivers are closed in an attempt to restrict the killer's range and permit a concentrated effort. Towers and machans, or tree-platforms, are constructed at strategic spots to permit sentries to guard paths and roadways. Inexplicably, armed men disappear from their stations, and, if they turn up at all, are little more than scattered bones and blood-soaked tatters of cloth when found.

At the height of the terror, the cat takes to raiding villages, ripping open thatched roofs, and clawing down barricaded doors. A cat that has reached the point where it will enter a village and ignore the screams and wailings of the inhabitants, has gone too far, and is usually killed soon after. However, as long as the cat keeps to the forest, it is nearly impossible to destroy. It avoids traps and poisoned bait with almost supernatural cunning. Once hunters think they have discovered a pattern to its behavior, the cat switches and does the unpredictable. If a man-eater happens to be a female with cubs, the situation can be even worse. First, it will require more food to feed itself and its family, and the cubs *may* grow up to be man-eaters themselves. It is not clear whether cubs raised on human flesh become man-killers once they start to hunt on their own. Even Corbett, an authority on man-eating tigers, never was clear on this point. He expounds both points of view in his writings.

Maj. Charles Simpson, of Black Rock Estate in southern India, wrote to the author of an encounter with normal tigers:

On my estate in 1925 I had a virago of a female who was always fighting with her husband. One evening their wordy warfare developed into fisticuffs, and the woman decided to leave her spouse, so she picked up her *cumbly* (a coarse blanket) and walked out into the night. After going a few furlongs, she found it too dark to see the path, so she laid herself down at the side of the path, under the tea bushes, and went to sleep. She was awakened later in the night by a nudge in the ribs, and on opening her eyes, found a pair of tigers sitting in the path looking at her. Petrified with fright, she stayed still, and the male tiger, after putting his paw on her again and sniffing her, walked away, with his mate following him. She stayed until light and then ran back to the quarters to tell her tale. This was so incredible that I went out at once to see if I could find the tracks, and sure enough, there were the plain imprints of two tigers, male and female, on the sandy track, and evidence that one had sat down within two feet of where the woman had lain.

Seven years later, an altogether different account was given of a wounded tiger:

In 1932, a party of four shikaris, armed with muzzle-loaders, sat up over the carcass of a cow killed and partly eaten by a tiger, in the hills at the foot of my estate. The tiger, returning at dusk to the kill, was fired at and badly wounded, but got away. In the morning, the hunters followed its tracks by the blood, and were charged by the tiger. One man was killed outright, one severely clawed, the two others escaped by jumping into a thorn tree, where the tiger could not follow.

In his book on the wildlife of India, G. P. Sanderson gives this account of a man-eater. It is condensed here from ten pages of text.

When I pitched camp at Morlay in September 1873, to commence the elephant kheddahs, the countryside was in a state of alarm from the attacks of a man-eating tigress. This tigress' fits of man-eating seemed to be intermittent, as after killing three or four persons some months before, she had not been heard of till about the time of my arrival, when she killed two boys. On November 30th, news was brought in that a man (about six miles from Morlay) had been carried off. On December 19th another man was carried off five miles from Morlay. The man had been following the cattle home in the evening. The tigress had been in the rocks, and in one bound seized him, dragged him to a small plateau, from which she jumped down into a field, and there killed him. She had then dragged her victim half a mile where we found leg-bones . . . nothing was heard of the tigress for a week. Whilst at dinner, I heard voices approaching my tent . . . the people were from a village a mile and a half away, and had come to tell me that their cattle had galloped back in confusion into the village at dusk, without their herdsman. At dawn we started on the back-trail . . . we found the man's remains; only the soles of his feet, the palms of his hands, his head and a few bones were left. We lost no time in taking up the tigress' track . . . she had recrossed the river and gone into the jungles where there was no chance of finding her. About a week after this the priest of a temple ten miles due west was jogging along on his bullock . . . tigress with her cub stepped into the path . . . seized the poojaree, and carried him off to a deep ravine. The next death was of a horrible description . . . several villagers were grazing their cattle in a swampy hollow when the tigress pounced upon one man. She missed her aim at his throat, seized the shoulder, and then, either in jerking him, or by a blow, threw him onto a thicket several feet from the ground. Here the wounded wretch was caught by thorny creepers; whilst the tigress, as generally happens when a contretemps takes place, relinquished the attack. Next morning the lacerated wretch was found. In his mangled state he had been unable to release himself; he was moaning and hanging almost head downwards amongst the creepers; and died soon after he was taken down. Shortly after this, work took me to Goondulpet and I returned on the 14th January 1874 . . . a woman had been carried off by the man-eater out of the village during the night. There was no jungle to cover the man-eater's advance. The attack had been most daring. At one end of the street stood a shady tree, round the base of which a raised terrace of stones and earth had been built . . . the tigress had crouched upon this terrace, from which she commanded a view of the street. The old woman had been going to her daughter's, and as she crossed the street the tigress seized and carried her off. The poor old creature was not missed till morning. The villagers concluded that they would now not be safe in their houses at night, and some of the out-lying hamlets would have been temporarily abandoned had the tigress lived much longer. But this was to be her last victim. Next day I determined upon a plan of hunting her. I arranged that Bommay Gouda and three trackers should go to one end of her usual range, whilst I remained at Morlay . . . one of them came running back to say that the party had met the tigress . . . she was then in a small hill two miles from camp. They were going across open fields and presently discovered a tiger on the far side partly hidden by a bullock which it was half dragging, half carrying towards the hill. They immediately ran shouting towards her, obliging her to drop the bullock. I need here hardly say, except for those who have had no experience of man-eating tigers, that they never refuse a bullock or other prey, if such offers, and that when opposed by man they give way at once. Their tactics in attacking man may be described in one word— surprise; and if discovered in their attempt they generally abandon it. The most confirmed man-eaters never lose the fear with which all animals regard human beings, and unless they can catch an unwary cow-herd or wood-cutter in their own fashion they are not to be dreaded. When the tables are turned they flee as readily as other tigers . . . a peahen which had been hidden amongst boulders on the hillside rose with a startling cla-mour and there we saw the man-eater, a handsome but small tigress. I fired at her shoulder, broadside on, with my express. On examining her we found that she was in milk . . . she was in the prime of life and condition, and had no apparent injury to account for her man-killing. I may here say that we never killed her cub. It was heard calling to its mother for several nights but we could not find it and it must have died of starvation.

The most complete and best-known accounts of man-eating tigers occur in the writings of Jim Corbett. *Man-Eaters of Kumaon* and *The Temple Tiger and More Man-Eaters of Kumaon* have certainly been the most widely read books on the subject. There would be little point in recapitulating Corbett's accounts here since they are most revealing in their entirety. Corbett agreed with most serious writers, and pointed out that most man-eating cases could be blamed on old age or injuries. Unlike lions who can turn to man-eating without understandable cause, tigers seldom do so unless forced into it. Tigers that are injured while killing porcupines, and end up crippled by quills and festering sores, have often become man-eaters because they are no longer capable of taking swifter prey. Hunters who wound a tiger and fail to follow it up may condemn a number of fellow humans to terrible deaths. Most of the man-eaters Corbett hunted—the Champawat, Chowgarh, Mahan Kanda, Pipal Pani, Thak, Temple, Muktesar, Panar, Chuka, and Talla Des tigers—were found to be partially incapacitated when finally destroyed. Corbett had great affection for the lordly tiger, but knew full well the chaos that ensues when an area becomes terrorized by an aberrant individual.

(During the period when the preceding paragraphs were written, a man-eating tiger was terrorizing several native villages in Sumatra. At the last count, seventeen victims had been claimed. Subsequently, the author visited Bangladesh where a man-eater was rampant in the Sunderbans, a group of swampy islands in the north of the Bay of Bengal. The Sunderbans have been more troubled by man-eating tigers, it is said, than any other area on earth.)

The Lion (*Panthera leo*) once ranged through all of Africa save the heavily forested and greatly elevated regions. In early historic times it inhabited Eastern Europe to Romania, and, quite probably, Italy, and ranged thence east through Turkey and the Caucasus to central India. All of the Near East was included in its range except Arabia. Today, a few apparently still occur north of the Sahara, reportedly in Morocco, and a small population enjoys a measure of protection in the Gir forest in the Gujarat region of India.

Popular literature frequently characterizes the lion as a creature of the jungle. Nothing could be further from the truth. It is an animal of the open bush and savannah, the great grass plains that cover so much of Africa. You are more apt to find one in a desert than a forest.

The lion is not the largest of the cats. That honor belongs to the Siberian tiger, which exceeds it in both length and weight. Second though it may be, it is still a large animal. It can approach eleven feet in length, measuring tip-to-tip, and forty-two inches or more in height at the shoulder. Four hundred pounds is a good figure for a large specimen, and some few exceed it.

Lions are anatomically very close to tigers. With their skins off, the two animals are all but indistinguishable to anyone but an expert. The two cats can readily interbreed, giving "Ligers" and "Tiglons," the former when a lion is the father, the latter when the tiger is sire. Not only do numerous subspecies of lions (*kamptzi, nyanzae, vernayi, goojratensis,* etc.) differ in appearance, but even closely related individuals show marked variations, so that the creation of subspecific designations is thought by many specialists to be a most dubious practice. In males, manes may be extremely luxurious (although seldom so in areas where thorny brush is found) or totally absent. Colors range from golden-fawn and silver-blond, through the entire spectrum of brown tones, to almost, but never true, black. Faces vary tremendously and individuals can be as readily distinguished by observers as can people. Game rangers come to know individuals and assign them pet names. They can pick them out of a pride as readily as the city dweller can identify his own bank clerk as he passes him on the street. They differ as much in disposition as they do in appearance. It is not only in children's books that we can find "lazy" lions, "happy" lions, "timid" lions, and "brave" ones. The author is not fond of attaching human emotions to animals, but however lion emotions can be characterized, the gamut is run. One lion will stroll down a well-trafficked street on the outskirts of Nairobi, indifferent to screaming mothers and honking car horns, while another will become panicked by a sheet on a clothesline. Some individuals will go placidly through life showing real animation only when really pressed by outside influences or internal stirrings, while others will fly off into regular tantrums at the least of causes.

When lions hunt in pairs, or groups as they usually do, cooperative effort is used. One or more approach a herd of hoofed animals in full view. The herd is panicked into an ambush of one or more females who have been stealthily circling the herd from behind as it focused its collective attention on the visible cats. It is a device that has been used by lions since time immemorial, but their hoofed prey has never learned how to avoid the trap. Once the herd is within striking distance, it is over very quickly, or the cats go hungry, for, when it comes to a chase, the lion must inevitably lose out because it can't match the speed of its swift and agile prey. If the lion once makes contact, however, a shattering blow is delivered with a forepaw, teeth seek the neck, and one bite usually brings the animal to ground for a few convulsive kicks. Occasionally, a lion will fail to land on the back of its prey, or won't get into position to strike a lethal blow, and will sink its claws into flanks or body and claw the prey down with its weight. Since lions hunt in the open, the whole hunting and killing procedure has been observed innumerable times. Rarely do lions hunt in dense cover, and dropping from a tree onto prey, characteristic behavior of the leopards, is unknown. Almost all killing is done by the female. The lion roars, the lioness kills. Dusk, dawn, and night are the usual hunting hours.

Lions, like many wild animals, have little stamina. Their speed is astounding for short distances, but one lightninglike rush is all they are capable of, however, and open-field running is not attempted.

Ivan Sanderson, in his *Living Mammals of the World*, says of lions:

They never molest men unless suddenly startled, bullied, wounded, or driven to regular man-killing by disease, excessive hunger, or a strange contagious delinquency that sometimes affects whole lion populations and notably the unmated juveniles. Senile individuals usually subsist on ... rodents ... and other little things rather than plump native women and children.

Most observers are in general agreement with Sanderson on this. Lions do not regularly become man-eaters, but confirmed man-eaters do crop up more often than is generally realized. Young, healthy animals, perfectly capable of taking normal fleet-footed prey, are often the culprits. This is the unexplained juvenile delinquency referred to, but why it approaches epidemic proportions at times is not known. Explanations are always available, but none hold up. Males and females are both guilty. Young and old, healthy and sick cats have been involved. Incidents have occurred in areas where game was scarce and where it was plentiful. There is no pattern to it. Quite simply, it is a kind of "disease" which may be contained within one animal, or spread to others. The author does not propose that disease indicates a bacterial infection, but rather a behavioral aberration for which there is no known prophylactic, and for which death is the only known cure.

C. A. W. Guggisberg has long studied the lion in his habitat. His book, Simba, contains valuable data and photographs. Included also is some important research on man-eaters. He gives the case history of "Chiengi Charlie" as one example:

Place: Chiengi, Northern Rhodesia.
Time: January, 1909.
Case: 1 woman taken from village at sunset.
1 woman taken from nearby village shortly thereafter, again at dusk.
1 man killed a week later and eaten while his wife watched helplessly from a nearby tree to which she had escaped.
2 women killed in front of their hut—one eaten.
1 man killed while working in his field.
The lion then moved off to start a reign of terror among the villages in the nearby hills.
1 boy, part of the retinue of the Chiengi medical officer, James Dunbar–Brunton, was killed and eaten on the night of February 17th.
1 kitchen boy taken in Chiengi itself.
Twice thereafter the large light-colored lion attempted to claw down the walls of native huts, but was driven off, once by a fire-brand, and once by being speared in the neck.
Then "Chiengi Charlie" joined forces with two other lions, and night after night they raided villages, while the list of victims mounted.
Finally, gun traps succeeded in ending the career of "Chiengi Charlie" and one of his cronies. Charlie turned out to be an old, very large male.

A young leopard in a South African game reserve. These cats are fast and smart and can never be underestimated, though they are generally shy and vanish at the first sight or sound of man. They are both nocturnal and diurnal, and will hunt or take carrion.
Courtesy South African Tourist Corp.

The leopard that (almost) wasn't: the extremely rare Sinai or Palestinian race that has managed to survive for thousands of years along the Israeli side of the Dead Sea. This photograph was made at night after a six-year watch by Israel's Nature Reserve Authority. It was taken at or near the oasis of Ein Gedi, less than twenty-five miles from the caves where the Dead Sea Scrolls were discovered.
Courtesy Holy Land Conservation Fund

The Bengal tiger, one of the most powerful of all land predators. These cats are solitary and require a large private hunting block in order to survive. There will probably be none left in the wild by the turn of the century—habitat destruction and sport hunting will have caused their final decline and disappearance from Asia.
Courtesy U.S. National Zoological Park

Left: The benign face of the king who isn't. The male is an indolent beast that sleeps as much as twenty hours a day. He is seldom up except to eat or mate. Although the ultimate in male chauvinism, he can hunt and kill as effectively as the female—he just chooses not to most of the time.
Courtesy South African Tourist Corp.

Right: The female lion and her killing equipment. It is these fangs that reach the spine of the prey or clamp its throat shut to suffocate it. This is not a threat "face," just a yawn.
Courtesy South African Tourist Corp.

Guggisberg comments:

The case of "Chiengi Charlie" cannot actually be considered as very exceptional, for man-eating lions turn up more often than is sometimes assumed. It also cannot be said that man-eating is restricted to a few isolated areas, for in the course of a careful study of the subject I have come across records from practically all parts of the lion's African range of distribution. . . .

Certainly the most famous man-eating lions of all were those of Tsavo. The reports of their depredations reached the floor of the British Parliament. They brought the building of a railroad to a halt for three weeks and the price in human terror and suffering cannot be calculated. The story was reported in full by Lt.-Col. J. H. Patterson, an engineer assigned to the construction of the bridge over the Tsavo River, who brought the career of the Tsavo man-eaters to an end by his skill and persistence, and not without considerable personal danger.

The Tsavo is a river about eighty miles long in southeastern Kenya. It flows from Mt. Kilimanjaro into the Sabaki River, a turbid run of 120 miles eastward into the Indian Ocean. The surrounding land rolls away to the horizon in unspectacular undulations of grassy expanse and scrub thorn, except for some hills near Voi. Some trees dot the seemingly endless plains, and rock outcroppings are relatively rare. Real lushness is reserved for the riverbanks and a few swampy lowlands. Game is plentiful during some seasons and relatively rare in others. Periods of flood alternate with arid months. It is lion country: the rolling savannah and scrub thorn combination is perfect hunting country for an open-plains cat.

In 1898 two things happened along the reaches of the Tsavo, one quite understandable, and the other without explanation to this day. The understandable change was the appearance of a railroad destined to run from Uganda in the northwest to the Indian Ocean. The unexplained part of it concerned two male lions who went on a rampage of slaughter which wasn't ended until twenty-eight Indians who had been imported to construct the line, and unknown dozens of African natives, had been killed, and most of them eaten. One European was injured. Often groups of laborers huddled together whimpering while they listened to the two cats fighting over and eating friends and relatives. The victims were not always killed outright, and their calls for help left the laborers half-mad with fright. Some nights, two victims would be taken. When Patterson finally killed the two man-eaters, he found them to be virtually maneless males of large size. Neither was incapacitated, and both were perfectly normal in all aspects save this behavior.

Patterson's account of the episode is quite naturally full of shredded flesh, bodiless heads with wide staring eyes, and all of the other gore found when the subject of man-eating cats is discussed.

After the two Tsavo man-eaters were killed, other cats took up the habit. Three months after the second Tsavo killer fell to Patterson's persistence, an engineer named O'Hara was killed. His wife and child were witnesses. That was March 1899. In June 1900 another man-eater appeared and hunted men with reckless abandon. It was eventually caught in a box trap, put on display, and later shot. None of the subsequent man-eaters who made life a living nightmare along the Uganda rail line came close to the original two in the extent of their depredations. Collectively, this episode at the turn of the century was one of the worst in history. Word of it spread around the world, it was thoroughly documented by reliable witnesses, and dozens of photographs are extant to prove quite conclusively what can happen when nature's great predators go on a rampage.

What happened at the Tsavo construction sites and subsequently in the surrounding territory has no known explanation. The cats involved were acting in an abnormal manner. For reasons completely unknown, they turned away from normal prey and took to human flesh. Unfortunately, there is no way of knowing when and where it will happen again. We know it has happened dozens of times since then; in Mgori, Tanganyika (now Tanzania) in 1958, in northern Tanganyika in July 1960, and periodically since then in a variety of locales. A wave of man-eating occurred in Ankole in the late 1930s; in southern Tanganyika in 1953; twenty-three known human victims were taken in Mahenge District in 1923–1924. Portuguese holdings in East Africa have been plagued with killers from time to time. Accounts exist by the score.

It is difficult to reconcile these stories with personal observations. The author has photographed lions in numerous parts of Africa on dozens of occasions and never once saw anything even resembling aggressive behavior. Following individual males and prides numbering as many as twenty-eight individuals (on the Serengeti) has failed to turn up a single cat that could be characterized as anything but *sleepy* most of the time and briefly animated only when mating or hunting perfectly normal lion prey. Yet, the records prove, some lions do go berserk or crazy, or into whatever mode properly identifies a man-eater who has become that by apparent *choice*. Man-eaters are, however, in a tiny minority.

Least catlike of all cats is the Cheetah (*Acinonyx jubatus*). With its nonretractable claws, a unique feature among the cats, and long straight legs, the hunting leopard, as it is sometimes called, is a very doggy feline. Once common to much of Africa below the Sahara outside the forests, as well as to some parts of India, it ranged through Syria, Mesopotamia, Persia, and the Caspian lowlands, but its distribution has been slowly contracting. (It apparently became extinct in India in 1952.)

There can be little question that the cheetah is far and away the fastest four-legged creature on earth. It has been clocked at speeds of almost seventy miles per hour, and claims have been made that it can go faster still. It is this remarkable speed that makes the cheetah the successful hunter it is, and restricts it to open savannahs. Such speeds would hardly be useful in wooded country.

Often seen in pairs, cheetahs are shy and inoffensive. They seldom bother domestic stock, and are nowhere as common as lions. Their prey consists of hoofed plains animals and they tend to take smaller species than does the lion.

For all its flash and speed, this handsome animal is not dangerous to man except under the most unusual and accidental circumstances. Unprovoked attacks on man are, as far as can be discerned, unknown. Even provoked attacks have been extremely rare and seldom, if ever, fatal.

The author has been fortunate enough to encounter cheetah on a couple of dozen occasions at least. So oblivious are they to a man in a Land Rover (or any vehicle) that on one occasion when the party was watching a mother cheetah teach her cubs how to stalk a gazelle the cats used the vehicle as a blind. They actually brushed against the side of the Rover while slipping into position by the front wheel to launch the attack. It would have been quite possible to reach out and pat the animals. Cheetahs simply are not aggressive except when they are hungry and then only to natural prey. In the Serengeti the author watched two cheetahs play with a young Thompson's gazelle the way a housecat might with a mouse. They released the Tommie unharmed and it promptly bounced over to its mother and began to nurse. Unfortunately, cheetah young are preyed upon by lion, leopard, and hyaena.

The one great cat of the Western Hemisphere is the Jaguar (*Panthera onca*), very often referred to in Latin America as *el Tigre*. This cat is truly one of the largest in the world, surpassed in size only by the African and Indian lions and the tigers. It is among the best of the tree-climbers, approaching even the leopard, but is not limited in its range to forested areas. Generally thought of as a jungle animal, it actually ranges from the desert and semidesert areas of the southwestern United States, where it is very rare, through the tropical rain forests of Central and South America to the open grasslands of lower Patagonia. It is an

A cheetah in Kruger National Park, Republic of South Africa. Attacks on man by this species are not known to have occurred. This cat is disappearing over most of its former range, and countries like South Africa are fighting to save those that remain. *Courtesy South African Tourist Corp.*

A magnificent jaguar in Venezuela. These cats, largest in the New World, range through South and Central America and occasionally even reach the American Southwest. They are large, powerful, and fearless, but reports of attacks on man are highly questionable in nearly all cases.

active, tenacious, aggressive, and beautiful creature of stocky build. It is easily distinguished from the leopard, with which it can come in contact only in captivity, by a series of spots enclosed in rings against a variety of ground colors, just as in the tiger and leopard. Albinism is known, and melanism is apparently fairly common in some areas, particularly in northern South America.

The jaguar swims exceedingly well and readily takes to water. It is essentially nocturnal in hunting habits. A big male can weigh 250 pounds. Its powerful, square chest and heavy hind legs make it a powerful jumper.

Of course, the jaguar is accused of attacks on man, although waves of man-eating are not reported as they are in India and Africa. It is said to follow hunters, perhaps out of curiosity, and to ambush natives. There is nothing to distinguish this cat's behavior in this regard from that of the leopard, according to most reports, except that it tends to hold its ground with more conviction, at least at times. It does tend to melt away when approached, but appears to be quick to resent intrusion, and to be rather easy to arouse. Like any of the big cats, it can be extremely dangerous if wounded, cornered, come upon when it is with young or when breeding. It has the advantage of living in extremely dense cover over much of its range. When it does ambush a man it has everything in its favor. Its camouflage is near perfect, and it has that great feline advantage—patience. Many people who have spent their lifetimes within the range of this powerful predator have never seen one outside of a zoo. The jaguar subsists on mammals, up to the tapir in size, birds, and fish.

Two characteristics of its behavior do occasionally lead to problems. First, although something of a wanderer, the jaguar establishes a range. Intruders in this area are challenged, and meetings between males frequently end in battle. Whether this hostility is transferred to humans who inadvertently blunder into a jaguar's hunting range is not clear, but it could explain the many reports of hunters, prospectors, and others whose interests have carried them into the jungles of South and Central America, who tell of being followed, or "tracked," for miles, then suddenly abandoned. In fact, the jaguar might have been "seeing them out." Tracking, in the usual sense, is not the case since the jaguar's sense of smell is probably no better than that of the other big cats. More likely, the cat follows the sounds of the intruders.

A second kind of problem can arise when jaguars take to raiding domestic stock. They can evidently become as possessive over a herd of cattle as they can over wildlife in a more natural hunting range. Laborers working near cattle herds that have been under attack have been mauled by jaguars lying up between kills. Although the literature on this cat is nowhere nearly as extensive or comprehensive as that on the other great cats, it does seem to indicate more man-killing than man-eating. More people appear to be mauled and killed from anger than are killed for food. This is not to say, however, that a hungry jaguar would not take advantage of a human kill, or indeed would not kill a man for food on occasion. Both apparently have occurred, though rarely.

There is no evidence that the jaguar is any more of a threat to man than any other great cat. Indeed, most reports of human deaths and injuries which the author has encountered involved wounded animals doubling back and attacking their attackers.

Few cats have been more falsely accused of being dangerous to man than the mountain lion or puma; known also as the cougar, panther, and even the catamount. Originally it ranged from southern forested Canada, the United States, and all Central and South America to the island of Tierra del Fuego, and, what is more, in both forests *and* open country. Today, extinct throughout most of its eastern range, it still extends through more degrees of latitude than any other wild feline on earth. It can be found above the tree line on mountain crags, below sea level in deserts, in tropical jungles, and on forested hillsides in temperate zones. Its adaptability is truly amazing. It is beyond doubt the most adaptable cat left in the wild state. It still occurs in the Okefenokee Swamp of Georgia, in Florida, and possibly in eastern Canada. There are annual reports from New Jersey and all down the Appalachians, but these are as yet unsubstantiated. It is barely possible, however, that this extraordinary animal may in fact be making a comeback in the East.

Known properly as *Felis concolor*, the Mountain Lion in the United States today is concentrated in the Rocky Mountain states and southward through the desert mountain ranges of Arizona, Texas, and New Mexico. The coastal ranges of California, Oregon, and Washington have a population. A specimen in the red-color phase, weighing an estimated 100 pounds, was taken in Somerset County, Maine, in January 1935 or 1936. A specimen was shot in Kent County, New Brunswick, in 1931. The last sighting from Vermont that has been substantiated occurred in 1881. The whole matter of where the mountain lion has survived man is a controversial one. The claims and counterclaims are difficult to sort out and evaluate. Quite simply, the mountain lion may possibly still survive in some areas no longer thought of as part of its range.

The amount of damage done by the mountain lion is a matter of much discussion. Those who fight for its preservation say it is a natural control on deer, and does little damage to domestic stock. Circular No.

6 of the U.S. Fish and Wildlife Service, *Mountain Lion Trapping*, on the other hand, reports:

> Stockmen suffer heavy losses through its depredations, for when game is scarce the mountain lion attacks young domestic stock, particularly colts, lambs, and kids, and even full-grown horses and cattle. It is practically impossible to raise young colts or sheep on open stock ranges in the rough, rocky, and broken country that forms an ideal habitat for the mountain lion.*

There can be little doubt that the second point of view, however foolish, has prevailed. This 100- to 200-pound cat has been hunted as vermin since white men first arrived. Once found on Manhattan Island, it is a tribute to the great cat's tenacity that it has survived anywhere. For over 300 years it has been classed as an outlaw, fair game for one and all to shoot, trap, poison, and otherwise destroy by any and all means. It would be sad indeed to see this great, beautiful cat finally driven to extinction. It is unique to our hemisphere, and deserves protection.

Early in the 1800s, a tribe of Sioux Indians living near what is now Cannon Ball, North Dakota, sent a young boy out to some buttes west of their camp to fast and go through a series of initiation tests. On the third night, some of the young men who were watching for his return heard cries. In the morning, they found his bones and blood-stained clothing, and the unmistakable pug marks of a large mountain lion. This story is still vividly alive in their oral history. To the people, and their number is legion, who insist that the puma is harmless this story is pure Indian hokum. But is it? Probably not. It is not the kind of story the Sioux would create and maintain. It contains no heroics, no vanquishing of a seemingly insurmountable foe, or any other ingredients the Indian might wish to insert and preserve to bolster up a sagging tribal image. Yet, its very preservation indicates that even to the Indians it was an unusual and memorable event, indicating that it must be an exception.

There is no doubt that the mountain lion prefers to avoid man. All cats do, even lions, tigers, and leopards. But, as we have seen with the big cats of Africa and India, this doesn't make a cat harmless. A cat will avoid trouble (and man usually means trouble for a big cat outside of protected areas), and it will hide, run, or do anything to avoid contact—*usually!* When a cat has young, when a cat is cornered or wounded, or is prone to aberrant behavior for any reason, it can be

*This is, in fact, grossly overstated; the stock killer is the exceptional animal.

extremely dangerous. The mountain lion can be described as an animal constantly and assiduously avoiding man, but it cannot be described as harmless.

In 1924 a thirteen-year-old boy in the state of Washington was sent on an errand to a neighboring ranch. He was waylaid, killed, and partially eaten by a mountain lion. This incident is reported by O. Earle Frye and Bill and Les Piper in a 1952 paper entitled "The Disappearing Panther." American big-game hunter, guide, and author Elmer Keith also refers to the same incident in his *Big Game Hunting.* Keith also reports that a twenty-one-year-old man in Colorado, a schoolmarm in Washington, and a boy in Oregon were killed by these cats. He refers to them as the only four authentic cases he personally knows of. Two of the four victims were eaten.

Theodore Roosevelt had a friend who was badly mauled in 1890 when a mountain lion sprang from a ten-foot-high sandstone ledge, bowling him out of the saddle. Another friend of Roosevelt's, Ed Smith, was charged by a wounded puma, but survived. General Hampton told Roosevelt that a laborer near his Mississippi plantation was waylaid by a mountain lion in a swamp and killed. These cases are reported by Roosevelt in his book *The Wilderness Hunter.* Roosevelt, like most experienced hunters, considered these cases to be exceptional, but does point out, " . . . it is foolish to deny that in exceptional instances attacks may occur. Cougars vary wonderfully in size and no less in temper. Indeed I think that by nature they are as ferocious and bloodthirsty as they are cowardly."

Bruce Wright, in his *Wildlife Sketches—Near and Far,* remarks that probably more people have been killed or injured by pet deer than by wild pumas. Nevertheless, in the January–March 1953 issue of *The Canadian Field–Naturalist,* Mr. Wright reports on three attacks in New Brunswick, where the cat, referred to locally as panther, apparently still exists in very small numbers. One took place in 1841, the second in June 1948, and one on November 22, 1951. In the second of the three cases, a resident of Kingsclear, New Brunswick, was lying flat on his face drinking from a stream "when an animal jumped on his back." The victims in all three cases survived. Wright observes, "It appears that truculent specimens are not unknown, so that the animal should be approached with caution. The great majority, however, are timid in the extreme. . . ."

W. A. Perry, in *The Big Game of North America,* reports that the six-year-old son of Mr. Farnham of Olympia, Washington, was seized in 1886. His twelve-year-old brother attacked the cat with his hands and a bottle he was carrying, and beat it off. Both children were badly scratched. In the 1880s, a Swedish sailor named Joseph Jorgenson jumped ship at Esquimalt, British Columbia, and went to work on the ranch run by Perry's father. He was attacked, bitten, and clawed by a mountain lion before he finally killed the cat with a shovel. A Miss Mary Campbell of York, British Columbia (later Mrs. John Kelly of Sumas, Washington) was attacked in 1884 but was saved by her father's dogs, Perry reports. Mr. Charles Harmon of Mt. Vernon, Washington; Mr. Cathcart of Snohomish, Washington; Mr. John Potter of Brownsville, British Columbia; the Hon. Orange Jacobs of Washington; and Mr. John Davis of the same state, were all reportedly attacked.

The following article was released by the Associated Press in March 1962:

FIGHTS COUGAR
TO SAVE BOY

HINTON, ALTA. (AP)—Mrs. Elsie McEvoy, a Hinton housewife, grabbed a cougar by the ears and pulled it off a 6-year-old boy Friday.

Brian Kilbreath was in serious condition in a hospital yesterday following the attack.

Brian was playing 200 yards from his home when the cougar jumped him. Mrs. McEvoy raced to the scene, picking up a stick on the way, but could not beat the animal off.

"I did the only thing I could," Mrs. McEvoy said. "I grabbed the cougar by its ears and tore it from the frightened boy." The cougar retreated, but the boy had suffered claw marks on the face and a severe scratch to one eye.

Such a report is inconclusive, however, since it is never stated if the animal was wild, a pet, or a captive specimen, the age and condition of the animal, namely, cub versus adult, and if any other factors were involved. Subsequently Bruce Wright informed the author that it was a half-grown cub in very poor condition, weighing little more than thirty pounds. It had evidently been abandoned by its mother and was starving, frightened, and quite apt to act in an atypical manner.

If it would appear in our discussion so far that we are displaying the mountain lion as an inveterate man-eater, such is not the case at all. We are trying to achieve a balance. Bravado is foolish and dangerous. The mountain lion is a large predatory animal equipped, as are all cats of this size, to kill fast, strong prey. It moves swiftly from ambush and kills with great efficiency. Such an animal is not to be toyed with. It apparently attacks man only on very rare occasions. When it does so it can be considered as acting in an abnormal manner.

It has been suggested by a number of observers that mountain lions suffering from rabies may attack men. As far as we know, all mammals can get the disease, and if the ailment can turn a pet Pekingese into a ferocious beast, it could certainly cause the normally retiring puma to act as badly. In the early 1960s, a female puma attacked two boys near Morgan Hill, California. A young woman came to their rescue and was badly torn. Seven weeks later the woman and one of the boys developed rabies and died. Certainly, rabies could supply a logical explanation why this particular species occasionally attacks the one creature that it almost always tries to avoid.

We have now covered the true big cats that can be even *potentially* dangerous to man. Undoubtedly, lesser cats have been involved in attacks, but they are exceptional. The little-known Clouded Leopard *(Profelis nebulosa)*, generally an arboreal beast, ranges from the Himalayas to Borneo and Java. It is a shy animal and has rarely, if ever, figured in accounts of man-killing. The other cats, the golden cats, the various Asian leopard cats, and numerous other desert, plains, and jungle cats, and all of the genus *Felis,* could be "bad news" if cornered in a cave or chicken coop, but any injury would be accidental.

A number of lynxes and bobcats have bad reputations for "viciousness" (never really an appropriate word when applied to animals). In the United States and Canada, the bobcat has been accused of causing considerable damage to livestock, by way of justifying the efforts being made to exterminate it. Circular No. 1 of the Bureau of Sport Fisheries and Wildlife entitled *Hints on Bobcat Trapping* reports that one cat has been known to kill as many as thirty-eight lambs in one night, although it couldn't have consumed more than one. Other cats have been known to go on an orgy of killing, but it is atypical of most species. Although these cats may be expensive and troublesome to man, they cannot be considered dangerous except accidentally, on rare occasions. The European Wildcat *(Felis sylvestris)* fits into this general category.

This abbreviated discussion of the cats has taken us from Siberia to South Africa, and from Canada to Argentina. We have talked of cats living on snow and ice, in desert wastes, on open savannahs, on rocky slopes, and in steaming jungles and swamps. All of these cats have much in common: they are clever, powerful, beautiful, and unpredictable. Among almost all species of big cats there seem to appear a number of abnormal individuals who seek man as food. They are exceptions to the rule, but, at least among some species, not so very rare as to be surprising. The fact that all of the big cats—except the African lion and the New World mountain lion—have been sought for their beautiful fur, and that all big cats have been adjudged fine sporting game, has kept man in close touch with them. Man's pursuits in animal husbandry have brought the big cats to his doorstep. Despite all of this, man can generally live pretty much in peace with these animals, and there is rarely justification for the degree to which their kind is hounded with firearms, traps, explosives, and poisons. Unfortunately, those individuals who turn bad have, in a sense, justified in many people's minds the treatment accorded the whole. The number of these cats must steadily diminish in the coming years with the decrease in game. Unless more reserves are set aside where the natural prey of these cats can flourish, and unless the ill-considered attempts at artificial predator control are reevaluated, even the most durable species will eventually vanish. Man may not be a good enough hunter to track down and shoot every great cat in the world, but he is an efficient enough butcher to starve their kind out of existence. It will be a much poorer planet when they are gone.

2 Wolves

"The eyes have a peculiarly sinister expression. . . . They are destructive brutes, and kill large numbers of sheep, goats and children. . . .
They are generally cowardly beasts, but they not infrequently take to
killing human beings. . . ." So wrote Brig. Gen. Alexander A. A. Kinloch
of the British Indian Army about the wolf of India, in 1892.

In 1958 Lois Crisler wrote, "The wolf's clear, intelligent eyes
brushed mine." And then, "The wolf is gentle-hearted. Not noble, not
cowardly, just nonfighting."

Both Mrs. Crisler and General Kinloch had kept wolves as pets, and
one must wonder at this strange diversity of opinion. Indeed, as we
survey large segments of the animal kingdom in this book, we will find
that while some animals are misunderstood, others little understood,
and yet others confusing, the wolf hides behind a smokescreen of
human invective, legend, symbolism and nonsense. The classic villain
of so much of the world's literature stands as one of the great enigmas
of the animal world.

The taxonomy (or classification) of Wolves (*Canis lupus*) is an
involved subject. They belong to the genus *Canis*, in which we also
place all domestic dogs.* Among their relatives are the jackals and the
foxes. There are those who consider the so-called Red Wolf of the lower

---

*The so-called Cape or African Hunting Dog *(Lycaon)* is not closely related. The Wild
Dog, or Dhole, of Southeast Asia, genus *Cuon*, is quite a different animal and belongs to
another subfamily.

Mississippi valley a distinct species and bestow upon it the name *Canis niger,* which, of course, means "black dog." The wolf, per se, once ranged all over North America, Africa north of the Sahara, and the whole of Eurasia apart from peninsular India (the domain of the Indian wolf) and the forested southeast of Indochina and the East Indies.

To establish a few significant points before discussing its behavior toward man, the wolf is a carnivore that will take what it can get, mouse to moose, quite literally. It hunts in large packs, small family units, or even alone. It is an intelligent animal and its brain is reportedly larger than that of a domestic dog of comparable size. Observers who have known the animal well speak of an extraordinary variety of facial expressions and a remarkable "language," or, at least, a capacity for vocal communication that ranges from a low and apparently affectionate whimper to the very familiar, but singularly variable, howl. More than one dedicated enthusiast has reported on his own ability to learn this language along with certain posturings, and thus be able to communicate directly with the animal in mutually understandable terms. This is, in fact, quite true to some degree, as the author can attest from firsthand experience.

The wolf becomes of special concern to man in two areas, the safety of his domestic herds and flocks, and his own personal safety. They are quite distinct considerations, though they are generally run together in popular writings of the past. Addressing himself to the secretary of the interior in 1914, the acting superintendent of Yellowstone Park wrote, "They are very destructive to game, and efforts will be made to kill them." In 1915 he reported, "Gray wolves are increasing, and have become a decided menace . . . several were killed last winter in the park." From October 6, 1915 to June 30, 1916, two special rangers were added to the regular staff on advice of the U.S. Biological Survey for the purpose of exterminating carnivorous animals in the park. The two men succeeded in killing twelve wolves, bringing the total for the year in Yellowstone to thirty-six. The story is much the same in other parks and livestock areas. The world over the wolf is an outlaw and is hunted with hounds, guns, traps, and poison. The U.S. Government Printing Office will sell you a handbook on coyote and wolf trapping. The booklet notes their acute sense of smell, alert hearing, and keen eyesight.

Still found in very small numbers in Michigan, and perhaps Minnesota, and, probably as strays from Mexico, in Arizona, New Mexico, Texas, Louisiana, Oklahoma, and Arkansas, wolves are rare animals within the lower forty-eight states. As recently as the turn of the century they ranged west of the Mississippi in great numbers. One would like to think, now that their number has been so drastically reduced, that the pressure on them would be eased a little. Such, unfortunately, is not the case.

In the eastern part of the United States, man has won the one-sided war. Reuben Cary is believed to have killed the last member of the great Adirondack packs in November 1893. Strays from Canada were killed in New York State in 1902, 1906, and 1923. The last-known Pennsylvania specimen fell to hunters in 1898. They disappeared from southern New England about 1850. The last wolf in Connecticut was killed outside of Bridgeport in 1837; 1877 saw the end of the species in New Hampshire. A specimen was shot by a Mr. White in Norway, Maine, in the winter of 1907–1908. Occasional sightings are reported even today, but they remain unsubstantiated. More likely, feral dogs (a term for a domestic animal gone wild) are what have been seen. It may be that many crimes laid to the wolf were in fact committed by dogs. There isn't a year that goes by without reports of feral dogs being hunted down. They are known to be very destructive to wildlife, livestock, and man himself.

In reviewing what has been written about the wolf, one can't help but be dismayed by the nonsense directed against this animal, even by knowledgeable people. No less a figure than William T. Hornaday, onetime director of the New York Zoological Park, wrote in 1904, "Of all the creatures of North America, none are more despicable than wolves. There is no depth of meanness, treachery or cruelty to which they do not descend."

Treachery to what cause, one can't help but wonder! Hornaday continues speaking of their being "without mercy," and being "rank cowards." This emotional anthropomorphism is without value, even if written by Hornaday. It is, however, rather typical of an attitude that has prevailed for untold generations, an attitude that, when coupled with the actual facts, necessitates what is virtually an obituary for a fascinating species.

These facts are reflected, if in a somewhat exaggerated manner, in the now famous story of the Custer wolf. This best known of American wild canines ended up with a $500 price on its head. It is said to have killed over $25,000 worth of stock in its ten years of hunting along the Wyoming–South Dakota line. Tales were told about it being guarded by a pair of attendant coyotes. Strangely, this story was apparently true, for a hunter by the name of H. P. Williams killed the two coyotes, and finally ended the remarkable career of the Custer wolf in 1920. There can be little doubt that the coyotes were more parasites than bodyguards, but the image of so successful a hunter attended by smaller canines is both dramatic and in several ways rather satisfying. It should

The author with Homer, a socialized male timber wolf weighing approximately 125 pounds. This was part of a "ceremony" initiating the author into the pack, for which Homer acted as Alpha Wolf. The author received a few minor cuts and bruises, but nothing remotely resembling an attack took place.

A timber wolf pup. Although vital in the natural order of things, in North America his future is bleak because of the monumental stupidity of man.
Courtesy Ontario Dept. of Lands and Forests

be stressed that the Custer wolf was an aberrant individual and not typical of the species.

The statistics of wolf damage to livestock are probably exaggerated and it is doubtful that control is necessary, or even advisable, in natural game areas. The wolf usually takes only weak and sickly individuals. To protect a herd of reindeer by killing wolves is to condemn the herd to a worse fate; weak and inferior animals live to breed and weaken the strain. Predator control of this kind is shortsighted and not at all in keeping with the best interests of any conservation project. There is no livestock area left in North America with a sufficient number of wolves to make this supposed threat anything but academic.

The charge that the wolf is a killer, not only of man's domestic stock, but of man himself is open to serious doubt. Although a great deal has been written on the subject, there always has been and still is an extremely fine line between fact and fiction in this matter.

The Associated Press released the following story on May 5, 1962:

WOLVES ATTACK VILLAGE
IN TURKEY, KILL BOY

Izmir, Turkey (AP)—A score or more of wolves, *believed to have rabies* [italics added], attacked a hamlet in Buca district last night, killing a nine-year-old boy and biting or mauling 14 other persons.

Press dispatches said the wolves attacked the 18-dwelling village of Kaynaklar four times during the night. The villagers fought the animals for seven hours with axes and scythes.

A medical team rushed to the village, placed it under quarantine and inoculated the residents against rabies.

Similar stories, old enough now to be legend, are told of villages in Sweden, Norway, Finland, Russia, India, the United States, and many other areas. These older tales do not stipulate rabies as an ingredient of the nightmare. They smack of fiction, and most can probably be discounted out of hand.

General Kinloch reported, "When impelled by hunger they sometimes become bolder, and when we were encamped at Jalalabad during the winter of 1878–79, sentries were on more than one occasion attacked by wolves, which nightly visited our camp."

In a letter to the author, American hunter-author Elmer Keith reported:

I know of one case on an island in S.E. Alaska where they found a man's skeleton and a rusted .357 S & W [The specifications of a .357 S & W by Keith, an arms expert, marks this as a recent report, possibly one of the most recent on record. The .357 Magnum caliber was developed in the mid-1930s. The first revolver designed to use this cartridge was presented to J. Edgar Hoover in 1935.], and three wolf skeletons together, no doubt on that one . . . [I] talked with several men who had been in Russia in the old days when they hunted wolves with sleds and 4 to 6 horses and used buckshot . . . sometimes whole outfits were not only run down, but eaten up, horses and men both, and the harness, where the wolves travel in big packs of 100 or more. No fiction about this.

It should be noted that a great many people disagree with Keith's last remark: they *do* think it is fiction.

In reviewing references to wolf attacks on man, two interesting points become apparent. Most such references are old, and relatively few come from North America. One is forced to two conclusions *if* the accounts are taken at face value: first, wolves vary in habit, at least in their attitude toward man, from place to place; and, second, attacks on man were more common in earlier days. The first conclusion is quite probable, the second is somewhat more difficult to accept since the reduction in the numbers of reports of attacks on man did not necessarily coincide with the decimation of wolf populations. Even in the last century, when thousands and perhaps tens of thousands of wolves ranged through the American West, reports of attacks on man were rare. It is entirely within the realm of possibility that an ingredient of the wolf's being considered as dangerous to man stems from man's own need to fictionalize the subject.

In their classic study of the wolf (*The Wolves of North America*), Young and Goldman cite many old references:

In the Scotland of James VI [sixteenth century], wolf attacks became so numerous that houses, called "spittals," were provided for travellers at night, specifically as places of retreat from the marauding packs [Harting, 1880].

Wolves, which, to the great damage of the country, not only furiously set upon cattle, but even upon their owners themselves, to the manifest danger of their lives . . . [Camden, 1586].

In 1875 one hundred and sixty-one persons fell victims to wolves in Russia [St. George Mivart, 1890].

Although the wolves of North America are the most daring of all the beasts of prey on that continent, they are by no means so courageous or ferocious as those of Europe, particularly in Spain or the South of France, in which countries they commit dreadful ravages both on man and beast; whereas an American wolf, except forced by desperation, will seldom or never attack a human being. . . . *

*The author believes this last statement to be true.

A small pack of wolves in
Canada. These animals,
although capable of pulling a
man down, will inevitably
flee or at least "dissolve" at
the first sign of man.
Courtesy Ontario Dept. of Lands and Forests

The submissive posture of a
female wolf in a highly
socialized pack. The woman
is Joy Adamson, author of
Born Free and founder of the
Elsa Wild Animal Appeal.

Young and Goldman themselves observe,

European comments of earlier times regarding unprovoked attacks on humans are numerous while those relating to North America are much fewer. Whether these stories are products of the fertile imagination, or are truth, is difficult to determine.

They go on to suggest that there is more than enough smoke to indicate that there exists or at least existed a fire of sorts.

In a twenty-five-year period of a wolf-control program, the U.S. Fish and Wildlife Service failed to substantiate a single reported unprovoked attack. A newspaper in Ontario, in an area known for bloodcurdling tales of wolf attacks, offered a $100 reward for proof of an unprovoked attack. It went uncollected for the fourteen years we know about.

There is no shortage of supposed records from North America, although, as we noted earlier, they are fewer in number by far than those from Europe. Experts rally to both banners, some claiming that no proved cases of unprovoked attack exist, and others countering with names, dates, places, and even witnesses, although most of these begin to thin out under closer scrutiny. There is very little substantiating evidence. Where human remains have been found on blood-soaked snow, laced unmistakably with wolf tracks, it is impossible to tell whether the person died from any number of causes and was later eaten as carrion, or whether he was attacked and killed. There is a distinct difference, certainly. Where human and wolf remains have been found together, unprovoked attack is extremely difficult to establish in a wilderness situation. In short, it is extremely difficult to come to any conclusion about this matter of wolf versus man. It looks very much like a small amount of fact liberally spiced with fiction.

There may be certain factors that affect the wolf's attitude toward man which could account for the contradictions. Wolves probably reproduce according to food supply since they are responsive to their environment. If a series of four or five very mild winters followed in succession, the hoofed prey on which the wolf depends might increase in numbers. Although this is not substantiated, the number of wolves in the area might increase correspondingly, not just as wolves from other areas drifted in for the easy pickings, but because the local animals might have increased their reproductive rate. Also, because of a plentiful food supply, their migratory, or at least far-ranging, hunting habits might be cut back as well.

If a particularly severe winter followed this period of increase and plenty, the needs of the wolves would be likely to exceed the food supply available to them. Desperation might bring on a whole series of bold attacks not attempted under other conditions. If a migration of hoofed animals was diverted, or failed to materialize for any reason, wolves that, historically, congregated along a migration route might similarly be driven to excesses of behavior. Whether hunger alone drives wolves to such attacks, or if other aspects of physiology and behavior are involved, is not known. Overpopulation, as is known to be the case with other mammals, could trigger mechanisms of which we know little or nothing.

The possibility of rabies being at the root of many or even most reputed attacks by individual animals cannot be overlooked. Coyotes, close relatives of the wolves and frequently their range mates, are known to be carriers of the disease, and wolves are certainly subject to it as well.

Several reports exist of smallpox epidemics ravaging Indian tribes and bringing scavenger wolves in droves. Wolves thus emboldened might have continued to seek human flesh when the available supply of corpses was used up. This is believed to be the case with leopards in India, as we have noted. Historically, wars in Europe, and epidemics of large proportions, have been followed by an intensification of the wolf problem. At least we are told this by early and not always accurate writers. Many such stories, when traced back, are found to be mere repetitions of earlier tales: the same stories told again and again give the impression of many stories.

The wolves of North America, when they were plentiful, had one of the richest harvests on earth available to them. Nowhere, save on the African plains, have there ever been such enormous herds of wild game, at least in recent times. Neither Russia nor Siberia ever boasted anything to equal the millions of bison and pronghorn that roamed the prairies of North America, while the woodlands were rich in deer and moose, and the uplands swarmed with the mountain goat and wild sheep. It is quite possible that these were prime factors in keeping down attacks on man. Even the large wolf populations had no need of man.

Literature on the subject can give the impression that attacks occurred only in winter. A wolf attack in the bleak winter night makes for better fiction, and people are more apt to sit around a fire and tell such stories in winter than in the summer.

Almost certainly, there are factors that can account for great differences of behavior in individuals of one species. One man's experience in a given place may be totally different from another's at the same place at a different time. The carnivores of the world are at the extreme end of a food chain. All the factors that affect the food sources of other animals eventually affect them. Carnivores must obtain their food in a way unknown to grazers and browsers, and a certain seasonal desperation is understandable. Just what the mechanisms are that trigger alterations in behavior are not known, but it can be assumed that the severity of the seasons and the available supply of hoofed prey lie at the root of it all. All that has been said and written cannot be discounted. Almost certainly, wolves have attacked men; probably provoked for the most part by the rigors of their environment or by rabies. But, it is equally certain that such attacks were exceptional at best. Wolves are shy and retiring animals unless sorely pressed. Except in rare and aberrant cases like the Custer wolf, these animals do not kill wantonly, they kill what they must to survive, and where carrion is available they will take that instead of killing.

To sum up the wolf, he has probably under unusual and stressful circumstances attacked both livestock and man himself. In either case the circumstances were at the least atypical. Now rare, wolves are hardly dangerous to anyone or anything. They live on wildlife and undoubtedly benefit those species by culling inferior animals. The wolves of the world are facing extinction, and their loss will be felt.

3 Bears

A review of the popular literature on the bears, and much of the allegedly scientific writing as well, makes confusing reading due to the amount of rhetoric employed to prove these animals harmless on the one hand and dangerous on the other. Bears tend to be cranky after they reach maturity, and are immensely powerful creatures. Any bear is harmless at a distance, and any bear is potentially dangerous at close quarters. Occasionally, moreover, an individual specimen will take the initiative in closing that all-important safety zone, and it is then that the animal must be considered dangerous to man. In dealing with these animals we must keep in mind that bears are individualists to an extraordinary degree. Experience with one is no guide in dealing with another. To be safe, one must take the position that all are dangerous and should be treated with respect.

The bears, or ursines, are a relatively recent development in the animal kingdom, and are very closely related to the dogs, or canines. Until modern times, bears were spread all over North America, from the Arctic to central Mexico; throughout the Andes in South America; and all across Eurasia, including Japan, Formosa, Borneo, Sumatra, and Java, and along the southern Mediterranean coast. Being far too tempting a target for anyone with a gun, they have been driven out of much of their range and, apart from the North American black bear, are generally found today only in remote areas. Yet, throughout most of the mountainous terrain encompassing their original range, they can still be found, and some lowland wilderness regions have limited populations. The far (American) northern populations are still comparatively intact, although the advent of private aircraft, high-powered rifles, and a class of big-game hunters who have all but exhausted the supply of other trophy-caliber game, probably mark the eventual doom of the more impressive species. The great Grizzly Bear *(Ursus horribilis)*— actually one of the American brown bears—once ranged throughout much of North America in large numbers, while today few are left in the United States exclusive of Alaska.

The classification of the group is a matter of controversy and at times appears to be rather arbitrary. Certainly, the space allotted to us here will not permit a presentation of the interesting taxonomic arguments, and we will say in passing that, except for the Sloth Bear of India *(Melursus)*, the South American Spectacled Bear *(Tremarctos)*, and the small-headed Polar Bear of the Arctic *(Thalarctos)*, most of the world's bears are remarkably similar.

For our purposes, the following list of genera will do:

Ursus	Brown bear including grizzly, Kodiak, etc.—North America and Eurasia
Tremarctos	Spectacled bear—South America
Helarctos	Sun bear—Southeast Asia
Selenarctos	Asiatic black bear—Middle to Far East, centered around the Himalayas
Euarctos	American black bear—North America
Melursus	Sloth bear—India
Thalarctos	Polar bear

There are wide variations in appearance, size, and behavior among geographic races or mere populations of individual species, but proportionately not so much among the species, or even genera, themselves. Animals as adaptable as bears do not need to differentiate into endless species to survive; individuals within a species or genus make the necessary adjustments. For instance, the American Black Bear *(Euarctos)* ranges through every type of terrain and environment found in the United States, from mountains to coastal swamps, and from deserts and plains to deep forests.

The Brown Bear makes a good starting point in our discussions of bear behavior, for not only is it the most impressive of the Ursidae, but one form constitutes the largest terrestrial carnivore left on earth. Thus, the Kodiak Bear *(Ursus middendorffi)*, limited in range to a few islands off southeast Alaska, can weigh close to a ton and have a maximum length of nearly a dozen feet. (While camping on Kodiak Island, the author encountered, tracked, or otherwise observed twenty-two Kodiak bears. One of them, an old chocolate bear, had a paw print seventeen inches across.) The so-called grizzlies belong in the genus *Ursus*. About seventy-five "species" have been supposedly described but, while these animals vary greatly in color from area to area, all may be varieties of but a single species.

Early American history and Indian lore are full of harrowing grizzly bear tales. In point of fact, the American Indian probably avoided the animal before the advent of white man and his firearms, though it once roamed the prairies in great numbers. Reliable accounts of large specimens taking several heavy slugs from big-bore rifles and still pressing home a determined defensive attack demonstrate how ineffectual even a tightly drawn bow must have been. Certainly, they were killed by Indians, but the toll that could be taken by an angry, adult grizzly probably limited its tormentors to the bravest of the braves.

Plantigrade, or flat-footed, and equipped with nonretractable claws (characteristic of all bears), the grizzly bear is truly omnivorous. It hunts, fishes, gathers, and browses, eating anything from grass, roots, berries, and fruits to insects, honey, reptiles, fish, and other meat. Essentially restricted to the Northwest today, most sleep away part of the winter, and all females normally produce two cubs in late January or early February. Indeed, two cubs constitute the standard litter among all of the world's bears. Single births occur, and triplets and even quadruplets may be born on rare occasions.

W. T. Hornaday said of the grizzly bear:

> Down to the advent of the breech-loader, the Grizzly was a bold, aggressive and highly dangerous animal. When attacked, he would charge his enemies with great ferocity, striking terrible blows with paws that were like sledge-hammers armed with huge hooks of steel. The combined swiftness and strength with which any large bear can strike must be seen or felt to be fully appreciated.
>
> I . . . am convinced that naturally the disposition . . . is rather peaceful and good-natured . . . no animal is more prompt to resent affront or injury. . . . The Grizzly temper is defensive, not aggressive. . . .

Lewis and Clark wrote a great deal about this animal, and at one point spoke of it as "a creature of extraordinary ferocity." Theodore Roosevelt wrote, "No Grizzly will assail a man now unprovoked . . . though if he is wounded or thinks himself cornered he will attack his foes with a headlong, reckless fury that renders him one of the most dangerous of wild beasts." John M. Holzworth described the animals as "fighting machines of the first order." The same author says that unprovoked attacks are all but unknown, and poses the very interesting question, Who is to say when a bear is provoked?

The people who have been hugged to death by bears in fiction are uncountable; the number who have met their fate this way in real life is almost certainly zero. Bears bite. They may take a swipe at an enemy in passing, or if the encounter occurs in thick brush, but a normal bear attack (if there is such a thing) generally involves a man running and a bear running after him. In such cases, teeth are the weapons used. Pulp magazine artists invariably have these impressive creatures wading into a fight in a standing posture like steel-clawed prizefighters. Since this makes for better composition on a page, it is in a sense understandable. However, a bear is an animal that moves on all fours, and it is in that position when it closes for combat. The bear goes up on its hind legs to reach for things, and to see over obstacles like dense brush, but generally not to attack.

Ernest Thompson Seton wrote:

> Notwithstanding the sinister reputation that has won for him the names "horribilis," "grisly," "ferox," etc., the Grizzly, according to all the best authorities, never attacks man, except when provoked. That is, he is a harmless, peaceful giant, perfectly satisfied to let you alone if you let him alone.

Seton quotes a number of sources discussing the reputation this animal has acquired down through the years. They are in general agreement with the observations already cited above. However, the World Wildlife Fund described the grizzly as "about the only really dangerous mammal in early America."

There can be little doubt that grizzly bears in the United States and Canada have made apparently unprovoked attacks on men, with fatal results to one or both parties. The problem, as presented by Holzworth, is that it is really impossible to determine if a bear has been provoked or not. A man on foot who approaches a thicket and is suddenly charged by a female bear may think himself unfairly set upon, never knowing that he approached two concealed cubs. A man on horseback who is attacked and sees his favorite mount killed by an enraged grizzly may similarly feel himself victimized, not knowing (or caring) that the last one, two, or three mounted men encountered by the animal had taken shots at it, possibly inflicting wounds. With man's record in mind, the term *unprovoked* has little or no meaning.

Provoked attacks have occurred in great numbers and have often been disastrous. Many men have survived attacks, mainly because the bear bit and ran, perhaps charging half by accident in the direction of the noise. Other men have been terribly mutilated. Bears, as we said, are immensely powerful and have extremely long claws which, while not razor sharp, are capable of inflicting great damage when employed. All indications are, however, that most injuries have been caused by the bear's impressive teeth.

The whole matter of grizzly bear attacks came into sharp focus one August evening in 1967. On that one night two girls, in two separate and unrelated incidents in Glacier National Park, were killed—both by grizzly bears. No mistake was possible—the bodies of both girls were recovered, and there were witnesses; it was a calamity not only for the girls and their families but for wildlife in America.

The *whys* of those two attacks have been expounded in scores of newspaper and magazine articles and in a first-rate book by Jack Olsen entitled *Night of the Grizzlies*. There was carelessness all around—on the part of park personnel who had allowed grizzlies to live on garbage, thereby conditioning them to be around people, and who had also failed to follow up reports of bears acting up in the days before the attacks; and on the part of the girls themselves, who were acting against good advice and practice in their choice of camping sites. There were other factors, too, and an overdose of bad luck.

There was, as might be expected, an immediate cry that the parks belong to people and not bears and that the bears had to go. The outcry was not tempered by the fact that the game parks of Africa contain lion, leopard, hyena, buffalo, rhino, hippo, elephant, and a host of other potentially dangerous animals. In African parks both people and animals are under control. Too much, obviously, is left to chance in American parks, and that is why the girls died.

At the height of the controversy the author was called upon to put some historic and statistical perspective to the matter. The National Audubon Society requested a rebuttal to the statements that the bears had to be destroyed. Putting aside for the moment the tragedy of the two deaths, let us consider the facts.

The National Park Service administers only sixteen areas where any bear populations survive. The national parks now log in close to 200 million visitors a year, and the system is now 103 years old. No one can really come up with a good figure of just how many hundreds of millions of people have entered the parks in the century of their being, but in all that time the number of people killed by bears in the national parks totals six. More people drown in the national parks on one July Fourth weekend than have been killed by bears in a century, yet no one says swimming, boating, and fishing should be banned on lands administered by the Department of the Interior. People are run down and chopped up by power boats more often than they are hurt by bears in our parks, yet the cry continues and the National Park Service has not quite decided whether the parks are for bears or for people. In fact, without the bears there wouldn't be parks at all.

In the final analysis, bear watching in an American national park is safer than boating, skin-diving, water-skiing, fishing, hunting, home carpentry, bathing, showering, hiking, climbing, gardening, and making love. There is almost nothing safer from a statistical point of view.

There are, though, too many people going into our parks to allow for any carelessness in the future. Hand-feeding bears from automobiles, or approaching them on foot with camera in hand in an attempt to "get a good picture," is a singularly foolish practice.* This is particularly true in park areas where protection reduces the animal's apparently natural fear of man. In wilderness areas, a bear will normally move off at the approach of man. In parks, specimens climb onto parked cars and often try to reach in through the windows to get handouts from the occupants. Clearly, the last set of circumstances is the most dangerous, and I would suggest that the more nearly tame a bear is, the more likely it is to cause injury. Furthermore, people who break park rules and feed bears are not only endangering themselves but the bears they feed, for brazen bears are marked with yellow paint, and if they continue to bother people, they are shot.

People who are caught discarding garbage, storing food improperly, or feeding bears should be fined and sent out of the park. We can have parks for people and bears, but if the 1967 Glacier National Park tragedy is not to be repeated, many American and Canadian tourists will have to act as adults, perhaps for the first time in their lives.

The North American Black Bear (Euarctos americanus) has a perfectly vast range, from northern Alaska to southern Florida; across all of Canada, south along the West Coast, down the Rockies all the way into Mexico, around the Great Lakes, through New England, New York, and, in fact, throughout just about every wilderness region left on the continent. They range into suburban areas in parts of North America.

The black is not big as bears go, but large males can approach 500 pounds and reach a length of over six feet. Nonetheless, it is the smallest bear on the continent, and the most common. Color phases include cinnamon and nearly white (in areas of British Columbia), with the black phase always having a brown muzzle and generally some white on the breast. (There is also a blue form—the glacier bear.)

*While visiting Algonquin Provincial Park in Ontario, the author spoke to a ranger who had come upon a provoking scene. A woman had lured an adult bear up onto the road with a candy bar, and while her husband photographed the scene she placed their 18-month-old son on the bear's back. The ranger punched the father and quit his job. He was reinstated the same day.

Like the other North American species, the black bear is omnivorous, shy, and short-tempered. It is a powerful animal and not to be toyed with. Protected today in many areas (although still a bounty animal in others), it tends to become more bold where not hunted. A close encounter could be disastrous and, indeed, a young girl was killed *and eaten* some years ago in Michigan. A specimen newly out of winter quarters or with cubs can be downright ferocious.

The National Observer for September 2, 1963, reported from Anchorage, Alaska, on four attacks made by black bears. One man was killed and two others severely mauled. The report suggests that the summer of 1963 produced a poor blueberry crop, driving the bears to seek other food. Charles W. Major of Fairbanks was dragged from his sleeping bag while on a hunting trip. A companion shot the bear, but not before Mr. Major was badly injured. A few days later, an electronics engineer from Fairbanks, George P. Roberts, was driven from his tent and badly bitten and clawed before a companion killed the animal. William Strandberg was killed and his brother found his maimed body with a bear standing over it. Larry J. Bidlake was chased up a tree and bitten on the legs. The Fish and Wildlife Service warned people in the woods to be alert until the cranberries ripened. It was taken for granted that the attacks—all of which took place within a space of a few weeks—were prompted by a lack of natural food.

The Polar Bear *(Thalarctos)* has often been implicated in seemingly unprovoked attacks. It is possible that some of these attacks have been prompted by hunger since, except in the brief Arctic summer, the animal cannot fall back on honey, berries, and other vegetable food when the hunting is poor. Bruce S. Wright says of them:

> The polar bear is truly one of the most dangerous land animals alive as they are the only bears that live entirely on meat. There is no other large land carnivore that has had less contact with man, and consequently has less fear of him. This is why they are so dangerous.

Kaare Rodahl wrote, in 1953, that the polar bear ". . . at times will stalk and attack a man, at other times he will flee like a ghost at the slightest scent of human beings." He goes on to tell the amusing story of a sailor who was charged on the ice and who threw off his jacket to be able to run faster. The bear paused to examine the garment and then took up the chase again. The sailor kept discarding diversionary articles as he ran. He arrived at his ship quite naked, at the same time as the bear who caught up with him and began licking his hand.

Stories of bears retreating and of others attacking balance each other

A massive grizzly in its winter coat. This is a zoo specimen in Washington's National Zoo. Grizzlies are becoming increasingly rare in the contiguous forty-eight states. This is one of the New World's most impressive animals.
Courtesy Washington National Zoo

A typical view of a black bear—in the black phase. The same animal could be cinnamon, blue ("glacier bear"), or even, though rarely, white. It is our most common bear and a species that generally minds its own business when not tempted into contact by man. Old-timers—usually solitary, except around good feeding areas—can be cranky. A mature black bear can weigh as much as four hundred pounds, still far less than a grizzly.
Courtesy Ontario Dept. of Lands and Forests

A typical view of the polar
bear, an animal that spends
much of its time in, or
immediately adjacent to, the
sea. On land this animal can
be aggressive and even
dangerous. It should be
treated with great respect.
*Courtesy Ontario Dept. of Lands and
Forests*

The Asian sloth bear, a
consistently dangerous
animal much feared by
natives. One such animal
kept the author at bay for
nearly an hour on a jungle
trail in Sri Lanka. Many
attacks on humans occur
every year, and mutilated
people are commonly
encountered.

out, it would seem, leaving no conclusion possible. Polar bears are often accused of attacking open boats, and almost certainly some of these tales are true. There are factors that enter into the picture that lend plausibility to even diametrically opposite opinions. First and foremost are individual differences. There can be little doubt that some polar bears are more shy than others.

Previous experience with man certainly could be a contributing factor, as could degree of hunger. Females will fight to protect their young, particularly since there is good evidence that they must protect them from males who will eat their own offspring. A very important factor is probably latitude. As Seton put it:

> The White Bear, like the Grizzly, has learned that guns are very much more dangerous than arrows or spears. Along his Southland, where he commonly meets whalers or explorers he is shy, fearful as a fox. Farther north, where he never meets a gunman, he is much more aggressive.

Most reporters point out that attacks on men more often occur in winter than in summer, which strengthens the theory that the polar bear can be regarded as a potential man-eater, at least in parts of its range.

Second in size only to the Kodiak, the polar bear is a formidable creature on the ice, or in the water. It is a true hunting animal, swift, silent, well camouflaged, and quite cunning. Under no circumstances should one be trusted. The unknowns that combine to create the bear's "personality" are too variable and the animal far too powerful to permit license.

Writing of the Indian sloth bear in 1896, G. P. Sanderson said: "Bears are dangerous to an unarmed man. Woodcutters and others, whose avocations take them into the jungles, are frequently roughly handled by them."

Dividing the bears of India into three species, snow, Himalayan black, and Indian or sloth, Brig. Gen. Alexander A. A. Kinloch wrote of each in turn:

1. I think I am justified in saying that it is very seldom indeed that one of this species [snow] will deliberately attack a man.
2. Occasionally, certainly, the Black Bear proves a formidable antagonist, and I have known more than one British Officer killed by them, while one constantly meets with natives who have been terribly mutilated in encounters with one of the species; but these accidents have usually occurred, when the animal has been attacked or suddenly met with, in thick cover where the bear had every advantage.

3. The Indian Bear has the character of being very savage, and in some parts of the country it is dreaded by the natives as much as, or more than, the Tiger.*

Kinloch then goes on to describe mutilated, faceless natives and similar living testimonials to the animal's reputed ferocity.

The Sun Bear (*Helarctos*), referred to earlier, ranges from the eastern Himalayas to Szechwan in China, and south to Burma, sections of Indochina, Malaya, and Borneo. It is a pleasant-looking creature between four and five feet long. Black, it has a light muzzle and a characteristic yellowish mark on its chest. Essentially arboreal, it has long claws, particularly on the forefeet. Often kept as a pet, reports vary as to its actual tractability and there is every indication that it is probably as unpredictable as the other bears. It would certainly be unwise to trust an adult specimen too far. Reputedly, at least, it has attacked men in the wild, without apparent provocation. It is probably one more case where proximity can lead to an unfortunate chain of events culminating in a dead bear or a badly mauled man.

In reviewing scores of references, and in corresponding with dozens of people with wide experience with one bear or another, the author has been unable to find any serious disagreement with the following capsule summary:

1. Bears are extremely adaptable, variable, and therefore individualistic. Generalizations or predictions about the behavior of an animal are hazardous.
2. Bears may vary in behavior from season to season in some parts of their range, and are equally variable from one range to another.
3. Bears do sometimes attack without any *apparent* provocation. In most cases, "hidden" provocation is probably involved.
4. Although bears can use their extremely formidable claws in devastating "swipes," biting is a more characteristic form of attack. Similarly, bears can and do rear up on their hind legs, but the quadrupedal position is more likely to be employed in an attack.
5. Bears are nearsighted, and do not have particularly good hearing. Their sense of smell is very keen, however, and the downwind position is the safest for man.

---

*The author was following a jungle track in a jeep some years ago and encountered a sloth bear that refused to move out of the way. It held its ground for fully half an hour, growling and threatening to attack. Only when another jeep approached from the opposite direction did the bear take off into the forest.

6. It is never safe to approach any bear, and this includes feeding them through the bars at zoos, or from car windows in national parks. More than one person has lost a hand or arm by disregarding posted warnings.

One point of clarification is needed while we are on the subject of bears. The two favorite "bears" of picture books, the koala of Australia and the giant panda of China, are not bears at all. The former is a marsupial much more closely related to the kangaroos than to the bears, and the latter apparently comes closest to the raccoons.

4 The Leopard Seal and the Walrus

Victor B. Scheffer estimates, in his *Seals, Sea Lions and Walruses*, that the total world population of pinnipeds is between 15 and 25 million individuals. There are currently recognized but three families, twenty genera, and forty-seven species and subspecies. Considering the vast pole-to-pole range of these active marine mammals, they constitute a small and highly specialized group.

Categorically, all of the pinnipeds are flesh-eaters. They dine variously on fish, squid and octopus, shellfish, sea birds, macroplankton, other seals, and, reportedly, some carrion. The reports of seaweed found in the stomachs of slaughtered specimens almost certainly represent accidental ingestion. With forty-seven seals, sea lions, and walruses to choose from, popular writers have generally chosen only a few to accuse of being dangerous to man, with the leopard seal and the walrus leading the list.

In fact, the Walruses (there are two subspecies, *Odobenus rosmarus rosmarus*, Atlantic, and *O. r. divergens*, Pacific) could be troublesome if cut off from the water. Like most intelligent animals, and walruses are quite intelligent, they fear man and generally seek to escape when approached on rocky shore or ice floe. Restricted both in distribution and numbers, they seldom range very far south of the Arctic Circle in summer, or south of Hudson Bay and Bering Sea latitudes—58 degrees north—in winter (one record indicates 42 degrees north). Walruses could have no interest in man as a potential meal for they eat shellfish, principally. With the exception of the characteristic tusks—actually enormously elongated canines—found in both sexes, their teeth are flattened or rounded, and adapted for crushing molluscs.

Walruses grow to great size, the male approaching a ton and a half, the female nearly a ton. During breeding season, or with young in tow, they can be quarrelsome, and attacks on small boats are reported from time to time. Certainly a wounded and enraged animal would be a handful. A staple item in the economy of the Eskimo tribes, walruses are hunted assiduously. To the Eskimo in a skinboat who misjudges his harpoon throw, or to the adventurer who stumbles into a harem during the breeding season, walruses can be a lot to handle. On the unlikely chance that you encounter one, and it doesn't flee, don't press the issue. In close quarters, the walrus would certainly prevail with all that weight, and those tusks, to throw around.

The Leopard Seal, or Seal Leopard of earlier writers (*Hydrurga leptonyx*), belongs to the subfamily Lobodontinae of the family Phocidae. It is believed to be represented in the world today by about a quarter of a million individuals, and all of these are resident in generally inaccessible Antarctic and sub-Antarctic areas. It is found, but never in great numbers, all around the edge of the Antarctic continent, off South Africa, the southern tip of South America, New Zealand, and Australia. Isolated islands in the southern Atlantic, Pacific, and Indian oceans have limited populations. The leopard seal is thus quite rare, retiring, asocial, and doesn't characteristically seek the company of man but like most seals is inquisitive.

There can be no doubt that the leopard seal is a fierce animal which could be dangerous to a man foolish enough to tangle with one at close quarters. Large males grow to ten feet in length and weigh over 600 pounds. Females grow to over twelve feet and may weigh half a ton. They have long, pointed, incurved teeth, and powerful jaws. Like most of the pinnipeds, they don't chew but rip and shake their prey apart when it is too large to swallow whole. Their teeth and jaws are made for grasping, but that would not keep them from giving a serious bite should the occasion call for one.

Swift and agile in the water, leopard seals are somewhat cumbersome on land or ice. They can, however, lunge with determination and even put on bursts of speed when pressed. The body is streamlined, the neck flexible and muscular. At best, out of the water, peak performance would still not be as fast as a man can run. In the water it would be another story.

Leopard seals eat ice-front marine birds, especially penguins, and other species of seals. When times are bad they undoubtedly take what they can get in the way of fish. In years past, some popular writers went so far as to suggest that they attack man as a potential meal. The suggestion was never taken very seriously, apparently, since such stories have had limited currency. The picture of a seal dining on an explorer is somehow more comical than ominous. An argument given in support of this theory was the very questionable claim that many Antarctic seals regularly hunted by the leopard seal are two and three times the weight of a large, full-grown man. It is much more likely that it is the young of these preyed-upon seals that are taken. In fact, there isn't a shred of evidence even to suggest that any leopard seal ever attempted to make a meal of a man.

It is interesting to note a few recorded encounters. On May 29, 1911, Capt. Robert Scott, with his companions Wilson and Bowers, came upon a young leopard seal on the ice off Inaccessible Island, an ice-locked, frozen area about three-quarters of a mile long. It lies about a mile and a half south of Ross Island, and not far off the Antarctic continent, just about due south of New Zealand. When Scott and his men spotted the young leopard seal, they decided to collect it for their scientific series. Antarctic explorers have never had reason to walk around armed, so they attacked the animal with clubs. In Scott's words, "This poor beast turned swiftly from side to side as we strove to stun it with a blow on the nose. As it turned it gaped its jaws wide, but oddly enough not a sound came forth, not even a hiss." On his earlier expedition, Scott had noted (March 1, 1904), "We have also passed two or three Sea Leopards asleep on the floes: one we surprised greatly by ramming the floe on which he was taking his siesta, whereat he opened his formidable jaws and threatened us in the most ferocious manner." In describing the animal in his report on Antarctic fauna, Edward A. Wilson, Scott's zoologist, commented: "This seal is a carnivore of the most aggressive type, and probably in the Antarctic has but one enemy to fear, and that is the still more aggressive carnivorous dolphin, the Orca or Killer Whale."

In his report of his Antarctic Expedition of 1907–1909, Sir Ernest Shackleton included a dramatic account of the leopard seal's tenacity:

When he [Joyce] got close he found that the animal was a sea-leopard. He was armed only with a club, and came running for a pistol, for the sea-leopards are savage and aggressive, and can move very rapidly on the ice . . . the animal was still in the same position, and he shot it twice through the heart, and then twice through the skull. It had remarkable tenacity of life, for it still struggled, and even after a fifth ball had been put through its brain some minutes elapsed before it turned over and lay still.

A mounted specimen of a Pacific walrus. These very large animals are, by nature, shy and retiring. If bothered or interfered with, they can of course be dangerous.
Courtesy American Museum of Natural History

The dental array of the leopard seal. Though a large and formidable animal, tales of it pursuing luckless explorers across the ice are pure nonsense.
Courtesy British Antarctic Survey

Shackleton went on to say that when they dissected the animal it appeared to have two hearts! Unfortunately, some sled dogs got to the specimen, and the doubtful matter was not verified. Elsewhere, Shackleton reported that one of his men was attacked when a leopard seal left the water for an ice floe and found he was not alone. Leopard seals have not had enough experience with men to get used to them. As aggressive carnivores they undoubtedly have a bullish attitude.

In the foregoing accounts and, indeed, in almost all reliable accounts that can be found, the topic heading would best be "Man Dangerous to Leopard Seals" since they inevitably report on man attacking the animal, and the animal attempting to remain alive. Aside from emotional adjectives like "ferocious," the worst that seems to be reported about this animal's behavior is that it does attempt to defend itself against being slaughtered and it apparently is capable of giving a rather good account of itself.

Is the leopard seal dangerous to man? In a letter written to the author on August 8, 1962, Philip Law, director of Australia's Antarctic Division, says:

> . . . we consider the Leopard Seal much maligned. . . . It is a shy creature on land and is generally only dangerous if you stand on the beach between it and its escape route to the water. It is curious in the sea and will follow a boat but we have no record of it ever having attacked one.

Victor B. Scheffer wrote to the author on May 11, 1962, from Seattle, Washington: "It does not seem likely that any pinniped would attack a man without provocation. . . ." Scheffer later added, "The approach of a man during the frenzy of the mating season may represent to the dominant male no more and no less than the approach of a 'rival.'"

What is provocation? Many seals, including the leopard seal, apparently have short tempers. They are carnivores themselves and are in turn preyed upon by killer whales and sharks. In some species the males are highly competitive during the breeding season and a "harem" system prevails in the social structure of most of them. These factors—being keyed to the hunt, being alert to attack, being quarrelsome about sex—make many of the pinnipeds dangerous animals to tamper with; worse, no doubt, during certain seasons. Most pinnipeds, and certainly the leopard seal, can inflict painful and even serious injuries. Many biologists have been badly nipped by species far less aggressive than the leopard seal. Provocation is quite simply a matter of giving an animal good reason to fear, resent, or otherwise object to your proximity. As a result, the leopard seal is dangerous to man only if molested or led to feel it is going to be interfered with.

5 The Killer Whale

Early in the morning of Thursday, January 5, 1911, six or seven large Killer Whales *(Orcinus orca)* surfaced aft of the *Terra Nova,* the Antarctic research vessel of Capt. Robert Falcon Scott. She was anchored to the floating ice shelf of McMurdo Sound, approximately 2,200 miles south of New Zealand. In the few minutes that followed, expedition photographer Herbert G. Ponting nearly lost his life. Using a cooperative pack tactic peculiar to these animals, the hungry whales smashed the ice on which he was standing in an effort to catapult some tethered Eskimo dogs and, presumably, Ponting himself into the freezing waters. Captain Scott recorded the incident in his journal, which was published and republished a number of times. Nearly every author who has discussed the killer whale at any length since has made some reference to the affair. I told the story in detail in my volume *Antarctica: Land of Frozen Time.* This celebrated adventure has stood for over half a century as proof that the killer whale is a man-eater. Other adventures, recounted on considerably less authority than Captain Scott's journal, could be disproved in almost any intelligent discussion, but Ponting's close scrape was always available to anyone who wanted to show the killer whale to be man's deadly enemy. Seeking the truth about the killer whale has proved to be the most intriguing investigation in all the research for this book.

John D. Craig tells a nonsense tale, in his book *Danger Is My Business,* of a killer whale trapping a diver in a submarine grotto and biting and battering at the rocks of the entrance to get at him. Before passing on to other deep-sea monsters, Craig retreats to the safety of the ice-battering business without actually naming Ponting. He goes on to say, "They will attack and smash small boats, and eat whatever falls into the water from them." Since man is the one animal currently building and using boats, we can assume that he means they eat men.

Frank T. Bullen, in his *Denizens of the Deep,* has the killer whale and Swordfish *(Xiphias)* joining forces to slaughter large whales and their young. This delightful fiction, I believe, arose from the fact that the name *swordfish* was reportedly once used for the killer because of its extremely long dorsal fin. Other writers have the orca swimming beneath large whales and slashing their bellies open with this same fin. That is an impossible claim since the six- to seven-foot fin is so limp it often flops over like a spaniel's ear.

Dr. Tedford L. Greathouse of Oxnard, California, writing in *Skin Diver* magazine for January 1960, says of the killer whale, "It has been known to bite holes in small boats in an attempt to get at its occupants." Writing in *Skin Diver* for July 1961, Aden F. Romine says, "The killer whale is the bitter enemy of man . . . because there is not a fact on record to disprove it." Of all the statements one encounters about the killer whale, that is probably the least logical! However, Mr. Romine's article is a classic collection of inaccuracies, and some of his other observations are equally suspect. He claims that there is one known incident of men being eaten by the killer whale and this involved one which smashed up a fishing boat off Cape Town, South Africa, and ate its four occupants. He mentions that another stove in the hull of a fishing craft off northern California but failed to get the two anglers.

Let us first identify and locate the animal in question, and then examine some of these stories in detail.

Orcinus orca is the largest of the dolphins. The name killer whale, however, is not inaccurate since the dolphins and porpoises are all small whales, members of the mammalian order Cetacea. The male grows to thirty-one feet while the female seldom exceeds half that length. They are communal animals traveling in small herds, packs, or pods, or in great convoys reportedly numbering in the dozens and even hundreds. Hundreds of killers together almost certainly represent a migration rather than a normal hunting pattern. They are, of course, warm-blooded, air-breathing mammals with, it is believed, a very high order of intelligence, perhaps the intellectual equal of the apes.

There can be little doubt that the killer whale prefers a diet of warm-blooded animals and its depredations on seal herds, penguins, porpoises, and dolphins have been too often recorded to warrant repeating here. They are stated to attack the largest animals that ever lived on this planet, the great Baleen Whales or *Mysticeti*. It is reported that they prefer the tongue, and will attack a 100-foot blue whale to get this choice two- or three-ton morsel. However, that claim is questionable.

It is also reported that an aggressive baleen whale can put a pack of killers to flight. The percentage of successes realized by the killers in their attacks on these giants of the sea cannot be estimated. They may succeed most of the time, or only rarely. There is no way of knowing. It may be a matter of individual disposition on the part of the big whale, and possibly a question of leadership among the killers. The social structure of a killer pack would be an interesting thing to study but the odds against such a study ever being done are enormous.

Certainly, the smaller mammals have no defense when attacked. Even their speed can be matched by these aggressive predators. Seals have the one advantage of being able to get out of the water. In the open sea, they don't stand too much of a chance, although their quick turning ability may save some. It is also reported that other whales will ground themselves and smother rather than face an onslaught by these powerful carnivores. Such reports are apparently speculative and are usually offered as a probable explanation for the periodic beaching of whales reported from all over the world. Since killer whales themselves are sometimes found high and dry for no apparent reason, the explanation may not hold up. From the British Columbia area alone have come several reports of killer whale strandings: twenty at Estevan Point, Vancouver Island, in 1945, and eleven at Masset on Queen Charlotte Island in 1941. There have been many others since then, some every year, in fact: 1972, Melbourne, Australia; 1973, North Carolina; 1971, California; 1973 again, Delaware; it is a frequent event and records are plentiful. Actually, the reason why whales, including killer whales, beach themselves is not known. When they do, they are condemned to death from suffocation. Even their muscles cannot keep pushing their weight up enough to allow their lungs to fill.

The killer whale ranges from the Arctic to the edge of the Antarctic continent. It has been reported from just about every sea in the world. It is reported in the open sea, in harbors and bays, and even along beaches in sheltered sounds.

Unfortunately, the literature on the killer is almost inevitably colored with misleading adjectives. Even the *U.S. Navy Diving Manual,* which gives the killer a 4 plus or top danger rating, describes it as "ruthless" and "ferocious." That is hardly more clinical than Romine's description of it as the "meanest thing in the sea." A rundown of the literature on this animal will reveal that it is cruel, heartless, vicious, treacherous, nasty, devilish, monstrous, and pitiless, to name a few characteristics, and that it has a violent "bloodlust" and "kills for the joy of it." I would suggest that before we start to investigate the crimes against mankind of which it has been accused, we discard all of these words and take the cool, zoological view that the animal is merely hungry. It has a huge body, it is very active and requires a lot of food. Because, even if the killer whale has eaten a man a day since the dawn of the age of mammals *(and it hasn't!)* it is not cruel, heartless, or any of the rest. Those are human emotions and however bright the killer may be, it does not possess them. The fact is that we have no yardstick for measuring the emotions of these animals; they are as foreign to us as are the mouselike squeaks with which they communicate among themselves. The danger in using human emotions to describe the ways of animals is not merely a semantic one. Their use has done a grave injustice, not so much to the animal (who certainly doesn't care what man thinks of him), but to our own powers of reason. So overpowering has been fictional invective that today it is universally taken that the orca is an incorrigible man-eater. As we shall demonstrate, few facts exist to support this belief.

Let us take a long hard look at the most celebrated case of a supposed killer whale attack on man. Only Ponting's adventure, as recorded by Scott, has received more attention. For two decades this story has been told and retold as final proof that the killer whale does attack man.

On the front page of the Seventh Sport Night Final of the Friday, March 28, 1952, edition of the San Francisco *Call-Bulletin* there appeared the following headline and story:

WHALE BITES CAL. BOAT; TWO MEN RESCUED
FISHERMEN WIN BATTLE OFF COAST

Two men in a small fishing boat were attacked by a killer whale off the Sonoma County coast today but escaped with their lives when one of them fought off the creature with an oar.

The deep-sea monster—a modern day "Moby Dick"—circled the pair's 14-foot craft several times as they rowed frantically to escape him.

Then he made one preliminary pass underneath the boat, turned, and charged, sinking his teeth into its hull.

"Poked Him in Eye"

He thrashed and twisted, his teeth grinding on the wood, until one of the men grabbed an oar and "poked him right in the eye."

With that he unclamped his teeth and drew away, permitting the pair— H. W. Van Buren, 50, and A. L. Anderson, 72, both Petaluma poultrymen—to reach safety on a nearby island.

Their boat, a six inch hole bitten in its hull, swamped just as they touched the shore.

They were picked up by a Coast Guard helicopter and carried to safety after waiting on the island about an hour and a half for aid.

Half Mile off Shore

The episode—almost unheard of in these waters—took place shortly before 8 A.M. about half a mile off the shore of Bodega Head, a peninsula jutting obliquely off the coast about 30 miles north of San Francisco.

Van Buren and Anderson were approaching the small island in their outboard motor boat with the engine stopped as they coasted toward an intended landing to gather abalone.

In another smaller craft nearby was their companion, George Stewart, also of Petaluma.

Van Buren—who confessed his knees were shaking a little bit after the rescue—told the story:

"We were just about 75 feet from the shore of the rock, about a half-acre island, when we saw him circling us.

"There were a lot of seals in the water, but he wasn't going for them. He seemed to be eyeing us.

"We started rowing as fast as we could to get away. But we didn't get more than 50 feet. Once he came close and went underneath, bumping the boat.

"Then he turned and charged right at us, and hit us as hard as he could.

"He sank his teeth in the boat, one set on the rail and the other underneath on the keel.

"He was hanging on and chewing and twisting, trying to break the boat.

"I was sitting down, trying to hold on. Anderson was doing the same.

"Then I grabbed the oar and I just jabbed him right in his eye. I don't know whether I ruined the eyeball or not, but I poked pretty hard. I sure did.

Dark Brown Whale

"His head was right there in front of me. He was kind of a dark brown.

"When I hit him, he just let go—opened his mouth and went away. I don't know where he went to. We didn't see him again."

Water began gushing in through the gaping hole in the hull and the two men just managed to make the final 25 feet to the shore of the rock.

The boat swamped as they reached it.

Stewart, in the other boat, joined them, but his craft was too small to take all three to the mainland.

In the meantime, a man who witnessed the deep-sea drama from shore notified Coast Guard boatswain's mate first class Norman Paulsen, in charge of the light at Bodega Bay.

Land on Island

He notified San Francisco headquarters and a helicopter piloted by Lieutenant Tommy Hynes with Lieutenant Milton L. McGregor as his aide, took off from the South San Francisco field.

Hynes landed the ship on the island itself, took Van Buren and Anderson aboard and landed them on a sandspit off Bodega Bay, where they had left their cars when they started their fishing trip.

Stewart returned in his own small boat.

Were the men scared?

"I sure was!" said Van Buren.

The Coast Guard said killer whales—one-ton creatures, from 15 to 20 feet long—are not uncommon in these waters. They ordinarily attack other whales, seals and other large sea creatures, but rarely man.

Outdoor Life magazine [vol. 119, no. 4 (April 1957), p. 36] recapitulated the story in a series of nine drawings under the heading, "This Happened to Me! Killer Foiled." The drawings show a killer whale biting a huge hunk out of the side of the boat. Presumably, it was this incident Dr. Greathouse referred to in his 1960 article when he said, " ... [It] has been known to bite holes in small boats." Romine probably referred to this episode when he said an orca stove in a fishing craft off northern California. Many other writers have referred to it and so the matter has stood, duly recorded in print, worthy of a banner headline in a large and reputable metropolitan daily. Hence, the killer whale must be a threat to men in small boats. But is it?

Clearly, if the mystery were to be solved, this was the case to study. It happened recently, it is clearly recorded, and the area involved is nearby. This was no rumor of sea monsters, drifting in tardily from some distant and mysterious clime! This happened less than thirty-five miles from San Francisco in 1952.

The first step was to locate and question the most reputable single source of the story. What was the most authoritative voice repeating it? The answer came in the Biology Laboratory of the U.S. Antarctic Research Program at McMurdo Sound on frozen Ross Island, just a few miles off the Antarctic mainland. There, several miles from the spot where Ponting had his big adventure in 1911, the author found a copy of what is almost certainly one of the most respected studies of the pinnipeds, *Seals, Sea Lions and Walruses*. The author of that book, Victor B. Scheffer, is a world-recognized authority on marine mammals and a scientist whose integrity is beyond question. Facing page 151 in the book was a photograph of the boat and a caption outlining the adventures of Anderson and Van Buren.

On May 5, 1962, the author wrote to Mr. Scheffer and on May 11 an answer was received which contained the following paragraph:

An important point: I am now convinced that the identification by the fishermen of the attacking beast as a killer whale was wrong. It was quite certainly a great white shark ... the dentition of the shark, clean and sharp, corresponds to the injury sustained by the dory. A killer whale would have left a coarser, more crushing kind of mark.

Mr. Scheffer's new view of the episode provided the key! Dr. Raymond M. Gilmore, another world-recognized authority on marine mammals, wrote from a whaling station at Richmond, California, on July 13, "The photo of a boat in Vic Scheffer's book, said to represent attack of killer whale, showed tooth marks of shark . . . I have spoken with two biologists who examined the boat and they agreed it was a shark."

With the permission of the *News-Call Bulletin,* a closeup of the boat is reproduced (see p. 66). In examining the photograph, keep in mind that the killer has large conical teeth, as much as two inches in diameter at the base. Such teeth, crushing down on wood, could not tear and puncture, but would crush. A shark has exceedingly sharp teeth, the kind that would penetrate, rip, and tear. Clearly, the boat was attacked by a shark.

That is only the conclusion. What of the facts of this story? How was such an error made? Both killer whales and very large sharks are found off California at the same latitude as San Francisco. A fifteen-foot Great White Shark *(Carcharodon carcharias)* was taken in a net off San Miguel Island in March 1958. The distance from Bodega Bay was about 260 miles. However, seeing either animal close up, at least close enough to poke with an oar, is an unusual experience. Although Mr. Anderson was seventy-two and Mr. Van Buren fifty at the time of the incident, it is unlikely that either man ever got close to a killer whale at sea before. A shark, particularly a large shark (and some sharks grow every bit as large as killer whales) partially submerged, with a hide discolored from age, and probably covered with scars and marine growth would look like a whale, particularly if you were under attack, scared half out of your wits, and fighting for your life. There is no question here of misrepresentation. Killer whales are known to appear in that area, they are believed to be a threat to man, and an attack by one would not be much of a surprise to anyone who hadn't stopped to question the matter before. The report in the *News-Call Bulletin* was not sensational and was probably close to the actual interview granted by the two terrified men. The account in *Outdoor Life,* five years and one month after the episode, was within the bounds of reasonable reporting although not quite as cautious as the original newspaper account. Apparently, Anderson and Van Buren made a very human error, and everybody followed suit, for a time at least.

Aden Romine referred to the eating of four men by a killer whale off Cape Town, South Africa, and it seemed only right to at least look into the matter. The search was a short one. A year and a half earlier, the same magazine, *Skin Diver,* carried an article by the world-renowned scientist, Professor J. L. B. Smith, an ichthyologist at Rhodes Univer-

A large killer whale—undoubtedly a bull—in Antarctic waters. Neither "bloodthirsty" nor "vicious," it is still not an animal to trust in open water, if for no other reasons than its size and the fact that it is carnivorous.
Courtesy U.S. Navy

The boat that was supposed to have been attacked by a killer whale off San Francisco. Clearly, the teeth marks are those of a large shark. A killer whale would have destroyed the boat with one bite.
Courtesy San Francisco News-Call Bulletin

sity, Grahamstown, South Africa. Fortunately, Professor Smith's article is more characteristic of this interesting and informative magazine than is Mr. Romine's. In his article, Professor Smith tells that on July 30, 1956, a large whale attacked a fishing boat in False Bay at the Cape and wrecked it; four of the six-man crew drowned. He further reports that it had been suggested that the attack was made by a killer whale. He discounts the idea on a number of points, mainly size. The attacking animal was a *large whale* and the killer is a small one, not even a third the length of a big Blue Whale *(B. musculus)*.

Professor Smith had been most helpful to this author in the preparation of other portions of this book, and another letter was dispatched to Grahamstown in an effort to find out if the killer who ate four men off Cape Town was, in fact, the nonkiller whale who drowned four men in the same area. It is not possible, of course, to determine this. Professor Smith did say, however:

> We certainly have no information here about the alleged attack and devouring of four men off Cape Town. While this may have occurred, I think it most unlikely that it would not have been greatly publicized and we should certainly have heard about it.

The author might add that Professor Smith knew his home waters well. It is very difficult to accept the idea that he would not have heard about such a significant thing as a whale, any whale, eating four men in his own backyard! Other reliable sources in South Africa report knowing of no such incident.

In the same letter from which we quoted above, Professor Smith wrote, "There have been attacks on boats by sharks in that area and in one case a large shark badly battered a fishing boat and so great a hole in it, . . . etc."

On this same point, Dr. V. M. Coppleson, an authority on sharks, wrote in a letter to the author from Sydney, Australia, ". . . an attack . . . occurred in Safety Bay, Tasmania, about two years ago in which some claims were made that the attack was made by a killer whale, but those who investigated the attack came to the conclusion that the attacker was a shark and not a killer whale."

Certainly, all of this reflects on the California incident of 1952. We will have more to say about this when we review the alleged shark menace and attempt to evaluate it.

Quite simply, there were no authenticated reports of attacks by killer whales on men, outside of the Antarctic, before 1972. On June 15 of that year Douglas Robertson was sailing his forty-three-foot schooner *Lucette* around the world. A few days out from the Galapagos Islands the *Lucette,* carrying four of Robertson's children as well as a twenty-two-year-old college student bound for New Zealand, was reportedly rammed by three killer whales almost simultaneously. The schooner was fifty years old, in very good condition, and weighed nineteen tons. She sank in a few minutes giving Robertson and his young crew time to make it into a raft. The killer whales (seen by some of the youngsters, but not by Robertson himself who was below deck) had by that time vanished. (The story is very well told, indeed, in a book entitled *Survive the Savage Sea,* by Douglas Robertson, published in 1973 by Praeger.)

It is hard to figure out just what did happen. It is possible the whales were not killers (I have seen sperm whales literally play with a fully manned dory south of the Hawaiian Islands), but let us assume the sighting was accurate and the animals that rammed the *Lucette* or collided with her were killer whales. Why, if they weren't going to eat what was on board, would they batter themselves against a metal-sheathed hull? One of the Robertson children reported that one of the whales had a big triangular cut on its forehead, and Robertson suggests that the others may have stopped to eat it. It is doubtful—that isn't whale behavior. Whales help each other when in distress, not eat each other as sharks do. Nor have I ever heard any other suggestion of cannibalism among killer whales. (Robertson makes another mistake when he identifies the killer whale as the largest carnivore in the world. It is a pinniped, not a member of the Carnivora, and the sperm whale, twice the size of a killer whale, is every bit as carnivorous.)

If we really must accept the suggestion that killer whales did hit the *Lucette* and caused her to sink, we must also accept the fact that the killer whales made no other attempt to harm the small group on the rubber raft. If everything else about the story is accurate, that fact is very difficult to understand. This is not to suggest that there is any misrepresentation in Robertson's fascinating account, but it should be noted that it was a very exciting few moments and the observers may have been mistaken about what they saw.

Let us accept, though, that the schooner *Lucette* was sunk by at least three killer whales in June 1972. It may be a unique case, and it should be noted. Surely this is a distinction—that a boat and not people were attacked. There is not the slightest evidence that the attacking animals associated a schooner's hull with fresh meat.

Back to the Antarctic, where the Scott–Ponting affair occurred. During Operation Deepfreeze, a young naval lieutenant, Morton Beebe, had a very similar adventure, also in the Ross Sea area. Here, then, are two cases where men on ice were endangered by killer whales. Why is it that man, who has been in contact with these animals for thousands of years, has recorded *authenticated* attacks (on men, not boats) only in the Antarctic?

The killer whale of the polar regions, north and south, is the same animal, as far as we know, as the killer whale of Long Island Sound, San Francisco Bay, and the English Channel. The difference lies not in the animal but in the behavior of man.

There is an axiom when dealing with large carnivores—if you act like their natural prey, you stand a chance of getting into trouble. Animals function, no matter how bright they are (if I may borrow a human value), on natural instincts. They respond to stimuli in rather rigid patterns, and when conditioned or instinctive reflexes are triggered in a hungry beast, trouble can ensue. We offer here the not altogether new theory that, in the Antarctic, man inadvertently acts like the normal prey of the killer whale, and that is how Ponting and Beebe, and a number of others, nearly got into serious trouble.

In the Antarctic, seals and penguins retreat to the questionable safety of the ice whenever killer whales are near. Killers have been photographed rising out of the water six or eight feet and looking across the surface of the ice for escaping prey. If they spy a meal, they may attempt to smash the floe or tip it up to spill the victim into the water. Ice has strange effects on vision, and even at short distances it is extremely difficult to get a clear outline of an object. We don't know how good the killer whale's eyesight is but we can assume it has the same problem. Its eyes are best adapted for use underwater and probably are less effective in the air. Man probably looks like a seal to the killer when it sees him on the ice. Many Antarctic seals are at least as big as man (they may outweigh man by 800 pounds), and even the emperor penguin is nearly four feet tall. It is a mistake a killer whale could make. Even if a man doesn't exactly look like a penguin, the killer whale probably doesn't have the mental facility to understand the difference.

Of course, if a man ever gets caught off guard and does fall to a killer whale, it will be purely academic that it was just a case of mistaken identity! It is important, however, in our effort to determine whether the animal is by nature a man-eater. Before concluding, let's see what some of the experts have to say. The following quotes are from letters received by the author on inquiry and are printed by permission:

Donald P. de Sylva, research assistant professor, the Marine Laboratory, Institute of Marine Science, University of Miami, writes, ". . . I know of no authenticated attacks . . . except to say that these animals are certainly potentially dangerous by their size alone."

Gilbert L. Voss, chairman, Biological Sciences Division, the Marine Laboratory, Miami:

Concerning the killer whale, I have been also unable to find any information concerning attack on man. Dr. Paul Hansen, at Charlottenlund Slot, Denmark, who is in charge of the Danish fisheries at Greenland, told me in conversation, that in his many years in killer whale infested waters there has never been a case of a killer whale attacking an Eskimo in a Kayak, regardless of distance from shore; although the Eskimos are fearful of them.

George Mack, director, Queensland Museum, Brisbane, writes, "I have no record of . . . the killer whale causing any harm to a human being. . . . In my opinion, the fanciful tales . . . are the creations of novelists and newspapermen. . . ."

Bruce S. Wright, director, Northeastern Wildlife Station, Fredericton, New Brunswick, writes, "I would still rate the killer whale to be as dangerous to a man in the water as any shark, although records of its attacks on men are almost non-existent."

John E. Randall, professor, Biology Department, University of Puerto Rico, Mayaguez, states:

I know of no injuries or deaths resulting from man's contact with killer whales. . . . I suspect that the killer whale is a very intelligent beast like the porpoise. It certainly has had ample opportunity to attack man. It is most distinctive in color pattern and morphology, as you know. If more than just a very rare attack on some poor Eskimo on an ice floe has occurred, I think we would have accounts of it. But I must confess that I would be more than just a little uneasy if I were to share the same part of the ocean with a hungry killer whale.

Victor B. Scheffer of the U.S. Fish and Wildlife Service, Seattle, notes:

. . . I have been aware of the need for documented accounts of attacks by killer whales . . . but do not recall having seen any. . . . I would feel very uneasy if I were in a small boat or were swimming in the vicinity of killers, particularly if the animals had just made a kill and were excited.

Paul Hansen, Ministeriet for Grønland, Grønlands Fiskeriundersøgelser, Charlottenlund, Denmark, replies:

[I] have never heard that Killer Whales have attacked human beings. The Greenlanders are, however, very much afraid of that whale, and we have heard that Greenland seal-hunters in many cases have taken refuge on small islands with their kayak, when Killer Whales have appeared.

It is an old experience of the Greenlandic seal-hunters that Killer

Whales do much harm to their hunting by chasing away the seals. Therefore Killer Whales are outlawed and all crews on board motorboats and schooners are asked to fire at them whenever they meet them.

A. S. Houston, assistant director, Fisheries Research Board of Canada, Nanaimo, British Columbia, replies:

Mr. Pike, who is in charge of our Marine Mammals Investigation, does not know of any confirmed incidences of attacks by any of these creatures in British Columbia waters. While we do not maintain a close check on these matters, it is unlikely that any such attacks would not come to Mr. Pike's attention. Since killer whales are relatively abundant in our waters, it appears unlikely that they are a great menace to man.

The Long Island Dolphins, Inc., a skin-diving club, issues a newsletter called "The Snorkel Snooper." Page four of the December 1962 issue carried the following account:

Fifteen killer whales showed up at the individual competitive spearfishing meet of the Greater Los Angeles Council of Divers. They just nosed around the divers and in the process turned one over with the swirl from his tail. Another diver pushed a bull away with his speargun. Now get this . . . only six divers of the 43 contestants left the water because of the killers.

[The author has not checked this story. It is repeated here as reported.]

A noteworthy addition to the above extracts is a brief report on a conversation the author had with Capt. Jacques–Yves Cousteau. From his own experiences with marine animals, from his observations, research, and general knowledge, Captain Cousteau feels that the danger from this creature is minimal. He has known of cases where skin divers were in the water with killers and were not bothered. He feels the tales of their so-called ferocity are exaggerated.

Antony Alpers, in his interesting book, *Dolphins: The Myth and the Mammal,* reports at some length on the fabled cooperation between a pack of killer whales and whalers of Twofold Bay, Australia. Men still alive swear that the stories of the orcas assisting the whalemen to get their prey in return for the tongue and lips are true. For over fifty years, the whalers of Eden on the bay were supposed to have been on the best of terms with three distinct packs of killers. In view of other seemingly incredible stories that have proved to be true about other cetaceans playing with children, it could be true.

What, then, can be our conclusion—if any?

The killer whale, particularly an adult bull, is a large and formidable creature. Although small as whales go, it is a big animal, the biggest of the dolphins. It is very fast in the water, and is armed with a really terrible array of teeth. The crushing power of its jaws is apparently immense. It can snap a seal or a porpoise in half with a single bite; or so it is reported. A man in the water would be absolutely helpless should one attack. Any small boat, unless especially designed, could be broken up by an orca. In brief, if a killer attacks, it is as dangerous to man as any creature on earth.

Does the killer whale attack? The temptation here is to reverse Romine's odd logic that the killer whale is dangerous because nothing proves that it isn't, and say that it isn't because nothing proves that it is. We will avoid that trap, however, and say that it is surprising, even startling, that there aren't reports of death and injury to man. It would seem that there would be enough rogue bulls on the prowl to cause at least some trouble! Eskimos in their skin boats are surely at the mercy of the killer every time they put to sea. Where are the reports of attacks? There is an extremely effective grapevine that operates on an international level carrying information of interest to biologists into libraries and laboratories from Sydney to Tokyo, from Bombay to London, Paris, and New York. Where are the reports of the killer whales? There are thousands of attacks by the big cats on record; a man killed by an elephant in the African forests is recorded sooner or later. Why, in thousands of years, has there been only one single attack by an animal whose appearance in the vicinity of small craft could be reported daily from some place on the oceans of this planet?

This author does not believe the killer whale is disposed to attack man unless it mistakes him for something else, something it normally eats. If there have been attacks on man, intentional or in error, they have been extremely rare. The killer's appearance is such that one would think that it must be dangerous; and, quite simply, this author believes that is how the stories started.

To those who may challenge this point by asking me if I would go over the side and cavort with a killer, my answer is, No, I would not. There is the danger of aberrant individuals, "rogues," extremely hungry migrants, nearsighted old-timers, sexually excited bulls, and mothers with calves. In conclusion, it should be noted that the author finally got to pat a killer whale at the Miami Seaquarium. The monster actually snapped at me. He didn't like me—bad chemistry, one must assume.

6 The Elephants

The following account was received from Maj. C. H. Simpson in April 1962. It was sent from Blackrock Estate, Nagercoil, Kanjakumar District, South India. Major Simpson is a hunter and planter with many years of experience in the forests of India.

In the same year [1932], six men went up into the Mahendragiri Hills to collect cardamoms. They had a muzzle-loading gun, although this was prohibited. They found a large male elephant feeding in a patch of cardamoms and the gunner of the party crept up close and let fly his weapon, charged with bits of iron and slugs, and propelled by country-made black powder. The pain of the wounds, the noise of the shot and the smoke, combined to cause the tusker to go crashing off down the hillside, trumpeting with rage. The cardamom pickers moved away some distance to camp for the night. Three of them slept under an overhanging rock, the other three put up a shelter of wild plantain leaves and slept just alongside. The elephant returned at dark, took up the scent of the men, and came to their camp. He rushed the camp and killed all three men under the shelter. Those under the rock, he could not reach.

Two years later this same elephant was walking through Woodlands Estate in broad daylight when he was seen by an overseer named Singarajan. The tusker was below on a steep slope, so thinking he was safe, Singarajan flung a large stone at him. The stone hit his tusk, and he immediately gave chase up the slope. Singarajan ran for his life, shouting warnings to other men who were working further up the hill. All scattered except an old man, who squatted under a bush beside the path. The tusker rushed after Singarajan, ignoring the others. As he passed the old man in the bush, his fore foot hit the man who rolled over into the path, and the tusker's hind foot came squarely on his head, squashing it. Singarajan, though young and active, had no chance, he was caught in the tusker's trunk, thrown to the ground, and torn in two. Not satisfied with this, the tusker trampled him until not one bone was left unbroken, and then left trumpeting his pean of victory.

Less than a year later, a party of men were going down from Mahendragiri Estate to their homes in the village in the evening. One man was running to catch up with the others, when he ran into the rogue tusker. He was immediately seized and killed. The other men heard his shrieks and the trumpeting of the elephant, and ran for their lives. The corpse was found next day.

I had been continually writing to the Government about this elephant giving them a detailed description of it, and asking for it to be declared a rogue, which would entitle it to be shot. Elephants being preserved in Travancore State, shooting one not proscribed would lead to prosecution. I was managing several estates, and was kept busy driving away the rogue when he was near.

On the morning of 16th April, 1936, the man who brought the morning muster from Seafield Estate, turned up late, and pitched me a harrowing tale of how he had been waylaid, and had escaped only because of his superhuman agility. I gave him a restorative in the shape of a tot of rum, and taking my 450/400 H.V. rifle told him to lead me to the spot. Getting on the slope overlooking the ravine in which the rogue was said to be, I sat scanning every clump of bush for a sign of it, and listening for the crack of breaking branches as he fed. Seeing and hearing nothing, I told the man to get back to Seafield, and that I would stay and cover him over the ravine. He had gone little more than half way when the rogue burst out of a clump of brush hardly big enough to conceal a cow, and made for the man with a scream. I roared to the man to run, at the same time firing two shots into the air to deter the elephant, but with no effect. I fired at the root of the elephant's neck, just as he stretched out his trunk to grab the man. He reeled and staggered a few paces and collapsed below the path. The man dropped a few yards further on, and I had to administer another tonic to bring him round.

In addition to these instances, there have been several cases of elephants causing deaths, the last being barely a year ago on the Mahendragiri Road, there was an instance of an elephant attacking a lorry and piercing the radiator with its tusks, when the hot water squirted out and put him off further mischief. A cart was broken up and the bullocks killed on the Baalamore Estate Road, the cart driver escaped by running for his life.

Let us examine the subject of this account, the largest land animals left on our planet, the elephants.

Of the more than 350 kinds of elephants (order Proboscidea) that once lived on earth, two species are left. The African Elephant *(Loxodonta africana)* has a range extending over the greater part of Africa south of the Sahara, but with large pockets excepted. The Asiatic or Indian Elephant *(Elephas maximus)* ranges through much of India, Ceylon, Bangladesh, Burma, Laos, Cambodia, Vietnam, Thailand, Malaya, Sumatra, and parts of Borneo, and has an indefinite number of subspecies. There is no way of accurately estimating the world's wild elephant population, but it is considerable. Vast herds still range wild, and majestically independent.

For many reasons, the elephant has long attracted the attention of man. To protein-starved populations, a slaughtered elephant is a cause for great rejoicing. Reports of natives descending on a still-warm carcass, and literally hacking and eating their way into the mountain of flesh exist by the score. Few observers have been able to resist a description of the event. In most cases, their own protein-rich diet has given their reports a rather supercilious air. Elephants have supplied a highly treasured commodity to the world's artisans since long before the dawn of history. One example of ivory carving, a mask from Nigeria, recently brought $20,000 at auction. In large areas, the elephant is essential to the logging industry, and performs other heavy industrial chores as well. Elephants pull man's vehicles, carry man at work and play, lift his loads, and assist in the capture of more elephants to help with the labors. Should the elephant suddenly disappear, local economies would suffer. When man hasn't been using the elephant to work or supply raw materials, he has used it as a symbol, as a sign of wealth, and as a mystic image. From the hardwood forests of Burma where it supports a major logging industry, to the national parks of Africa where it supports a major tourist industry, to the circuses of Europe and America the elephant is an animal close to the hearts of men.

All of the attention directed to these magnificent beasts has resulted in a veritable mountain of legends, beliefs, and misinformation. In India, they still dress their ceremonial elephants in lavish tapestries. Everywhere in the world, primitive and sophisticated people alike dress elephants in robes of finespun fiction. Why it is more enticing to repeat nonsense than sense when dealing with such honestly amazing animals will forever remain a mystery.

Although someone will almost surely mount an expedition within the next twelve months to find the great, secret elephant graveyard, it doesn't exist. The lure of untold tons of free ivory has caused this particular legend to persist right up to the present day, despite all evidence to the contrary. Elephants may at times wander away from the herd to die, but the idea that they trek to some secret valley is without foundation.

Elephants do not live to be hundreds of years old, not even to a hundred. To the best of the author's knowledge, there isn't a record known to prove that they pass seventy years on any but rare occasions. Some almost certainly do, of course, but a seventy-five- or eighty-year-old elephant would be very old indeed.

The idea that elephants never forget *is*, surprisingly, close to *a* truth. Of course, *never* is a strong word, and elephants differ as individuals. They are not improvisers but function well within certain confines, and can learn an astounding variety of tasks. They learn slowly and apparently retain what they have learned almost indefinitely, and they keep learning all their lives. These animals are slow to be born (twenty-one months is normal gestation), slow to grow up (they are kept on milk for years), slow to learn, and slow to forget. Just what the memory span and the saturation level are has not really been determined, but certainly there are limits to both.

Reports of charging elephants leaping ravines and galloping or trotting in pursuit of man mark themselves as fiction. An elephant cannot leap or jump under any conditions. If the maximum stride of an individual is six feet, it will burn to death before it will cross a moat six feet six inches wide to escape a fire. Quite simply, it can't; its body does not have the bone—muscle—tendon combination necessary for any form of saltation. As for running, trotting, or what-have-you, never! An elephant has one form of locomotion on land, it can walk! It can walk fast, to be sure, faster than a man can run by a very good margin, but nothing more. At the height of a charge, an elephant is walking despite a thousand adventure stories to the contrary.

The question of maximum size is often discussed, and some really fantastic claims have been made. The African elephant actually does grow to be slightly over eleven feet at the shoulder, and weighs around seven tons. (However, a thirteen-foot-two-inch specimen is in the Smithsonian Institution.) The Asiatic animal is somewhat smaller. There are any number of differences between the two genera, but these are of significance only to the specialist. It is enough, generally, to be able to distinguish between the Asiatic and African elephants, and this can be done at a glance. The African elephants have huge ears, the Asiatics' are very much smaller. The Africans give the impression of having little or no neck, due largely to their great ears; the Asiatics appear to have their heads set out well in front. African elephants have sloping foreheads, while the Asiatics have two very pronounced bumps at the top and front of the head. The other differences are less apparent at a distance but are nonetheless quite distinctive. Side by

Freshly captured elephants near Mysore, India, in the "old days." Still exceedingly dangerous because they were badly frightened, these animals were beaten and bullied by trained elephants, or *koonkies*, starved and denied water until their spirit was broken. Only then could their training as working elephants begin. It was a brutal process.

By three o'clock in the afternoon, working elephants are brought in from the forest and scrubbed down by the mahouts. This constant contact helps the mahouts keep a measure of control over their enormous charges. It doesn't always work—mahouts are sometimes killed. When that happens the elephants are not destroyed, the men are replaced.

The true king of beasts—the African elephant. This interesting photograph was taken by Osa Johnson near Lake Paradise in northern Kenya and given to the author when he was ten years old.

side, the two types of living elephants are obviously very different animals, even to the most casual observer.

Are elephants dangerous to man? Under certain conditions, decidedly so. They have enormous strength and are capable of a speed estimated at twenty miles per hour. Left alone, they generally won't bother man, but man very often does not leave them alone. When he hasn't been hunting them for their flesh, hide, and tusks, he has been capturing them for use as work animals. When he hasn't been tracking them down for any sensible use, he has hunted them mercilessly to prove his own manhood. The mystic rite of slaying a magnificent beast that has taken nature forty or fifty years to mature, to prove that you are brave, is not generally practiced by primitive people. Only supposedly civilized people seem to feel that manhood can be obtained at the expense of our most impressive land animal. This endless and aggressive pursuit of elephants has resulted in a lot of dead and mutilated hunters, but we won't consider the animal dangerous in this context. If an individual wishes to pit his skill and his $4,000 double rifle against the biggest and potentially most dangerous game in the world, there is always the chance that he'll be rather the worse for the experience. We'll consider the danger posed by these animals in a different light here.

An adult elephant will consume up to four hundred pounds of food a day, it has been estimated. Much of this is wasted since a great deal of undigested matter is passed out. The enormous stomach of the creature indulges in endless churnings and rumblings known as borborygmus. The digestive process is quite staggering in its proportions. All of this attention, however, is lavished on vegetable matter. Elephants, of course, do not eat meat, and reports of their turning carnivorous are without substantiation. Although the elephant is therefore never a man-eater, its appetite can make it dangerous to man in another way. Elephants like many of the same foods enjoyed by man, and this puts them in direct competition with hunting–gathering tribes, and makes them particularly troublesome to agricultural people. The invasion of cultivated lands by wild elephants is a common occurrence, and human deaths have resulted from the practice. A herd of wild elephants trampling through a farm can lay waste many acres in a single night. Farmers often find it necessary to hunt them down, or bring in professionals to do it for them. Elephant control is still a major problem in many places. An inexperienced hunter attempting the job himself can get into serious trouble. Elephants move like ghosts through the thickest of cover, and can hide most expertly in almost any cover at all. Knowing how far you can push a foraging herd before triggering a charge, or even a stampede, and how far a bull will retreat before turning and waiting in ambush, are calculations for the expert to make. Should the herd have young, and since the young are not weaned until years after their birth and most herds always have young around, the cows can be very touchy. A herd of wild elephants, in or out of your garden, is a thing to be respected. These animals are shortsighted, and short-tempered. They have incredible hearing, and a most delicate sense of smell. They are quite fearless, and if really provoked will attack anything in sight, trucks and cars included.

Oscar "Ed" Pearson of the South African Tourist Corporation told the author of a successful attempt to enclose an area near a national park with an elephant-proof fence. Railroad track was driven deep into the ground with a pile driver, and laced with elevator cable. It apparently worked, although it was never put to the test of a charge or stampede. Even if it did resist the determined efforts of a herd (and that is very doubtful), it would hardly be a practical way to enclose a farm of many thousands of acres. The systematic control of elephants by trained naturalists and really expert hunters is essential to all agricultural areas within their range. Surely, there are few jobs requiring a higher level of skill in the ways of the wild than this. Some friends of the author do it in off seasons in Africa when the safari trade is slow. They confess that even the most skilled of professional hunters approach a herd of wild elephants with their hearts in their throats. Only novices, and slightly deranged old-timers, like killing elephants. That last squeeze of the trigger is accompanied by a thunderous roar, and a feeling of real guilt in all but the most unfathomable of minds.

The fearlessness and temperament of wild elephants are in part demonstrated by an adventure enjoyed by friends of the author. Christian and Barbara Hansen, a team of nature photographers, returned from their fourth African safari with some priceless motion picture footage. Late in 1961, having negotiated the Sahara Desert by car, they were motoring south through East Africa. They camped in a clearing in a heavily forested area, and spent an uneventful night although there were signs of elephants all around. The following morning, while Chris was checking some camera equipment, Barbara set up breakfast on a folding camp table outside their tent. Chris looked up, and shouted for Barbara to run. An enormous bull was striding out of the forest directly for her. She ducked into the tent, the nearest available cover, and prepared to escape through the back should matters get any more dangerous. Chris took up his rifle, but, reluctant to kill, he held fire until he could determine the bull's intent. The animal made no signs of charging, nor did it hesitate in the slightest from its apparently predetermined path. While the Hansens, now more amused than terrorized, watched, the bull polished off their oranges, took a full box of cereal into its mouth and spat it out empty, rummaged around for a minute or two and then moved off, doing no real damage.

The story of the Hansens' breakfast makes the elephant sound like an amusing, if somewhat oafish, fellow. Nevertheless, it would have been a serious mistake for the Hansens to have relied on that quality at such close quarters. A precipitous act by either of them could have enraged the bull, and set it off into an orgy of destruction. An elephant is not an easy creature to kill, and even if Chris had used his rifle, there would have been no guarantee that Barbara would not have disappeared underfoot before a telling shot could have been placed. On the other hand, a snap of the fingers might have frightened the beast and set it crashing off into the forest in headlong flight. The trouble is, with elephants you can never be sure.

The author has been chased by both Asian and African elephants on a number of occasions but cannot say with certainty that he was ever actually charged. On the island of Sri Lanka he was chased repeatedly by a large cow because, as it was later discovered, another female was giving birth nearby. Our ancient diesel Jeep kept stalling and each time it did the cow hauled up and gave all sorts of warning displays. These were clearly alternatives to a real charge. The cow kept it up until the Jeep and its occupants were well out of the area. In Mozambique the author and his wife inadvertently drew what appeared to be a charge of six elephants at the same time. A great deal of arm waving and shouting split the small herd with half passing to the right and half to the left. Again, an alternative to an actual showdown was elected by the elephants. In fact, despite encounters with perhaps a thousand wild elephants over the years, the author cannot honestly recall a single incident where he was actually endangered. Of course, the elephants weren't endangered either, since the author doesn't carry a gun.

Theodore Roosevelt, in his *African Game Trails*, describes the graves of two hunters at Nimule, in British East Africa. Both men were killed by elephants; one was dismembered by an infuriated bull. Carl Akeley, father of modern taxidermy, was seized by a bull and terribly mutilated. A series of miracles, not the least of which was the great hunter's astounding stamina, enabled him to survive. One can believe that the incident contributed to Akeley's belief that the elephant is the most dangerous game in the world.

In his *Large Game Shooting in Thibet, the Himalayas, Northern and Central India*, Brig. Gen. Alexander A. A. Kinloch writes:

Elephants usually go in herds, varying in number from four or five to sixty or seventy. When in herds they are generally quite harmless, and a child might put a hundred to flight; but a solitary bull is often a savage and dangerous brute, attacking and killing everyone he can. Occasionally one of these "rogues" will haunt a certain road and completely stop the traffic as long as he remains. There was one which used to haunt the Dera Dun, and which was said to have killed many people, and even destroyed houses. I fancy, however, that the depredations of several Elephants were laid to the charge of one.

A. Blayney Percival, of the former Kenya Colony Game Department, in his *A Game Ranger's Note Book*, wrote, ". . . it was impossible to know what the herd might do; elephants have been known to charge a camp at night when they blunder on it thus in the dark. . . ."

G. P. Sanderson wrote, in his *Thirteen Years Among the Wild Beasts of India*,

Single male elephants spend their nights, and sometimes days, in predatory excursions into rice and other fields in the immediate vicinity of villages. They become disabused of many of the terrors which render ordinary elephants timid and needlessly cautious. These elephants are by no means always evilly disposed. A solitary elephant I knew intimately at Morlay was a most inoffensive animal, and, although bold in his wanderings, never injured anyone. Some male elephants, however, as much wandering herd tuskers as really solitary animals, are dangerous when suddenly come upon, but rarely wantonly malicious.

Of cases recorded of really vicious animals perhaps the most notable is that of the Mandla (near Jubbulpore, Central Provinces) elephant, an elephant supposed to have been mad, and which killed an immense number of persons about five years ago. It is said to have eaten portions of some of its victims, but it probably only held their limbs in its mouth whilst it tore them to pieces. The Mandla elephant was shot, after a short but bloody career, by two officers.

One is unlikely to read a book by a hunter, game conservator, missionary, or just plain traveler who has known the habitat of the elephant, without finding some reference to the depredations of so-called rogues.

Since this special kind of elephant is the one generally accused of being the man-killer, it is on it that we should concentrate in our discussion of danger to man. Webster defines a rogue elephant as "a vicious elephant that separates from the herd and roams alone." Semantically, this may be correct, but it is not clear if it is an accurate zoological description. The only thing that is certain is that some elephants spend part of their time away from the herd, and tend to be more dangerous than a normal herd animal. Perhaps the solitude they endure, not characteristic of a highly social animal, makes them uneasy and defensive. Perhaps some infirmity keeps them from staying with a herd on the move; and most herds, generally, are transient. This same infirmity could make them unusually cranky. Since all solitary animals are not old and not bulls, the idea that rogue elephants are old bulls past their sexual prime is open to question. A herd bull past his prime, and who was displaced by a younger and more vigorous male, might quite readily develop a personality disorder. This may account for some so-called rogues but not all.

Male elephants fight among themselves, the sexual drive probably being at the base of most disturbances, and very extensive wounds often result. These puncture wounds and lacerations undoubtedly fester and cause great pain. Many rogues have been identified as "pain-maddened," once shot and examined.

Jokes are often heard around the elephant pen at the zoo to the effect, "How would you like to have a toothache in that?" To an elephant whose tusk has been injured and is decaying, that is hardly a joke. The nerve in the base of the tusk is immense, as big around as a man's arm, and an ache there must be monumental. Certainly, an elephant with a tuskache might very well be disposed to attack.

The elephant has a surprisingly small brain for an animal so large. It is set low, and far to the rear. Most of the massive frontal portion of the skull is given over to air pockets to help reduce the load of the broad foundation required to support the tusks. For this reason, the brain shot so often attempted by the hunter is frequently unsuccessful. When successful, the brain shot is the best way to stop a charge, but it is a difficult assignment. Many bulls go through life with heavy particles of metal imbedded in their skulls. The loads used in elephant rifles, .450 to .600 caliber, fire projectiles weighing from 480 to 900 grains. Since most big tuskers who wander outside of game reserves get shot at sooner or later, one can wonder just how many majestic headaches an old bull will endure before taking a dislike to all mankind. A number of rogues have been shot and found to have one or more old bullet wounds. Such an animal can almost be excused for its disposition, except by the innocent victim who is plucked off a path en route to market. It cannot be demonstrated at this point that the elephant is capable of so complex a motive as revenge. It would seem that way, however.

What is an elephant charge really like—not a chase or a bluff, but a real charge? The enraged elephant tastes the air with that wonderful trunk, casting it up, from side to side, and then straight out. Its ears are spread wide, many feet across at the extreme, to force every small sound into its ear canals. Its wholly inadequate eyes glisten, and its feet practice a nervous little prancing shuffle as it takes one step forward, and then two back. Suddenly, rocking slightly from side to side, the first charge is made. A cloud of dust and debris billows up around its chest and forelegs, and a shrill blast issues forth with stunning impact. The first charge, a last bluff, carries it twenty feet or so before it hauls up and half turns. It snorts, shuffles, and tastes the air once more. Any structure or vegetation at hand is apt to get smashed down as the rage mounts. Perhaps it holds its advanced position and shrieks again, or perhaps it turns in a small circle, or backs off a few steps. At any rate, it is soon again facing the cause of its irritation. Its ears snap forward again, its trunk seeks the direction its eyes can't locate, and then it comes, with all the force of an express train as the giant presses home the charge. The first few strides are misleadingly slow; in a moment the pace is far in excess of any speed a man can approximate. In a moment, the elephant is either dead with a bullet in the heart or brain, or the man is in grave peril.

Reports of just what elephants do to their victims vary. Some animals evidently catch their victims in their trunks and dismember them, smash them against the ground or an upright object, or simply toss them into the air or back over their shoulders. Some elephants impale their victim on their tusks, while others simply run over people; others totally mutilate their enemies. Some angry beasts are satisfied with one crushing charge, while others return again and again to their victim after he is dead.

Thousands upon thousands of elephants are slaughtered every year, so the animal is not beyond the destructive powers of our midget race. Nonetheless, a charging elephant is as dangerous to man as any animal can be.

In this chapter, so far, we have concentrated on the danger these animals *can* represent. It now remains to put this into perspective. The elephants are one of the most magnificent natural heritages we have left on earth. Basically, they are orderly herd animals, very intent on minding their own business. An adult has no natural enemies save man and disease. Other animals, even the great predators, leave it alone for the most part, although an unguarded calf may be taken. The average elephant in normal circumstances is not dangerous to man. It confines its attentions to herd behavior, migrations, foraging, and seeking water. Although quick to go on the defensive, it is normally a peaceful animal. Most elephants will flee the sound or smell of man. They will frequently vacate an area if man moves in. From their earliest days, baby elephants come to associate the smell of man with great agitation and nervous rumblings within the herd. Nature teaches her young how to survive; what the mother doesn't like, the baby learns to dislike from the disturbance in routine that it causes.

On occasion, a herd will ignore man and raise havoc. Crops are ruined and structures destroyed. For reasons not clearly understood, lone animals will become killers with behavior as far from the norm as the cunning of a psychopath among humans. These aberrant individuals must be dealt with, naturally. Elephant control is essential to agricultural areas, and few people can argue with the logic of a game ranger tracking down a known insane specimen. Sometimes a herd becomes diseased, and it is essential that it be destroyed before it can migrate to new areas, carrying diseases like anthrax. For the most part, however, there is little excuse for considering the elephant a threat or a crop (to be harvested). We have perfectly good plastics from which to make our piano keys and billiard balls, and these magnificent creatures are worth any and all efforts to preserve. Fortunately, they respond well to sensible control and are for the moment not in danger of extinction in many areas. Surely, if there is an animal on earth worth preserving as a monument to nature as it once was, the elephant is the prime candidate.

7 Venomous Mammals

Everyone knows there are venomous snakes; a great many people realize there are venomous fish; but few people, apparently, are aware of the fact that some mammals are equipped with venom.

There are venomous mammals; just how many is not yet known. To the author's knowledge, the ability is limited to two groups, the extremely isolated, egg-laying monotremes of Australia, Tasmania, and New Guinea, and an unspecified number of specialized soricids, or shrews and related animals. All of these animals are shy, retiring, and, if not actually rare, extremely difficult to find. By no stretch of the imagination can any of them be considered dangerous to man and they are discussed here only to establish this fact, and because a review of the world's venomous animals must logically make some note of them.

Blarina brevicauda, the Short-tailed Shrew of North America, has red-tipped teeth. It is a minute creature with infinitesimally small eyes and a perfectly foul disposition. It makes its home under trash and vegetation and builds a cozy little nest where it hibernates and where the young are born. It eats an absolutely amazing quantity of insects, worms, arachnids, slugs, and other animal prey, and will turn to cannibalism if denied other food for a few hours. It is apparently almost constantly in a "rage" which is magnified by its atom-splitting metabolism. Its shrill shriek is partially beyond the range of human ears, and it is evidently seldom still. Although superficially mouselike, it is really related to the moles and is an insectivore. If it were as big as a collie, and kept the same rate of metabolism, it would be far and away the most dangerous animal alive, venom glands or no. What a really large shrew could do to the natural balance of any region is terrifying to contemplate.

Near the base of the short-tailed shrew's lower incisor teeth is an opening to a pair of ducts. These ducts lead to a pair of modified salivary glands where the venom is produced. The two pairs of lower incisors project forward, forming a groove along which the venom flows. No great amount of venom is stored, but it has been demonstrated that mice can be killed by a small fraction of the available dose. Partial paralysis, protruding eyes, and convulsions occur in small mammals injected with an extract prepared from the glands. Death follows these symptoms in a few minutes. There have been no recorded human deaths resulting from the bite of any of these animals; only a few mild, localized reactions.

The folklore of Central Europe contains many references to venomous shrews. It is known that at least the European Water Shrew (*Neomys fodiens fodiens*) and the British Bicolored Water Shrew (*N. f. bicolor*) are also venomous. The Masked Shrew (*Sorex cinereus*) is also almost certainly in this special group. The squirrel-sized Haitian Solenodon (*Solenodon paradoxus*) is definitely known to belong. Once again, there is no danger to man unless one takes gypsy legends as truth. They have reportedly been stirring shrews into their magic broths for generations. Aside from that, a shrew could hardly bite a man who wasn't handling it, and even if a venomous shrew did manage to bite, the venom is too mild to have any meaningful effect on humans.

The Monotremata are generally represented in most people's minds by the famed Duck-billed Platypus (*Ornithorhynchus anatinus*) of Australia. This single member of the family Ornithorhynchidae has close relatives in the family Tachyglossidae, the so-called echidnas, or spiny anteaters, of Australia, New Guinea, Tasmania, and some adjacent islands. Although quite different in appearance, the echidnas and the platypus share certain remarkable characteristics: they lay eggs, and have only one body opening for all eliminatory and reproductive purposes. They have hearty appetites, and are shy and retiring. They are among the most fascinating animals in the world, representing a number of reptilian as well as mammalian features.

On the inside of the male platypus' rear ankles are matching spurs that lead to ducts running down from the animal's thighs. The females are not so equipped. These spurs can be driven deep into the flesh of anyone handling the creature by a convulsive little kick. It would seem to be a defensive device only, and of little threat to man. As a matter of fact, as shy as this animal is, it is hard to see how anyone could become involved with the device without picking the platypus up. And picking up a duck-billed platypus has to be one of the more unlikely activities in which one might expect to engage. It is also suggested that the spurs play a role in mate selection but little, really, is known about the evolutionary impetus behind this venom system.

David Fleay of Queensland, Australia, the outstanding authority on the platypus, kindly responded to a letter from the author by publishing a request for platypus envenomation case histories in the *Brisbane Courier-Mail*. He himself told of a Mr. Warrian of Injune who accidentally hooked a platypus in 1950 while fishing in the Dawson River. While attempting to free the creature, he received both spurs in his hand. He was in great pain and dangerously ill for weeks. Ten years later, his arm was still "useless." In reply to Mr. Fleay's column, two letters were received, attesting, as Mr. Fleay pointed out, to the rarity of incidents. A Mr. Richards wrote from Liston in New South Wales and told of a nine-year-old girl named Gillespie who was struck on the arm by a platypus caught in a fish trap. The incident occurred in the tiny village of Vacy near the junction of the Allyn and Paterson rivers, in 1895. Mr. G. H. Sargent wrote from Currumben to tell of his own adventures fifty years ago. As a boy of twelve, he caught a young male platypus in the North Pine River and tucked it in his shirt. From 9:00 A.M. until 1:30 P.M., it cuddled up against the boy's body without any sign of aggression. He then transferred the animal to a wooden crate. He removed it several times to show it off, and never encountered any difficulty. Toward evening, he took the creature out to show to some people from a traveling circus. Among them were "three very brightly dressed, rather loudspoken ladies." Their effect on the young platypus was evidently electric, and young Mr. Sargent received one spur in the front of the wrist and the other in the back of the hand. Mr. Sargent describes his injury in this way: "The pain was very severe, like a nerve pain, and left me feeling shocked and sick for some minutes. The hand immediately began to swell and was soon so 'puffy' that no knuckles were visible. The whole arm became very hot and a lump developed in the arm pit." A doctor at Sandgate who had previous experience with platypus envenomation prescribed hot baths for the arm. Mr. Sargent concludes, "My arm was O.K. again in a few days and except for stiffness, for a day or so longer, in the hand and fingers, no lasting ill effects occurred." The platypus was lucky in that young Mr. Sargent was a real animal lover. Despite his injury, the boy returned the animal to its river unharmed. One can speculate that the youngster was lucky to have picked on an immature specimen.

There is reason to believe that the echidnas may also be similarly

The short-tailed shrew *(Blarina brevicauda)*, a species whose bite is known to be venomous, though not dangerous to man.
Courtesy U.S. Dept. of the Interior, Fish and Wildlife Service

The duck-billed platypus under water. When submerged the platypus depends on its sense of touch, for both its eyes and ears are covered by watertight lids. It is not known if the platypus uses its venomous spurs under water except, possibly, when seized.
Courtesy Australian News and Information Bureau

equipped. Mammologist Ernest P. Walker suggested that the spines of the echidnas *may be* venomous to a degree. He developed a localized reaction after being jabbed and writes that a Japanese researcher reported a case of envenomation from the spines. Stanley P. Young of the U.S. Fish and Wildlife Service reported that all monotremes have venom glands. The question is as academic as the case with the platypus. It is interesting information, should be noted in a book dealing with venomous creatures, but must be offset with the statement—*Within the context of this book, it is not dangerous to man.*

8 Other Mammals

The dog-faced monkeys are a widely varied group. They are found from Gibraltar in the west to Japan in the east and far to the north (Amuria) in the eastern part of their range. They are, though, for the most part, restricted to south of the great desert belt in Africa and Asia. Their range is quite enormous and their habits as varied as their appearance. Though by nature retiring, some forms grow large enough to be dangerous to lone people, while a high degree of social organization among some species has led to apparently deliberate attacks on even parties of people. Of the dog-faced group, the Baboons *(Papio)* have the most advanced social organization and have a remarkable level of intelligence. They mass attack in self-defense, and can put a marauding leopard to flight. They are powerful creatures with enormous canine teeth. They do kill livestock, notably sheep, and are omnivorous. Their raids on gardens, and even homes, have made them a real pest animal. Human children have been stolen by them on at least a few occasions, although the motive was more likely adoption of a new baby than intended harm. Eugene Marais recounts such an incident in *My Friends the Baboons.* In those cases where an overstimulated troop attacked a man, the punishment they inflicted was quite appalling. Wise enough to be afraid of man, they are nevertheless damaging to man's enterprises in many areas, and are altogether too much animal to be taken on bare-handed.

A Salvation Army medical missionary with forty years of service in India told the author that monkey bites are more common in many parts of that country than snakebite. The significance of that observation will be appreciated more fully when we examine the venomous snakes. Rhesus Monkeys (*Macaca*) in India, because they are emboldened by the freedom granted to them by the Hindu religion, do attack and bite children. Buttocks and leg muscles are torn in these ill-tempered assaults, but rarely will death occur. Monkeys enjoy various degrees of protection in a number of social orders erected by man within their range, and they are generally nuisances in all such situations. For the most part, monkeys are shy and quite harmless when unmolested. And the larger species definitely discourage molestation by any but the most skilled animal handlers.

The anthropoids, or apes, are among the most dramatic (and overdramatized) creatures on earth. Their range today is strictly limited to parts of forested Africa south of the desert and the Oriental region. The lesser apes are generally regarded as seven species, six Gibbons (*Hylobates*) and the Siamangs (*Symphalangus*). The gibbons range from the Himalayas to Hainan, throughout Indochina, Borneo, Sumatra, and south to Java. They are superficially "monkeylike" but tailless, are equipped with very long arms, a rolling bipedal gait, and a normally gentle disposition. They are shy but very intelligent.

The great apes are much better known. The Gorillas (*Gorilla*), Chimpanzees (*Pan*), and Orangutan (*Pongo*) constitute this group. The orangutan, found in Borneo and Sumatra, although immensely strong is retiring and peaceful. There is every indication that it is extremely intelligent. Unless actually attacked or threatened it never bothers man. Even when molested it is much more apt to retreat than to take the offensive. It is within the realm of reasonable speculation to suppose endangering the young might bring on an attack, but it is an unlikely set of circumstances that would elicit such behavior on the part of these large, and now seriously endangered, creatures. In dealing with captive specimens, however, their normally docile behavior should not cause their great strength to be overlooked. In one case, a newly caught specimen was crated for shipment to a zoo. It was packed in a crate made of teak held together by tenpenny spikes. The creature managed to wrap a finger around an inch or so of one spike that had been left protruding. The startled keeper, assigned to its care, watched the orang draw the spike out of the wood, with one digit!

Chimpanzees, still found in the equatorial forests of Africa, are brash creatures as individually variable in behavior and appearance, it would seem, as men. Normally retiring, they watch the movements of human beings within their realm from a safe distance, and with great interest. It is reported that they can be annoyed into attacking, but surely these are exceptional cases. Among the brightest, best-known, and most engaging animals on earth, they should be respected for their great strength, strong teeth, and occasional outbursts of bad temper. They are not, however, normally any threat to man. Young specimens displayed in circus acts and on television are quite misleading. Old males grow to be very large, extremely strong, and cranky, particularly during parts of their sexual cycle. The bite they can administer is seriously damaging, although a zoo keeper is far more likely to be the victim than even a traveler in their natural habitat.

The mighty gorillas are among the most maligned of all animals. Two forms of the same species, Mountain and Lowland, are restricted today to equatorial Africa. The gorilla is apparently at least as intelligent as the other apes, but the somewhat sullen attitude of adults in captivity has frustrated efforts of investigators to determine what the real level of that intelligence is. They are very large animals (an adult male will have an armspread of nine feet), and outweigh man by several hundred pounds, although they are generally shorter in stature. Their strength is prodigious, their teeth formidable, and their behavior when encountered in the forest conducive to wild flights of fantasy, which indeed has marked much of the literature on them.

The nature libraries of the world were enriched in 1963 by the publication of George B. Schaller's *The Mountain Gorilla*. This study examines these fascinating animals from all angles, and in depth. Not ignored is the matter of danger to man, and Dr. Schaller's findings are in keeping with most of the serious writing of recent years. Apparently, man is coming to his senses as regards, at least, some of our wild creatures, and tales of gorillas raping women and carrying off living victims to sacrifice in some mystic jungle rite have become increasingly scarce.

Gorillas are generally harmless animals. Attacks on man have been made when the troop was pressed too far, but these were exceptional cases. Gorillas, like so many large and formidable-looking creatures, are big bluffs. Their actual powers of destruction are so marvelous that they seldom have to employ them. They do quite well by simply threatening to do so. They *do* pound their chests, they *do* roar and bellow, and they *do* make terrifyingly realistic charges. This great show usually puts all but the most persistent or best-armed observer to flight. Those who have witnessed these anthropoid histrionics, who have shot the animal, or turned tail and run, have come away with harrowing tales (and even motion picture footage) of matchless ferocity. Those observers who were interested enough in the animals to steady their nerves and call the bluff, came away with a true evaluation of these remarkable melodramas. Until recently, this latter type of

observer was lost in a rash of fiction about these apes and their supposed homicidal tendencies.

Like the bear, the gorilla has been worked into an erect posture by
pulp magazine illustrators and is usually depicted as a hairy gladiator
wading into battle. Gorillas generally travel on all fours, using their
knuckles in front. They certainly travel that way when in a hurry; and
when they charge, in bluff or in earnest, they are in a hurry. In the
words of Dr. Schaller, "Prolonged bipedal locomotion is rare." On
those occasions when the gorilla actually presses home and attacks, the
subject may receive a perfectly devastating sideways slap or a rending
bite with enormous teeth and powerful jaws. The gorilla usually makes
one punishing pass and is satisfied to move off into the thick forest near
which it is always found. These attacks are rare, however.

Certainly, only a fool would knowingly involve himself with a
gorilla at close quarters because one of these animals has the strength of
a number of the biggest men. The chances of being injured by an
unmolested specimen are very slight. Although man did not "descend"
from these apes, as so much popular literature would have it, the
common ancestors we shared with them were sufficiently recent to
make looking into the eyes of these fascinating animals a haunting
experience.

In several chapters preceding, we have discussed the most impressive of the meat-eaters: cats, wolves, and bears. Many of these forms are
on occasion dangerous, and some of the lesser creatures remaining in
the order can be troublesome as well. Aside from those already discussed, the carnivores include: the remaining Felidae, the lesser cats;
the Viverridae, or civets, mongooses, and their allies; the hyaenas or
Hyaenidae; the raccoons and related forms such as coatis and kinka-
jous, called the Procyonidae; the other Canidae—the true wild dogs
and jackals, foxes, and fennecs; and the Mustelidae or weasels, minks,
martens, badgers, wolverines, skunks, and otters.

The Cape Hunting Dogs of Africa (Lycaon) are reputed to occasionally attack lone humans, but certainly these are rare instances. These
animals, as hunters, live by their wits and are intelligent enough to fear
man. It is a rare carnivore that doesn't give man a wide berth. The
author has observed a number of packs of hunting dogs in Africa and
was never threatened in any way.

The case of the hyaena is a particularly interesting one. Once widespread throughout Europe, Asia to eastern China, and all of Africa, they
are today restricted to that latter continent, India, and the Near East.
They are strictly meat-eaters and scavengers as well as hunters.
Together with the African aardwolf, a harmless, aberrant hyaena, they

constitute the group known as Hyaenidae which apparently falls closer to the felines than the canines, despite appearances.

Hyaenas are frequently characterized as "cowards." They supposedly slink about, cackling in a demented fashion, and eat only carrion. While the "laugh" of the spotted hyaena does have a deranged quality, and while the hyaenas do clean up carrion, they are animals equipped with some of the most powerful jaws in the class Mammalia. They can crack bones that would resist efforts by much larger and apparently more formidable forms. They also appear at times to be aggressive as the following reports show.

9 CHILDREN CARRIED
AWAY BY HYENAS

BHAGALPUR—Nine children have been lifted away during nights by beasts of prey, believed to be Hyenas in six weeks in Bhagalpur town and its outskirts.

The last, a six-month-old child, was carried away from Waraligunj Mahaila on Sunday night.

The police have been trying to locate and liquidate these beasts but without any success so far.

That report, from the Madras *Mail* of May 5, 1962, does say "believed to be Hyenas," but no surprise is expressed at the idea. Some years ago four-year-old Terry Anderson, son of Baptist minister Douglas Anderson of Kroonstad, South Africa, was dragged from his father's tent in Kruger National Park by an adult hyaena and carried thirty yards into the brush before his screams brought rescue. Other such reports are on record and it does seem fairly certain that a helpless human being, small child, or invalid might occasionally be taken. It is believed that old lions eventually fall prey to them. An animal given to cleaning up derelict carcasses may not necessarily wait for a body to be dead before starting to feast. It is now known that hyaenas do hunt in packs and at times lions scavenge after them.

Theodore Roosevelt said of them, "The hyena is a beast of unusual strength, and of enormous power in his jaws and teeth . . . on occasion the hyena takes to man-eating after its own fashion . . . it will enter native huts and carry away children or even sleeping adults." In 1908 and 1919, Uganda was scourged by sleeping sickness, and hyaenas, emboldened by the supply of corpses; took to raiding native villages, graduating from corpses to the sick and helpless, and eventually to healthy people as well. A native hunter working for Sir Alfred Pease was seized by a hyaena and had part of his face torn away. Maj. R. T. Coryndon, administrator of northwestern Rhodesia, was attacked in

The siamang gibbon is an agile, active, and essentially arboreal animal. Highly social, it is given to extremely elaborate vocal displays and posturing. It is not dangerous to man in the wild, though it can, of course, bite most effectively. But that would be likely to happen only in captivity or during attempted capture. Like all apes the siamang would rather shout than fight.
Courtesy Zoological Society of London

The huge shoulders and arms of the lowland gorilla. The enormous strength of these animals can hardly be overstated, though they are by nature peaceful and retiring. Fights among them are more display than battle, and attacks on man are very rare and virtually always provoked.
Courtesy New York Zoological Society

The cape hunting dog, an aggressive species that runs in packs, can pull down most African hoofed animals with relative ease. Attacks on man are all but unknown.

The spotted hyaena, one of the several species of Hyaenidae. An active hunter—not a cowering scavenger, as so many writers have had it—this animal has the most powerful jaws of any land predator. This form is the "laughing hyaena." Neither the striped nor the brown variety is as noisy when it hunts, kills, or eats.
Courtesy South African Tourist Corp.

The Australian dingo (here a bitch and her puppy) is an introduced animal that has become feral—that is, returned to the wild. Is this approximately what all feral canids come to look like in time? Probably so.
Courtesy Australian News and Information Bureau

his sleep, and, in 1910, a hyaena entered the outskirts of Nairobi and carried off a man. Many other such reports are on record.

Many of the other carnivores such as viverrines (mink, weasels, badgers, wolverines, and ratels are good examples) can give very bad bites, and, indeed, do so when mishandled. Few, if any, however, can be accused of attacking man, unless rabid.

Carnivores are among the "cleverest" animals on earth, second, perhaps, only to the primates and whales. Few ever really are dangerous to man unless cornered, captured, or otherwise molested.

The Rodentia is the largest of mammalian orders. A third of all the known genera and half the total species belong to it. Five thousand is the current estimate for species, and 352 for genera. They are among the world's most adaptable animals and certainly range farther than any other mammalian order. There are very few natural habitats without some, and their reproductive rate is so great and so easily accelerated that often, when a new area is involved, unless predators or starvation conditions are present to exercise control, the population explodes and the area is overrun. Rodents are the most destructive mammals on earth, except for man, and the annual toll amounts to billions of dollars. Crop spoilage by rats* alone reaches a staggering figure. The U.S. government estimates that there are over 50 million rats on farms today, 30 million in towns, and 20 million in large cities. It further estimates that each rat costs over $10 per year, or more than $1 billion in damages. One state alone conducted a survey of cereal grain storage facilities and found 43 percent had infestations by rats, and 59 percent by mice. In one section of the United States, only 3 percent of the corn shipped to terminal markets was free from rat and mouse filth. A state chemist found rat hairs in thirteen out of forty-three different canned food products. A single recorded incident involved the spoilage of 1.8 million pounds of sugar by rat urine!

The government of the United States issues warnings that hundreds, and perhaps thousands, of baby chicks, ducks, and geese are killed by rats every night of the year. Small pigs, lambs, and calves are injured and killed. Among the diseases carried and spread by rats, or the fleas they in turn carry, are plague, typhus, amoebiasis, infectious jaundice, salmonella food poisoning, tapeworm infections, and rat-bite fever. Discounting the people killed by these diseases, and the people who die in fires caused by rats eating the insulation off electrical wiring, rats

---

*That is, the Black Rat (*Rattus rattus*) and the Brown Rat (*Rattus norvegicus*); both originated in Asia.

are dangerous by direct assault. Hundreds, and perhaps thousands, of people, particularly children, are attacked each year and bitten. Some are injured badly enough to die.

A man and wife on Manhattan's upper East Side were awakened by the screams of their eighteen-month-old son. They approached his crib and found him bleeding from several bites on his ear, cheek, and neck. Glowering defiantly from a position on the child's pillow was a rat measuring "nearly two feet long." The father took a broom and attacked the rat which in turn attacked the man and bit him deeply on the leg. The wife was similarly attacked by the maddened animal, and all three members of the family required medical attention. The family's cat, kept as protection against rats, had been killed by one the week before! Exterminators, ordered into the building at the cost of the landlord by an outraged judge, killed forty-three rats in the one tenement with no guarantee that the infestation had been eliminated. Such cases are not in the least unusual, unfortunately.

No mammal on earth causes man more pain, discomfort, and food and money loss than does the rat. It is far and away the most troublesome, and at least indirectly, the most dangerous mammal. Rats travel aboard ships and evidently have for a very long time. An area visited by an infested ship soon has its own population. Unless checked by predators, the rats soon destroy the natural balance of the area by killing off native species. Many of the world's ground-nesting and flightless birds were wiped out largely by rats.

Rat control is an essential and costly process for which man must pay each year. With the breeding cycle as short as it is, a single year without control would seriously endanger many of man's enterprises, and life. Few city dwellers realize that their welfare is in such critical balance with so small an animal, but such is the case.

Compared to rats, the other rodents are harmless, save for rabid specimens. All can give nasty bites, but few if any attack man.

One of the most remarkable adaptations made in the world of mammals is the modification of the forelimbs as organs of flight. This power is restricted to members of the order Chiroptera—the bats. Some rodents (the so-called flying squirrels) and a few other mammals soar rather effectively, but the true power of flight is limited to these almost mythical creatures. Only rodents, among mammals, outnumber the bats in actual numbers and kinds. Bats are harmless to man with one odd exception, and this only secondarily—as a disease-carrier. These are the blood-lapping Vampire Bats (*Desmodus*, *Diaemus*, and *Diphylla*), animals that feed only on blood and will take that of any animal from man to toad. The wounds they make are small and not damaging; and the amount of blood consumed, although disquieting, does not approach a dangerous level. One can suppose that an unprotected infant could be set upon by a number of vampires and bled to death, but this is stretching a point too far, though a ten-year-old boy once sustained a dozen bites in one night. Indeed, it must be something more than annoying to wake up in the middle of the night to find a bat enjoying the seepage from a freshly gouged big toe, but the bat itself will do no real harm. Secondary infections are certainly possible, but here again the real damage is a result of microorganisms, and not bats. The very real harm that *can* result from these encounters is discussed in Appendix B, "Rabies."

Many bats are capable of giving a good bite if handled, but the group as a whole is harmless. Most of the stories that exist about them are pure fiction and, except perhaps in appearance, they are entirely inoffensive. In plain fact, the world would be a sad place without bats, for the quantities of insects consumed each night of the year by the insectivorous varieties must be measured in tons. Bats have a very important place in the natural scheme of things. (Incidentally, they will not descend upon, or stick in, women's hair.)

Collectively, all of the hoofed animals of the world are called ungulates. Those with an odd number of toes (including the horses, asses, zebras, tapirs, and rhinoceroses) belong to the order Perissodactyla, and those with an even number of toes (pigs, peccaries, hippopotamuses, camels, llamas, chevrotains, deer, reindeer, okapis, giraffes, cattle, buffalos, bison, antelopes, gazelles, sheep, goats and dozens of related forms) to the order Artiodactyla.

Whereas the rodents are the most significant mammals to man from a negative point of view, the ungulates are so on the positive side. It is safe to say that man could not have reached his present state of social development without the domestication of these animals. Leather, wool, and meat, and uncounted scores of other products come from this group. Fortunately, a great many ungulates are easily domesticated and bred into new and more productive forms. Early overland transportation was entirely dependent on members of this order and, in many parts of the world, they are still essential to the economy. The ungulates are truly the animals that carried the primates to a place of dominance on earth today.

Most wild ungulates are shy. They are the primary food source of not only hunting man but of many of the world's carnivores. As a group, the bears alone of the great carnivores are not largely dependent upon ungulates for survival. As browsing–grazing animals, the ungulates

The African black rhinoceros. This animal will characteristically rush an intruder in what is really a mock charge, usually stopping short with a lot of snorting and huffing. The author has been subjected to dozens of such "charges" and has never once been really threatened.
Photograph by Roger A. Caras

The author with a captive square-lipped or white rhinoceros. This degree of familiarity might not be wise with a so-called black or prehensile-lipped rhino. The white rhinos, although massive animals, do tend to be less aggressive in the wild and more tractable in captivity.

The peccary or javelina is a small but powerful piglike animal of Mexico and the American Southwest. Hunters' tales abound, and there is no doubt that when molested these animals—in packs or "sounders"—can be aggressive. When wounded they can give a good account of themselves, but left alone they tend to mind their own business.

Courtesy Arizona Game and Fish Dept.

The vampire bat (*Desmodus*) does suck blood and, in some areas, does transmit rabies. While a rather unpleasant nocturnal visitor, it hardly warrants centuries of horror tales. It may be difficult to love a vampire bat, but even hatred should have its limits.

Photograph by Charles E. Mohr, courtesy National Audubon Society

Hippos as they are usually found—all but submerged. Inadvertent intrusion on the social structure of this seemingly random collection of animals can bring on a fatal charge. Sexual prerogatives are intensely protected.
Courtesy South African Tourist Corp.

The impressive jaws and teeth of a bull hippopotamus in a South African game park. These jaws can easily crush a boat, or a man.
Courtesy South African Tourist Corp.

have developed the skill of escape rather than that of attack. Some few have learned how to fight back, and some of these are dangerous to man under certain conditions, and not always in mere defense.

Our planet once swarmed with rhinocerotine animals of great variety, and, frequently, great size. Today, only four genera and five species are left. Two genera are in Asia and two in Africa. Having either one or two "horns," depending on the species, the rhinoceros is a formidable animal. (The so-called horn of the rhinoceros is not a horny substance at all, but a matted, hairy conglomeration akin to human fingernails.) These creatures are nearsighted, and short-tempered. Most of them will at least bluff a charge when disturbed, and they can be dangerous at times. They are powerful, thick-skinned animals and have been known to overturn cars and trucks when in a particularly truculent mood. This behavior, however, is defensive and predictable, although their habit of going for the first thing they detect, when they charge, makes it quite hazardous to get too near to them, unless you really know what you are doing. Except on rare occasions when they are encountered by unwary men on foot, there is little excuse for getting into trouble with them. Most of their charging is sheer bluff,* pulling up short of contact, or veering aside, and if you are downwind you won't be detected even a few yards off unless excessively noisy. They are, by and large, inoffensive brutes of no great intelligence, but they are best avoided by anyone not familiar with their rather odd behavior and habits, particularly the African black rhino.

The swine have many wild members and many of these are decidedly dangerous to encounter at close quarters. Various Wild Hogs (Sus), and particularly the related Peccaries (Tayassuidae) of the New World are very well equipped to take care of themselves. Large cats have more than enough to do in making a kill, and a man on foot who threatens a sounder can find himself the object of slashing tusks and fierce determination. Although not strictly vegetarians, the wild pigs and peccaries do not kill large animals for food, but have developed a formidable counterattack—a characteristic that advises caution.

Men have had their horses killed out from under them by White-lipped Peccaries (Tayassu pecari) if reports from Central America are to be believed. (Something that is optional to say the least!) Writing of the collared peccary, or javelina, of the southwestern United States, Hornaday commented: "An enraged Peccary, athirst for blood is to any one not armed with a rifle or a first-rate spear a formidable antagonist."

*The author has been "charged" at least half a dozen times by black rhino in Africa and it always proved to be nothing but bluff, a way of saying "go away and leave me alone."

A report published in 1940 tells of a camper who was run up a tree by a pack of 200 javelina and held at bay for twenty-four hours. The pack refused to move off although the man killed two dozen before he ran out of ammunition. The same report warns against attacks on riders where tendons were ripped on horses' legs.

In 1880 hunter A. G. Requa was run up a tree by a pack of collared peccaries in Sonora, Mexico, and observed the following, "They were chewing the tree, and climbing over each other trying to get at me. Each shot laid one out, and each shot seemed to make them more and more furious, as they would rush at the tree, and gnaw the bark and wood, while the white flakes of froth fell from their mouths." He finally had to tie himself in the tree to keep from falling out. He never hunted javelina again. Similar reports are told of Wild Boars (Sus scrota) in Europe, Red Forest Hogs (Potamochoerus) of Africa, and feral "razorbacks" of southeastern United States. The wild swine of the world, while not man-eaters, or even man-hunters, are dangerous to approach. They are at least as smart as domestic dogs and a lot less dependent on human affection.

The great and ponderous Hippopotamus (Hippopotamus) of Africa (except for a pygmy form—Choeropis—on the same continent) is unique. Of great bulk, they are fast swimmers and quite dangerous in the water. When man does get into trouble with them, however, it is usually through his own ignorance. A herd of hippos is a matriarchy. The females rule from a central sandbank or sandbar in the middle of the established herd territory called the "crèche." Only the babies and very young are allowed in the crèche area with the grown females and an intruder on foot can bring on a charge. Surrounding the crèche are refuges inhabited by the older males of high social standing. Farther out, and less accessible to the crèche and therefore breeding possibilities, are the less well-defined refuges of the younger males. The hundreds of photographs that have been published showing hippos "yawning" are actually pictures of hippos warning others of their kind who have intruded on a refuge. If this warning is not heeded, a violent fight can ensue. A man in a boat who unwittingly paddles from the refuge area of the younger bulls into the refuge of a cranky or insecure old bull, can find his boat suddenly broken in two. Also, lonely "rogues," usually old males, seem to occur in certain areas.

Hippos are generally peaceable creatures, despite their seemingly rigid social structure and territorial divisions. Most often a herd will scatter, or at least submerge, at the approach of man, but attacks are not uncommon, and because of their sudden and violent nature, it is well to avoid them.

The deer of the world are of great variety, and great numbers. They are usually the last big animals to die out once civilization starts to impinge on a wilderness area and their high reproductive rate keeps populations fairly intact even close to urban centers. Usually retiring and shy from overhunting (as they once were from predation), these large sharp-hooved, often well-antlered animals can be most formidable under certain conditions. They can be dangerous once they reach maturity and a sexually excited stag, triggered to fight off challengers to its harem, will readily charge an intruder. The occurrence of these sometimes damaging and rarely fatal charges seems to vary from place to place. In areas where there has been a great deal of hunting, fear is the dominant factor and a charge is unlikely. In very remote wilderness areas, such an occurrence is more possible. Moose (Alces), called elk in Europe, are particularly quick to take offense, and a fatal encounter is reported from time to time. Generally, the victim is a hunter who has placed his shot badly, and the incident cannot be looked upon as unprovoked.

Discounting wounded specimens for the moment, charges are evidently made when a man on foot infringes on an established territory. A couple of years ago, two automobiles were attacked and wrecked by moose in Canada, and in one instance the driver was killed. Approaching 1,000 pounds, with antlers as much as seven or eight feet across, the moose is a formidable animal. Some years ago, six lumberjacks on Clear Water River, Idaho, attacked a swimming moose from an open boat with axes. They wanted the animal for meat. Turning on the boat, although over its head in the fast-running current, the moose destroyed the heavy wooden craft and killed two of the men. Hunter-writer Newton Hibbs shot badly, on one occasion, and broke a bull moose's shoulder. Although floundering, half-crippled, in snow seven feet deep, the animal charged again and again, until finally dispatched with a bullet between the eyes.

The ubiquitous White-tailed Deer (Odocoileus virginianus), found over much of the United States and southern Canada (and replaced by the Mule Deer—Odocoileus hemionus—in some of those areas where the former is not found; their ranges overlap in many places) is truly a creature of the shadows. Alert, shy, with extremely keen senses, it is the most heavily hunted big-game animal in North America. Twice-a-year hunters who never even see another species of big game seem, eventually, to all get their buck. This onslaught (even bows and arrows are used on them by sportsmen today) has made the animal shy in most areas. Still, the animal can be formidable and reports of attacks are not uncommon. One evening in 1961, a housemaid left her place of employment in Westchester County, just north of New York City, and was waiting for a bus on a dark street corner. A white-tailed buck charged out of some bushes and pinned her to a tree. Only the arrival of the bus kept the woman from being killed. The white-tailed deer is equipped for flight. It can clear high obstacles with graceful, arching leaps, can run with remarkable speed even in dense cover, and has excellent camouflage. However, caught in unusual circumstances, the whitetail will turn and fight with sharp hooves and slashing antlers. Territorial infringement during the breeding season undoubtedly accounts for most attacks.

Ernest Thompson Seton wrote, in "The Whitetailed (Virginia) Deer and Its Kin," ". . . the bucks not only fight among themselves, but occasionally attack man; and more than one unfortunate person has been gored to death by them."

T. W. Merriam, Jr. reported:

> I was once sitting quietly on a log in a Deer park when a buck approached and, making a sudden spring, dealt me such a powerful blow on the head, with the hoofs of his forefeet, as to render me unconscious. No sooner was I thrown upon the ground than the vicious beast sprang upon me, and would doubtless have killed me outright had it not been for the intervention of a man, who rushed at him with a club and finally drove him off.

Field and Stream magazine, on December 26, 1898, carried an account by J. Park Whitney of a similar incident that occurred in Maine. Seton adds, "If, however, the Deer is the conqueror, he never ceases to batter, spear, and trample his victim as long at it shows signs of life." Reports like these are quite common. The deer, as a large animal, should be treated with due regard for its capabilities in the art of close combat.

Similar incidents are reported of the magnificent American Elk or Wapiti *(Cervus)*. A Mr. McLaughlin, a rancher in Stinking River Valley, Wyoming, barely escaped with his life when charged by a stag. His pack horse was thrown off a cliff to its death by the impact of the assault. John Fossom of Gardner, Montana, had a similar narrow escape when attempting to photograph a wapiti.

It seems fairly apparent that any large hoofed animal can be dangerous and should be approached with caution; this applies most particularly to males in the autumn when mating pressures predispose them to fighting.

The true buffalos (not to be confused with the bison of North America and Europe) are without question among the most potentially dangerous of the ungulates. The great "Buff" of Africa *(Syncerus caffer)* is considered by many to be the most dangerous animal on the continent, exceeding even the elephant, rhinoceros, leopard, and lion. Their great bulk is not a deterrent to speed, and their charge is apt to be carried through. It takes great skill to get a bullet into a fatal spot when the head is down with its spread of heavy, deflecting horns meeting across the skull. Stories are told of men driven into low trees and held at bay there by an infuriated buffalo until death came in a most unorthodox fashion. Parts of the body exposed to the buffalo were rasped clear of flesh by the animal's filelike tongue. Such stories are quite common, but I find them questionable at the very least. Suffice it to say, the buffalo is a particularly cunning ungulate, with great slashing horns, a penchant for lying in ambush, and a very short temper. The author, however, has photographed literally thousands of buffalo in Africa and was never at any time threatened. Perhaps buffalo are less antagonistic toward men with cameras than with guns.

Speaking of buffalo, Theodore Roosevelt described them as "tough animals, tenacious of life and among the most dangerous of African game." He also said, "The list of white hunters that have been killed by buffalo is very long, and includes a number of men of note, while accidents to natives are of constant occurrence." In some areas, destruction to crops and attacks on people have reached such proportions that buffalo have been ranked as vermin. Writing in *Harper's New Monthly Magazine* in 1898, Arthur C. Humbert commented, "My guide who has lived in this country for the past ten years, relates many stories of men who have been mauled by lions, and who have escaped death, but he knows of no instance where the African buffalo has left a human being until the life was trampled out of him." References, observations, and reports like these exist by the thousand, the only conflict being whether the buffalo is the most dangerous animal in all of Africa, or only the second or third most dangerous. As is commonly the case in Africa, animals are rated on a very personal level. If one has killed your father or your brother it is the most dangerous.

The mighty Gaur *(Bos gaurus)*, the wild ox of India, Burma, Thailand, and Malaya, is another animal given to charging molesters; and being hit by one is almost certain to prove fatal. The gaur or gaor is the largest member of the bovine family, and in India, in height at least, is second only to the elephant. Kinloch wounded one on a hunt in the Satpura Hills, and, in his words, "Back he came, at a fast gallop, evidently looking out for some one on whom to wreak his vengeance. I was ahead of my men and stood my ground, while they, being unarmed, very wisely scrambled up trees. I allowed the bull to come on to within forty yards, when I fired my right barrel at the point of his shoulder. . . ."

The Water Buffalo (*Bubalus*) of the Oriental region still exists in many areas as a wild animal. It is powerful, and short-tempered. Accidents with them and apparently unprovoked attacks by them have been reported, strengthening the thought that no wild bovine can be trusted. All of these great bovines are hunted as trophy animals and many hunters have paid with their lives for badly placed shots.

There are a number of reports on record of antelope charging their tormentors with extensive damage done by their often spectacular horns. Certainly, some of these stories are true but it is, once again, stretching a point to call them dangerous to man. Many species, indeed, could be hazardous at close quarters, most because they would thrash around in blind panic. Spectacular accidents have occurred when hunters have approached animals they thought dead. Supposedly dead antelope can come to life with amazing speed and energy!

Whales do not generally seek issue with man, but man has been hunting the whale for many hundreds of years, in fact, thousands. Whaling from open boats was a hazardous occupation at best because of the size of the prey-animal. Stories of stove-in boats and lost harpooners are legion. The great historic period of American whaling was well reported. Many, many such stories were true, and are occasionally reported today as witness the following UPI release of January 1963:

WHALE SMASHES FISHING BOAT

SYDNEY, AUSTRALIA—A 70 foot whale smashed a fishing launch off Coogee Beach near here yesterday, killing one man.

Police said William Morris, 64, was killed. Companion Jack Banning, 39, was pulled out of the water.

The mighty Sperm Whale (*Physeter catodon*) is one of the most formidable creatures on earth. Males reportedly reach a length of more than sixty feet, although fifty is the average size of a large bull. In his definitive work, *Whales*, E. J. Slijper writes, "Sperm Whales, like elephants, have the occasional rogue male, i.e., a solitary individual which obviously cannot fit into any school, and which is therefore particularly aggressive. Such rogues were Moby Dick, New Zealand Jack, and many other famous whales from the great days of Sperm Whale hunting, all of which tore up men and boats alike. . . ."

In August 1851, the *Ann Alexander* out of New Bedford lowered two boats on order of Capt. John S. Deblois. Both were sunk by an angry sperm. A few minutes later the ship itself shuddered as she was struck below the waterline by the infuriated animal. She sank in a few minutes. Capt. George Pollard took the *Essex* out of Nantucket in 1820, never again to return. A sperm twice smashed her bow, sinking her. Most of the crew perished. There are dozens of such stories on record, with no reason to doubt them. Sperm whales are apparently sound sleepers and are often encountered floating on the surface in deep slumber. In 1956 alone, three ships are believed to have collided with sleeping sperms; the Russian whaler *Aleut*, the American liner *Constitution*, and the Dutch ship *Willem Ruys*. The S.S. *Amerskerk* collided with a sleeping thirty-two-footer while doing seventeen knots in March 1955.

Approaching whales in light watercraft is generally not a wise practice. If the animal is a cow with a calf nearby, a charge is likely in many species, especially in relatively shallow water. Old bulls can be quite short-tempered, the great size of these creatures alone suggesting that they are dangerous to molest. Most whales will sound and disappear at the approach of man, but if one doesn't, it is usually an indication that something is wrong, or may be so very shortly thereafter. However, the author, in a small boat off the coast of Oregon, has approached gray whales to within thirty or forty feet and has never encountered signs of aggression.

Most marsupials are harmless to man. While a kangaroo at close quarters can deliver a stunning clout with its powerful hind legs, these animals are extremely shy. But two forms reputedly were involved in attacks on human beings; both are today apparently on the brink of extinction. The Tasmanian Devil *(Sarcophilus harrisii)*, now restricted to Tasmania, once ranged over much of Australia. The last specimen there is believed to have been killed about sixty miles from Melbourne, at Tooborac, in 1912. Although small, the creature attacked larger animals including domestic stock. Occasionally caught in the act of raiding farms, it reportedly turned on its would-be tormentors with a reckless fury. Quite possibly this is so, and some settlers may have received painful bites, but no deaths are known to the author.

The Tasmanian Wolf or Thylacine *(Thylacinus cynocephalus)* was roughly the marsupial equivalent of the wolf, although far removed from any true canine. The animal is now probably extinct, although it may possibly be found in the most remote regions of Tasmania. Once, like the Tasmanian devil, it inhabited mainland Australia. When cornered, the thylacine is said to have counterattacked, and human injuries are on record. However, although an active predator, its hunting of man was never reported.

With this brief survey, we have reviewed the great order of mammals. Many others have behavioral characteristics unpleasant to man, but, all in all, mammals cause fewer deaths and injuries today than do most other groups of vertebrates containing dangerous forms. The great size and often colorful behavior of many mammals will continue to attract the attention and imagination of man. As long as this is so, whatever danger they do represent inevitably will be exaggerated. Sadly, each year sees more and more such reports added to the files of the quaint and historically interesting. We have brought so many of these great forms to the brink of extinction that to think of them threatening us is a kind of supreme irony.

Part II The Birds

9   Birds—Are Any Dangerous?

At the top of the so-called tree of life there are two main branches, the mammals and the birds. Birds are actually nothing much more than warm-blooded reptiles with some odd features such as feathers instead of scales, and a four-chambered heart like our own. It is the latter development that has given them, like mammals, a great advantage over their cold-blooded ancestors, the reptiles. Are any of these forms dangerous to man? The answer is a qualified "possibly." This, however, requires some explanation.

Unlike mammals, birds are, as the old expression goes, "bird-brained"—and this despite the fact that some birds have respectable brain capacities. Nevertheless, whether actual gray-matter capacity does or does not indicate intellectual capacity, there is no doubt that birds do have very different "brains" from mammals. Anybody who has handled animals professionally will tell you that if you are attacked by a bird, you cannot expect any respite. A bird, unlike a mammal, won't give up.

Man's dealings with wild mammals are almost wholly provocative, even if only by infringement of territories, as I have pointed out. With birds this is not so, for we keep many birds around us that are not truly domesticated. In various parts of the world, these include ostriches, swans, eagles, and peacocks. And it is these that are the most dangerous and the most likely to attack.

Astonishingly enough, while all but a handful never molest man, there are a few that will do so deliberately. They are the Cassowaries

115

(Casuariidae) of New Guinea and Australia. There are six known species of the *Casuarius*, all from Australia, New Guinea, and adjacent islands. They reach a height of five feet or more and have strong legs. Few people are likely to come in contact with these strange distant relatives of the ostrich and emu, except natives of the countries where they live. However, during World War II, Allied troops encountered them in dense scrub in New Guinea, and several times confirmed native reports that they may attack by leaping into the air and slashing down with their enormously long and powerful first claws. Oliver L. Austin reports that "many" natives have been killed by these pugnacious creatures. Whèther such attacks are truly unprovoked, or just random panic on the part of these remarkably stupid and hysterical animals, is difficult to say, but, judging by accounts given by zoo keepers, they must be formidable to say the least.

It is manifest that, to be truly dangerous, attacks must be by large birds. An interesting case is the largest—the Ostrich *(Struthio)*. Not only are these birds now farmed, they roam about in considerable numbers in game reserves visited by tourists. Thus, man is in contact with them. Like all birds, and perhaps more so, they are a bit balmy, and if they get particularly excited they kick out. They can give a terrible kick with their huge, pistonlike legs that end in a shaft of almost solid bone and two toes with strong claws. It is a curious fact that, if for some extraordinary reason you find yourself confined with a lot of hysterical ostriches, you should fall flat on your face. Even in extreme panic these strange creatures will not tread on you! The cock ostrich in the mating season is, in the opinion of Peter Ryhiner, a big-game collector, probably one of the most dangerous animals on earth, and not, according to him, only in a zoo enclosure.

For centuries the Mute Swan *(Cygnus)* has been semidomesticated, but there are greater numbers of truly wild ones. There is little doubt that they will attack if their nests are too closely approached either deliberately or by mistake, and they can and have broken people's arms, and the legs of some children. They half-jump, half-fly directly at you and then pound you with their half-folded wings. Their "elbow" joints are hard knobs of bone, and their wing muscles are very powerful so that they can deliver a terrific wallop. Like all birds, they keep at it once they have launched an attack. Swans, moreover, seem to be of rather high "intelligence" for birds, and appear to employ real strategy when they fight. A child was killed in Ranelar Park, England, it was reported some years ago in *The Field*, and a very young child was killed in Methuen, Massachusetts, in 1938, when a swan forced it under water after it approached the bird's nest. In 1972 a man was killed or at least

The bald eagle. Stories of these birds flying off with children in their talons are plain nonsense. They are scavengers and fishing birds and are harmless to man.
Photograph by Wilford L. Miller

Schlater's cassowary. Note the nails on the powerful feet. Raking and kicking, these birds can do a great deal of damage if cornered or crowded in close quarters. In the wild they are shy and retiring.
Courtesy Smithsonian Institution

died in Montauk, New York, when attacked by a cob. It was determined that he died of a heart attack after being severely pummeled by the bird. He had been trying to catch some cygnets and that, no doubt, prompted the attack.

The so-called game birds include the fowl, peacocks, partridges, and their like; they are lumped together as gallinaceous birds. Many are armed with long, sharp spurs on the backs of their legs—hence cock-fighting—and they can do extraordinary damage with them. A lone man so attacked by a Peacock *(Pavo)* is at a disadvantage because he has to protect his eyes at all costs, and at the same time ward off a sort of living hovercraft that usually goes for the back of his neck.

The birds which have from time immemorial been most feared by people, though notably by those who know little about them, are the eagles. The stories about eagles carrying off human babies, and even small children, are absolutely endless. It is pure myth; yet the stories persist. Applying logic, these stories are false. An eagle attacks small mammals, reptiles, fish, and, perhaps, some other birds. It is not equipped by nature to lift great loads and the tales of these birds acting like giant helicopters airlifting army supplies, are not at all in keeping with their actual physical structure. I recall seeing a scene of an eagle carrying off a child in an old movie. This badly stuffed and rather moth-eaten prop, suspended from the studio roof by an all-too-visible wire, was about as convincing as the stories one encounters!

Eagles, as a matter of fact, are, of all birds, probably the calmest and most serene. They are also really rather timid. I have photographed specimens in many parts of the world and can testify that it is extremely difficult to get near enough to make a 200 mm. lens pay off. People examining or robbing eagles' nests may have received some attention from the mother and sometimes also the father, but I do not know of any case where the "attack" was carried through to the point of actual physical harm to the intruder.

The lesser cousins of the eagles—the falcons and hawks—can some-times give a very good account of themselves if molested; and they probably don't hesitate to do so. I do not know of an unprovoked attack that resulted in a significant injury. Occasionally, a handler engaged in falconry will get clawed by one of his charges.

If you deliberately walk up to a group of vultures when they are feeding, you may, according to some people, be confronted by a lot of hissing avian monsters that will even run at you. For the most part, they are very wary and just flop up into the nearest tree and wait for you to go away; but sometimes, it is alleged, they do not. You have to be very wary of certain individual vultures in captivity as they don't wait to be provoked, and it may be possible that some in the wild would adopt the same attitude toward interference.*

There remains then a somewhat different aspect of danger from birds. This is in handling them. Many birds can give really terrible bites. Many of the long-billed birds, like the Maribou and Jabiru storks (Ciconiidae), can make a nasty puncture wound and there is always the danger, in handling birds, of damage to the eyes. Never hold any bird with a long neck and sharp, pointed bill at less than arm's length.

The Skua (Catharacta skua), an aberrant gull-like bird, ranges from the Arctic to the Antarctic, and is the southernmost vertebrate animal on earth. Specimens have mysteriously appeared within a few miles of the geographical South Pole, over 800 miles from the nearest possible food source. It is a powerful predatory bird of the coastal regions, and preys on young penguins. It has earned an unfortunate reputation for itself by attacking men who approached its nest. I do not know of any injuries received, but attacks do occur. One can suppose that eyes could be lost, and other painful injuries inflicted if an explorer failed to duck in time.

The Parrots and their allies (Psittaciformes), have powerful beaks. Anyone who has ever handled them to any extent can testify to the kind of bite they can give. This is a defensive measure, though, and hardly a danger in our context.

The birds of the world are a source of never-ending joy. They are color, life, and movement personified, and their very being graces the natural world in a way typified by no other class of animal life. It is tempting to discuss them here at great length, but hardly justified in light of our purpose. Mountain climbers may have been toppled off cliffs by "dive-bombing" eagles defending their aeries; zoo keepers have been hospitalized by ill-tempered ostriches; men have been variously pecked, scratched, even bullied by geese, swans and other forms, but, all in all, birds are not dangerous to man. In rare cases this may not be an accurate generalization, but the threat, when it does exist, is so slight statistically (and generally a result of human molestation, or at least provocation) that we will stand by it as a conclusion.

*South African Scope (vol. 6, no. 7, Summer 1963), an official government organ of the Republic of South Africa, reports that on March 3, 1963, Miss Bessie Smit on a farm named Aminnis was attacked by a large southwest African vulture. The deliberate assault carried Miss Smit to earth, but a rock within her reach enabled her to escape.

Part III The Reptiles

10 Venomous Lizards

There are surviving today approximately three thousand known species of lizards, suborder Sauria of the order Squamata. There are a few hundred more species of lizards than snakes, but while more than two hundred species and innumerable subspecies of snakes are more-or-less dangerous to man, only two species of lizards are known to be so.

Antarctica is the only continent on our planet that hasn't been accused of housing a venomous lizard, but so far as anyone has been able to demonstrate, the family Helodermatidae, found exclusively in the United States and Mexico, has the world's only venomous lizards.

The family is respectably old, with fossils dating back 40 to 50 million years (Oligocene strata—*H. matthewi*) in Colorado. Today, there is only one genus, *Heloderma*, with two species and five subspecies.

Until quite recently an earless Monitor Lizard from Borneo *(Lanthanotus borneensis)* was also thought to be venomous, or at least potentially so since it was placed in the family Helodermatidae. It has since been given its own family, Lanthanotidae, and is now known to be harmless. The legends persist in Borneo, however.

The origin of the venom apparatus in the Helodermatidae is the same as that of the snakes'—that is, modified salivary glands. There, however, the similarity stops. While the venom glands of snakes are *above* the upper jaw, those of *Heloderma* are in the *lower*. While the snake's venom is channeled from the producing glands to the injecting teeth, the venom glands of *Heloderma* have no connection with the animal's

Table 1. The Venomous Lizards of the World
(Family: Helodermatidae, Genus: *Heloderma*)

Species	Common name	Range
H. horridum horridum	Mexican beaded lizard	Pacific drainage of Mexico—sea level to at least 5,000 feet—coastal regions to at least 170 miles inland
H. h. exasperatum	Rio Fuerte beaded lizard	Very limited—drainage of the Rio Fuerte and Sonora Rio in Mexico
H. h. alvarezi	Black, or chiapan beaded lizard	Very limited—Rio de Chiapa drainage in Mexico
H. suspectum suspectum	Reticulated Gila monster	Arizona, New Mexico, and Mexican state of Sonora
H. s. cinctum	Banded Gila monster	Arizona, Nevada, and Utah

teeth. *Heloderma* have grooved, not hollow, teeth in both upper and lower jaws. Between eight and ten upper teeth, and six and eleven lower ones are grooved, always on the front but sometimes on the rear edge as well. Instead of one duct, as in the snakes, the venom glands each have a number of ducts which open into a mucous fold situated between the lip and the lower jaw. The venom flows along this groove until it reaches the teeth where it is then literally chewed into the victim, not injected. The whole system is quite diffuse when compared with the crisp and efficient hypodermic system used by snakes.

To replace the neat injection apparatus they never had, *Heloderma* use tenacity. Almost everyone who has had anything to do with them has used the comparison, "like a bulldog," to describe this trait. When a Gila (hee-lah) monster or beaded lizard grabs, it hangs on. At times, it is reported, pliers have been required to make them let go.

It is not characteristic for bites by animals with essentially neurotoxic venom to be particularly painful at the site of the injury. The bite of the Gila monster, although a nerve toxin is involved, has been described as very painful. The pain is caused by the chewing and tearing as the animal works its venom into the flesh and by a substance known as *serotonin*—a powerful pain producer.

The Gila monster is not a large animal, about twenty inches being the record length. The beaded lizard reaches thirty-two. They are generally slow-moving, rather sluggish animals with blunt heads, beady eyes, and powerful digging claws and digits on short legs. They have a very thick tail which is, in fact, a storage vault from which they draw nourishment during hibernation. One of the more inane legends that has grown up around these animals has it that the poor creatures are unable to dispose of body waste, and that it is stored in the tail. The putrefaction of this fecal matter is said to supply the animal with its venom. For the record, the Gila monster and kin dispose of their waste quite naturally.

We have said that these animals are sluggish. They are, unless pressed. If escape is not practical, or if the creature is injured or teased, it is capable of swift and determined lunges and twists. When it does grab hold, its mild and noncombative disposition undergoes a sudden reversal.

Heloderma feed on nestling birds, baby animals, and perhaps some eggs. They do not attempt to catch fast-moving prey. They have highly developed chemical senses—smell and taste—and use these to track down their prospective meals. They are great bloodhounds.

If disturbed, *Heloderma* generally seek cover under rocks, or in scrub. They will, on occasion, hold their ground with loud hissing and short lunges.

To round out our capsule description of these interesting animals, they are egg-layers, take readily to water although they are essentially a desert animal (some Mexican beaded lizards are found in Colima, Mexico, in an area not unlike the western Ozarks) and hibernate during the colder seasons. Their scales do not overlap, but have a beaded look. The differences in marking are quite distinct, and apparent when different subspecies are placed side by side. Actually, they look like no other lizard and are easy to recognize. It is almost inconceivable that a case of mistaken identity could account for an accident, except where it involved a small child.

In their exhaustive study of these animals, *The Gila Monster and Its Allies*, Charles M. Bogert and Rafael Martin Del Campo supply some of the vernacular names by which these animals have been known. The list is a long one, but most important is the fact that the animal has for long been known by variations of the Spanish name *Escorpion*. One can't help but wonder if some of the deeds of which *Heloderma* have been accused aren't, in fact, the results of confusion in popular litera-ture with the scorpions which inhabit the same region, and which are much more dangerous to man, at least statistically.

We have already written off the comic notion that these animals are without elimination processes, but it might serve to examine a few other long-standing legends about them. The breath of *Heloderma* is harmless. The animal can cause damage only by biting. They do not spit venom, although they may spray a little saliva around when pushed into their defensive-hissing attitude. Although these animals can pivot rapidly on their hind legs, and lash out to either side with startling agility, they do not leap on their prey. They aren't built for

The fabled Gila monster *(Heloderma suspectum)* is equipped with powerful jaws, efficient venom-producing glands, and a lethargic, almost benign disposition. Dangerous to handle, the animal is easy to avoid in the wild. Its aggressiveness is overrated in adventure stories, but its venom isn't.
Photograph by Roger A. Caras

The Mexican beaded lizard *(Heloderma horridum)*, a seriously venomous but inoffensive lizard, now quite rare in most parts of its traditional range in Mexico.
Photograph by Roger A. Caras

saltation. The teeth of these animals are made for grasping, and not for cutting; they are incapable of cutting out a piece of flesh as they have been accused of doing. Their tongue is harmless although if you are close enough to be touched by their tongue you may be in for a bit of trouble. They are essentially immune to their own venom. Heloderms are not a cross between a lizard and an alligator, but have a respectable lineage as pure, albeit rather singular, lizards. As far as is known, the Gila monster possesses no magical powers and is quite killable, although it *is* tenacious of life. All in all, these animals are just about what a sensible person might expect them to be; they are all lizard, not terribly bright, not at all affectionate, very poor pets, very intent on minding their own business, but different in that they are (1) large, as North American lizards go, and (2) venomous. They have many distinctive features, of course, but these are of interest mainly to the specialist.

In answer to the question, Are the Gila monster and its allies dangerous to man? we must give a qualified yes. Bogert and Martin Del Campo discuss thirty-four known cases of injury to man, eight of which were reportedly fatal. It is pointed out that most of the fatal cases involved men in poor health, or drunk at the time of the incident. Most of the victims were handling the animals either in laboratories, zoological collections, or displays of some sort. Two cases involved the victim carrying the creature in a shirt pocket, or inside a shirt next to the body. A number of cases occurred when drunks or near drunks were teasing or otherwise maltreating captive specimens. Very rarely are cases recorded involving a chance encounter in the wild. One victim was bitten when he pushed or struck at a Gila monster that crawled over him as he slept in a cave.

Even with all of the above before us, we should not be deluded into thinking of *Heloderma* as harmless. They possess a powerful neurotoxin, and can cause respiratory paralysis if they get sufficient venom worked into the tissue of a human being. Their venom, though, unlike the snakes, is poor in enzymes, making it extremely doubtful that it ever was important to the lizard's feeding pattern. Records indicate eight human deaths attributable to this cause. Symptoms of the bite include swelling, pain, loss of consciousness, vomiting, accelerated heart action, shortness of breath, vertigo, numbness, weakness, and swollen tongue and glands. Not all symptoms need necessarily appear in one victim.

The qualification of our yes in answer to the question, Are these animals dangerous? is this—you almost have to *try* to get bitten in order to become a victim. The Gila monster and its allies are not often encountered. They are peaceful animals and generally do not invade areas inhabited by man. They avoid human beings whenever possible, and almost always try to retreat rather than fight. They can't strike out like a snake, can't do any damage unless they get a good hold, and can't bite through a shoe or a boot. It is a rare person who ever sees one outside of captivity (where they live well), and they represent no real threat to a normal, well-oriented human being. As a matter of fact, if you ever see one in the wild state you are more lucky than threatened.

11 Giant Snakes

Felix Kopstein, a trained naturalist, studied the reptiles of the East Indies, and knew them firsthand. In a 1927 nature journal, he reported that a fourteen-year-old boy had been killed and swallowed by a Reticulated Python *(Python reticulatus)* approximately seventeen feet long. The story is probably true, if for no other reason than because Kopstein believed it. Very often, when logic is not apparently neglected, we can evaluate secondhand information only on the basis of source.

A great many other people have reported human deaths attributable to giant, constricting snakes. Most of these tales were probably not true because the people reporting them were unable to establish any facts in connection with the alleged events. Tales so fanciful that they are downright shocking to the senses are repeated again and again. The literature of the great constrictors is not without its out-and-out lies. Some tales are so ridiculous one can speculate that they were told originally in jest. Repeated time and again, they unfortunately gain currency until, with time and inevitable change, they emerge as fact.

A book was published in England in 1962 which describes "water" snakes 3 feet *round* and 140 feet long. A specimen (Anaconda) forty-five feet long, according to the author, wrapped its tail around a submerged root and used its "head and neck coils" to drag a grazing cow into the water. A native porter is said to have severed the monster's head with *one bullet.* One might speculate that to sever the head of a forty-five-foot snake would require quite a bullet—a howitzer shell, for instance. The author, however, doesn't give you time to wonder how the porter managed to wield such artillery, because he has the severed head attacking him and his men. The head, he says, was "hideous" and "cat-like." The snake's smell, according to this adventurer, is used to numb and hypnotize prey. The author manages to snap out of his odor-induced trance just in time—the severed head was only three feet away and closing fast. Later on, he is induced to vomit by the touch of a boa constrictor's coils. At another point, the largest anaconda he ever saw wraps its tail around a tree and "whips" its coils at him. Again, army ordnance must have been handy because he decapitates the beast with that single shot. Another water serpent has a head three feet wide. Two baleful eyes as large as tennis balls, eighteen inches apart, appear. It must have been a particularly colorful reptile since these impressive orbs are described as violet blue, lit with streaks of scarlet fire!

This was not Marco Polo speaking, but an author in 1962 describing "personal adventures" [sic] in a book of nonfiction! In a book copyrighted in 1920, *Trapping Wild Animals in Malay Jungles* by Charles Mayer, the frontispiece is captioned, "The native screamed and the snake constricted suddenly, breaking nearly every bone in the man's body and crushing the life out of him." These words, in a book of ostensible fact, are pure fiction. Constrictors do *not* constrict suddenly. Some of their movements are quite rapid but the pressure applied by a coiling constrictor is a slow, inexorable process. Constrictors do *not* break "nearly every bone" in their victims' bodies; indeed, they seldom break any at all except by accident. They do *not* crush the life out of their prey.

The author has been unable to trace anyone who has witnessed the death of a human being in the coils of a giant snake. All of the information available is secondhand—at the very best. We shall have to tread lightly. It is a subject that has delighted the fictionalizers of natural history for centuries, and our path is fraught with danger, not from giant snakes but from people who have written about them.

Clifford H. Pope, in his excellent and reliable book, *The Giant Snakes,* numbers the true giants at six. He places them all in the family Boidae. It should be noted that approximately 85 percent of the sixty to seventy members of the family fail to achieve a length of twelve feet at full growth. Other specialists prefer to split the true giants into two families, Boidae and Pythonidae. The six giants named by Pope are:

1. Anaconda *(Eunectes murinus)*—South America—37–38 feet maximum
2. Boa constrictor *(Boa constrictor)*—South and Central America—18–19 feet maximum

The Australian carpet python. Lengths are variously reported at ten and twenty feet—ten is probably more nearly correct. These constrictors are essentially harmless to man unless handled inexpertly, when they can give a painful but nonvenomous bite with their long recurved teeth and powerful jaws.
Courtesy Australian News and Information Bureau

3. Indian python *(Python molurus)*—India, Asia, East Indies—18–20 feet maximum
4. Reticulated python *(P. reticulatus)*—Tropical Asia—32–33 feet maximum
5. Amethystine python *(P amethystinus)*—Australia to Philippine Islands—22–25 feet maximum
6. African rock python *(P. sebae)*—Africa—30–32 feet maximum.

The question of maximum length is a subject on which reams have been written. There is no end to the stories that have been told. The anaconda, particularly, has been said to reach astronomical proportions. In his extremely interesting book, *On the Track of Unknown Animals,* Dr. Bernard Heuvelmans recounts the unsuccessful attempts that have been made to capture, or even locate, the gigantic anacondas, reports of which have been filtering out of the South American forests for centuries.

Maj. Percy Fawcett was on an assignment for the Royal Geographical Society of London when, in 1907, he shot an anaconda on the Rio Abuna. His claim was, "As far as it was possible to measure, a length of forty-five feet lay out of the water, and seventeen feet in it, making a total length of sixty-two feet." Other observers allow for forty-five feet as maximum; some nineteen!

The anaconda is not the only one of the giants believed by many to achieve these huge sizes. Similar stories can be found for each of the others. Are they true? To the best of the author's knowledge, there is no natural factor in the snake's anatomy that would make it impossible for them to achieve these seemingly incredible lengths. On the other hand, there is no evidence that can really be accounted reliable to support claims that they do. It is all speculation. Knowing something about the photographic equipment and film speeds now available to the explorer, the author would prefer to see photographs. One thing is certain, if any explorer does encounter such a monster in a remote swamp, photographs are about all we can expect to see. The weight of an animal that large would make it very difficult to transport, though the skin and skull could be preserved. Skins alone are not to be trusted since they can be stretched to a remarkable degree before they are dried. A snake a dozen feet long will weigh between fifty and seventy-five pounds, depending upon species and condition. The pounds-per-foot factor increases with length as the girth increases. A seventy-five-foot snake would be a mighty load overland, or downriver in a native canoe.

Are the true giants, at the maximum lengths given in this chapter, capable of killing a man? Depending on the man, of course, a snake twenty feet long probably could, without too much trouble. Women or children could certainly be taken with even greater ease, and reports that seem reliable generally involve one or the other. The question of whether or not the giant snakes *can* kill a human being is not as important, however, as the question *Will* they? Being able to do a thing and doing it are quite different.

The giant constrictors kill large prey, naturally enough, by constricting. They can give a vicious bite which, indeed, they generally do before coiling. Their recurved teeth and powerful jaws enable them to get a firm grip. The bite is nonvenomous. *Constricting* does not mean *crushing*, as is so often contended. The constrictors do not normally crush their prey, they suffocate it. Once firmly around the victim's rib cage, the snake has only to wait. Each time the victim exhales, as it must to retain consciousness, the snake need only exert a slight increase in pressure. In good time, the victim is unable to draw in enough air to feed the brain the oxygen it requires. Once the victim has passed out the snake may continue the pressure until the heart stops, or may swallow the still-living but now inert animal. A really large snake firmly wound around a man could certainly exert the pressure necessary to kill him. It would require, quite probably, nowhere near a maximum effort. The big question in a hypothetical contest between a constrictor and a man would be the man's ability to stand up under the weight of the snake initially. If the man could remain standing, the snake might very well give up before getting a firm hold. If, on the other hand, the man buckled under 250 or 300 pounds of snake, he would be hard put to defend himself. This is all rather academic, however, for although this may in fact have occurred from time to time, we still haven't answered the key question, *Do* giant snakes attack man?

Snakes are shortsighted and are without ears. They can detect movement close by, and almost certainly "hear" with their whole bodies. Even though they do not receive much in the way of vibrations through the air as do the eared animals, they can feel vibrations carried by the ground. A snake is generally well aware of a man long before it sees him. Quite literally, it *feels* his approach. By a system far more complex than our own, snakes "smell" the presence of other animals with keen accuracy. To say that they smell prey is not quite descriptive enough—they "smell-taste" the world around them. Their tongue, a device known as Jacobson's organ, and their nasal passages all play a part. This sense is very keen: it is chemical reception at its best.

This brief discussion of a snake's senses has as its purpose the point that, when a man approaches a giant snake, he does not generally do so unannounced except in rare and unusual circumstances. (Snakes do take to trees, of course, and a constrictor asleep on a branch would not get the vibrations of footsteps on the ground. A snake hanging from a

The eastern diamondback rattlesnake *(Crotalus adamanteus)* is one of the largest of all rattlers and one of the most seriously venomous of all snakes. Specimens can be very cranky and quick to strike, and have been known to reach eight feet.
Photograph by Roger A. Caras

The very common, very cranky, and very dangerous Texas or western diamondback rattlesnake has been responsible for a number of human deaths. *Crotalus atrox* may, in fact, have killed more Americans than any other species of rattlesnakes.
Photograph by Roger A. Caras

The timber rattlesnake *(Crotalus horridus horridus)* is a widespread and short-tempered eastern species. Bites are usually serious but sublethal.
Photograph by Roger A. Caras

The rattlesnake's rattle is a unique device found in no other group of snakes. The number of segments *is not* an indication of the animal's age, but rather of its luck crawling over rocky ground. Rattlers are broken off over rough terrain and are replaced a button at a time with each shedding of the snake's skin.
Courtesy National Museum of Canada

The very widespread, very populous prairie rattlesnake, *Crotalus viridis viridis*, has at least nine subspecies. Its bite is not usually lethal to man.
Photograph by Roger A. Caras

The Northern Pacific rattlesnake, *Crotalus viridis oreganus*, one of the subspecies of the prairie rattlesnake, in the process of swallowing a rat it had previously killed with its venom. The venom in the rat's body began acting as a digestive enzyme at the moment of the bite.
Courtesy National Museum of Canada

limb could be surprised.) The chances are a snake on the ground will sense a man's approach far enough in advance to determine a course of action; that is, whether to flee, hold ground, or attack.

It seems fairly certain that some giant snakes have attacked human beings. It is equally certain that a very few people have been eaten after having been killed. These attacks, however, are most assuredly rare. They probably represent not so much a fair estimate of these animals' normal behavior as further evidence that, in the wilds, any combination of unfortunate circumstances is possible, sometimes with tragic results, just as on the highways of the modern world where gruesome mistakes can be made. These attacks are probably accidents at the outset.

There are some indications that snakes are a bit brighter than most of us have generally given them credit for, but they still function pretty close to the reflex level. If a snake sensed the approach of a man and failed to clear out before an encounter was forced upon it, it might very well strike out. Once it caught hold and felt the man's struggles, it might press the attack by reflex. The snake's whole feeding mechanism is designed to respond to specific stimuli and a man could provide the necessary stimulation in these circumstances. The more violent the contest became, the more the snake might be stimulated. Compared to some of the animals to which the giants are known to give battle, man is a relatively easy mark. He does not have teeth or claws he can bring into play with any purpose beyond hysteria, and he is without hoofs and horns to interfere with swallowing, not that these matter much to the constrictors, it seems.

Schmidt and Inger (Living Reptiles of the World) refer to an "authentic" case of a Malay boy of fourteen falling prey to a snake on Salebabu Island, in the Taland group. He was killed and swallowed. (This is the Kopstein case referred to at the beginning of this chapter.) Herpetologist Arthur Loveridge, in a 1931 issue of the Bulletin of the Antivenin Institute of America, reported the death of a young mother on an island in Lake Victoria. She was found still in the coils of an African Rock Python (Python sebae) about fourteen feet long. Although it probably killed her, it almost certainly could not have swallowed her. There have been other such reports, but very few from reliable sources. The author does have recent reports of two presumed incidents. When in Mozambique in 1973, he was shown a newspaper account of the death of a Portuguese soldier. The youth vanished while on guard duty one evening and was said to have been recovered from the stomach of a large python. Efforts to obtain further information were not fruitful. Then, two years later, having just arrived in Pretoria for a survey of the game areas of South Africa, he encountered the following story in the *Pretoria News* for February 26, 1975:

MAN'S STRUGGLE WITH PYTHON

DURBAN—A Durban gardener fought a life-and-death struggle with a huge python when it dropped on to him from a tree and tried to squeeze him to death while he was cutting a hedge in Greenwood Park yesterday.

The man, Mr. Tinkosa Ngurta, was almost strangled as he desperately tried to remove the 2.2m snake which had coiled around his neck and waist.

His screams brought a neighbour, Mrs. G. Adams, who called an ambulance.

After about five horrifying minutes, Mr. Ngurta finally managed to free himself from the snake by wriggling out of his overalls.

A teacher at the Greenwood Primary School, near where Mr. Ngurta was attacked, Mrs. C. McPhearson, said local children had reported seeing a large snake.

"This plot is frequently used as a short-cut by children at the school. I hate to think what would have happened if the snake had got hold of one of them," said Mrs. McPhearson.

The giant snakes are not particularly rare, for the most part, and many live in close proximity to man—some within city limits of large urban centers like Bangkok, and along busy waterfronts where the human traffic is heavy. Pythons in the Orient and, reportedly, boas in South America are encouraged to take up residence under houses because they are a natural control on vermin.

While stories of attacks do exist, calling the giant snakes dangerous to man is stretching a point. All reliable observers report that the snake's first move is almost inevitably an effort toward escape. They either take off as fast as possible or freeze, instinctively taking advantage of their really excellent, and frequently quite beautiful, protective coloration. Active at night, they may tend to bite when suddenly approached in the dark. If a few human beings have been unfortunate enough to encounter a snake whose escape route was cut off, we can pity the experience they must have had. These almost certainly extremely rare occurrences do not, however, indicate that the giants are naturally man-eaters, or even man-killers.

Before going on to discuss our next group of animals, it might be worthwhile to dispose of a few legends that have grown up around these animal giants. Although a snake may be able to strike from close quarters faster than a man can recoil, particularly if the man is caught off guard, they cannot outspeed a man in an all-out race. It is difficult to imagine a large constrictor chasing a man across an open field, but if such a thing did occur, the man would win, hands down. It would take an exceptional swimmer, however, to outswim an anaconda. They move well in the water.

Further, these snakes do not have to anchor their tails in order to constrict. Wrap a small specimen around your arm and invite him to give you a playful squeeze, and you will see just how unnecessary an anchor post is.

The giant snakes are about as adept at milking cows as is the American milk snake. It is a ridiculous legend but one that is still believed. The best way to disprove it is to ask the believer to milk a cow himself. After he has finished ask him to recall the pressure he had to apply and the tugging he had to do. Then, ask him what would have happened to the cow if each of his hands were lined with a hundred or so needle-sharp, recurved teeth. Unless you are dealing with a fool, he should concede the point.

No part of a giant snake's anatomy is venomous at any time of the year. These animals are not immune to fire; cannot remain under water indefinitely; and they reproduce in a very normal reptilian way. The pythons lay eggs; and the boas, including the anaconda, give birth to living young.

The larger snakes will continue to fascinate man as they have always done. They are truly giant forms and, as such, carry a certain mystical aura about them. Although there will be no more of a basis for fear then than now, our great-great-grandchildren will still look at them in the zoo and recall, with delicious, tingling horror, tales of man-eating serpents. If your child asks you, as I once heard a little boy ask his father in the Reptile Wing at the Staten Island Zoo, "Do they just feed bad people to the snakes?" don't be upset. It is evidently an inevitable part of our folk-legend heritage.

12 Venomous Snakes: The Rattlers

As should have become clear from the preceding chapter, snakes potentially dangerous to man fall into two groups—those that can cause mechanical damage and those that can cause chemical damage. The former are the boas and pythons; the latter, which are much more numerous and widespread, are also more diverse. It will serve our purpose to place these creatures in a comprehensive framework.

There are living today some 2,700 kinds of snakes, divided among ten or more families of varying size and importance—both from the naturalist's and our more specialized points of view. These are:

1. Typhlopidae (blindsnakes)—200 species (at least); harmless*
2. Leptotyphlopidae (slender blindsnakes)—40 species; harmless
3. Aniliidae (pipesnakes)—11 species; none venomous
4. Uropeltidae (shield-tailed snakes)—43 species; none venomous
5. Boidae (pythons and boas)—65 species; none venomous
6. Colubridae (very diverse group)—1,400 species; most harmless or nearly so, two very dangerously venomous
7. Hydrophiidae (sea snakes)—50 species; all seriously venomous

*The word "harmless" should be qualified. Some snakes rated as harmless do have venom glands but do not have an advanced fang system with which to use that venom against another organism, at least one the size of a human being.

8. Elapidae (cobras, kraits, coral snakes)—230 species; venomous
9. Viperidae (vipers)—58 species; venomous
10. Crotalidae (pit vipers)—122 species; venomous

In this listing, we find that 412 species are recognized as potentially venomous to man. That is 15.2 percent of the world's living species of snakes. It should also be noted that some herpetologists may list the Crotalidae (here accorded full family status) as a subfamily under the Viperidae. To them it would be, then, Crotalinae, and would raise the number of species in the Viperidae to 180. In any case, whether the pit vipers* are a family or a subfamily really doesn't matter all that much if you get bitten by one of its representatives.

The order in which the families are listed above may be best described as standard practice among herpetologists, but that order may be altered without affecting its usefulness. And, for several reasons, we propose to do just this.

The crotalids are, as regards the development and complexity of their envenomating mechanism, the most advanced. In fact, the families as listed above show a progressive development in this respect from the colubrines through the others listed—and in that order—to the crotalids; and the rattlers appear to be the most "advanced" and specialized of these last. Thus, an explanation of the envenomating apparatus of this group will lead to a better understanding of the other groups.

There are six genera recognized in the family Crotalidae. These are listed in Table 2.

Although there is room for discussion, we are on reasonably safe ground in stating that there are thirty existing species, subdivided into sixty-six subspecies of rattlesnakes—of two genera: *Crotalus* or *Sistrurus*. Of the two, *Crotalus* is by far the most important from a number of points of view. Sixty of the rattlesnakes are in this genus (as compared with six in *Sistrurus*); its members are spread over a much wider range, and they are generally larger, carry more venom, and have longer fangs.

One of the characteristics the two genera have in common is a definitive identification point for rattlesnakes. Of all the snakes that exist on this planet, only the rattlesnake has a true rattle. (No other snake has this device, and no snake is a rattlesnake unless it has one,

*The group is known as "pit" vipers because its representatives have openings between the eyes and the nostrils (slightly below lines drawn between the two) with which they sense prey and enemies by body heat. Its range is very much exaggerated, and is probably only really effective up to eighteen or twenty inches. Stories of these snakes sensing people yards and even scores of yards away are pure fiction. The heat sensor simply enables the pit viper to make a highly accurate inclose strike.

Table 2. The Family Crotalidae

Genus	Members	Range
Crotalus	Rattlesnakes	North to South America
Sistrurus	Massasaugas and pygmy rattlesnakes	North America
Lachesis	Bushmaster	
Bothrops	New World pit vipers	Central and South America
Trimeresurus	Asiatic pit vipers	Central and South America
Agkistrodon	Cottonmouth water moccasins, and copperheads,* Old World pit vipers**	Asia
		North America, Southeast Europe, and Asia

*The Australian "copperhead" is not related, but is an elapid snake, far more dangerous than this crotalid.

**Old World members of Agkistrodon usually have no other popular name than "pit viper." This can be rather confusing.

except *Crotalus catalinensis*, the Santa Catalina Island Rattlesnake.) Here, at least, no confusion appears possible.

Snakes, because of their light bone structure, do not fossilize well. It is difficult to pin down the periods in which types first emerged, but C. W. Gilmore places the first venomous snakes in Europe somewhere between 8 and 20 million years ago. Rattlesnakes have been positively identified in deposits in North America between 4 and 12 million years old. This is enough to tell us that man never existed on this planet at a time when there weren't rattlesnakes. We can't however, place the time when the two first met.

Appendix Table C-1 lists the sixty-six recognized rattlesnakes now in existence, alphabetically by Latin name, gives a popular name for each, and provides a brief description of its range. It must be recognized that the descriptions of the ranges are sketchy. Frequently, only small isolated areas in the regions listed are today populated by a species or subspecies. A continuous population, blanketing the regions listed, is seldom the case because of varying geographic features and human intrusion.

When you glance over Table C-1, it is easy to see where the rattlesnake has developed most sucessfully. In all of South America, only three forms are presently known. Compare that continent's area of 7,035,357 square miles with Arizona's 113,909, and the fact that Arizona has seventeen species and subspecies seems all the more astounding. Although this animal has been known in every state except two (Hawaii and Alaska), and has been exterminated, it is believed, in only two (Maine and Delaware), it is primarily an animal of the Southwest.

Mexico's thirty-five mainland species and subspecies, and her additional insurlar variations, when coupled with Arizona's seventeen, New Mexico's nine, California's ten, and Texas' ten pretty much places rattlesnake headquarters of the world in the southwestern portion of the North American continent.

The apparatus with which a rattlesnake inflicts injury consists of two highly specialized teeth, and their attendant mechanisms. Contrary to legends, which surprisingly still have currency, the breath of the rattlesnake is harmless, as are its forked tongue and unique tail. Rattlesnakes cannot spit their venoms as do some cobras.

A rattlesnake cannot poison a suckling infant through its mother's milk by biting the mother, nor has a rattlesnake any hypnotic powers beyond causing hysteria in individuals with an unnatural fear. A garter snake can do as well, generally, in these cases. Categorically, the only way a rattlesnake can cause an injury is to puncture the skin with one or both of its fangs. What is involved is a bite or scratch, a stab, if you wish, but not a sting. No snake stings. That is left to bees, and a host of other creatures we discuss elsewhere in this book.

One strange belief is apparently well founded in fact. A rattlesnake can "bite" after it is dead. Reptiles, it seems, have prolonged reflex actions. James A. Oliver, former director of the American Museum of Natural History, reports that people have actually been bitten by snakes handled after they were dead. The reference is in a pamphlet he prepared for the New York Zoological Society entitled, "The Prevention and Treatment of Snakebite." This author has noted other reliable references to this fact.

The mechanism with which a snake can cause injury can readily be divided into two parts: (1) a system of venom production and storage, and (2) a system for the introduction of that venom into the victim. We will discuss the latter part first.

Not all snakes have the same tooth system. There are the solid-toothed types without any fang differentiation sometimes known as aglyphs. Snakes with *fangs* at the back of the mouth—that is, with enlarged and grooved posterior teeth—are frequently called opistho-glyphs. Here, the venom is chewed into a wound, as opposed to injected. Snakes with strongly differentiated fangs in the front of the mouth are either proteroglyphs—snakes with permanently erected fangs—or solenoglyphs—snakes with fangs that fold or rotate back to the roof of the mouth. Clearly, the most advanced and efficient biting mechanism belongs to the animals in the last of the four categories. They have their venom injectors in front where they can be most readily brought into play, and can accommodate longer fangs because they can fold them away. They actually carry fangs that are far too big for their mouths because they only bring them forward when the lower jaw is in a position close to 180 degrees from the upper. It should not be assumed, however, that the most efficient biting mechanism automatically indicates the deadliest bite. As we shall be noting, the most dangerous snake venoms belong to the third group, the front-fanged, permanently erect type, and not to the viperine, folding-fang group.

The highly developed biting mechanism of the viperine snakes involves two modified maxillary teeth, and the means for swinging them downward. They move down with their protective sheaths from the roof of the animal's mouth, through an arc of roughly 90 degrees, to a position about perpendicular to the upper jaw. The fangs are greatly elongated, curved inward and canaliculated, or equipped with an enclosed canal. As the animal's fangs penetrate the victim's tissues, the sheaths are pushed back up along the fangs.

One of the most remarkable things about the rattlesnake's fangs is that they are always present for the animal's needs. Although they are fragile and easily lost in action as well as by periodic shedding, the rattlesnake has immediate replacement provisions. In a system not unlike a cartridge clip in a semiautomatic pistol, the animal has as many as six additional fangs in various stages of development on each side of his head. As soon as one is lost, the most mature of the replacements goes through a few brief changes and the animal is again fully armed, as it was at the moment of birth, for action. There is an overlap in the schedule of change. In a letter to the author, Dr. Klauber pointed out that, for a short time, venom can be injected from both fangs on one side of the head. When the new one is fully operative, the old one drops out.

The fangs themselves curve back at an angle of 60 to 70 degrees. An entrance lumen at the top front of the fang, near where it joins its bony support, allows venom to enter a hollow canal. The venom comes out through a discharge orifice slightly up from the point, and on the *front* of the fang. The fang has cutting edges also on the front to assist in effective penetration.

Of particular importance is the size of the fang. If the fangs are very small and frail, the chances of the animal's breaking them on striking are increased, and the chances of its injecting its venom are reduced. Short-fanged animals are also hindered by even light clothing. Klauber reports fang lengths all the way up to $11/16$ inch, and he estimates some specimens have $7/8$ inch of exposed, functional fang. However, rattlesnakes do not have the longest fangs in the world. African Vipers (genus *Bitis*) undoubtedly hold the record. The Gaboon Viper (*Bitis gabonica*) probably outdoes all other species with fangs approaching two inches in length. However, fangs of $11/16$ or $7/8$ of an inch in length, and even smaller, are capable of reaching well-blooded tissue below the fat layers. Quite plainly, the rattlesnake's fangs are long enough to be dangerous.

Just how dangerous are these, America's best known and most frequently encountered, venomous snakes?

Wyeth Laboratories, a major producer of antivenin specific for the Crotalidae, publish a very informative booklet entitled "Antivenin (Crotalidae) Polyvalent." In discussing the Florida or Eastern Diamondback (Crotalus adamanteus), it refers to it as " . . . one of the most dangerous (rattlesnakes), ranks among the world's deadliest snakes." Discussing the Texas or Western Diamondback (Crotalus atrox), it says, "Bold and aggressive, it often crawls in the open and is commonly seen in cultivated areas, even in or near farm buildings. It is responsible for more serious and fatal accidents than any other North American snake."

James A. Oliver says in his booklet, The Prevention and Treatment of Snakebite: "The Western Diamondback kills more people than any other snake in the United States. Babies can deliver a lethal bite."

Dr. Herbert L. Stahnke, former director of the Poisonous Animals Research Laboratory at Arizona State University, says in his booklet, "The Treatment of Venomous Bites and Stings," "This is due to the fact that nearly all venomous snake bites in the United States are inflicted by Pit Vipers, i.e., rattlesnakes, copperheads, and cottonmouth moccasins. These snakes are not only abundant but their habits and habitats conflict with those of man. . . . Serious tissue destruction can result from the bite of even the youngest pit viper." We could easily cite several hundred such references from equally reliable sources.

Information on rattlesnake venom is incomplete and much research remains to be done. As closely related as different species are, there are apparently widespread variations among their venoms, and there is no one description that will accurately cover both genera. Since laboratories like those of Wyeth are able to produce a polyvalent antivenin for all pit vipers, however, we can describe certain things they have in common. The variables between the venoms of different species may often be at least in part a matter of amount, and not of kind. As the Wyeth booklet says, "Venoms are structurally complex substances; none has been completely analyzed."

It is generally accepted today that all pit viper venoms, or almost all, are both neurotoxins and hematoxins; viz., they attack the nervous and the blood and circulatory systems of the victim. It is also generally believed that each venom is predominantly one or the other, with the remaining characteristic secondary. This is certainly true of the rattlesnakes.

The venom of snakes developed from saliva, and the venom-producing system grew out of salivary glands. Many species completely harmless to man have toxic qualities in their saliva linking venomous and nonvenomous snakes. This all makes good sense, since saliva plays a large part in the digestion of food in animals, and the venom of a poisonous snake is used, not only to kill prey, but also to begin the digestive process before it is swallowed. In fact, the venom of these animals is first and foremost a prey-killing and digestive substance, and only secondarily a defensive one. The evolutionary development of venom from saliva is linked initially with these primary functions. The entire complex of the snake's envenomizing apparatus was designed to get food and utilize it, and not to injure animals too large for it to feed on.

In appearance, venom is generally yellow in color (although some colorless samples are on record) and usually cloudy when first obtained. Since the cloudiness settles out if the venom is allowed to stand, we can assume that it is caused by cellular debris of some sort. It is usually described as odorless. It has a slightly sweet taste, but this is not very strong. Klauber says there is a slight tingling sensation on the lips when the venom is tasted. It should be noted that no harm will generally come from tasting, or even swallowing, venom as long as there are no open sores in the mouth, or in the digestive tract. (Cobra venom, on the other hand, may be injurious if swallowed.) Similarly, venom on unbroken skin is harmless although it should be washed off as soon as possible. Venom is a poison but, like all poisons, it can be safely handled by people who know what they are doing.

Since venom is so complex, and so difficult to analyze chemically, many researchers have concentrated on breaking it down, not by chemical constituents, but rather by the effects it produces. Quantitative analysis usually involves a description of which effect on the victim is most pronounced. Even a brief survey of the work that has been done in this field would far exceed the limited space we have here. Keep in mind that a wide range exists even among the rattlesnakes; the venom of the South American Rattlesnake (Crotalus durissus and subspecies) is closer to the venom of the Indian cobra in effect than it is to that of the Florida and Texas diamondbacks. And the Mojave Rattlesnake (C. scutulatus) has a venom not only different from, but much stronger than, that of any other species of either rattlesnake genera.

What all this amounts to is that the venom of the rattlesnake is most definitely dangerous to man. Just as it is certain that some rattlesnakes can cause death by their bite, it is equally certain that some do not or may not. Since only the specialist can tell one rattlesnake from another with any certainty, the practical attitude is to leave them all alone.

Anyone can learn to tell the very different species apart—the massa-sauga from the Texas diamondback, for example—but since the color phases are so erratic, and since it is almost certain that the young of some species are more dangerous than the adult forms of others, the rule still applies. Reading about the use of the "T" or "Y" stick does not equip a person to attempt to catch and handle a dangerous reptile. This should be left strictly to the experts. If you encounter a rattlesnake in the wild, unless you really blunder into it, the chances are you will not be injured. Don't try to kill or capture it; leave it alone. It will soon go its own way.

We have, then, an animal that is, at least in many of its forms, dangerous to man in direct contact. What of the statistical potential, how much of a threat is the rattlesnake?

Dr. Klauber estimates that the mortality rate from rattlesnake bite is between 1.5 and 2 percent. The U.S. Department of Health, Education, and Welfare reports annual death rates running from five to fifteen.* The states where these bites occur most often are, in order of incidence, Arizona, Florida, Georgia, Texas, and Alabama.

How great, then, is the nationwide danger from rattlesnakes? With approximately 1.5 million deaths a year in the United States, fifteen to twenty deaths from any one cause is inconsequential. In Mexico, with a large rural population, much of it barefoot, the snakebite incidence is bound to be higher. If you live, work, or play in Arizona, Florida, Georgia, Texas, or Alabama, you have a better chance of being fatally injured by a rattlesnake than in any other state in the Union. Of course, there are parts of New York and Massachusetts where you are more apt to be bitten than in parts of the five states listed above. We are speaking now of statewide statistics, for whatever they may be worth. The five states that do lead the field probably do so because of the occurrence of the Florida and Texas Diamondbacks (C. adamanteus and C. atrox), two of the most aggressive and dangerous of all rattlesnakes. Neither Florida nor Georgia has anywhere near the variety of rattle-snakes that California has (three and five as compared to ten), and California is not on the top-five list.

If you are a man you have a much better (or worse!) chance of being bitten, and the reason for that is obvious; it is because of the places where you are most apt to work and play. If you are a child under seventy-five pounds in weight your chances of dying are much greater, although this is not to suggest that obesity is a practical defense against a rattlesnake.

*Sixteen to twenty may be closer to an accurate annual average for the United States.

Klauber lists a number of other variables that influence the ratio of injuries to death:

1. Age, size, sex, vigor, and health of the victim.
2. Allergy complex; susceptibility to protein poisoning.
3. Emotional condition and nature of victim.
4. Site of the bite. (Fortunately, you have a better chance of being bitten on the extremities than near the vital organs.)
5. Nature of the bite: full, direct stroke, as opposed to glancing blow or scratch.
6. Protection afforded by clothing.
7. Number of bites; *occasionally* more than one is involved.
8. Length of time the snake holds on. Usually rattlesnakes hit and run, but there have been cases where they got hung up and even had to be pulled or shaken loose. Certainly, these cases are exceptional.
9. Extent of the anger or fear of the snake. While there is no truth to the old legend that a snake's *virulence* increases with his rage, it is true that a rattlesnake will not generally discharge all of its venom, which it needs for food-getting. If injured or violently excited, however, it might really let go and give all it has, or nearly all. . . .
10. Species and size of the snake. (We have already indicated that this is a major factor.)
11. The age of the snake is also a factor; very young and very old snakes are likely to be less virulent. However, this is relative.
12. Condition of the venom glands; full, partially depleted, etc.
13. Condition of the fangs.
14. Presence of various microorganisms in the snake's mouth; venom contains an antibactericidal constituent that can lead to serious and even fatal complications.
15. The kind of first aid, and eventual treatment given.

Klauber reports that, drop for drop, some rattlesnake venoms are sixty times as powerful as others. Item 10 above would be the author's choice for the most important single consideration, though this is, of course, open to argument.

The medical text, *Principles of Internal Medicine*, states that "The minimum lethal dose of dried rattlesnake venom for man has been postulated to be 1 mg. per 6 pounds of body weight. The average Diamondback yields 220 mg. of venom, the Moccasin 150 mg., and the Copperhead 45 mg. Since these venoms are qualitatively similar, the larger quantity injected appears to account for the greater deadliness of the Diamondback." Of course, all rattlesnake venoms are not necessarily qualitatively similar, although the end result of a massive dosage might be. For the purposes of the practitioner, the statement would appear to be accurate enough. One other point, however: we can assume the three dosages given, 220, 150, and 45 mg., were measured from snakes artificially milked under laboratory conditions. If that assumption is correct, the information is slightly misleading, since rarely would a snake evacuate its fully supply on a single bite.

Dr. Herbert L. Stahnke, in his booklet, "The Treatment of Venomous Bites and Stings," describes and illustrates with case photographs terrible tissue destruction from essentially hematoxic crotalid venom. This localized destruction, on occasion requiring amputation, would not be typical of neurotoxins with their slight or absent localized effects.

What, then, can our conclusion be about the rattlesnake, and the danger it poses to man? Individually, the rattlesnake is a dangerous animal and one best avoided. Certain areas of the country realize more dangers than others by a tremendous margin, due to large rattlesnake populations and more dangerous species. Statistically, your chances of being bitten are very low almost everywhere, and nonexistent in most places. The chances of your being killed by a rattlesnake are lower yet. If you are a calm person who takes normal precautions you are even less likely to get bitten, and less likely to be killed even if caught off guard and struck. Individually, the rattlesnake can be very dangerous; nationally, it isn't much of a health menace.

The rattlesnake, however, is not just a mass of statistics, nor is it simply an excuse for constructing a probability graph. The rattlesnake is an integral part of the natural economy of American wildlife. It is a durable, adaptable, and even a useful animal. It is an important cog in the machinery nature set up on this continent to control fast-breeding rodents. Without the rattlesnake, our natural balance in many parts of the United States would be quite different. Ironically, this dangerous animal helps keep many harmless animals harmless. Without the rattlesnake, many animals now harmless would be much more destructive and expensive to deal with.

The rattlesnake can probably survive just about everything that will happen on this continent in the foreseeable future except expanding urbanization and the resultant increase in suburban construction. This rapid spread of urban and suburban development has no natural limits other than altitude and the coastlines of the continent. Cliffsides and sand dunes that were once considered totally unfit for human habitation are today the wellsprings of new architectural schools. Man's conquest of microscopic animals has led to immense population expansion. To this growth, the rattlesnake must eventually bow. It is hunted, its natural prey is hunted and starved, and eventually it, like the mountain lion, lynx, bear, and other species which do not sit well with man, will be a zoological curiosity. For the time being, however, it is here in quantity, and we might well heed the ancient admonition, "Don't Tread On Me!"

All of Canada, from the Arctic to the U.S. border, has only four species of venomous snakes, all of them rattlesnakes. Alberta has the Prairie Rattlesnake *(C. viridis viridis)* in the southeastern sector; British Columbia has the Northern Pacific Rattlesnake *(C. viridis oreganus)* in the south-central and eastern areas; Ontario has the Eastern Massasauga *(Sistrurus catenatus catenatus)*, the Timber Rattlesnake *(C. horridus horridus)*, and both in the southern parts, and Saskatchewan has the prairie rattler in the southwest. Manitoba and Prince Edward Island each *may* have a rattlesnake in very limited populations. No venomous sea snakes are known to visit Canadian waters. Snakebite, as a problem, is negligible. The mortality rate is between one and two per year for the entire nation of 3,610,097 square miles. No other nation of even comparable size is so free from this problem.

There are more than forty species and subspecies of rattlesnakes in Mexico. The aggressive and dangerous Western Diamondback *(C. atrox)* occurs on the Baja California peninsula, on San Pedro Mártir, Turner and Tiburon islands, and in ten or eleven Mexican states. Although figures verifying this are not available, rattlesnakes alone are probably a much bigger health problem in Mexico than they are in the United States. Overall snakebite mortality appears to run ten times as high, but rural Mexicans have a larger variety of venomous species to contend with.

As we have seen, the rattlesnakes are not absent from South America, although they appear in nowhere near the variety found in Mexico and the United States. At the present writing, aside from *Crotalus unicolor,* the Aruba Island Rattlesnake (found only on tiny Aruba Island), only two subspecies are listed for all of South America: *C. durissus terrificus* and *C. d. vegrandis.* In a letter to the author, Dr. Klauber said that he is sure further taxonomic breakdowns of *C. d. terrificus* will be recognized once more work has been done on the group. The range of this rattlesnake in South America is considerable, Chile and possibly Ecuador being the only exceptions, and even Ecuador is not positively known to be free of them. They are known by many dozens of names because of the number of linguistic groups in this vast area. Among the best-known colloquial names are: South American diamondback rattlesnake, boicininga, boiquira, maracaboia, cascavela, and cascabel.

On December 3, 1775, Commander-in-Chief Esek Hopkins was piped aboard his flagship, the *Alfred*, and took command of the fleet constructed by the new American Congress. Capt. Dudley Saltonstall, commanding officer of the vessel, accepted a flag from his superior. The flag, a gift to Hopkins from a Colonel Gadsden, was hoisted at the main mast of the *Alfred*, and the first of a long line of "rattlesnake flags" felt the pull of the wind.

The flag had a yellow field with a coiled rattlesnake in the center, and the words, "Don't Tread On Me," at the bottom. On the same day, the U.S. Navy jack was raised on another ship in the fleet picturing a rattlesnake crawling across a field of thirteen stripes. A similar flag was the emblem of the South Carolina navy. The Minutemen of Culpeper County in Virginia carried a flag showing a coiled rattlesnake with the additional legend, "Liberty or Death." The Massachusetts navy had a rattlesnake coiled around a pine tree, and the words, "An Appeal to God," before the ubiquitous, "Don't Tread On Me."

The rattlesnake, whether hoisted as a flag and leading British colonists in their battle against their king, or held alive and squirming between the teeth of a Hopi Indian as the symbol of lightning in the intense Hopi snake ceremony, has never been very far away from American folklore, symbology, and imagery. Ranging from southern Canada past our own southernmost boundaries deep into Central and South America, the rattlesnake, in its currently recognized sixty-six species and subspecies, is solidly implanted in the American ecological scene. Encountered in mountain crags, in deserts below sea level, and in steaming coastal swamps, this animal exists, or did exist before hunting and human invasion somewhat restricted its range, in every state within the continental limits of the United States. Alaska and Hawaii alone, of the fifty American states, have not known the readily distinguishable *whirrrr* of the rattlesnake's tail. Surrounded by legend, accredited with powers that bring it to the very threshold of deification, and scientifically studied more than any other group of reptiles, the rattlesnake appears to have a firm hold on popular fancy and full title to the role of American animal archvillain.

13 Venomous Snakes: The Other Crotalids and the Old World Vipers

There are four genera of pit vipers we have not yet discussed: *Lachesis, Bothrops, Trimeresurus,* and *Agkistrodon.* The Bushmaster *(Lachesis muta)* is the only species in its genus. It is probably the largest of all pit vipers, but fortunately is not particularly abundant in any part of its range. It inhabits abandoned burrows of mammals in hot, damp lowlands and jungles. It is found from Nicaragua south through Central and into northern South America. Costa Rica, Panama, Colombia, Venezuela, the Guianas, northern Brazil, and Trinidad all play host to this impressive animal. S*urucucu, mapepire z'ananna* and *la cascabel muda* are some of its common names. The last means "silent rattle," and since it is a native name we might assume it isn't based on the scientific relationship the creature actually does bear to the rattlesnake. It has the habit, as do some other rattleless pit vipers (and some harmless snakes), of rapidly vibrating its tail when disturbed. On a bed of dry leaves, the sound produced can sound much like a rattlesnake.

The bushmaster has the distinction of being the only egg-laying pit viper of the New World. The others give birth to living young. Lengths in excess of twelve feet have been reported for this rasp-skinned, reddish-brown serpent, but nine to ten feet is closer to average. The *shusupé,* as it is sometimes called, has particularly long fangs 1⅜ inches having been reported, with 1 to 1⅛ inches probably being average for an adult specimen.

As to aggressiveness, the picture is confused. The American traveler, Leonard Clark (*The Rivers Ran East*), has the bushmaster "fatal to man in five minutes,"* and "it will follow a man and kill either by day or by night," not to mention "will continually strike until the victim is dead." Karl P. Schmidt, late curator of zoology emeritus at the Chicago Natural History Museum, wrote an amusing piece called, "Anent the 'Dangerous' Bushmaster," for the August 1957 issue of *Copeia*, the journal of the American Society of Ichthyologists and Herpetologists. The story is interesting in the sense that it contradicts so much of what has been written about the bushmaster.

To the best of available knowledge, Leonard Clark lost his life on the Amazon in 1957, and he can't defend his opinions. We will allow them to stand on their own merits as they face comparison. In his article, zoologist Schmidt cited a letter received from his friend, herpetologist Raymond E. Stadelman, dated April 17, 1957. Mr. Stadelman was formerly curator of a serpentarium in Honduras. He was an early contributor to the *Bulletin* of the now defunct Antivenin Institute of America. The letter concerns the capture of a bushmaster between eight and nine feet long in Colombia. An employee of the Villa Artega rubber station near Antioquia was bathing in a stream with his wife when he spotted the snake. Mistaking it for a harmless boa, he decided it would make a nice addition to the Stadelman collection. The amateur collector tied a shoestring around the snake's neck and together with his wife started to lead the bushmaster home on the improvised lead. Then the snake got stubborn about being dragged along like a dog in Central Park; the shoestring broke. While the man retied the fragile leash, his wife shoved and pushed from behind. The couple encountered an Indian who told them that their harmless boa was a dreaded bushmaster, and the wife left the scene. The husband picked the snake up with the help of another workman and carried it to the site of the Stadelman collection, nearly strangling the reptile in the process. (Bushmasters have very fragile neckbones and if treated roughly during capture and handling may not survive.)

Stadelman commented in his letter to Dr. Schmidt,

> I have always had doubts about the famed aggressiveness of the Bushmaster, and believe this reputation is unwarranted. While I consider the Fer-de-lance to be very dangerous because it is nervous and apparently bites through fear, I think the Bushmaster just doesn't give much of a damn about anything. . . .

*After that one, everything the man says is immediately suspect.

He goes on to describe how he frequently handled bushmasters without the snakes assuming a threatening attitude. Dr. Schmidt does point out at the end of the article that a pit viper with inch-long fangs is dangerous, whether aggressive or not.

Certainly, the bushmaster must be rated as potentially dangerous to man. It has extremely long fangs, it carries a massive dose of venom and has caused deaths. We have discussed it at some length here because reliable reports list this snake as sluggish and generally not aggressive. Folk legends, however, have it actually pursuing man. Somewhere between total indifference and constant murderous intent lies the truth. The nature of this truth determines how dangerous the animal is, its ability to kill being readily established. Bushmasters, like all other snakes, vary from specimen to specimen. Certainly, some individuals may be combative while others are apparently quite docile. We can assume, based on the observations of qualified individuals, that the bushmaster is not the monster it is so often described as being. Left alone, it doesn't look for trouble.

It is with the remaining three genera of crotalids that we encounter real problems. Of the three, *Bothrops* is found only in the New World, *Trimeresurus* in the Old World (but not Africa), and *Agkistrodon* in both North America and the Old World.

These North American species are known, commonly, as the copperheads, the cottonmouths, and the Mexican cantil (see Table 3).

Table 3. *Agkistrodon* **in North America**

Scientific name	Common name	Distribution
Agkistrodon bilineatus	Cantil	Mexico through Central America
A. contortrix mokasen	Northern copperhead	Massachusetts to Kansas, south to Alabama, west to Texas
A. c. contortrix	Southern copperhead	Virginia, Florida to Alabama, Texas north to Illinois and Missouri
A. c. pictigaster	Trans-Pecos copperhead	Trans-Pecos Texas
A. c. laticinctus	Broad-banded copperhead	Kansas, Oklahoma, Texas
A. piscivorus piscivorus	Eastern cottonmouth	Virginia to Key West and Alabama
A. p. leucostoma	Western cottonmouth	Illinois to Alabama, west to Kansas, Oklahoma, Texas, Missouri

The copperheads and cottonmouths are obviously closely related, with the cottonmouth being almost certainly the more dangerous. Statistically, it is generally known as the third most dangerous snake in the United States; only the Eastern and Western diamondbacks cause more fatalities. In fact, the cottonmouths are about as dangerous as most rattlesnakes of comparable size, although the venom of the copperhead is weaker than that of the rattlesnake. The copperhead, though, undoubtedly bites more people in the United States than does any other species. Fortunately, its venom is relatively mild.

The cantil is a highly toxic snake and, although rarer than other *Agkistrodon*, it does figure in public health statistics. It prefers damp areas and may be quite common in some places.

Between ninety and one hundred snakebite deaths are reported for Japan each year. (A number of the sea snakes range that far north, but cases of injury or death to man from them are as rare in Japan as everywhere else.) The Mamushi or Pallas's Pit Viper (*Agkistrodon halys*) is probably the chief villain in Japan. The mamushi belongs to the same genus as the copperhead and cottonmouth of North America. It ranges through a variety of terrains and in many places is quite common. During the spring and summer months, large numbers are collected and shipped to the cities where they are displayed alive in drugstore windows. A medicine is made from them that is used for a variety of complaints ranging from impotency to asthma. The author noted windows full of these animals in several Japanese cities. Some of the cases of snakebite reported probably come from the fact that the mamushi is handled frequently, in large numbers, and with singular carelessness.

There are eight other species of *Agkistrodon* in the Old World. The mamushi range from northern China to extreme southeastern Russia; other forms are scattered over Southeast Asia as far west as the Himalayas and south to the island of Sri Lanka and to Malaya. These snakes are commonly called pit vipers, which is most misleading since the same general designation is given to the Old World representatives of the *Bothrops* and *Trimeresurus*.

Turning now to this other group, we will again take the New World forms first. These are now commonly all called *Bothrops* by herpetologists, and the best known is undoubtedly the Fer-de-lance (*B. lanceolatus*). This is a much-feared snake with very large venom glands, long fangs, and a rather active disposition. The venom is said to be fast-acting and to cause internal bleeding, both around the bite and, in surprisingly short order, in other parts of the body. First aid is of course indicated in the case of a bite from this snake, but antivenin is called for

The bushmaster
(*Lachesis muta*) is
a large and highly
venomous South
American species.
Mild-mannered
and retiring, it
seldom figures in
human mortality
statistics.
*Courtesy American
Museum of Natural
History*

The copperhead (*Agkistrodon mokasen*) bites more
people in the United States, it is believed, than does any
other species of venomous snake, yet deaths are all but
unknown. They are venomous, but mildly so. The author
inadvertently stepped on one in Texas, and it didn't even
attempt to strike.
Courtesy American Museum of Natural History

The cottonmouth water moccasin *(Agkistrodon piscivorus)* is a dangerous snake of the American South. Its bite can result in gross tissue damage, and amputations are not uncommon after a bad bite. The species can be aggressive at times and is densely populated in some areas.
Photograph by Roger A. Caras

The cantil or Mexican moccasin *(Agkistrodon bilineatus)* is a relatively small, handsome reddish snake that seldom causes human death. It can be short-tempered, though, and is feared in some parts of Mexico more than is justified.
Photograph by Roger A. Caras

at the earliest possible moment. The species is found only on the one island of Martinique.*

The incidence of venomous snakes in the West Indies constitutes something of a mystery. Although surrounded on three sides by lands more than amply provided with snakes, they are strangely barren of venomous snakes. Trinidad and Tobago, islands that are really parts of South America, have the bushmaster, some pit vipers, and a coral snake; all the remaining islands, except Martinique, are without venomous snakes.

This lack may indicate an early separation from the mainland. Where geological evidence is otherwise, you have mainland species, *Bothrops* and *Lachesis*. Rattlers, being more recent evolutionary products, perhaps weren't around when they could have invaded the land that now makes up these islands.

Some of the close-in coastal islands of the Caribbean undoubtedly have acquired strays that floated across on vegetation carried downriver from the highlands, but these are exceptions. To find hundreds of tropical islands, some covered with dense jungle, free of these animals is a most unusual situation.

Dangerous pit vipers are found not only on the West Indian island of Martinique, but also from central Mexico south through Central America to northern South America. They are a particular problem to native laborers since they thrive on rats that normally infest sugar plantations. Their venoms are hemolytic and even young vipers (born in litters reportedly as high as thirty or more) can be dangerous. The various names for these relatives of the true fer-de-lance include *barba amarilla* ("yellow beard"), *el tercipela* ("the velvet one"), *barcin*, *caissaca*, *macagua*, *guayacan*, and many more. Although more of a problem in Panama and other areas than in Mexico, there can be little doubt that many of them are among the more dangerous venomous animals. Some species achieve a length of eight feet (some reports say twelve). They are denizens of both moist and dry regions, forested as well as open country, and some forms are dreaded throughout their range. Their frequent irritability is not the least factor contributing to their reputation as bad citizens. Ten species of *Bothrops* occur in Mexico, but none match the fer-de-lance in disposition, virulence, or size.

It is an interesting fact that the pit vipers of this group are divided both in the New and Old Worlds into two distinct subgroups—arboreal species with prehensile tails and, in most cases, displaying green coloration; and ground-dwelling forms, without prehensile tails and of

---

*Many related mainland pit vipers (*B. atrox* and others) are also called fer-de-lance, for its "lance-shaped" head.

various color combinations, but in no case vivid green. Even more strange is that some of the former on both sides of the Pacific have red tails. There are some thirty-five forms in the New World and twenty-five in the Old World.

Apart from the fer-de-lance the best known in the New World are probably the Jararaca (B. jararaca) and the Jararacussu (B. jararacussu) of Brazil, both of which can exceed five feet in length and deliver strikes that can result in death. In some respects the most unpleasant form appears to be the Tommygoff or Jumping Viper of Central America (B. nummifer), a thick-bodied, short animal with a tiny tail held high off the ground. This snake can climb, though it is not prehensile-tailed, and its strike is so violent it can actually launch itself off a low branch or even, it is reported, the ground.* Actual case histories of envenomation by this and most of the other tropical American Bothrops are few and inconclusive, but we must assume that collectively they account for a large proportion of the deaths caused by snakes in this area. And this is quite a serious problem as demonstrated by the following extracts or information from C. C. Swaroop and B. Grab, "Snakebite Mortality in the World":

Argentina: "It is believed that snake bite constitutes a problem of real importance in the rural sections of certain regions. . . ."

Bolivia: Statistics are apparently not available.

Brazil: "On the basis of the 1929 figures, it is estimated that there are 4,800 deaths from snake bites annually in Brazil. According to an indirect source, the number of annual deaths was estimated at about 2,000 in 1949."

British Guiana: Statistics for deaths from venomous animals (there were fifteen from 1944–1948) are not broken down as to type of animal.

Chile: "It is believed that there are no venomous snakes in Chile."

Colombia: From 1945–1949, there were 821 known deaths caused by venomous animals. It is not known how many of these were caused by snakes, but Swaroop and Grab observe: "A great variety of poisonous snakes are known to be present in Colombia, the most common species and the one causing the largest number of deaths being B. atrox."

Ecuador: "From 1900 to 1946, 2,182 cases of snakebite were treated at the Luis Vernago Hospital, Guayaquil; of these 87 were fatal. Mortality data for snakebite for the country as a whole are not available."

French Guiana: No mortality figures. Bushmaster known to exist.

Paraguay: No available statistics.

*Some people who dread snakes are really phobic about them, and have recurring nightmares about snakes "jumping" at them. Although this species is far from being one of the world's most seriously venomous, it does appear to live up to these phobic expectations.

Peru: Well-provided with venomous snakes, but no statistics available.

Surinam: No figures, but problem believed to be slight.

Uruguay: Fifteen known snakebite deaths from 1935–1946. Largely *Bothrops*, it is believed.

Venezuela: During the three years, 1947–1949, there were 1,295 snakebite cases reported, with 419 deaths, a mortality rate of nearly one-third. (This figure is so inconsistent with those from the rest of South America that this author would tend to question it.)

Central America, 228,578 square miles of tropical mountainous territory with limited coastal lowlands, includes six republics: Guatemala, Honduras, El Salvador, Nicaragua, Costa Rica, and Panama, and the colony of British Honduras. Like Mexico, Central America has a wide variety of venomous snakes.

British Honduras reports a low incidence of snakebite, with rare fatalities. This is in part accounted for by the relatively small population—under 100,000. Costa Rica has a considerably higher rate; El Salvador a reportedly low rate; no meaningful figures are available for Guatemala or Honduras; and Nicaragua is believed to have a low rate. Isolated populations and depressed areas without medical records in part account for sketchy, nonexistent and unreliable statistics. Yet, reportedly, snakebite is prevalent both in the forested lowlands of the Caribbean coast of these countries and also on the dry coastal plains of the Pacific where crotalids abound. Palm vipers, and certain ground vipers (all *Bothrops*), contribute to whatever problem exists.

The genus *Bothrops* is very well represented in South America, although much work is left to be done in what appears to the nonspecialist to be a perfect muddle. Some herpetologists apparently feel the genus should be broken down into several genera, at least.

Among the *Bothrops* in South America, Schlegel's or the eyelash viper, a prehensile-tailed creature, is probably the southernmost member of the genus, reaching well down toward the bottom of the continent. There are many more species, a number we have already mentioned, and some of them figure rather prominently in the statistics of snakebite incidence, while many more figure in locally consumed and exported fiction. Endless vernacular names cause confusion that is all but incurable.

The remaining crotalids are Old World forms and are of the genus *Trimeresurus.* They are distributed over a great triangle in eastern Asia, from the Ryukyus west to the forested limits of the Himalayas and south to Sri Lanka and the Indonesian islands. One of the most popularly known is the Habu (*T. flavoviridis)* of Okinawa, which became well known to Americans during World War II. This species appears to be extraordinarily abundant on both that and other islands of the group, while subspecies are found in southern Japan. There is also an apparently different and smaller species called the Kufa. (T. okinaven- sis) found on the same island.

During military operations on Okinawa Shima during World War II, a twenty-year-old marine private was lying in some bushes at the side of a tomb, peering down on Japanese soldiers below. He thought he felt a twig poke him in the cheek, and when he turned to see what it was, he was struck a second time below the left eye by a habu, supposedly the most deadly snake in the Ryukyu Islands. This man and nine other victims of the habu recovered and were eventually returned to duty. The habu, long feared as a particularly dangerous snake, is not known to have taken the life of a single American during the campaign when tens of thousands of GIs poked into virtually every cave and brush pile on the 579-square-mile Pacific Island.

While all of the snakes of this genus are venomous, and some may be potentially lethal to man when antivenin is unavailable, Schmidt and Inger note the very interesting fact that the arboreal, prehensile-tailed members of the Oriental group do not appear to be lethal or even seriously dangerous to man. They report, for instance, that Wagler's Viper (T. wagleri) of the greater East Indies is "very sluggish and gentle during the day, not at all prone to bite . . . is not dangerous to man, though it produces severe pain and local swelling. Venom relatively innocuous to man appears to characterize all of the arboreal pit-vipers of the Asiatic region."

In this and the preceding chapter we have noted nearly all of the venomous snakes of the Western Hemisphere. We have gone from Canada to southern Argentina, reviewed all the world's rattlesnakes, and many other pit vipers, and we did not find one animal whose bite means inevitable death. Taking the whole Western Hemisphere (from the Arctic to the Antarctic) we found snakebite a problem, for the most part, from Texas to Brazil. North and south of these two areas, snake- bite diminishes rapidly as a statistical cause for concern. This "snake- bite belt," we will find, carries on around the world. Venomous snakes are, indeed, dangerous to man, more often so up to 35 degrees of latitude north and south of the equator than anywhere else, but nowhere have we yet seen that snakes are necessarily lethal when they do bite. What of the rest of the world?

The other large family of snakes, which have venom fangs that can be folded back, are the true vipers of the Old World. This is an extremely numerous group both in forms and individual populations. Only a very few have adopted the arboreal habitat but these, like the climbing pit vipers, have also developed prehensile tails. Most of the ground-dwelling forms have comparatively short tails, but some have exceedingly abbreviated ones. Their colors run the gamut of the earth colors, with all manner of dark and light patterns. Some of the desert forms are almost cream-colored and all are masters of camouflage.

Since both systematic zoology and the scientific study of snake envenomation were started in Europe, we may legitimately start our survey of the group on that subcontinent. Europe proper has a very limited variety of poisonous snakes. All are true vipers of the genus *Vipera*. The Common Viper *(V. berus)* ranges from the Pyrenees to 67 degrees north in Scandinavia and is almost certainly the northernmost, and most widely distributed, venomous land snake on earth. It is the only venomous snake in the British Isles and ranges from those Atlantic islands right across Eurasia north of the Desert Belt to Korea, where in the southern part of its range it is found to an altitude of 9,000 feet. Table 4 outlines the venomous snakes of Europe.

Europe, generally speaking, suffers less than most other temperate areas in the world. The death rate from accidents with venomous snakes, when compared with the population involved, is negligible. Some of the vipers *(V. ammodytes,* for example) are reportedly more seriously venomous than the ubiquitous common viper, but not enough so to cause a problem of significant proportions. Even one death, of course, is "significant," but in examining an area as large as Europe, and as heavily populated, snakebite cannot be called a matter of grave concern.

There are some thirty true vipers in Africa of several genera. The Puff Adder *(Bitis arietans)* has a wide range and a dangerous, relatively slow-acting venom. It is nocturnal, slow to move away, comes near human settlements in search of rats, and it is easy to step on in the dark. The Night Adder *(Causus rhombeatus)*, the best known of four night adders in this genus, is reportedly timid and slow to anger, but its habit of invading human habitation at night results in accidents. The Rhinoceros Viper *(B. nasicornis)* is said to be inoffensive for the most part. It does, however, have a particularly potent venom, and ranges across the continent from Ghana to Kenya.

The Gaboon Viper *(B. gabonica)* is probably the one snake that comes closest to delivering the "sudden death" so often accredited to most venomous reptiles. It can be especially dangerous to man, since it has the longest snake fangs known. It has a massive head and, if it hits squarely, the fangs are planted dangerously deep. It is altogether a very formidable animal. Happily, it has a mild disposition, and bites are not common.

Two Horned Adders *(B. cornuta* and *B. caudalis)* are accredited with waspish dispositions and dangerous venom. The Berg Adder *(B. atro-*

Table 4. Venomous Snakes of Europe

Country	Partial list of species	Extent of the problem
Austria	Vipera ammodytes (long-nosed viper)	Very slight.
Denmark	V. berus (common viper)	Seven deaths in forty-seven years—all victims twelve years old or younger. In all, 1,200 cases of snakebite.
Finland	V. berus	Very slight.
France	V. berus and aspis	Probably higher in the south of this country than in most other European areas.
Germany	V. berus	Very slight.
Great Britain	V. berus	Seven deaths in the past fifty years.
Greece	V. ammodytes meridionalis	Not known.
Hungary	V. berus	Not known.
Italy	V. berus and aspis	May be slightly higher than most areas.
Netherlands	V. berus	Practically nonexistent.
Norway	V. berus	Practically nonexistent.
Portugal	V. berus and latasti	Not known.
Russia	V. ammodytes and renardi	Not known.
Spain	V. berus and latasti	About five deaths a year.
Sweden	V. berus	About 1,300 people bitten per year. Fifteen deaths from 1915–1944.
Switzerland	V. berus and aspis	Twenty-five deaths between 1881–1930. Between five and ten bites per year.
Turkey	V. a. meridionalis	Not known.
Yugoslavia	V. berus and aspis	Not known.

pos) of South Africa is also dangerous. The Sand Viper of North Africa (Cerastes vipera) and the Saw-scaled Viper (Echis carinatus) are common in desert areas. The saw-scaled viper ranges from Africa through Arabia and Iran to India.

Writing from Pakistan to Dr. Laurence M. Klauber, Dr. Sherman A. Minton, Jr., said of the saw-scaled viper:

> While not wishing to talk down Echis as a dangerous snake, I believe some of the factors that keep the fatality rate relatively high concern the human population at risk. The average snake-bite victim here is apprecia-

The Central American tree pit viper (*Bothrops schlegeli*) is one of many arboreal Central and South American pit vipers. Just how dangerous each species is, is not clearly understood. There is a great deal of legend attached to these snakes and scores of common and vernacular names.
Courtesy Chicago National History Museum

The dangerous South American jararacussu (*Bothrops jararacussu*) is a much-feared snake with a seriously venomous bite. There is still much confusion over the venoms of many Central and South American species.
Courtesy Harvard Institute for Tropical Biology and Medicine

The common European viper
(Vipera berus) is much
feared in some areas,
although its venom is quite
mild. Rarely does a human
death occur as a result of its
bite.
Photograph by John Markham

The puff adder *(Bitis arietans)* kills more people in Africa than do all
other species of snake combined. Lethargic during the day, it
approaches human habitations at night in search of rats. If
approached, it does not move out of the way. A very common snake
south of the Sahara, it has enormous fangs and a very serious venom.
Photograph by Roger A. Caras

Echis carinatus, the saw-scaled viper, may kill more people every year than any other single species of snake. It is small but extremely aggressive and highly toxic. It ranges all across the arid portions of Africa, the Middle East, and Asia. A congener in Israel is *Echis coloratus.*
Photograph by Dr. P. J. Deoras

Pallas's viper *(Agkistrodon halys)* is widespread—Eastern Europe to the Far East—and is related to the cottonmouth and the copperhead of North America. A very common snake, deaths are seldom attributable to it, although it is certainly a venomous species.
Photograph by Roger A. Caras

bly smaller than the average American or European, is to some extent malnourished and anaemic, and may well be suffering from chronic malaria and/or tuberculosis. The treatment he gets at a village dispensary may be positively harmful (e.g., permanganate injections). He may fare better at the hands of the local hakeem or snake charmer who will use his snake-stone, incantations, and herbal remedies. Even if the victim makes it to one of the relatively few modern hospitals, the best he can hope for is intelligent symptomatic and supportive treatment. Incidentally, the fatality rate in hospitalized cases here seems to be about 10% rather than the higher figures that have been reported particularly from parts of Africa.

Today, the principal habitat of the true vipers is undoubtedly Africa. The distribution of the various forms may perhaps best be understood if we regard the equatorial forest area of central and west Africa as the hub of their territory, and then consider a number of circular belts around this—belts incomplete only to the southwest which is, of course, occupied by the Atlantic. Within the hub are to be found such small-headed types as *Causus* and the great puff adders. It also contains the burrowing *Atractaspis* which, though also having a small head that looks more like that of a nonvenomous snake, has long fangs.

All around the deep forests lie, first, open woodlands; then savannahs; then semideserts; and finally the great expanses of true deserts that reach from the Mauretanian coast on the west, to North Africa, the Near East, and thence northeast right across central Asia to China, east to India, south into Arabia, and southwest in a great curve through the Sudan and Ethiopia, to lower Somalia. This desert belt contains its own hosts of vipers. Outstanding among these are the horned vipers of the eastern Mediterranean, three large species in Asia Minor and the Levant. There are also dangerous forms in southern Russia, Iran, Pakistan, and Jordan. Iraq has the Levantine Viper *(Vipera lebetina)*, the Horned Viper *(Cerastes cerastes)*, and the saw-scaled viper common farther to the east. This last-named snake is one of the most dangerous in the world, from all indications, due to its numbers, range, aggressiveness, and a toxic venom.

Beyond this arid belt, we have, to the north, the little adders of Europe and Middle Asia, and, to the east, large tropical forms in India, Burma, the Indochinese peninsula, and several of the Indonesian islands. The most notable of these Oriental forms is perhaps the *Daboia* or Russell's Viper *(V. russelli)*, which is found all over the Indian peninsula and beyond to Thailand and Java. It is dangerously venomous and can on occasion display a savage disposition. It is one of Burma's archvillains and a threat to barefooted farm workers. It is found in great numbers in the Irrawaddy River valley. It is reported that even a very small specimen can inject the amount of venom required to kill a healthy full-grown man. Incidentally, this was Sherlock Holmes's famous "Speckled Band."

Among the most venomous (for their size) of all the vipers, and the most potentially dangerous due to their abundance and habit of lying in depressions in paths in open, intensely hot places, are the horned vipers of Egypt and Arabia, and the saw-scaled vipers, which range from North Africa to India and south to the island of Sri Lanka. The saw scales have exceptionally potent venom, are touchy, and have a lightning strike. The number of deaths caused by them cannot be assessed but, judging by their numbers even in areas of heavy population, it must be extremely high. The vipers, in fact, though creatures that normally lie and wait for prey, and which are sluggish compared to many other venomous snakes, constitute a real menace to man especially in the arid areas of the Old World where the human inhabitants do not wear thick, tough foot-coverings, or where they go barefoot altogether.

14 Venomous Snakes: The Sea Snakes, Elapids, and Poisonous Colubrines

The remaining venomous snakes, as may be seen from the list given on pp. 139–40, fall among three great families. These are, first, the sea snakes or hydrophids; next the elapids, which include the cobras and the coral snakes and their allies; and third, the colubrids, among which there are but few menaces—in fact, in the case of man, probably only two species. Although the second group contains the snake that most experts agree is potentially the most dangerous—the king cobra—it appears that the real danger (of the venom itself) is in descending order from the hydrophids to the colubrids. The degree of "danger," "menace," and "potential danger" to man cannot be assessed by the same criteria. As we have constantly tried to point out, so many factors are involved it is impossible to say that this, that, or the other snake is the one most dangerous to man.

Sea snakes, venomous creatures all, members of the family Hydrophiidae, are almost all residents of the western Pacific and Indian oceans. The one exception is the Yellow-bellied Sea Snake (*Pelamis platurus*), and this species reaches the western coast of Central America and Mexico in not inconsiderable numbers. Its range, from eastern Africa to western America, makes it the most widely distributed reptile in the world. Equipped with a particularly virulent nerve toxin, this snake has reportedly caused human deaths.

The family Hydrophiidae includes fifteen genera, and approximately fifty species. Some members of the subfamily Laticaudinae, the more primitive sea snakes, do come ashore to lay eggs, although they live most of their lives in the sea and eat fish exclusively. Members of the subfamily Hydrophinae have adapted to the point where they are totally marine, and, giving birth to living young, never venture out onto dry land. Indeed, they can't, for their ventral scales have been reduced to a degree where they cannot be used to move on land. Agile and swift in the sea, they flop and squirm ineffectually once removed from it. They have also adapted to life in the sea in another strange way. They generally have an exceedingly slender neck and anterior half of the body, while their posterior end is much heavier, terminating in a flattened, vertical, paddlelike tail. Since these snakes hunt fish, which they obtain by means of their potent venom, they have to strike much the same way as any other venomous snake. Floating in a liquid medium, however, they have no fixed fulcrum. Nature has made the necessary adjustments and the heavy after-end supplies the inertia while the slender forward-end is designed to reduce the effects of resistance in the heavy medium of seawater. All of these snakes are air breathers and will drown, as will any other lunged animal, if held under water beyond their limit. Like the whales and seals, the sea snakes are derived from land animals who returned to the easy life of the sea.

With the exception of *P. platurus*, the sea snakes are limited to the southwest Pacific and Indian oceans. This one wanderer not only reaches Central and South America, but has been captured in Posieta Bay, Siberia. It is likely that the few specimens taken there were carried by the Tsushima branch of the Kurosiwo Current which flows northward into the Sea of Japan. No other sea snake is know to travel into deep waters. They are generally coastal animals with a strong preference for river mouths, harbor and beach areas, and coral reefs. A few are occasionally seen somewhat farther at sea, and some travel up brackish tidal rivers for short distances. One species, *Hydrophis semperi*, apparently got caught by a geological upheaval and dwells in freshwater Lake Bombon on Luzon Island. *Laticauda crockeri* is also a lake-dweller being found in brackish Lake Tungano on Rennell Island in the Solomons. All others are strictly coastal animals.

As a group, these seagoing snakes are not large. Eight-, nine-, and ten-foot specimens have been reported, but most species achieve nowhere near that size. Four to six feet is apparently about average. All are venomous, although there exists a difference of opinion as to how dangerous each of them is. At least one species is known to have venom fifty times as potent as that of the king cobra. They have venom glands located just below the eye. Their fangs are cobralike, being permanently erect, hollow, and not very large.

There are reports of these animals occurring in vast numbers at certain seasons. They evidently congregate for breeding and reports exist of ships sailing through seas literally alive with them.

The U.S. Navy Diving Manual (NAVSHIPS 250-538) has a hazard table for marine life: one plus means minimum danger, and four plus means maximum. Collectively, sea snakes are rated three plus. Under the column marked "Behavior" is the comment, "Boldness varies." Despite the fact that these snakes are venomous, often dangerously so, and even though they are plentiful in some parts of their range, bites are not common. The determining factor appears to be aggressiveness and, although reports vary, the relatively few cases reported would tend to support the idea that they are more retiring than pugnacious. Most snakes prefer to give ground rather than take on a foe as large as a man, and the sea snake has a better chance to retreat before a showdown is forced upon it than has a land form. A swift whisk of its paddlelike tail with a single side-to-side movement, and the serpent is gone. It is reported that they are particularly aggressive during the breeding season.

Most accidents reported with these animals are tied in with fishing activities. They appear to hunt by night, and have been known to take bait and suddenly appear at the gunwales much to the chagrin of some poor angler. They are very often taken, and sometimes in large numbers, in nets. Over a hundred were taken in a single seine-haul off Luzon. Some fishing peoples, it is reported, refuse to report or discuss accidents with these animals on superstitious grounds and good statistics aren't available. Many of the areas inhabited by the Hydrophiidae are remote and underdeveloped. It is impossible to get a reliable population count, much less a reasonable estimate of snakebite mortality. This, however, would appear to be a fair consensus: they are often extremely venomous; they do on occasion bite, although they are not generally aggressive. It would be best to leave the water when they are around, and they certainly shouldn't be handled by anyone who isn't an expert. They have a limited economic value since some are hunted for their skins, from which a good grade of leather is made; they are bottled in chunks, and sold as an aphrodisiac and a general medicine, and they are smoked on bamboo skewers and used in Japan and parts of the Ryukyu Islands, where they are highly esteemed as a delicacy.

Dr. H. A. Reid of the General Hospital in Penang, Malaya, has consented to the use of the following extract of a case history of a sea-

Blue-ringed sea snakes *(Hydrophis cyanocinctus)*, one of about fifty species of highly specialized, highly venomous marine snakes. Note the laterally flattened tails and the small, streamlined heads.
Courtesy New York Zoological Society

The common and widespread banded sea snake *(Laticauda colubrina)*, another dangerously venomous marine species.
Courtesy Australian News and Information Bureau

snake bite which appeared in his paper, "Three Fatal Cases of Sea Snakebite," in Venoms, the 1956 symposium of the American Association for the Advancement of Science:

A Chinese fisherman, aged 54, was admitted to the Penang General Hospital on November 24, 1952, in a semi-paralyzed state. Eight days previously, he had returned from fishing off the west coast of Penang Island about 4:00 A.M. and, while kneeling down on the seashore sorting his nets, he felt a bite on the left knee. With the aid of a torch, he found that he had been bitten by a snake which he killed with a stick and threw back into the sea. It was about 2 ft. long and black and white in color with a flat tail. He noticed two teeth marks with small clots of blood at the spot where he had been bitten. He returned to his house and during the following few days the left, then the right leg, and finally the whole body became progressively weaker. He was eventually found by Security Forces operating in that area and carried by chair about 2 miles to transport by which he was brought to Penang General Hospital.

On admission bite marks were observed above the left knee. Intelligence, speech, and memory were noted as normal. All the limbs were weak and painful, and he was unable to sit up.

The following day, November 25, 1952, he was quite conscious though restless. At times he appeared mentally alert, answering questions reasonably, but mostly he seemed confused and uncooperative. He then complained bitterly and constantly of thirst. The pupils were small, equal, and reacted to light. Eye movements were normal. There was generalized loss of power and tone in all limbs. He could move somewhat feebly but was unable to lift his head off the pillow or sit up in bed. Involuntary movements were not seen. All tendon reflexes including the jaw jerk were absent. Abdominal reflexes were not obtained, plantar responses were flexor, and he was incontinent of urine and feces. No reliable estimation of sensation could be made but he responded to pinprick on the face and elsewhere, and no gross hyperesthesia was observed. Two pairs of puncture wounds were seen above the left knee, 5 mm. and 4 mm. apart respectively. There was no swelling, bruising, or tenderness, and the marks might well have been made by a hypodermic needle. The remaining physical examination was not remarkable; blood pressure 100/65, respiratory rate and fundi normal. The urine was normal apart from a trace of albumin. No abnormal color was seen. Cerebrospinal fluid was normal.

During the next two days, his condition remained essentially unchanged. He was restless and noisy, constantly complaining of thirst despite intragastric drip of 5 pints milk daily. His respiratory rate and rhythm appeared to be within normal limits. He died in the early morning of November 28, 1952, 4 days after admission and 12 days after the bite.

The same paper presents two other cases, both involving bathers. They were both bitten on the same day at the same beach. The first, a boy of eight, lived for thirteen hours. The second, a man of twenty-six, lived for seventy-seven hours. Evidently, cases of bathers being bitten are almost unheard of. These two cases are the first fatal cases involving bathers on record, and it may be more than a coincidence that they occurred at the same place on the same day. Dr. Reid does not draw this conclusion in his paper, and I must be held responsible for it; *possibly* it was aberrant behavior on the part of a single animal. The bites are reported as having been administered about two hours apart. The adult was the first victim (3:00 P.M.), and the child the second. A small boy would have less tolerance, generally speaking, than an adult and could have been killed even by a snake that had delivered a lethal bite only two hours earlier, assuming that sea snakes, like land snakes, do not tend to discharge their full load unless wildly agitated. This, however, is pure speculation, and I repeat, must be laid at my door and not Dr. Reid's.

It is interesting to note that the bite of the sea snake is virtually painless and slow-acting. The lack of reports of accidents may be due to the failure of victims to associate the two, or even to realize they have been bitten. Here, again, this is speculation. Turning now to the elapids, we come to the animals which probably do represent more potential danger to man than any other snakes on earth. I would stress that this does not mean that they are any more aggressive than other kinds; it is that they happen to be extremely common throughout extensive areas where there are large barefoot human populations. Also, the same areas lack modern medical facilities to a large extent, and in several places they are rife with superstition, which is inimical to both the prevention and cure of any ailment or injury.

Although the greatest potential menace to man by snakes is in areas where there are the most people; and although the elapids take first place as this menace, their headquarters, though surely not their place of origin, turns out to be Australia. This continent has more kinds of venomous than nonvenomous snakes, and no less than eighty-five different kinds of elapids are found there. These land-dwelling snakes are close relatives of the cobras, with fixed, relatively short fangs in the front of their upper jaws. According to D. M. Cochran, the larger Australian snakes are "outstanding for their abundance, insolence, and high toxicity."

As long ago as 1894, in Melbourne, Australia, Dr. George Britton Halford wrote:

A gentleman residing in South Yarra . . . rang me up at about midnight in May, 1868. He told me he had been bitten by a snake, that he did not want my advice, only that he wished to know if it was a poisonous snake or not.

With that, he opened a parcel and let the snake, which had been cut in halves, fall upon the carpet. The fall made it, although dead, wriggle about a little. I saw the punctures on his arm, examined the head of the snake, and found it to be that of a vigorous Tiger snake. Presently he asked leave to go on the verandah, where I heard him vomiting, and an hour or so afterwards, at his home; he coughed up into his cambric handkerchief, bloodcolored sputum. I felt sure he would die, which he did, twelve hours after the bite. His intelligence remained nearly to the last. The devitalised blood . . . was no longer capable of carrying on the processes of life. It was as if one were looking at St. Paul's Cathedral, and seeing it from some mysterious cause tumbling into dust. Such were my thoughts watching the passing away of this fine man.

On June 13, 1960, *Life* magazine carried an article about a twenty-two-year-old snake-handler in California who was bitten by a Tiger Snake *(Notechis scutatus)*. The article says the young man was "the first person outside of Australia ever bitten by the rare tiger snake, deadliest of all land serpents." It is not exactly certain that this creature is the deadliest of all venomous snakes (and it is not rare in Australia), but C. C. Swaroop and B. Grab point out, "It has an extremely toxic venom . . . is one of the most aggressive reptiles found in Australia . . . is reported to be responsible for a high proportion of the deaths from snake bite in the country."

Of the more than eighty-five varieties of venomous snakes that occur in Australia, F. G. Morgan of the Commonwealth Serum Laboratories pins the appellation "most deadly" not on the tiger snake, but on the Taipan *(Oxyuranus scutellatus)*. In a paper he did on this serpent for *Venoms*, Morgan describes it as a large, active, highly dangerous snake "capable of injecting at a bite an enormous dose of highly potent neurotoxic venom."

In his paper, Morgan describes the case of a young man from Sydney named Kevin C. Budden. While visiting Queensland in July 1950, Budden collected a taipan for research purposes. He was carrying the specimen to his car when "the snake managed to bite him on the thumb and hung on, biting savagely, being removed only with great difficulty by the victim." Budden managed to save his specimen, but he died the next day from the bite.

The taipan is reported as rarely encountered since it is scarce, shy, and quick to escape. It grows to a length of over ten feet.

Morgan lists the Death Adder *(Acanthophis antarcticus)*, the Tiger Snake, the Australian Copperhead *(Denisonia superba)*, the Common Brown Snake *(Demansia textilis)*, and the Red-bellied Black Snake *(Pseudechis prophyriacus)* as the main contributors, along with the taipan, to Australia's snakebite mortality. Swaroop and Grab agree, describing the death adder as especially active and dangerous.

It should again be pointed out that the Australian copperhead has nothing whatsoever to do with the American snake of the sane name. They are not at all related. To the lay reader who may object to the use of Latin names following the popular name of each animal, as it appears for the first time in this text, this example will demonstrate the necessity of that practice. Here is the case of two English-speaking nations on opposite sides of the world. They both have venomous snakes known throughout their respective ranges by the same name, "copperhead." The snakes have nothing to do with each other. Without the refinement of scientific names, confusion would be supreme!

Interestingly enough, although 60 percent of Australia's land snakes are venomous, and elapids, very few are deadly to man. In addition to its venomous land snakes, Australia has twenty-seven species of the sea snakes in its coastal waters.

Australia is frequently described in pulp literature as the home of the deadliest snakes in the world. This may well be the case, but when these treasuries of inaccurate herpetological lore go on to describe Australian snakes as creatures whose bite no man can survive, they pass over into fiction.

The very dangerous death adder of Australia is found also in New Guinea and in the Moluccas. A number of relatives of the brown snake and the taipan also occur in New Guinea along with great numbers of sea snakes along the coasts. New Zealand is free of venomous snakes, as are Norfolk and Nauru islands. The snakes listed as most deadly for Papua and for New Guinea are the death adder and the brown snake. Records for these areas are too scattered to have any real meaning. Although scientists working on New Guinea report that the area is anything but crawling with snakes, there are a number of dangerous species, and still a lot of barefoot people. Another factor that might contribute to a high incidence of snakebite is the fact that the natives use snakes as food. Rather than being avoided, they are hunted. In British Papua alone, from 1949 to 1952, 118 persons were admitted to hospitals for snakebite of whom nine died. In the same three-year period in New Guinea, 123 people were hospitalized, with no deaths recorded.

The Fiji Islands have no recorded snakebite mortalities although sea snakes appear in coastal waters. Eastern Samoa is free of this problem, and the 2,140 individual islands of the Pacific Island Territories have no dangerous species.

All the snakes we have discussed so far as residents of the United

States have been members of the family Crotalidae, the pit vipers. There are two genera of snakes in the United States that are related to the cobras. The coral snakes are proteroglyphs, that is, having strongly differentiated fangs in the front of the upper jaw which are permanently erect. These fangs are of necessity much shorter than the fangs of the vipers and pit vipers. This fang system is more primitive than the viperine system, but efficient enough to cause damage. Fortunately, the highly venomous American elapids are small and retiring animals.

Cases of snakebite involving the coral snakes are relatively rare, and almost inevitably result from people handling specimens. Coral snakes are so small, rarely much over two feet long, that they have to chew to get a firm grip and penetration with their small fangs. Elapids such as corals, unlike the vipers and pit vipers, do not have enlarged heads, but are proportionate throughout their entire length. A very small snake has a very small head. It would be *almost* impossible for an average-sized coral snake to "strike" and penetrate clothing. People have been bitten, however, and the venom is a particularly dangerous neurotoxin. The effects are widespread over the body rather than localized, and although death is neither inevitable nor immediate, as so often reported, the bite of these snakes is very dangerous.

Coral snakes can readily be listed among the deadly venomous animals of the world, but cannot be considered much of a health menace. If you spent your whole life within the geographical boundaries of their range, death by their bite would still be one of the least likely climaxes to your career. Your chances of even seeing one would be very slim since they are seldom encountered. And even if you came running home all out of breath announcing that you had just seen "the American cobra," the chances are you would be mistaken. The Scarlet King Snake (*Lampropeltis doliata*) and various of its subspecies, mimic the corals to an extraordinary degree, and since part of their range coincides with that of the Southeastern and South Florida coral snakes, there can be little doubt that confusion often results. Of course,

Table 5.   North American Elapidae—The Coral Snakes

Scientific name	Common name	Distribution
Micrurus f. fulvius	Southeastern coral snake	Florida north to North Carolina, west to Mississippi River
M. f. barbouri	South Florida coral snake	Southern Florida
M. f. tenere	Texas coral snake	Arkansas to southern Texas
Micruroides euryxanthus	Sonoran coral snake	Southern Arizona, possibly New Mexico and west Texas

it works both ways, and mistaking a coral snake for a harmless scarlet king snake would be a dangerous error to make. The king snake ranges farther north than the corals, and reports of coral snakes from Tennessee and Kentucky are apparently products of this confusion. The easiest way to tell them apart is the order of color; if the red is bordered by black, it's harmless; if the red is bordered by yellow or white, it's a coral.

In a word, the American members of the cobra family are among the most colorful animals on the continent, but also the least likely venomous reptiles to cause the average citizen any concern. If you don't go looking for them or pick them up, the chances are many uncounted thousands to one against your ever becoming a statistic.

Micrurus, the genus that gives North America a few unoffending coral snakes, reaches full flower in South America. There are more than forty species and subspecies of *Coralitos* on the continent. *M. spixi* of Brazil is the most impressive. It is the giant among coral snakes, and specimens measuring over five feet have been taken. Even so none of the group represents much of a threat to man when compared with the pit vipers. They do occasionally appear in the statistics as having delivered a lethal bite, but, as in North America, they are seldom involved unless handled carelessly, sat upon directly, or trod upon by someone with bare feet.

There are a group of especially slender coral snakes separated into another genus *(Leptomicrurus)* which occur from Peru to Colombia. Like all coral snakes, the venom is essentially neurotoxic, very potent, but seldom involved in human deaths.

The situation in Southeast Asia is somewhat different. Both the mainland and the islands are inhabited by a large number of snakes known as coral snakes. All develop venom, but the incidence of bites in humans is low, and few cases are on record. One caused by a species of *Maticoar* is on record and produced strange intermittent symptoms, but was not fatal.

The next group of elapids—though not necessarily their nearest relatives—are the Kraits *(Bungarus).* Col. William A. Noble of the Salvation Army, for forty-one years a medical missionary in India, told the author in a personal interview that the natives of Madras State in southern India called the krait (pronounced "krite") the "seven-stepper," believing that, if bitten, a man can take only seven steps before dying. This belief is not true, although the krait carries a particularly potent venom. Legends of almost instantaneous death from one snake or another are found almost everywhere venomous snakes are known. No such tale is true, although some venoms certainly act more swiftly than others.

The very venomous, very aggressive Australian tiger snake *(Notechis scutatus)*, clearly one of the most dangerous venomous animals in the world. Although chance of fatalities is very high, bites are relatively rare.
Courtesy Australian News and Information Bureau

The coral snake *(Micrurus sp.)* is a species surrounded with legend. Extremely shy and retiring, it is so small that bites are apt to occur only if the snake is handled carelessly. It does have a serious venom that is essentially neurotoxic.
Courtesy American Museum of Natural History

The banded krait (pronounced krite, not crate) *(Bungarus fasciatus)*, is one of Asia's most dangerously venomous snakes. The mortality is many, many times that of the Indian cobra.

Naja naja, the common Indian cobra, is widespread and often responsible for bites. The mortality rate from its bites is much lower than most people realize, however, and may not exceed 5 percent among people properly treated after the incident.

The Egyptian cobra (Naja haje) is widespread in Africa. Both aggressive and dangerous, it does not spit as do some other African cobras.
Courtesy Transvaal Snake Park

Milking or extracting venom from a green mamba (Dendroaspis angusticeps). This is work only for experts.
Courtesy South African Institute for Medical Research

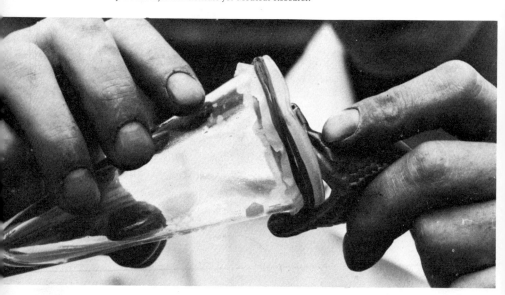

The boomslang (Dispholidus typus) from Africa south of the Sahara is the world's most potently venomous rear-fanged snake. Largely arboreal, it is mild-mannered and not prone to strike unless molested.

Two highly venomous kraits, the Malayan or Blue *(B. candidus)* and the Banded *(B. fasciatus)*, are very common in Burma, but their fortunately passive disposition keeps mortality low. Actually, it is the incidence rate that is low, and the mortality rate high—much higher than that for cobra bites. The snakes are nocturnal and much less likely to bite in the daytime.

The two remaining groups of elapids are more closely related. These are the famous cobras and mambas. The former are spread all over tropical Asia and Africa, the latter are confined to Africa. Among cobras, there is one species that stands out in every respect, and which is held in awe by all who know it or have heard of it. This is the King Cobra *(Ophiophagus hannah)* which may grow to almost nineteen feet in length. The venom is potent and, due to the size of the animal alone, massive, but fortunately this snake is not too common and has a rather retiring nature. It is snake-eating snake and generally keeps to wild, uncultivated areas. Unlike many other cobras, it does not usually approach human habitations.

There are other cobras in Asia, the best known being the famous Indian or Common Cobra *(Naja naja)*, the stock-in-trade of snake charmers and the central figure in countless stories ranging from true to false to utterly absurd. (The incidence of bites and deaths caused by this species is discussed in Chapter 15.) The group is represented in the Near East by the very closely related Egyptian Cobra *(N. haje)* which is the classic asp of Egypt. This can also be a potentially deadly species.

There are many other kinds of cobras in Africa, most notable among which are probably the Spitting Cobras (N. *nicricollis* and *Hemachatus haemachates*). These snakes can hit a man's face from a distance of six feet and temporarily blind him. The pain is reportedly severe, and permanent injury can result. There are also Tree Cobras *(Pseudohaje)* in many parts of tropical Africa.

The other African cobras, including the Black *(N. melanoleuca)* and the Egyptian *(N. haje)*, do not spit. The Egyptian is possibly the most widely distributed cobra on the continent. The Cape Cobra *(N. nivea)* and several others have a more limited range. The cape cobra has a particularly potent venom, one of the worst among cobras. The Water Cobra *(Boulengerina)* is known from the Cameroons, the Congo, Zaire, and Lake Tanganyika.

Closely related to the cobras are the mambas. During the past century these snakes, some of which may grow to fourteen feet in length, have become almost as notorious, if not more so, in the Old World than are the cobras. In the Western world their reputation has long since surpassed that of our rattlers or even the dreaded fer-de-lance. It is true, moreover, that the mambas are exceedingly agile, fast, and often aggressive snakes; and it may perhaps be said that, if any story of a snake deliberately attacking a man be true, it is more likely to have been a mamba than any other—the taipan, fer-de-lance, and king cobra not excluded. Their venom is known to be very potent. It is, however, their agility and speed combined with their climbing abilities, and the fact that they prefer long grass and other thick ground cover, that makes them so dangerous. Not only may you literally run into or kick them in such an environment, you may well panic if one comes along the top of the ground cover, and it is then that you are in most danger, for they tend to strike at moving objects in their path.

Writing in the December 1956 issue of *African Wild Life,* J. A. W. Bennetts tells of his father's dispatching a Black Mamba *(Dendroaspis polylepis)* with a shotgun on his farm on the south coast of Natal. The snake, measuring over fourteen feet in length and between three and four inches in diameter, had reportedly killed several natives. Legends about this particular snake had been known for over twenty years at the time the elder Bennetts killed it. There are several species of dangerous green mambas as well.

The last major group of snakes to develop venom are in the family Colubridae. A number of forms have fangs at the back of their jaws through which poison can be injected into their food as they start to swallow it. Rear-fanged snakes or opisthoglyphs are found in the Orient, Africa, and South, Central, and North America. In the last are the lyre snakes and some others; in South America there are other genera. By no stretch of the imagination can these be considered a threat to man, though we may speculate that accidents could occur if the animals were handled carelessly. The author has not encountered a single case where a native rear-fanged snake caused a human death in the Western Hemisphere. However, the situation in Africa is different.

On that continent there are at least two rear-fanged snakes known to cause human deaths, the Bird Snake *(Thelotornis kirtlandi)* and the notorious Boomslang *(Dispholidus typus).* This latter is an inhabitant of open country and varies in color from various browns to bright green. It has a habit of inflating its neck when aroused, and then may bite, but it is, on the whole, a retiring beast. The venom is potent, but reaction to it may be much delayed. It is essentially an arboreal animal and most accidents have resulted from people attempting to capture or handle the snake in trees. The venom acts on the blood and excessive internal bleeding precedes death. The boomslang is by all odds the most seriously venomous, rear-fanged snake in the world and is never to be approached or handled lightly. Its venom is far too potent to rely on the snake's usually placid disposition.

15 Snakes: How Dangerous Are They?

There can be no argument that, of all animals that are potentially dangerous to man, snakes are second only to the insects. This is odd, when you come to consider the matter, for one could hardly imagine two terrestrial creatures more distant in appearance and habits than man and snakes or—one would have thought—less likely to come into contact. Yet, throughout the temperate and tropical areas of the world, the two forms do constantly come into contact and, the more people there are, the more such contacts occur. Snakes are no more aggressive than any other animal, and no animals are truly aggressive unless sick, molested, injured, or unless man infringes upon their territory or privacy. There are exceptions such as the curious matter of so-called man-eaters and rogues, but no animal today hunts man for food deliberately except, perhaps, certain fish and crocodilians.

Since snakes do constitute the greatest single menace to man among vertebrates, I consider it worthwhile to assess this menace. This can be an exceedingly difficult thing to do.

Case histories, comments, and editorial observations are available by the thousands. Pulp magazines and medical journals, military manuals and health organization reports, books, booklets, pamphlets, and scientific reports exist in bewildering quantity. Man, quite obviously, has always been concerned with venomous snakes. As remote as a venomous snake may seem to a city-dweller, people in many parts of the world are daily faced with the reality of their existence. Just as the reader may look both ways before crossing a street, as a matter of course, other people must take comparable precautions before reaching into a cupboard, putting on their shoes, or stopping to pick a flower. Just how much of a reality the venomous snake is can be judged from the fact that the best available statistics put international snakebite *mortality* at between 30,000 and 40,000 per year! We will consider these figures in this chapter.

1. About 400 of the 2,700 currently recognized species of snakes are at least potentially dangerous to man. It can be assumed that all of the 400 are capable of killing a man, but the mortality rate shows a tremendous spread. With some snakes, the bite is extremely unlikely to cause death (there are *no* deaths recorded for a number of species); in others it is *almost* a likelihood. There is no known snake the bite of which is certain to cause death, nor is there any snake whose bite causes immediate death except under exceptional conditions.

2. The factors that determine the extent of the effects felt by the victim have been dealt with in Chapter 12 (p. 139). There is a long list of factors all tied in with the health and condition of the snake, the health and condition of the victim, and the circumstances of the bite itself.

3. To cause death, the bite of a snake must deliver a lethal substance into the tissues of a victim in such a way that it will be distributed to the vital organs. Most venomous snakes are capable of doing this under the right conditions.

4. The number of people bitten each year cannot even be guessed. The majority of the victims are in remote and underdeveloped areas where no records are kept but enough is known to state that snakebite is a major problem.

5. The sea snakes, about which so much has been written, are decidedly dangerous on contact, but contact is so unlikely that they represent a minimum threat. The snakebite mortality figure for the world is the result of contact with terrestrial animals.

6. Many areas of the world have a population of venomous snakes, but these cause no real health problem. Areas like Canada, the United States, and most of Europe are representative of this fortunate condition. Relatively few countries are entirely free of venomous serpents.

7. In a few areas (India, Burma, Mexico, Brazil, and possibly parts of Africa) snakebite is a major health problem. Unfortunately, there

is a disproportionate percentage of deaths among children. There are several reasons for this: children are more apt to go charging off into dangerous or potentially dangerous situations without thinking, children are less likely to recall physical characteristics of venomous snakes, children's curiosity is apt to get the better of their common sense, and children have less body weight and therefore generally less resistance to the effects of the venom.

8. Available statistics indicate that more men are bitten than women, the ratio is probably close to 4:1. The reasons for this are apparent: men work and play outdoors more than women. In underdeveloped areas where women are engaged in agriculture, this ratio probably doesn't hold up.

9. No snake always attacks, no snake is always deadly, and no venomous snake has the power to do anything but bite, that is, sink its fangs and inject a noxious substance. If a venomous snake can't bite you, it can't harm you, except in three cases where it can impair your sight by spitting. This statement is categoric!

So where does this leave us? Despite these remarks which, on analysis, almost amount to platitudes, we are still left with the inescapable fact that a very large number of people are bitten by snakes every year all over the world and that a not inconsiderable number of them die as a result.

We have now (I hope) learned which are the venomous snakes and where they live, albeit very sketchily, since it would take many volumes to describe their appearance, habits, and distribution in detail. But what of the other side of the coin? What is known of these animals in various parts of the world—in terms of human envenomation, suffering, and death? Here the picture becomes, perhaps, even more hazy because we really still know so little of what is actually going on in the world, while modern medical practice has still to penetrate the major part of it, and medical statisticians are still way behind that procedure. For some countries we have statistics that we assume to be reliable; for others we have educated estimates; others still, educated guesses; and others again mere guesses or no facts at all. Let me therefore review what is known—or, rather, published—on this facet of life. I will start out with tropical America, then proceed to the Oriental region, and, finally, to Africa, assuming that Europe and North America have already been adequately dealt with.

Mexico has its share of venomous snakes, and the resulting mortality rate is considerably higher than in the United States. Still, scorpions probably kill ten times as many people each year in Mexico as snakes do.

All five genera of venomous snakes found in the United States (not counting rear-fanged snakes), *Crotalus, Sistrurus, Agkistrodon, Micrurus,* and *Micruroides,* are also found in Mexico.

This is not a complete list for Mexico, but does clearly demonstrate that, with its wide variety of rattlesnakes, its moccasin (the cantil), a selection of *Bothrops* pit vipers, and about a dozen species of coral snakes, this country has more than its share of venomous snakes; and, as a consequence, an unfortunate number of snakebite mortalities.

South America has more unexplored territory than any other inhabited continent. Only the map of Antarctica exceeds this vast continent in unpopulated areas. Darkest Africa is bright and sunny by comparison. Certainly, all of the reptiles have not yet been collected and identified. Many areas are exceedingly remote and statistics on snakebite incidence and mortality are simply not to be had. This much is known: those parts of South America that have been thoroughly examined by qualified zoologists have yielded a rich variety of venomous snakes. In all of South America, Chile alone (it is believed), is free of these animals. What of their threat to man?

As is the case everywhere in the world where there are venomous serpents, there are so many variables involved in assessing the danger that we must restrict ourselves to approximate and generalized observations. Certainly, there are some species that appear more frequently on the statistical tables (like the Eastern and Western diamondbacks in the United States, the various cobras in Asia, etc., and in South America there are the lance-head vipers, and the jararacussu).

Let us next consider the situation in what is customarily called the Far East, and start beyond Japan. In this area, all existing families of venomous snakes are represented and often by a large variety of species and incredible numbers of individuals.

There are, of course, no reliable statistics from Mainland China, but the area is known to have something of a problem. Kraits, cobras, including the king cobra, pit vipers, and true vipers are known to occur. Projecting the general Asiatic picture to its logical conclusion, the snakebite incidence and, correspondingly the death rate, may be high in some few parts of China, notably the warm south.

The island colony of Hong Kong has at least two of the venomous sea snakes offshore: the four-foot *Acalyptophis peroni,* and *Hydrophis cyanocinctus,* which achieves a length of over six feet. As might be expected, bites from these two animals are rare, but can be quite serious when they do occur. It is estimated that about one hundred cases of snakebite occur each year in Hong Kong (including its mainland New Territories), although this figure is not reliable as a statistic. The Chinese often treat such problems at home with native remedies. A

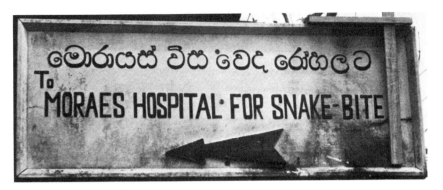

In some parts of the world snakebite is not an academic subject. This sign in Sri Lanka—in two languages—is as normal there as a traffic light is in our lives.
Photograph by Roger A. Caras

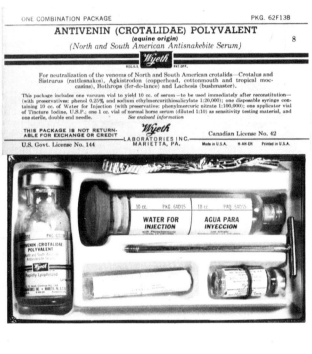

ONE COMBINATION PACKAGE   PKG. 62F138

ANTIVENIN (CROTALIDAE) POLYVALENT
(equine origin)
(North and South American Antisnakebite Serum)   8

Wyeth

For neutralization of the venoms of North and South American crotalids—Crotalus and Sistrurus (rattlesnakes), Agkistrodon (copperhead, cottonmouth and tropical moccasins), Bothrops (fer-de-lance) and Lachesis (bushmaster).

This package includes one vacuum vial to yield 10 cc. of serum—to be used immediately after reconstitution—(with preservatives: phenol 0.25% and sodium ethylmercurithiosalicylate 1:20,000); one disposable syringe containing 10 cc. of Water for Injection (with preservative: phenylmercuric nitrate 1:100,000); one applicator vial of Tincture Iodine, U.S.P.; one 1 cc. vial of normal horse serum (diluted 1:10) as sensitivity testing material, and one sterile, double end needle.   *See enclosed information*

THIS PACKAGE IS NOT RETURN-
ABLE FOR EXCHANGE OR CREDIT   *Wyeth*   Canadian License No. 42
                          LABORATORIES INC.
U.S. Govt. License No. 144   MARIETTA, PA.   Made in U.S.A.   N-AH-EH   Printed in U.S.A.

The two American kits are available, on prescription, through any drugstore. The upper kit from Wyeth is for all North American venomous snakes except the coral snakes. The lower kit from Merck, Sharp & Dohme is for the black widow spider. Wyeth also makes an antivenin for coral snakes, but it cannot be purchased (it is stocked in nine southern states and is available without charge in the event of an emergency).
Photograph by Roger A. Caras

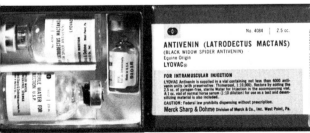

No. 4084 | 2.5 cc.

ANTIVENIN (LATRODECTUS MACTANS)
(BLACK WIDOW SPIDER ANTIVENIN)
Equine Origin
LYOVAC®

FOR INTRAMUSCULAR INJECTION

LYOVAC Antivenin is supplied in a vial containing not less than 6000 antivenin units (with preservative: Thimerosal, 1:10,000). Restore by adding the
2.5 cc. of pyrogen-free, sterile Water for Injection in the accompanying vial.
A 1 cc. vial of normal horse serum (1:10 dilution) for use as a test and desen-
sitizing material is also included.

CAUTION: Federal law prohibits dispensing without prescription.
Merck Sharp & Dohme Division of Merck & Co., Inc. West Point, Pa.

Green Tree Viper, often called the Bamboo Snake (*Trimeresurus albol-abris*), a close relative of the Central and South American *Bothrops* pit vipers, causes most of the cases of snakebite in Hong Kong. *Naja naja*, the Common Cobra, is another snake found there.

On several trips to the Crown Colony the author visited snake medi-cine shops where cobras and other venomous forms are used to prepare all manner of potions. Everything from tuberculosis to psychological disturbances are treated with cobra organs. The snakes are handled with great indifference, and this in itself could account for some bites.

The king cobra and several other cobras are found in the Philippine Islands. Two Coral Snakes (*Doliophis bilineatus* and *D. philippinus*) are found, but bites are rare and deaths rarer still. Wagler's Pit Viper (*T. wagleri*), a stout, short animal (about three feet is average) is found on some of the islands in the group. It is not considered very dangerous. *Aipysurus*, *Hydrophis*, *Laticauda*, and *Pelamis* sea snakes are found in Philippine waters, and are hunted for their skins and for export to Japan as food. Figures are not available, but possibly the active hunting of these animals may result in some bites. However, that is speculation.

Java and Sumatra have large venomous snake populations with viperids and elapids in abundance. Most interestingly, snakebite does not appear to be much of a problem.

There is reportedly a very low incidence of snakebite in Borneo (including Sarawak, Brunei, and other states therein) although the common cobra and king cobra and a viper abound in some areas. A wide variety of sea snakes are found in the surrounding waters and have been reported in astounding numbers during certain seasons. The Red-headed Krait (*Bungarus flaviceps*), marked with scarlet patches and six feet in length, occurs, but few cases of its biting man are known. Sarawak, particularly, is known to have large numbers of venomous snakes.

Indonesia has its share of venomous snakes. A variety of kraits are common, and the very dangerous king cobra is responsible for a num-ber of deaths each year.

The Malay Peninsula has its kraits, cobras (including the king), coral snakes, sea snakes, and pit vipers, but the death rate is low. The average is probably lower than ten per year.

Thailand, too, has the common cobra, the king cobra, Russell's viper, and kraits. *Calliophis* and *Doliophis* coral snakes, although not con-tributing to the death rate, are found, as well as a number of *Trimeresu-rus* pit vipers. The common green or bamboo viper is most often seen, though not particularly dangerous.

Herpetologist Carl Kauffeld pointed out the following interesting facts in a note written after reading a rough draft of this chapter:

The reptiles of Sarawak, the rest of Borneo, and all the greater Sundas, along with the Philippines, are extremely well known, and we know that all the dangerous venomous snakes of the Asiatic mainland, and then some, abound on these islands.

For a very long time, efficient colonial Dutch government prevailed on these islands. Java is one of the most densely populated spots on earth and 90 percent of the population is agrarian. How come then snake bite is so rare? This has been pointed out more than once as a reason for questioning the Indian statistics on snake bite. There is something decidedly fishy about the Indian reports. They exceed anything on earth, yet we have an almost identical situation in Java and where officialdom has had its finger on native health problems for years, with negligible incidence of snake bites and mortalities.

Burma is one of those unfortunate areas where there are large numbers and many species of truly dangerous snakes. The death rate is said to be exceedingly high. From 1935 to 1940, there were 12,733 reported deaths. These figures are so extraordinarily high that some question must be raised. For an area with a population of just under 30 million, the reported snakebite mortality rate is almost impossible to accept.*

Two species of Cobra (Naja), the spectacled and the monocellate or Burmese, are probably responsible for a good many deaths. Both animals deliver large doses of a dangerous neurotoxin. The tremendously impressive King Cobra (Ophiophagus hannah), also known as the hamadryad, is found deep in the Burmese jungles.

The beautiful island of Sri Lanka is another area with a high death rate. Three of the dangerous forms found in Burma, Russell's viper, the common cobra, and the common krait, cause much of the trouble. Deaths from these occur at an average rate of three hundred per year. In the dry northern areas of the island the Saw-scaled Viper (Echis carinatus) is common.

No country on earth, if we accept available figures, comes even close to matching India for snakebite mortality. Every year, anywhere from one-half to two-thirds of the world's victims reportedly come from this one overcrowded country. The estimate is frequently put at 20,000 deaths per year! While it will be a long time before a better figure will be available, this figure contains so many unknowns that it is little more than a guess. Some of the predictable error factors are: (1) most snakebites will occur in rural areas where medical facilities and medical records often range from crude to nonexistent, (2) in very underde-

*During the period reported on, the population was considerably less than 30 million—perhaps not much more than half that. More recent statistics are not available, or are even less reliable.

Snakes: How Dangerous Are They? 189

veloped areas, the importance of statistical information is impossible to convey, and reports given to visiting medical teams will be avoided, falsified, or exaggerated. A number of sources suggest that snakebite is a convenient explanation for an awkward death, and quite possibly some crimes in rural areas are covered up with this device.

Some cases are reported and authenticated, and Swaroop and Grab state that, "Before August 1947, snake bite was responsible for about 15,000 deaths each year. . . ." Dr. P. J. Deoras of the Haffkine Institute in Bombay, in his booklet "Snakes: How to Know Them," says, "in the former Bombay State alone 1,300 persons died of snake bite in 1955." Clearly, snakebite in India is a problem of considerable magnitude.

Of the 2,700 species of snakes in the world, India has 400, and of these 80 are venomous, although only about a dozen are seriously dangerous to man. Various species and subspecies of cobra, various kraits, Russell's viper and an *Echis* viper apparently account for most of the accidents (Table 6). Death-rate statistics from these bites are difficult to come by, but if an average of 10 percent can be accepted (and it is a reasonable figure), about 200,000 people a year are bitten in India. In one table of statistics, the fatality rate for the cobra was given as 4.8 percent; for the krait, 88.9 percent; and for the Russell's viper, 8.3 percent.

M. L. Ahuja and Gurkirpal Singh, in their paper "Snakebite in India" (in *Venoms*), give the number of bites per year at 300,000 with an overall mortality of 9.5 percent. The highest mortality occurs among children under ten years of age.

Maj. C. H. Simpson has written to the author relating personal

Table 6.   India's Dangerous Snakes

Scientific name	Common name
Ophiophagus hannah	King cobra
Naja naja	Cobra
Bungarus caeruleus	Krait
Vipera russelli	Russell's viper
Echis carinatus	Saw-scaled viper
Pseudocerastes persicus	Triangular-headed horned viper
Agkistrodon himalayanus	Himalayan pit viper
Trimeresurus malabaricus	Green pit viper
T. gramineus	Bamboo pit viper
Callophis beddomei	Coral snake
Enhydrina schistoma	Sea snake
Hydrophis spiralis	Sea snake

experiences with snakes and kindly granted permission to quote from his letter. Speaking of venomous snakes in general, he says:

I have had only one case of a fatal snake bite on my estate, this was a girl who was plucking tea leaves, she trod on a krait, which bit her on her toe. I sent her as fast as possible to the nearest hospital with antivenene, but she died before reaching it.

There have been many cases of bites from snakes which were not fatal. I myself have been bitten by a pit-viper, and a ratsnake, with hardly any effect. It is usually said the king cobras will attack on sight, but my experience is otherwise, I have killed over 20, and in no case was there an attack by the snake. But a king cobra will not run if it sees a human approaching, unlike all other snakes, which do run.

Nothing can convey the experience of meeting a venomous snake so well as a well-related personal adventure. Major Simpson is particularly adept at this, and I think the following excerpt from one of his letters gives a more accurate impression of the venomous snake in India than a volume full of statistics:

I was driving a patch of jungle for a sambhur stag, and I took post in a dry watercourse to await the expected arrival of the stag. I became aware of a rustling in the dry leaves lining the water-course and saw to my horror that it was caused by a very large king cobra (Hamadryad), which was coming along methodically stirring the heaps of leaves in the hollows. The line it was taking would bring it within a few feet of me. So I quietly covered it with my rifle, not wanting to fire unless it was absolutely necessary, as the stag would then be warned. Although my movements were slow and silent, the snake saw me and raised about two feet of its body from the ground and looked at me. I was quiet and tried to make my friendly feeling felt by it. In a few seconds it lowered its head and continued hunting in the leaves, passed me with only a casual glance, and went on down for about twenty yards. Here it found what it was looking for, a large rat snake, and then I saw at what speed it could travel, for although the rat snake had a start, it overhauled it and caught it in a few seconds. Had it attacked me, I do not think I could have shot it, it was too quick.

Africa, as I have tried to indicate, has a wide variety of dangerous species, although the relatively small population in many areas keeps snakebite from being the health problem it is in India and Burma. The African snakes occur in just about every kind of terrain, leaving only the high snowcapped mountains and the heart of the burning desert wastes free. There are terrestrial, aquatic, and arboreal species.

There are no reliable figures on snakebite incidence and mortality for Africa as a whole. Some few areas have been subject to intensive study, but these are the exceptions. As we note statistics here and there, we must keep in mind that these represent only reported cases. There are still areas virtually untouched by anything resembling modern medicine. It is difficult to find out what people there are doing, much less snakes. Any figures we do find can only represent a part of the whole. Europeans who have spent years in these regions, however, report that snakebite is not a major problem. It is not always clear if they are speaking only for themselves or if they are referring as well to the indigenous population.

Egypt reported 170 deaths between 1944 and 1948. The large, barefoot population probably suffers at a higher rate than 34 deaths a year, since both the grassy and the desert regions have cobras and vipers. Suicide with venomous snakes goes well back in Egyptian history, and the symbology of the region has apparently always included the venomous snakes, including the extremely venomous Desert Black Snake (Walterinnesia). Libya has a cobra and a couple of sand vipers, but probably not much of a problem overall. Much of the area where the snakes are found is uninhabited. Six to eight deaths a year were officially registered for a number of years. Ethiopia doesn't seem to be too badly troubled although there are cobras and true vipers in the less mountainous parts of the country.

Uganda, Kenya, and Tanzania have a full complement of typical African species, and a snakebite problem in some areas. Southern Rhodesia has a wide and interesting selection of venomous snakes, but poor statistical records.

The Republic of South Africa has no snakebite records of any consequence. To the adders, cobras, and mambas can be added the Ringhals (Hemachatus haemachates) and a few other species with restricted range. The boomslang is particularly common. This snake carries a virulent poison and although it is a rear-fanged animal, it is dangerous to man. It is one of the very few snakes of this type that does constitute a real threat, as stated earlier.

Zanzibar has few dangerous snakes and no snakebite cases reported in recent years. British Somaliland, Lesotho, and Swaziland all have a variety of dangerous species but few reliable records.

Mozambique has the full range: cobras, mambas, and true vipers. There are occasional fatalities among fishermen from the Sea Snake (Pelamis platurus).

The islands of Madagascar, the Comoro Archipelago, and Mauritius are free of poisonous snakes. The sea snakes are found offshore, but no cases of attack on man are known in recent years.

Angola, another area with fractional statistics, has a rather impressive number of potentially dangerous species. The puff adder, Gaboon viper, and the Green Night Adder (Causus) occupy the area along with several of the cobras and the greatly feared mambas.

Gabon, particularly, has a minor problem with the two dangerous cobras, the black and the water. The latter might occasionally be a threat to fishermen attending their nets and traps. It frequents the edges of lakes and uses small caves among the rocks in shallow water.

French Equatorial Africa formerly consisted of three territories: Middle Congo, Gabon, Ubangi-Chari-Tchad. Today, they are autonomous republics, Gabon, Chad, and the Central African Republic. Some 959,-256 square miles are involved with an estimated population of 6 million. The area runs from dense forest to desert; there are a number of mountain ranges, and many lakes and rivers. In hospitals, from 1947 to 1951, 155 people died from snakebite. The mamba and the puff adder caused many of these deaths. The Gaboon viper and the spitting cobra are problems in the savannah country. The colorfully marked rhinoceros viper is common in the forests. The night adder is common around human dwellings.

Nigeria has a large population (60 million) in vast, frequently under-developed areas. Snakebite cases *may* be comparatively high in some regions. To the usual African complement of true vipers, cobras (spitting and nonspitting varieties), and mambas can be added the Burrowing Vipers (Atractaspis) and several other venomous species which are harmful but probably not lethal to man.

Ghana is yet another region with a wide selection of dangerous snakes and useless statistics. The saw-scaled viper and a wide variety of cobras are responsible for a number of accidents in this country.

Statistics for what was French West Africa* are extremely fractional. The night adder abounds, the rear-fanged boomslang is common, and the spitting cobra is often seen. The Egyptian cobra, the black, and one or two other members of the hooded tribe add to the local problem.** The forested regions have a number of vipers: the Gaboon, rhinoceros, and puff adder are among the species often reported.

That concludes our review of the venomous snakes of the world. As

---

*Now the republics of Ivory Coast, Niger, and Senegal with an estimated combined population of between 13 and 15 million.

**The hood of a cobra, by the way, appears when the animal spreads a number of its ribs outward and stretches the skin. It has nothing to do with the creature's head. Cobras are so often photographed with the hood spread that some people believe they always look that way, while in fact they generally don't. The cobra spreads its impressive hood in defensive posture, and while expressing interest in its mate. There are other stimuli, certainly, that can prompt the cobra to put on a show, but generally it looks like a rather dull, sleek, harmless snake.

to just how dangerous to man they really are, remember that all the other vertebrate animals we discuss in this book, marine and terrestrial, *combined*, come nowhere near causing the suffering and death for which the snakes are responsible. Snakes almost certainly kill more people in a year than sharks do in a century, more people in a month than man-eating cats do in a hundred years, and more people in a day than rogue elephants have since time began. No area in the world is crawling with venomous snakes intent upon killing man despite the nightmarish proportions indicated by some of the statistics reported in this chapter, but venomous snakes are still the most dangerous vertebrate animals in the world. It is therefore difficult at first glance to put the situation in perspective. Venomous snakes are a critical part of nature in balance. The more of these forms that occur in a region, the more rodents are destroyed, for rodents constitute a major item in the diet of the majority of species. If the venomous snakes of the world should suddenly vanish, the rodent population would run wild and possibly, in the long run, through the spread of disease and the destruction of crops, cause much more suffering than the snakes ever could. When venomous snakes invade populated areas, then, of course, they must be eliminated. However, it is a decided mistake to think of them all as man's inveterate enemies. Unlike the situation with so many other potentially dangerous animals, the argument for conservation is not so much aesthetic or scientific as economic. Snakes, venomous as well as harmless, are of great importance in maintaining the balance and order of the natural world.

The U.S. Army Field Manual, *Jungle Operations* (FM 31-30, 1960, p. 15) puts it succinctly:

There is altogether too much fear of snakes on the part of the soldier without jungle experience. The wide spread fear of "the snake infested jungle" is an entirely imaginary picture. Poisonous snakes will be encountered in most of the jungles of the world, but not as frequently as pictured. The soldier's inherent fear of snakes reduces his efficiency in the jungle to a great extent. It is important to remember that relatively few people die from poisonous snake bites.

16 Crocodilians

The ancient order of reptiles known as the Crocodilia encompasses all the living alligators, crocodiles, caimans, and gavials, and related, extinct forms known from fossil finds. The order contains some of the most persistently dangerous animals in the world, animals that are *by nature* man-eaters. With the possible exception of a few sharks, I know of no other animals that are normally so disposed; and men, of course, don't live in the sea.

Allowing for the usual quibbles among systematists, Tables 7 and 8 cover all of the presently recognized species.

If we accept this breakdown (suggested by Schmidt and Inger, and modified after conversations with Kauffeld), we find an order with eight living genera and twenty-five species, about evenly divided between the Old World and the New. The genera *Alligator* and *Crocodylus* are found in both hemispheres, while *Caiman*, *Melanosuchus*, and *Paleosuchus* are only in the New, and *Gavialis*, *Tomistoma*, and *Osteolaemus*, only in the Old. We have, then, two genera worldwide, and three exclusive to each half of the world.

As Tables 7 and 8 indicate, the largest living crocodilians may not exceed twenty-three feet. There are strong arguments to the contrary, however. Fossil remains, often indistinguishable from contemporary species, or nearly so, show that these animals once grew to a much greater size. A skull in the American Museum of Natural History is over six feet long, and undoubtedly belonged to an animal fifty feet or more in length. Occasional reports of crocodiles "as big as submarines,"

Table 7. Crocodiles of the Western Hemisphere

Scientific name	Common name	Range	Maximum recorded length (feet)
Alligator mississippiensis	American alligator	Southern United States	19–20
Crocodylus acutus	American crocodile	Southern United States, Central America, West Indies, northern South America	23
C. intermedius	Orinoco crocodile	Orinoco complex	23
C. moreleti	Morelet's crocodile	Mexico and Guatemala	8
C. rhombifer	Cuban crocodile	Cuba	12
Paleosuchus palpebrosus	Smooth-fronted caiman	Amazon Basin	4–5
P. trigonatus	Dwarf caiman	Amazon Basin	4
Melanosuchus niger	Black caiman	Amazon Basin and adjacent territory	15
Caiman crocodilus crocodilus	Spectacled caiman	Amazon Basin	8–9
C. crocodilus fuscus	Central American caiman	Central America and northern South America	6
C. latirostris	Broad-nosed caiman	Eastern Brazil	6–7
C. yacare	Paraguayan caiman	Paraguay River and tributaries	8

Table 8. Crocodiles of the Eastern Hemisphere

Scientific name	Common name	Range	Maximum recorded length (feet)
Gavialis gangeticus	Gavial	India	21–22
Tomistoma schlegeli	False gavial	Malay Peninsula and East Indies	16
Alligator sinensis	Chinese alligator	Eastern China	5
Osteolaemus tetraspis	Congo dwarf crocodile	Upper Congo	3–4
Osteolaemus sp.	West African dwarf crocodile	West Africa	6
Crocodylus niloticus	African or Nile crocodile	Africa and Madagascar	16*
C. cataphractus	African slender-snouted crocodile	Congo Basin	8
C. porosus	Saltwater crocodile	Southeast Asia to Australia	20
C. mindorensis	Philippine crocodile	Philippine Islands	8
C. johnstoni	Australian crocodile	Northern Australia	8
C. novae-guineae	New Guinea crocodile	New Guinea	9–10
C. siamensis	Siamese crocodile	Southeast Asia and Java	12
C. palustris	Mugger crocodile	India and Sri Lanka	13

*Some records indicate that this figure may be too low.

while obviously hyperbole, may, when coupled with the fossil record, suggest that some specimens exist today far larger than the presently known record lengths. For our purposes, such matters are academic, because a man-eater fifteen feet long is as dangerous as a thirty-foot specimen.

The crocodilians are true remnants of the age of reptiles, and monsters like *Phobosuchus* (of the six-foot skull) undoubtedly hunted young dinosaurs. All crocodilians are egg-layers, exclusively eaters of flesh, well adapted to life in the water as well as on land, and very primitive. They are witless brutes with a high reproductive rate. Despite their penchant for eating their own young, they respond to protection, and the American alligator has increased rapidly in recent years now that hunting is forbidden.

Most, if not all, species hunt at least some prey that is too large to swallow, and, since they cannot chew, they have to tear it apart. They grasp a limb of their prey and rotate rapidly on their own axis, dismembering the animal. Sometimes they wait to drown the victim before starting the dismembering; sometimes they do not. Reportedly, they may "store" food, viz., wedge a large animal into rocks or vegetation under water for a few days until the body softens and becomes easier to pull apart. I do not *know* whether this is true or not, but it is so often reported it is recorded here as a possibility.

Claims of great longevity among crocodilians are unsubstantiated. Specimens reportedly hundreds (and even *thousands*) of years old are rigged as tourist attractions. Records are incomplete, but it appears certain that some alligators, at least, pass fifty years. The crocodilians apparently have no maximum size. They grow as long as they live. Admittedly, the rate of growth toward the end of their lives is slow, but a very large specimen is a very old one.

Which species are dangerous to man, and under what circumstances? Schmidt and Inger report: "The African crocodile . . . attacks human beings in some areas and not in others. This is somewhat mysterious, or at least has not been explained satisfactorily." They go on to describe how native villages in some areas find it necessary to build stockades to protect women going for water or to wash their clothes at the river's edge. Other villages live in peace with the same species. Larger specimens, they suggest, do become habitual man-eaters.

The author led a safari up to the Lake Rudolph region in northern Kenya in 1974 and there found numbers of Turkana tribesmen who had gathered around the western shore of the lake to live. Once very warlike nomadic cattle herders, they had come on bad times and had taken to fishing and crocodile hunting in order to survive. The lake fairly teems with crocodiles in some parts and they get to be very large and some do not want for boldness. Stories of man-eating were regularly told, but in Africa you get used to hearing almost any story you want to hear—sometimes created just for your benefit. There is no doubt, though, that some Turkana have lost their lives to the crocodiles in Lake Rudolph.

An outstanding book on Lake Rudolph and the crocodile was published in 1973 by the New York Graphic Society. With text by Alistair Graham and photographs by Peter Beard, it is probably the most interesting single book on the crocodile that has ever been written—and easily the most fascinating from a visual point of view. Called *Eyelids of Morning*, it includes, among many tales, stories of man-eating incidents. One chapter entitled "These Serpents Slay Men and Eat Them Weeping" should be read by anyone who has ever doubted the man-eating potential or capacity of the Nile crocodile. Particularly gruesome and exceptionally well documented is the death of a Peace Corps worker, twenty-five-year-old William K. Olsen. On April 13, 1966, Olsen was taken by a crocodile in the shallow, muddy Baro River in Ethiopia. Five fellow Peace Corps workers watched the attack. Police subsequently killed the crocodile and recovered parts of Olsen's body.

The Saltwater Crocodile (*C. porosus*) of Asia and the Pacific is probably even better known as a man-eater, and authentic reports are readily available demonstrating attacks on man. Since specimens of these animals can approach a ton or more in weight, an attack is a very serious matter. Philip J. Darlington, Jr., an entomologist, served in New Guinea during World War II in the Army Medical Corps. He was seriously injured by a ten-foot specimen that caught him by the arms. When young Michael Rockefeller tragically disappeared off the southern coast of New Guinea, the saltwater crocodile became a subject of discussion in every newspaper in the country, although it now appears certain that Mr. Rockefeller was not in fact killed by crocodiles but by natives. I attended a meeting in New York shortly thereafter and listened to endless discussion by men with experience in the field summarizing the saltwater crocodile as one of the most dangerous animals in the world. A subsequent issue of the *Explorers Newsletter* (January 1962, vol. II, no. 6) reported these observations:

At that time, the disappearance of young Michael Rockefeller was making headlines of the papers, and someone asked Dr. Gilliard, who probably knows New Guinea better than any of our other members (and possibly as well as his own back yard), his opinion of the chances of the early rescue of young Rockefeller, a fine youngster and promising anthropologist. Dr. Gilliard, in his always very charming, unassuming, and yet very learned manner, made most interesting comments and expressed his personal concern.

He stated that, as distinguished from the fresh water crocodiles of the rivers of the hinterland of the region which are found as high as 5,000 feet above sea level and are not very large in size, the monstrous salt water crocodiles, of the shore, are among the most vicious animals in the world—fearless and bloodthirsty—in fact, far more deadly than the sharks investing these waters. Dr. Gilliard also stated that he considered them indeed a cause of great danger as far as young Michael was concerned and did not reflect much optimism.

Noel Monkman was trapping specimens in northern Australia for a zoo when he had to go over the side to repair some damage done to his boat by a submerged log. Evidently his shirt billowed out behind him in the current, and it was suddenly grabbed by a saltwater crocodile and Monkman was jerked to the bottom. He was barely able to rip himself free of the shirt and make it to shore.

Writing of the Great Barrier Reef and its inhabitants, and the saltwater crocodile in particular, Dr. Paul Zahl said: "Even if these monsters had not killed and eaten many men in Australia and the East Indies, their size and fearsome dentition would set them apart as objects of dread." He suggests that the species in question is the bulkiest of living reptiles, and reaches thirty-three feet!

In her book, Six-Legged Snakes in New Guinea, Evelyn Cheesman reports an episode in 1939 when a group of natives gathered to dispatch a sixteen-foot crocodile found hiding under a riverbank overhang, suspecting it of being a man-eater. Inside the creature they found the torso of an adult male villager who had vanished from the river's edge the day before when he had gone there to wash some fish. The man's limbs were never found.

However, no account of the saltwater crocodile matches that given by Bruce Wright in his Wildlife Sketches, Near and Far.

In the winter of 1944–1945, British troops had over 1,000 Japanese infantrymen hemmed in at the edge of a mangrove swamp on Ramree Island, off the west coast of Burma, in the Bay of Bengal. From the air, the eighteen miles between the southern inshore edge of the island and the mainland of Burma appears to be solid vegetation. A trip through it by boat, however, reveals that there is no dry land, just miles of muck and waste-deep water inhabited by the great Crocodylus porosus. The Japanese commander expected units of the Imperial Fleet to rescue them but the Royal Navy intervened and the Japanese were cut off. Aerial reconnaissance by the British revealed that the Japanese were streaming into the impassable swamps on foot in an effort to escape capture by British troops swarming across the solid part of Ramree

Island. British units were dispatched in canvas boats with mortars and machine guns mounted on railroad ties, and they paddled into the open water leads in an effort to contain the doomed Japanese units. By February 19, 1945, the route to the mainland had been effectively sealed and the Japanese were locked up inside the swamp. Heavy gunfire from both sides ensued, and, in Wright's own words:

> The din of the barrage had caused all crocodiles within miles to slide into the water and lie with only their eyes above, watchfully alert. When it subsided the ebbing tide brought to them more strongly and in greater volume than they had ever known it before the scent and taste that aroused them as nothing else could—the smell of blood. Silently each snout turned into the current, and the great tails began to weave from side to side.

As the tide slipped out from between the island and the mainland, it left hundreds of both wounded and uninjured Japanese troops mired knee-deep in water and muck. The crocodiles moved in about nightfall. Wright goes on to describe a night of pure hell, as dead, wounded, and unwounded men alike were grabbed by the crocodiles. The uproar of thrashing as the great animals "spun" to dismember their prey was clearly audible to the British anchored just outside the swamp. The screams of the Japanese soldiers continued throughout the night.

Of the 1,000 men who stumbled into the swamp, just 20 survived. Some of course fell to gunfire, some drowned, and others perhaps died of yet other causes, but there can be little doubt that this night, February 19–20, 1945, revealed one of the most deliberate and wholesale attacks on man by large animals that is on record.

Had the story come from a source other than Bruce Wright, I would be tempted to discount it. Bruce Wright, a highly trained professional naturalist, was there at Ramree.

The caimans of South and Central America grow to great size, and take an immense toll of domestic cattle. During the dry period, November–December, hundreds of caimans congregate in small pools, and the cowboys of the Amazon delta kill them in great numbers. Reports vary as to ferocity and danger to man, but some accidents at least have probably occurred. The huge Black Caiman (*Melanosuchus niger*), achieving a length of over fifteen feet, is more often accused of attacks on man than other species. They are often seen sunning themselves on riverbanks and in muddy streams in the dense jungle. They appear to be more active than the American alligator found to their north. However, I know of no actual attacks on man by an unmolested caiman.

An Indian mugger or marsh crocodile, a species that may reach twelve feet in exceptional specimens. The author was "cruised" by one of these animals, when he attempted to swim in a small pond. Despite their primitive intelligence, they are wily when it comes to hunting. Their jaws have enormous strength.

The black caiman, an often densely populated species, has been accused of attacks on man. These are young animals on the banks of an Orinoco tributary. There is no doubt that these animals prey on livestock as well as on wildlife, for which they are often heavily persecuted.
Photograph by Karl Weidmann

An alligator (right) and a crocodile (left). Note the marked difference in the snouts. Strangely enough, this pair of animals mated in an Australian game sanctuary.
Courtesy Australian News and Information Bureau

The Nile crocodile, found over much of Africa south of the Sahara, is a true man-eater. Growing to enormous sizes it takes virtually any prey it can get, including man.
Photograph by C. A. W. Guggisberg

A young saltwater crocodile, *Crocodylus porosus*, showing its ample teeth. These animals may approach thirty feet at maturity, and there is little doubt that they are naturally man-eaters. Quite possibly the saltwater crocodile is, aside from the shark, the world's only natural hunter of man.
Courtesy New York Zoological Society

Hornaday rated the Nile Crocodile (*C. niloticus*) as second only to the saltwater in danger to man. He cites William Harvey Brown as saying people have been pulled from boats in Angola. Lest geographical confusion arise from references to Nile crocodiles and Angola, the Nile and the African crocodile are the same animal, and is found all over the continent south of the desert. James F. Barclay, who travels the world making films on missionary work, told me a story about crocodiles in Ethiopia. An advance unit moved into that country to scout film locations for a forthcoming production and attended a baptismal ceremony. They watched guards, posted on high ground near the river for the duration of the ceremony, shoot crocodiles as they moved in on the crowds of worshippers being baptized in the stream. It was evidently a very normal day in the life of the congregation.

Emil Ludwig described the Nile crocodile as: "Hated with genuine passion by the natives, and even by the dog, who realizes the danger; it is the enemy of all animals and all men . . . it drags man and beast into the river." Kermit Roosevelt shot a twelve-foot crocodile in East Africa, and found, among other things, the claws of a cheetah in its stomach. Apparently, anything that moves, except the very largest species, is a potential meal for the great saurians. Reports of man-eating come from all over Africa, and date back to ancient times. It is impossible to estimate the number of people who have been killed, but certainly it is enormous. (Crocodiles in Africa, as elsewhere, also take carrion, so things found in their stomachs don't *always* mean a kill.)

Virtually all reliable reports have the alligators as less active and aggressive than the crocodiles. As with the giant Gavial (*Gavialis gangeticus*) of India, there are no authentic records of man-eating by American alligators. Attacks, certainly, are known and have been widely publicized. A small girl was grabbed by a gator in Florida in the early 1950s, but was saved; in April 1950, another girl was severely bitten on the legs; and in 1949, two large males were trapped and removed from the Okefenokee Wildlife Refuge because they had begun stalking fisherman and tourists.

In the 1930s, a hunter shot a large American Crocodile (*C. acutus*) near Biscayne Bay, Forida. Thinking the animal dead, the man kicked the fifteen-footer which lunged at him and caught him in the midsection. The man died of the injuries inflicted by the teeth. It is the only known death attributable, in the United States, to the American crocodile.

Young caimans of several species were, until recently, imported into Florida and sold to tourists as alligators, the native species being protected. These caimans, set free by disgruntled recipients who find them to be something less than ideal pets, may be establishing a population here and, in a few years, the United States may, as a result, find itself with a more broadly diversified saurian population than in the past. There are stories, sworn to by many, that these "alligators" brought or sent from Florida resorts have established themselves in the sewers of New York where they feed on rats. I have never noticed any, but then I am seldom in the sewers; and I have not been able to obtain any verification of these assertions which have persisted for years.

There is no question that some of the twenty-five currently recognized species of crocodilians are extremely dangerous to man. The great saltwater crocodile is probably at the top of the list, with the African or Nile form second; and several others of the genus *Crocodylus* are not too far behind. Other species, like the American alligator and crocodile, the gavial and several others, apparently seldom attack man and must be considered harmless unless molested. Any large crocodilian, however, is capable of inflicting serious injury with its large teeth and formidable jaws. These animals are primitive with a very low intelligence. They are interesting to watch, certainly deserving of protection where they are not a menace, but are best left alone. They are remnants of life as it once was on this planet, and an important part of our wildlife heritage.

Part IV Amphibians and Fish

17 Frogs, Toads, and Salamanders

Because they occupy a position halfway between aquatic and land animals, the amphibians form a class that, to the average person, is mostly shrouded in mystery and generally blurred by abundant misinformation. Salamanders emerge from flames, toads and frogs are spontaneously generated in a variety of natural conditions, and specimens of both get mixed into all manner of broths and brews, sometimes to revitalize the human reproductive process, or to poison a foe. While it is true, as we shall discuss here, that the chemical properties of the skins of some amphibia are quite remarkable, beliefs concerning the group are absurd.

The class Amphibia contains the descendants of the first group of vertebrate animals to emerge from an aquatic environment and spend most of their adult life on land. Fossils date back at least 280 million years, and the class is undoubtedly older than that. Today, there are more than 3,000 species, spread all over the tropical, subtropical, and warm temperate zones.* The amphibians are probably the least harmful class of vertebrate animals on this planet. They do not compete with man for food, they destroy nothing, and they neither transport nor transmit any known diseases to man. No known species has been

---

*One salamander occurs as far north as southern Alaska.

demonstrated to have a venomous bite, although some few are poisonous in another and unique way. They are beneficial in that they consume quantities of noxious insects.

Amphibians, as a class, consist of: the coecilians (pronounced see-sil-ians) (order Gymnophiona), tropical, subterranean, primitive, and legless; the salamanders (order Caudata), secretive animals, most of them small; and the frogs and toads (order Salientia), certainly the best known of all. While the range of form and structure from the coecilians to the frogs is great, all amphibians are relatively primitive creatures with a low level of intelligence. They are creatures of instinct and reflex.

The coecilians can be ignored for our purposes here, although they are an interesting group of primitive animals. They are not known to be venomous, are not reported as significantly poisonous, and no grounds exist for considering any dangerous to man.

The salamanders are mostly terrestrial but some are aquatic. Some are eaten by man, but they are of little economic importance. The giant forms (family Cryptobranchidae) reach five feet in length (*Megalobatrachus japonicus*) and reportedly can give a firm bite when handled carelessly. The story of a zoologist requiring several stitches after being bitten by one recently came to the author. However, these nonvenomous, generally nonpoisonous (some few have a very mildly poisonous skin secretion), exceedingly shy creatures can hardly be considered a threat to man. Conceivably, a Japanese fisherman collecting the huge *Megalobatrachus* for the market (they are esteemed as food) might be bitten, but the animals are not aggressive.

The frogs and toads form the largest living order of amphibians. Some bite and some are extremely poisonous (not, however, venomous). Unknown numbers of human beings may have been killed by frogs, *indirectly*. Natives in Central and South America make a poison from frogs of several species. Some researchers have expressed the opinion that these skin-secreted poisons may prove to be among the most lethal, animal-produced substances in the world. The fact that these substances are highly poisonous has been known to science for many years.

The vast majority of the frogs and toads are completely harmless, but members of several genera can give a very bad bite if carelessly handled. The *Ceratophrys*, the toad-shaped "horned" frogs, are a South American species found in forested swamps. They are generally aggressive and feed on other frogs. Bell's *Ceratophrys* (*Ceratophrys ornata*) is very prone to bite. The Colombian Horned Frog (*Ceratophrys calcarata*) is particularly aggressive and apparently quite reckless in assaulting much larger animals. Contrary to local legends, it is

The giant salamander, *Megalobatrachus japonicus*, is not venomous but capable of giving a painful bite.
Courtesy Smithsonian Institution

A seriously poisonous dendrobatid frog from Central America. These frogs produce one of the most potent biotoxins known to man. It is their skin, though, and not their bite that is dangerous. You have to bite them.
Courtesy American Museum of Natural History

not venomous, just touchy. A Brazilian relative *(C. varia)* is reportedly similarly inclined. They are a bizarre group of irritable but harmless beasts.

The skin of nearly all amphibians secretes some poison but this protective device (it discourages other animals from eating them) is very much more highly developed in some forms, and reaches a peak, it is believed, in the tropical American families Atelopodidae and Dendrobatidae. Some frogs, and a number of toads (notably the genus *Bufo*) have large glands located behind the eyes that secrete a milky fluid. This does not exude but has to be squeezed from these glands through a number of small pores, and is poisonous. The poison involved is an extremely complex chemical, and, when extracted and processed, is deadly to animals up to the size of a cat or dog. Presumably, a massive dose of this foreign protein could be harmful to man as well.

The North American Pickerel Frog *(Rana palustris)* is covered with a poison deadly to other frog species. The mucous glands of all frogs secrete a lubricant from the skin that is more or less dangerous to small animals. Other glands, also located in the skin, secrete a wide variety of other poisons that seem to have a similar effect: this effect is like digitalis, speeding up the heart action, until it stops. Convulsions and several other symptoms are noted in smaller animals when kept with this attractively spotted frog.

A number of South and Central American frogs of the families Atelopodidae and Dendrobatidae are, as has been said, probably the most poisonous in the world, and the latter family—known as the "arrow-poison frogs"—is apparently the worse of the two. Notably poisonous are the species listed in Table 9. There are many more, and some probably still unknown.

South American Indians impale the poisonous species on sticks and roast them over a fire. The poison drops secreted as the skin contracts are collected and fermented. Arrows are dipped in the resultant concoction and used in hunting. It is decidedly deadly against smaller animals but the danger to larger species, including man, is not clearly defined. Some sources refer to it as harmless against man; others say that it is deadly. For years, reports have been coming out of Central and South America of species that not only provide an arrow poison lethal to man but that are extremely dangerous to handle while alive. The number of these reports is quite astounding, but, for the moment, the author does not know of a species, a victim *(by name)*, a place, or a date of any such occurrence.

If these stories are true, as told, then it may turn out that certain amphibians do indeed produce the most potent biotoxin in the whole animal kingdom. For the moment, however, the matter must rest as

Table 9. Some Poisonous South and Central American Frogs

Scientific name	Common name	Range
Atelopus zateki	Zatek's frog	Panama
A. planispina	Flat-spined *Atelopus*	Ecuador
A. boulengeri	Boulenger's arrow-poison frog	Peru and Ecuador
Phyllobates bicolor	Two-toned arrow-poison frog	South America
Dendrobates flavopictus	Yellow-spotted frog	Brazil
D. auratus	Golden arrow-poison frog	Central America
D. trivittatus	Three-striped arrow-poison frog	South America

unsubstantiated. Research is in progress on these problems, and this is not all academic, for such a biotoxin would have great interest for the pharmaceutical houses. Important medical discoveries may be waiting in the skin of a frog.

However, to sum up, aside from a few poisonous species, and a few giant frogs ("One will fill the bottom of a bucket," I was once told by a noted herpetologist at Harvard) which can bite quite effectively, the amphibians of the world, as a group, are more colorful and musical than dangerous.

18 Sharks

In this chapter we will examine the record of some of the most dreaded creatures in the world, fishes of the subclass Elasmobranchii, the sharks.

In 1848, R. M. Ballantyne reported in his book, *Hudson's Bay*, that an Indian had set out along the coast of the Gulf of St. Lawrence in a small canoe. His wife and their several small children were with him. A large shark began battering their frail craft and brought it to the point where it was about to break up. In desperation the Indian took his youngest child, an infant of a few months, and threw him into the water. While the shark was devouring the child, the Indian managed to get the rest of his family ashore in the sinking craft.

At 4:30 P.M. on July 27, 1958, eight-year-old Douglas J. Lawton was wading in less than four feet of murky water off Longboat Key, Sarasota, Florida. He was not ten feet from shore when his terrified screams brought his twelve-year-old brother who was in the water with him, and his parents and some friends who were on the beach, to his rescue. They found a five-foot Tiger Shark *(Galeocerdo)* hanging on to the inside of the boy's left leg. The shark continued to bite and hang on until it was literally torn and beaten off its hysterical victim. Dr. J. O. Ferguson amputated the leg that same evening at Sarasota's Memorial Hospital.

On June 14, 1959, thirty-three-year-old Robert L. Pamperin was diving for abalone in twenty-five feet of clear water about two hundred feet north of Alligator Rock, La Jolla, California. He suddenly rose to the surface, screamed for help, and then disappeared. His friend and companion dove after him and saw the top half of his body protruding from a shark's jaws. The animal's length was estimated at twenty feet and it was able to engulf the man whole. The body was never recovered.

Between July and September of 1959, a six-foot shark killed five, and injured thirty, victims at Machagon near the mouth of the Devi River, India.

On November 26, 1959, thirteen-year-old Mauama Mari swam beneath a native house set on pilings at Kaparoka, Papua, New Guinea. The child succumbed to shock and loss of blood when a shark tore off his right leg.

In October 1943, a fourteen-foot Leopard Shark (Negaprion) was caught and brought ashore at Miami Beach. When it was opened, a man's hand, portions of a forearm, leg, and pelvis were found in its stomach. The FBI identified the victim from fingerprints. He was Clyde Kelly Ormond, a member of the armed forces on a tanker that had collided off the Florida coast six days before. No one will ever know if Ormond was fortunate enough to have drowned before he was eaten.

Why is it necessary to retell these tales? Because, from reports such as these, it is hoped, some understandable pattern of the shark's behavior will one day emerge.

Sharks have been described as "beasts without a bone in their bodies or a brain in their heads." This is almost true. A shark's skeleton is composed of cartilage and the animal as a whole is exceedingly primitive. Ancestors of the sharks date back to the Devonian period of the mid-Paleozoic era, nearly a quarter of a billion years. As for brains, the sharks' are small and relatively poorly developed. About two-thirds of the brain's total mass and capacity are given over to the sense of smell.

Although the group is still imperfectly known, there are at least 300 species of shark recognized today. They range in size, at maturity, from six inches to an estimated fifty feet. Teeth identical to those of the Great White Shark (Carcharodon) have been dredged up that were over five inches long. A conservative estimate would put the shark who lost such a tooth in the neighborhood of one hundred feet in length. The teeth involved are not fossils, but recent. To the best of the author's knowledge, no one has ever recorded the sighting of a white shark anywhere near one hundred feet long. There is evidence that they might exist, however. Twenty-footers have been taken and a one-hundred-footer could be really no more dangerous to a man in the water than his cousin, one-fifth that size. The great white shark, known in some places as the death shark, is the most dreaded of known man-eaters.

The sharks currently thought of as being the biggest in the world, the almost fifty-foot Whale (Rhincodon) and forty-foot Basking Sharks (Cetorhinus), are inoffensive plankton strainers, harmless to man. They are relatively rare and retiring, but when spotted floating placidly along only inches beneath the surface of the sea are an easy mark for a man with a harpoon. Presumably, they could damage a boat if they thrashed around after being stuck, but there is no conceivable ground for considering them dangerous to man. Swimmers have grabbed onto their fins and been towed along. Small boats have cruised along beside them for hours and excellent motion picture footage has been taken of them from above and below the surface. Like the baleen whales, these sharks cruise along like massive vacuum cleaners filtering high-protein plankton from the sea.

Table 10 gives maximum sizes for some sharks based on data from the U.S. Bureau of Commercial Fisheries of the Fish and Wildlife Service's Fish and Wildlife Circular 119—"Sharks, Skates, Rays, and Chimaeras." These figures have been challenged, with a tendency to upgrade them, particularly in the case of the great white shark.

Great Hammerheads (Sphyrna tubes) and Thresher Sharks (Alopias vulpinus) of eighteen-foot lengths have been taken off U.S. coasts. Tiger Sharks (Galeocerdo cuvieri) nearly 14 feet long, 15½-foot Sixgill Sharks (Hexanchus sp.), and 16½-foot Greenland Sharks (Somniosus microcephalus) have also been caught along the U.S. coastline.

The skates, rays, sawfish, and the chimaeras, which are strange-looking creatures tapering sharply from a broad head to a threadlike tail, are closely related to the sharks. Of these forms, certain rays alone are believed dangerous to man, by reason of venom or electricity, and

Table 10. Maximum Sizes of Some Sharks

Scientific name	Common name	Maximum length measured U.S. coast	Maximum length recorded world	Traditional maximum size in literature
Cetorhinus maximus	Basking shark	32 ft. 2 in.	45 ft.	40–50 ft.
Rhincodon typus	Whale shark	38 ft.	45 ft.	45–50 ft.
Carcharodon carcharias	Great white shark	18 ft. 2 in.	21 ft.	36 ft. 6 in.

A six-ton specimen of the whale shark (Rhincodon typus), enormous but harmless to man—a plankton strainer. Note the size of the man to the right of the fish's head.

Photograph by Walter Bitterling

One of the hammerheads. Despite the seemingly awkward placement of their jaws, these sharks are capable of man-eating, and a number of species have been implicated in attacks on man. They are among the small percentage of shark species rated dangerous at all times.

Courtesy U.S. Dept. of the Interior, Fish and Wildlife Service

A shark cage for use by photographers and other divers working in shark-infested waters. This equipment was used by Capt. Jacques-Yves Cousteau's team in the filming of the underwater classic, *The Silent World*.

Courtesy Columbia Pictures Corp.

are treated in other chapters. The others are harmless. Some giant rays attain a length of seventeen feet and a "wingspread" of twenty-two feet. They characteristically propel their massive forms into the air and crash back onto the surface in monumental belly flops. The reason for this behavior is not known, but it is suggested that they do it to rid themselves of parasites. Again, a presumption could be made that they might land on a swimmer, diver, or small boat, but this farfetched hypothesis is about the only danger these inoffensive species might pose to man. The giant rays, or mantas, are spectacular but harmless plankton-feeding animals.

It is often suggested that a twenty-foot sawfish could slice a man in half with his toothed beak. Perhaps this is so. I have been told it has happened in the coastal fisheries of the Guianas. I could locate no specific cases, although the matter was investigated.

Sharks are marine creatures for the most part. Some species do invade rivers, and some seek fresh water in which to give birth to their young. One species, the Lake Nicaragua or Freshwater Bull Shark (*Carcharhinus leucas*), believed very dangerous to man, lives land-locked in Lake Nicaragua, 3,089 square miles of water, as much as 200 feet deep and 135 feet above sea level. This may be the only true freshwater shark, although there are reports of a New Guinea species.

Sharks are typically, but by no means exclusively, tropical and subtropical fishes. The Greenland and Pacific Sleeper Sharks (*Somnio-sus*), at least, range into very cold seas. The hammerhead, tiger, and great white shark are fairly common in Canadian waters during July and August. On July 9, 1953, a shark attacked a boat that was tending lobster traps off Cape Breton Island, Nova Scotia. It bit a two-inch hole in the wooden craft and sank it. John McLeod survived, but John Burns drowned. His body was found untouched sometime later. The attack took place less than 20 degrees south of the Arctic Circle. On April 3, 1940, the warden of a bird sanctuary on Canada's Basque Island was stalked by a shark while ice floes still littered the surface of the sea. He had shot some small animals to use as fox bait and the blood was dripping into the water. He escaped unharmed, but the tall dark dorsal fin of a shark threading its way between ice floes is not the typical picture in most people's minds. It is not, however, an uncommon sight.

The often-heard statement that the water has to be 70 degrees or warmer for a shark to attack man is *not* true. It is true that the vast majority of shark attacks do occur in waters above 70 degrees, but this is so because it is in the warmer waters that you are most likely to find swimmers. That fact gives us both our statistics and the misconception that warm seas are the only seas in which a man must fear the shark.

A great many sharks, just how many is not known, live in the deeper parts of the ocean. Catches have been made at over 9,000 feet and there is no reason to believe that this is the limit. These deepwater sharks are not a threat to man for obvious reasons. It is in the littoral, or surface zones, of the sea that the trouble begins.

However inadequate the shark may be intellectually, there is nothing wrong with its senses. Its ability to home in on prey from great distances is uncanny. The area of the brain generally associated with the thought process is completely lacking in sharks and any learning they do is on the reflex level. Their sense of smell is believed to be very well developed, but the value of their eyesight is still a matter of discussion. Their sense of taste is believed to be very important in the location of prey and they are equipped to taste with organs located all over their heads and parts of their bodies as well. Their use of this sense is imperfectly understood. Another puzzling sensory function is the shark's hearing. They are apparently extremely sensitive to water-borne vibrations and tests are being made that may help define the role this plays in their behavior toward man. They may "hear" with the lateral line that extends the length of their bodies as well as with organs in their heads.

The shark is a beautifully designed predator. It is a killing machine with a voracious appetite. However much it may be feared and hated, it is just plain silly to think of it as "cruel" and "heartless." Sharks have no emotions, and it only clouds the issue to try to pin these human qualities on them. They do what they must to stay alive, and it is in this context that we must examine their behavior and relate it to ourselves. We know enough not to touch the spinning blade of a buzz saw or plunge our hands into a roaring fire. Let's see if we can learn enough to stay out from between the shark's jaws. One thing is certain, it doesn't matter a bit to the shark whether we like the idea of being eaten; to a shark, lunch is lunch.

Psychologically speaking, that is what is so horrifying about any man-eating animal. As human beings we have come to rely heavily on the quality of mercy, however often it has been strained. In one's mind is the reserve idea that if things get too bad, we can always humble ourselves, beg for mercy and be spared. Instinctively, we know that no such plan will work with a mute, carnivorous beast. We have no reserve, nothing to fall back on. If we are caught by such an animal, tears will mean nothing. It is a nightmare of terrifying proportions. This unconscious knowledge colors much of our thinking, and only a clinical approach can give any real perspective to these animals. This is a major reason that so much of the layman's experience and observation of shark attack are of little or no value to the scientist. They are too colored by hidden fear and too often by conscious revulsion.

In 1974 a novel appeared called, simply, *Jaws*. In it author Peter Benchley skillfully wove a tale of sheer horror out of a series of attacks by a great white shark off the coast of Long Island, New York. The book was a bestseller and was purchased for production as a feature film. For a period *Jaws* and shark attacks in general were the object of conversation and endless conjecture throughout the country. More than one person was heard to say, "That's the last time I go swimming outside the pool." *Jaws* successfully capitalized on a very old, very deep, and virtually universal dread. It was, in fact, a nightmare made into entertainment.

Man has long been concerned with his relationship with the shark. From earliest times, in one place or another, there have been commercial shark fisheries. Sharks are still fished for their hides, some of which make a good-quality leather, once the sharply pointed placoid scales are removed. Some make excellent eating, and, reportedly, some Mako (*Isurus*) and Blue Shark (*Prionace glauca*) is still marketed as swordfish in the United States. The liver of the shark, a very large organ, is rich in vitamins A and D, and was an important source for the pharmaceutical houses before synthetics were developed. It is still collected for this purpose in some areas, although, as reported elsewhere in this book, it can be poisonous to eat.

However important the shark-fishing industry may be or may have been, on a worldwide basis, man's major interest in the animal has been defensive. Recreation takes man into and on the sea, and man's surface and airborne craft sometimes fail him and expose him to the dangers the shark represents. Sharks, too, are damaging to the fishing industry. Anyone who has tried to fish an area where fins are cleaving the surface can tell you the effect this animal has on the habits of other fish.

Reports of devastating attacks by swarms of sharks on shipwreck victims and downed fliers led to great efforts during World War II. The U.S. Naval Research Laboratory, stepping in where others left off, helped to develop a shark repellent consisting of 80 percent dark, water-soluble dyes, and 20 percent copper acetate. Original authorization for the experiments came from the U.S. Bureau of Aeronautics. Tests went on for years, and even though a large tea bag-like device containing the repellent, designed for attachment to life preservers and vests, is still being issued, reports vary as to its effectiveness. In other parts of the world, beaches have been uselessly bordered with perforated pipes emitting streams of bubbles. Antisubmarine nets have been tried, in some cases with a degree of success. Australia and South Africa, particularly, have made extensive efforts to protect their beautiful public swimming areas. Meshing with regularly attended nets has dramatically reduced shark populations, and attacks in meshed areas are relatively rare. Nothing, however, really works against the individual shark near a swimmer. Sharks still swim through clouds of dissolved repellent, sport almost playfully in streams of bubbles, navigate nets at high tide, and investigate experimental sonic devices. Nothing is presently known that can guarantee the safety of a man in the water when hungry sharks are near.

What makes the large shark such a dangerous animal? First of all, it *is* tough. The author has fought a ten-foot blue shark for over an hour and a half, brought it to gaff, shot it through the head several times with a large-bore pistol, and had it hung up out of the water. Over two hours later, it was still alive! Peter Ianuzzi, a fellow enthusiast in marine affairs, after a stiff fight caught a large blue, which the author shot through the gills with a soft-point bullet from a .303 British carbine. Two hours later, out of the water, the shark was alive. Dragging a shark backwards through the water is supposed to drown it. The author saw a 350-pound mako fight like a demon after being dragged backwards for over four hours, at speeds up to ten knots. The sharks are tough and tenacious animals.

A second factor making many sharks dangerous to man is limited visibility. Most people who have been attacked have been partially submerged, with their heads above the surface. It is true that calm water around coral formations is amazingly clear, but, for the most part, the shark's attack is a silent and secret affair. On some occasions, the fin circles the victim and closes in slowly, giving away the shark's intent. Too often, however, the attack is sudden, swift, and unexpected. In the final analysis, it is the shark and not the man who is at home in the water. Experts, like members of the diving teams of Jacques-Yves Cousteau, have the presence of mind and self-confidence in the water to fend off sharks without panic. But few swimmers, surf riders, and shipwreck victims have the opportunity to develop such aquatic savoir faire. When the average man in the water sees an attacking or nosy shark—if he sees it—he panics. A panicky human being has no defense against a graceful marauder with 350 million years of experience behind him. A shark attacks when instinctive behavioral patterns are triggered. It takes all of man's self-confidence to contend with the situation.

Perhaps the greatest difficulty in dealing with sharks arises from their unpredictability. You can't tell what they're going to do, or when they're going to do it. A U.S. Navy survival manual for fliers, called "Shark Sense," refers to them as having one-cylinder minds. This is true, as we have seen. The amusing manual goes on to describe the shark as a kind of subaquatic maverick who specializes in doing the unexpected. The pamphlet waxes poetic with,

How strange, the tiger of the sea;
He runs from you and dines on me.

Quite simply, most generalizations about shark behavior have proved to be valueless. Some sharks are driven off by shark repellent (in some areas) while others ignore it. Some sharks flee from streams of bubbles emitted by divers, while others frolic in them. Some sharks turn tail when an intended victim thrashes the water, or beats the surface with his hands or an oar. Other sharks bore right in, ignoring the fuss, or perhaps attracted by it. Divers have reported driving off sharks by yelling underwater, but you can't depend on it. To date, none of these differences in behavior can be explained by species, sex, size, water temperature, or time of day. Reports of shark attack and shark behavior cross all lines. Our understanding of their behavior and our ability to predict their actions will come only from a more profound knowledge of the physics and chemistry of their senses than we currently have.

One of the most nightmarish aspects of shark behavior is the so-called feeding frenzy. It is known that blood and certain other substances attract sharks from great distances. They are known to be able to home in on blood and fish oil from a distance of at least a quarter of a mile. When a number of sharks close in, a pattern of behavior may be triggered that can only be described as manic. They bite and tear at anything, including themselves and each other. Throw tin cans into the water and they will be gobbled up. Reports exist of sharks being ripped open by gaff hooks during a feeding frenzy and turning around to eat their own entrails. It is evident that nothing could survive such an onslaught. The lack of survivors from downed aircraft and sunken ships almost certainly results from behavior of this kind in some instances. Sharks are known to be attracted by explosions in or on the water. No repellent is of use during these frenzied mass attacks.

The author had read of this mass-feeding pattern a number of times and set out to witness it firsthand. With three friends, he chartered the shark-fishing boat of Frank Mundus of Montauk, New York. Mundus has earned a worldwide reputation as a shark fisherman. The forty-five-foot *Cricket II* sailed from the tip of Long Island at 6:30 A.M. on Saturday, September 22, 1962. The plan was to drift with the current, periodically ladling chopped-up fish, or "chum," over the side. Drifting away and sinking at the same time, the chum would pave a neat path of fish oil from the sea bottom to the boat. The mate never had a chance to start the chumming. Within thirty seconds after the engine was cut, a ten-foot blue shark passed beneath the stern. A minute or so later it was followed by three or four others. Within ten minutes, there were at least

Shark authority Dr. Perry Gilbert of Cornell examines a subject at a shark research station in the Caribbean. Note the teeth and consider their tearing action if the fish bit down and pulled away.
Courtesy Dr. Gilbert

A small corner of a shark-feeding frenzy. A blue shark attempts to eat the head of another blue shark, just caught and still alive, as it is dragged out of the water.
Courtesy C. M. Caras

twenty big blue sharks circling the boat. Before the group gave out from exhaustion, they took five sharks, on 50-pound test line, totaling nearly 1,300 pounds. Some fought for over an hour, while others were brought to gaff in a matter of a few minutes. As the sharks were brought in close enough to gaff and lasso, others closed in so rapidly that it was impossible to tell which shark was on the line and which were trying to eat it. As the diesel winch pulled the captured specimens out of the water, others grabbed hold and were pulled clear of the surface as they hung on and shook loose huge chunks of meat from their still-living hunting partners. Six of us aboard the boat leaned over the side and beat sharks on the head with gaff hooks, chum ladles, rifle butts, and anything else that could be used as a club. The author shot several through the head at a range of a foot and a half with a 9-mm. pistol as they tore at our hard-won prizes. One that was hit between the eyes went over backwards and started to sink with a few convulsive flicks of its tail. Before the water it splashed landed on the deck, two other sharks closed in on it. Frank Mundus leaned over and grabbed one by the tail. Infuriated, it struck out at another shark that brushed against it. Mundus stabbed one in the face, drawing blood and condemning it to be eaten alive. A shark that had been caught, gaffed and roped, grabbed another and started to tear out a chunk of meat while it was being dragged backwards around the boat to where the pulley and winch could lift it out of the water. This was an unusual experience where all of the sharks were large—mostly around ten feet long. It was easy to picture what would have happened to anyone who fell overboard at such a time.

It is often suggested that, except for feeding frenzies, most shark attacks are attributable to rogue individuals. One shark, so the theory goes, will move into an area and attacks on man will continue until the animal is caught or moves off. There is evidence to support this theory, or at least to indicate that it is true in some cases. Some individual sharks may be much more disposed to attack man than others of the same species. One well-known episode makes a good case for this theory. Ten-year-old Lester Stillwell was swimming in Matawan Creek, twenty miles from the ocean behind Sandy Hook, New Jersey, on July 12, 1916. He was seen being attacked by what was apparently an 8½-foot White Shark (Carcharodon). Stanley Fisher attempted to save the boy but was attacked himself in three or four feet of water. Stillwell was lost, but his body was later recovered. Fisher was rushed to the hospital, but died while being carried into surgery. Twelve-year-old John Dunn was swimming about half a mile downstream from Fisher and Stillwell, with his brother and several friends. They heard of the attack and rushed to get out of the water. John Dunn was not quite fast enough and his leg was barely saved at the hospital. Three people were attacked in a matter of minutes by what was, from all appearances, one shark. The shark itself was atypical, since it was so far from the ocean and in rather shallow water. The word *rogue* would seem to fit such an individual. Just how many shark attacks can be attributed to these lone marauders is not, however, known.

Sharks can injure man not only with their teeth but by rubbing against exposed skin. Densely distributed over a shark are placoid scales, or dermal denticles. These consist of dentine over a pulp cavity. If the lacerations they can cause are not in themselves disabling, they can cause the victim to bleed, triggering attack behavior in the same and other sharks. Whether sharks deliberately rub up against potential victims for any reason is not known. There have been suggestions made that they do.

Sharks, like most reportedly dangerous animals, have a number of legends that have developed around them. When an animal, like a shark, is truly potentially dangerous, misinformation ceases to be amusing; it can be downright dangerous. As we have pointed out, sharks do not need 70-degree water in which to attack. Although many more men than women have been attacked, sharks are no respecters of sex, and women are certainly attacked. Sharks do *not* have to roll over on their backs to bite. Although most species known or believed to be dangerous have their mouths underneath and set well back from their snouts, all are perfectly capable of getting their snouts up and out of the way; hence it is sheer folly to presume that a shark in a normal swimming position is harmless. Also sharks can and do attack at night. Sharks can and do attack in bright sunlight, on stormy and rainy days; and they do not need water ten-feet deep to be dangerous. A freshly caught shark, high and dry, can bite your head off.

Sharks are fish, although they are admittedly far removed from the mainstream of development of the world's bony fishes. No littoral species of shark is blind and they are not led around by pilot fish. Pilot Fish (*Naucrates*, etc.) are free-loaders who clean up the scraps that the shark, a messy eater at best, leaves behind. Nor is the pilot fish immune to attack if it gets too near the shark's jaws.

There can be little doubt that large sharks do attack boats, and sink some. In Chapter 5 on the killer whale are several references to attacks by sharks so large that whales and not fishes were blamed. In each case, careful examination has demonstrated that a shark was the offending animal. A large shark can smash a small boat with its great bulk, tip over a boat by placing part of its weight on the gunnels, or simply tear one apart with its teeth. Just how big a boat has to be before it is immune to attack depends simply on how big the shark is. It is certain that the great white shark does attack both men and boats. Here again, however, there is no way of knowing whether attacks of this kind are apt to be made by any large shark of a dangerous species, or only by an aberrant individual. Indeed, there may be something crudely equivalent to insanity among certain sharks that makes them individually far more aggressive than the norm. Higher forms of animal life—elephants, big cats, and bears, among others—are known to vary greatly in their individual attitude and disposition. This may be true of sharks as well. The answer may come when the chemistry and mechanics of the feeding frenzy are better understood. There is a great deal still to be learned about these dangerous and interesting animals.

Writers of fiction, and even many so-called nonfiction writers, have accused just about all sharks of being man-eaters. This, of course, is baseless. Probably not more than 10 percent of the currently recognized species have ever been implicated in attacks on man. Even some species that have been involved in human injuries, such as the Nurse Shark (Ginglymostoma cirratum), are not demonstrably true man-eaters. Almost always, attacks by these sharks have been brought about by divers and spear fishermen disturbing the normally peaceful animal and getting nipped. Not by any stretch of the imagination are all sharks dangerous to man. Most are not.

As silly as it may be to hear someone accuse all sharks of being man-eaters, at least it isn't a dangerous claim. At the opposite end of the spectrum, however, we have quite a different situation. In recent years, the lure of the sea and the freedom to it given by self-contained underwater breathing apparatus has brought thousands of novices into the surf with cameras and spears. The scuba and skin divers have come into their own. They follow in the wake of their ideals, the expert diving teams of France and Italy. Unfortunately, these novices are very often not as serious about their sport as were their forerunners. If anything, they treat their newfound freedom beneath the sea a little too matter-of-factly; though this is not true of all divers by any means. Many are keen sportsmen with a decidedly scientific bent. Excellent work has been done, and is being done, by serious-minded divers assisting in rescue and salvage work, submarine archaeology, and biological surveys. There are, though, an unfortunate number who seem to feel an uncontrollable urge to prove that there is nothing dangerous in the sea. The "I Kissed a Man-Eating Shark" kind of article litters the pages of the world's pulp magazines. In these monuments to literary mediocrity, the distinguishing feature seems to be that the line separating fact from fiction has been totally obliterated. The articles themselves are really amusing and harmless, but collectively they may one day bring about a lot of damage. There is a growing cult of uneducated divers whose common denominator is disrespect—disrespect for the very real hazards of their sport. Once again, these "Saturday experts" on everything aquatic are not to be confused with the thousands of fine, serious-minded sportsmen who are putting their newfound skill to work on constructive projects. The claim, so often heard, that all sharks are cowards and of no danger to a man in the sea, is as patently ridiculous as the counterclaim that all are dangerous. The difference is that the former claim may very well lead some new adherents of the sport down a marine garden path to destruction.

What sharks *are* dangerous to man? Somewhere between twenty and thirty species have been authentically implicated. Information is far from complete and a reliable and authoritative list cannot be compiled at this time. Too often, even where it can be demonstrated that an attack has taken place, there is no way to determine the species. Even victims who survive are uncertain about what they have seen.

Table 11 represents data collected from a number of sources. The species listed have been known to attack. There is no significance to the order in which they appear. Halstead notes these four families as being, in the order given, most dangerous: Isuridae—mackerel sharks, Carcharhinidae—requiem sharks, Carchariidae—sand sharks, and Sphyrnidae—hammerhead sharks.

There are some conflicting, confusing, and sometimes confounding reports, opinions, and legends about at least another dozen kinds of sharks. We purposefully say *kinds* here instead of *species* because the matter of species is particularly confusing. Some species of shark in one part of the world are known to be dangerous while related species elsewhere are believed harmless. Common names (more often encountered in literature than scientific names) are very confusing. The Blue Shark *(Prionace)* of the eastern coast of North America is not the Blue Shark *(Isurus)* of Australia. The shark known to Australians as the blue or blue pointer is called mako in other places, and mackerel in still others. The Mackerel Shark (properly *Lamna*) is any number of different animals depending upon where you live. To top it all off, the scientists are not all agreed on family and generic breakdowns, or on subspecific designations. Not all species of sharks, it is safe to assume, have even been scientifically examined.

How many human victims do sharks claim each year? No answer is possible. Primitive people fishing and diving off remote islands might very well fall victim to sharks without reports ever reaching beyond the coral reef that surrounds the atoll. Native people from isolated coastal zones of Africa, India, the Malay Peninsula, South America, and other areas do not keep records, and do not necessarily pass information about mortality along to people who do. During 1959 there were thirty-

Table 11. Sharks Known to Be Dangerous to Man

Scientific name	Common name	Remarks
Carcharodon carcharias	Great white or man-eater*	Oceanic—probably most dangerous single species
Isurus oxyrinchus and other species	Mako*	Oceanic—notable game fish, large and fast
Lamna nasus	Porbeagle	Continental
Galeocerdo cuvieri	Tiger*	Coastal and oceanic—global—particularly dangerous
Negaprion brevirostris	Lemon	Coastal—Atlantic
Carcharhinus [leucas] nicaraguensis	Lake Nicaragua	Lake Nicaragua only
Carcharhinus obscurus	Dusky	Atlantic—probably minimum danger
Pterolaminops longimanus	White-tipped*	Atlantic and Mediterranean—oceanic
Carcharias taurus	Sand	Global—coastal—probably minimum danger
Carcharhinus sp.	Bull	Coastal, ascends rivers
Carcharias arenarius	Gray nurse	Australia
Carcharias gangeticus	Ganges River*	Indian Ocean to Japan—aggressive—ascends rivers
Sphyrna sp.	Hammerhead*	Oceanic and coastal—global—unpredictable
Galeolamna macrurus and others	Whaler	Australia
Carcharhinus maculipinnis	Great black-tipped	Follows fishing craft—some attacks known
Carcharhinus zambezensis	Zambezi	South Africa—coastal—responsible for most attacks in Durban area
Ginglymostoma cirratum	Nurse	Not to be confused with Australia's gray nurse—harmless unless provoked
Prionace glauca	Blue	Coastal and oceanic—sometimes found in large concentrations

*These species are believed to be the most often implicated and are, therefore, probably the most dangerous.

six unprovoked and three provoked attacks known. Approximately a third of these were fatal. Coppleson reports that, between 1919 and 1949, there were seventy-seven attacks in Australian waters: forty-two occurred in the surf; thirty-one in harbors, rivers, and estuaries; and four on swimmers far offshore, or in the open ocean. The seventy-seven do *not* include thirty-three on pearl divers between 1926 and 1938, or several attacks at Darwin and along the north coast of Australia. Forty-seven attacks between 1913 and 1959 are reported for Florida waters by the Florida Board of Conservation. There are reports of eighty-seven attacks for all U.S. waters between 1907 and 1960. It is probably a safe estimate to place the annual incidence of unprovoked shark attack—worldwide—at between forty-five and fifty-five. It has been in that range for many years. The list is almost certainly incomplete. The number of attacks is small when compared with the number of swimmers in the water every sunny day, or the number of small boats that set out each year. As most researchers point out, however, the death or injury caused by a shark attack is particularly gruesome. The victims of these attacks must know terror in its most extreme form. Few more horrible deaths can be imagined than being eaten alive.

Shark attacks most often occur between 11:00 A.M. and 6:00 P.M., the peak bathing hours on the world's beaches. Of all recorded attacks, 94.3 percent occurred between sunrise and sunset. Still, it is probably more dangerous to swim at night than during the day. The number of swimmers at night is less than 5 percent of the daytime total. However, 5.7 percent of the known attacks have occurred after dark. Peak months are summer months for two reasons, migrating fish moving north, plus more people exposed during the warmer season. In the final analysis, dangerous sharks probably attack when they are hungry, when there is a victim handy, and when the attack mechanism, whatever it is, is triggered.

There are all kinds of free advice on what to do when a shark starts nosing around. Hitting it on the nose, sticking your finger in its eye, yelling, staying still, splashing and kicking, swimming calmly, grabbing its fins and riding it, or charging it and playing "chicken" have all been suggested. In individual cases some of these tactics undoubtedly have worked. Still, nothing can be depended on. A shark intent on attack is apparently insensible to pain and is apt to maintain the initiative no matter what you do. The best advice is still the most obvious: get out of the water as quickly as possible. If this is not possible, keep as calm as you can under the conditions and *keep facing the animal.* It is usually wise to stay under the water as much of the time as possible and do whatever you can to fend the marauder off without drawing blood, yours or his. If an injury has been sustained, everything should be done to stop the bleeding, since blood in the water may attract other sharks. Many people have managed to survive actual attacks, and many more have been able to chase off inquisitive sharks before the attack began, but too little is known about these animals to permit any really reliable generalizations. If you are in the water when a dangerous shark approaches, you are in grave peril. Whether or not he does attack will be more up to him than you. The following advice could prove helpful:

1. Always swim with a companion.
2. Stay out of the water if dangerous sharks are even suspected of being in the area.
3. Do not remain in the water with a bleeding wound.
4. Avoid swimming in water where underwater visibility is poor.
5. Avoid swimming at night.

If skin-diving:

1. Never dive alone.
2. Do not molest a shark. To provoke even a small and seemingly harmless one is to invite trouble.
3. Remove speared fish from the water immediately. Do not tow them around.
4. If a shark starts to circle you, a common prelude to attack, get out of the water using a rhythmic beat. Do not cause undue disturbance. Stay submerged until the last moment if wearing scuba.
5. If a shark moves in before you can retreat, do not panic but try to keep the shark in view. Try releasing bubbles, try charging it, try clubbing it on the snout. Try to avoid hitting it with bare skin. Try shouting, under water.

If you are a survivor of an air or sea disaster:

1. Do not strip. Clothing can be protection against a shark's rough skin.
2. Get wounded survivors out of the water onto a raft or float if possible.
3. Remain quiet; conserve energy.
4. If swimming is necessary, use rhythmic strokes.
5. Do not hang arms or legs over the side of a raft.
6. Do not jettison blood or garbage.
7. Do not fish when sharks are around. Abandon hooked fish if a shark comes near.
8. Use shark repellent if available. It sometimes works.
9. If in a group in the water, form a tight circle facing outwards. Hit sharks on the snout if they move in, but with bare hands only as a last resort.

Sleek and powerful, insensitive, insensible, and efficient, the great marauding sharks are among the world's most dangerous animals. They kill nowhere near the number of people that snakes do, only a fraction as many as are killed by lightning, and fewer in ten years, worldwide, than die in motor accidents in the United States on a single Fourth of July or Labor Day weekend.

Nevertheless, care and watchfulness are indicated when one is exposed to any danger of attack from a shark.

19 Skates and Rays

The stingrays cause more injuries to man each year than all other species of fish combined. Estimates for the United States alone range from 750 (Findlay E. Russell) to about 1,500 (Bruce W. Halstead) victims per year.

Rays of many kinds are common inshore inhabitants of all tropical, subtropical, and most temperate seas. Only one of the seven families of so-called stingrays is found regularly in fresh water. The others are marine forms that only occasionally enter brackish and sweet water. One factor in the number of human injuries is that stingrays are mostly shallow-water animals. Some deep-water species are known, but most of the stingrays of the world can be found in waters where humans might seek recreation or have to wade in shallow water as part of a fishing industry.

Stingrays are found along almost all of the coastline of the United States, all of Central, and most of South America. Europe as far north as central Scandinavia, all of the Mediterranean, all of Africa, and the Indian Ocean play host to these animals. The Pacific coast of Asia as far north as central Japan, and all the coasts of Australia and the Pacific islands are infested with them. A belt of stingrays runs around the world, and the number of human injuries must run into many, many thousands each year. Unfortunately, the world is not compensated for this misery by the enjoyment of stingray flesh. They are seldom eaten and are rated by most commercial fishermen as "junk fish."

The rays are elasmobranchs, closely related to the sharks. Like the sharks, they don't have true bones, and are extremely primitive. They have been swimming about the world's varying coastlines for hundreds of millions of years.

The seven families known to contain dangerous species are listed in Table 12. It should be noted that of the seven families listed as dangerous not all species are necessarily so.

Rays feed on worms, crustaceans, and molluscs, and can generally be found partially submerged in sandy or muddy bottoms where they excavate for living prey. None of these primitive creatures are known to be prone to attack man. Almost every case ever reported involved the victim stepping on or attempting to handle a specimen. Although the victim may not realize it, he has to be the aggressor in order to get stung. The insidious aspect of the whole business is that such aggression by man is almost always unintentional. Accidents with stingrays are generally all but unavoidable. And accidents can be very serious with some species. The Australian Giant Stingray *(Dasyotis brevicaudata)*, for example, grows to a length of fourteen feet, a width of seven feet and can weigh 750 pounds.

In all stingrays, the animal's weapon is in its tail, and the unwary wader who treads on the animal triggers reflexes that bring the tail up and forward in a powerful slashing motion. The stingray is the only truly venomous fish that causes extensive tissue injury in addition to injecting a toxic substance. Lacerations five to seven inches long are not unusual, and many is the stingray victim who has had to have his foot sewn up after an encounter.

In his handy guidebook, *Dangerous Marine Animals,* Dr. B. W. Halstead breaks the stingrays' envenomizing apparatus down into four main types (Table 13).

All of the stinging organs are located on the top or dorsal aspect of the tail, and all are essentially the same kind of device. There is a rough, barbed spine or spines enclosed in a sheath of skin. Although two or more on some species are known to exist, one is the usual

Table 12. Dangerous Stingrays

Scientific name	Common name
Dasyatidae	True stingrays or whiprays
Potamotrygonidae	River rays
Gymnuridae	Butterfly rays
Myliobatidae	Eagle or bat rays
Rhinopteridae	Cow-nosed rays
Mobulidae	Devil rays or mantas
Urolaphidae	Round stingrays

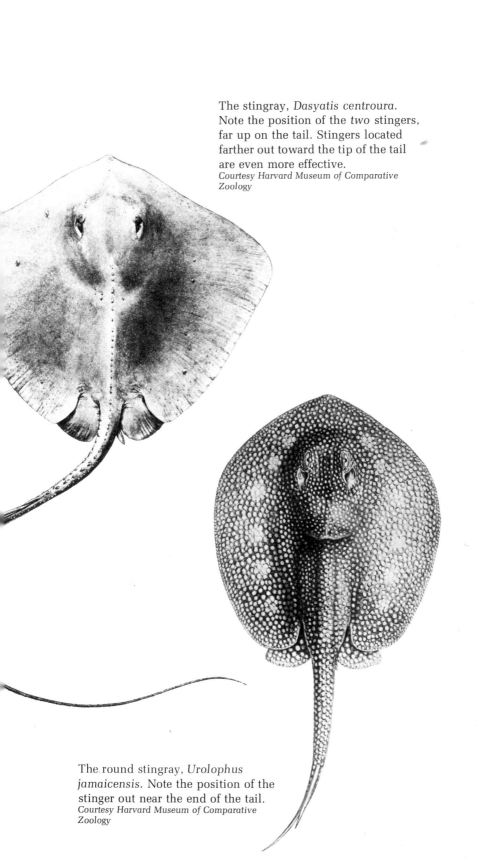

The stingray, *Dasyatis centroura*.
Note the position of the *two* stingers,
far up on the tail. Stingers located
farther out toward the tip of the tail
are even more effective.
*Courtesy Harvard Museum of Comparative
Zoology*

The round stingray, *Urolophus
jamaicensis*. Note the position of the
stinger out near the end of the tail.
*Courtesy Harvard Museum of Comparative
Zoology*

Table 13. Main Types of Envenomizing Apparatus Found in Stingrays

Type	Found in	Description
Gymnurid	Butterfly rays (*Gymnura*)	Not well developed. Close to base of short tail. Not very effective weapon.
Myliobatid	Bat or eagle rays (*Myliobatis, Aetobatis, Rhinoptera*)	Large; situated at base of whip-like tail. Can be effectively used.
Dasyatid	True stingrays (*Dasyatis, Potamotrygon*)	Very well developed. Set far out on whiplike tail—most danger ous type.
Urolophid	Round stingrays (*Urolophus*)	Dangerous. Set in short power-ful tail.

number. The sheath of skin is known as the integumentary sheath, and it covers the spine until it is brought into play. The spine is hard, but it is not true bone; it is properly identified as vasodentine.

On the underside of the spine, running its length, are a series of shallow furrows, the ventrolateral-glandular grooves, lined with soft, spongy tissue. It is this tissue, and perhaps parts of the integumentary sheath, that produce the venom.

The venom consists of soluble proteins, and ten different amino acids have been found in the chemical analysis of the substance. The immediate effect of the venom (and the often gross injury occasioned by the introduction of it) is pain; throbbing, sharp or shooting pain, and it evidently can be extreme. Eventually the venom can affect the heart and circulation, as well as the respiratory, nervous, and urinary systems of the victim. Frequently, portions of the sheath are left in the wound, and it is not uncommon for the barbed spine to break off and remain lodged in the victim. The removal of these foreign bodies, particularly the spine which cannot be drawn out with forceps, is painful and necessarily increases the size of the wound. Swelling and discoloration generally accompany the injury, and may last for several weeks. Weakness, nausea, and extreme nervousness are usual complaints. Cramps and violent pain can occur, and, rarely, death. Dr. F. E Russell reports that 2 out of 1,097 reported cases along the coastlines of the United States in a five-year period died. Sixty-two of 232 cases examined by physicians were hospitalized.

An additional problem can arise from the fact that the tetanus bacil lus, *Clostridium tetani*, may be injected into the wound along with the venom. The introduction of this bacillus and related bacilli isn't too much of a problem in relatively sophisticated societies where a tetanus booster is given as a matter of course for injuries of this general type. In undeveloped areas where proper medical facilities are lacking, the tetanus factor can cause more deaths than the venom itself. Russell and Lewis report that not all stingray spines contain the venom-producing tissue. Some stings produce nothing more than a stab or slashing cut. As painful as this may be, and as prone to secondary infection, it is not as dangerous as the injection of a venom.

Although the South American Freshwater Stingray (*Potamotrygon motoro*) is reportedly extremely dangerous, as are a number of other species throughout the world, death from an encounter with one of these tropical fishes is rarely reported, due in part to low populations in their areas. However, all stingrays have been recognized as dangerous since the time of ancient civilizations. (In early American history, Captain John Smith got badly stung in Chesapeake Bay, in June of 1608.) Yet deaths are not often recorded.* The animals themselves are not aggressive unless molested, and would certainly rather (if we can infer they are capable of choice) avoid man than become involved. Still, it remains an undeniable fact that accidents with them are frequently difficult to avoid, and will continue to occur as long as man fishes, swims, collects seashells, or just plain wades. They are dangerous animals in that they do cause a great many injuries, an enormous amount of pain, expense, and wasted manpower, and some deaths. The best defense against them is the power of observation. In areas where they are believed to exist, it is a good idea to carry a stick and probe ahead as you walk in the water. If you touch one, the chances are it will scoot out of the way.

If you do see a stingray, and have no immediate business with it, leave it alone unless you want to hasten it on its way with some long implement, other than your naked toe. If you accidentally net or hook one, beware of the tail! The hand, arm, and even face and neck of the fisherman are as susceptible to that slashing, serrated barb as the foot of the wader. Injury can be particularly dangerous for children whose small bodies react to the effects of the venom more rapidly and more completely than do those of adults. Even without intent, the stingray, although seldom deadly, can be dangerous to man.

---

*In February 1945, thirty-three-year-old Arthur Biggins, an Australian army sergeant, died at St. Kilda City Baths, Victoria, when a stingray drove its spine into his heart. It has been substantiated, but is certainly a freak accident. A Miss Jessie M. Laing of New Zealand died the same way. Both cases are reported in the supplement to the *Bulletin of the Post Graduate Committee in Medicine* of the University of Sydney, March 1963.

20 Venomous Fish

A distinction must be made between *poisonous* and *venomous* fish. The two words are generally used interchangeably but that can be confusing. For our purposes, *venomous* refers to the ability (by an animal) to introduce a noxious substance by means of a special device; while *poisonous* refers to animals whose substance or parts thereof are dangerous to man as food. In other words, a toadstool may be poisonous, whereas an arrow dipped in poison is venomous.

There are numbers of fish in tropical, subtropical, and even temperate waters equipped to administer a toxic substance on contact. We have discussed some of these, the stingrays, in Chapter 19. They are described separately because injuries caused by them are much more common than by any of the others, and contact with them is much more likely.

The forms we will discuss in this chapter use their venomous devices in self-defense, at least so far as humans are concerned. Categorically, none of these forms attack humans with these devices unless threatened at close quarters. Aggression in their direction, however, is met with a startlingly effective defense. The devices are not used in food-getting. The venoms involved vary greatly in toxicity; most are merely painful while others can be lethal.

The introduction of a venom into human tissue can constitute a medical emergency of the first magnitude. Effective antivenins for fish venoms are not generally available, and proper first aid measures are not always easy to determine. Injury by many forms under discussion in this chapter is an agonizingly painful affair. A man can be rendered either unconscious, or at least sufficiently shocked as to be disabled while still in the water. The only preventative is recognition. Before entering the water where these forms are found, the individual should learn the appearance and habits of indigenous species, and give them wide berth. Some, like the Stonefish (*Synanceja* sp.), are difficult to avoid because of their incredible powers of camouflage. Others broadcast their presence by their bizarre appearance. But, contrary to one ridiculous fable, these forms are just as dangerous out of the water as in. If netted or hooked, they should be treated with the utmost respect. Handling one in a boat can be just as hazardous as stepping or sitting on one in the water.

Writing in *Animal Kingdom* in November 1960, James W. Atz said:

The Stonefishes are the world's most venomous fishes. Such categorical statements are seldom safe to make when dealing with such biological variables as the strength of animal poisons and the health and immunity of creatures subjected to them, but there is no question that Stonefishes are in a class by themselves.

After reviewing the evidence, we would tend to agree with Dr. Atz. There can be little doubt but that the stonefishes are the most venomous fishes known.

There are three species of true stonefish currently recognized, *Synanceja verrucosa*, *S. horrida*, and *S. trachynis*. These grotesque creatures range from the east coast of Africa, east to the mid-Pacific. They are common and found as far north as the Red Sea and as far south as Australia. They are shallow-water, bottom dwellers, although few people get to see them, not even their victims. Wherever they are known, they are greatly feared.

The stonefish have none of the sleek grace of other fishes. The head is broad and quite flat, the body sharply tapered, and the tail blunt. They don't have normal piscine scales, but are warty and covered with slime. All of this supreme ugliness has a definite purpose, however, since a six- to twelve-inch stonefish in its natural surroundings—coral and rocky bottoms—is all but completely invisible. Your chances of seeing one as you wade in even shallow water are practically nonexistent. Add to perfect camouflage a reluctance to move that amounts to inertia, and you have an animal virtually impossible to detect. Even a great fuss in the water inches away will fail to disturb one beyond inducing it to erect its venomous spines. They remain frozen and invisible until it is too late—for their victim.

The stonefishes administer their venom by direct contact through the

The stonefish, *Synanceja,* member of the most deadly genus of venomous fishes known to man. Thirteen spines protect this lethargic fish, and an encounter with it produces agonizing pain and, in some well-documented cases, death.
Courtesy Australian News and Information Bureau

spines in their fins. They don't squirt anything, and they don't taint the water around them. There are thirteen spines along the back, three in the anal fins, and one in each pelvic fin. All the animal has to do is erect its spines and wait. Each spine has two sacs well toward the tip, which secrete venom when pressure is applied to the tip of the spine. The fluid flows along grooves into the wound—the insertion of the spine having stripped back a sheathing that covers the whole apparatus. Most injuries to humans result from a brush with the dorsal spines, almost invariably resulting from stepping on a specimen. Occasionally one is kicked, bringing the anal or pelvic spines into play. Since stonefish were around and venomous before man evolved, the device is apparently protection against other sea creatures. The stonefishes do not use their envenomizing apparatus to procure food. For that process they rely on camouflage. They lie waiting until a likely meal happens along. Literally faster than the human eye can see, they lunge forward, snapping the prey up in their cavernous mouths. Even other fish, it seems, can't spot a stonefish amid coral rubble.

Stonefish can live out of water for surprising lengths of time. Dr. Saul Wiener reports that specimens have survived as much as ten hours out of their natural environment. They have developed a secondary respiratory system to cover their needs when exposed in small pools at low tide. Even apparently dead specimens encountered along the shore should be handled with extreme care, or not at all. This would be particularly true if the encounter took place below the high-water mark.

Certain writers have attempted to deny the danger of the stonefish, citing cases where people have been jabbed and suffered no ill effects beyond a slight puncture wound. These cases are undoubtedly true, since examination of captured specimens will reveal an inevitable percentage of dry spines, that is, spines without venom sacs. Whether certain individuals fail to develop sacs for all of their spines, or whether these dry spines are the results of previous encounters is not clear. One thing is certain, many, and probably most, stonefish carry a full, bristling array, and it would be hazardous to be careless with one of these creatures. (No doubt some reports of stonefishes were cases of mistaken identity.)

All reports of injuries from these creatures emphasize one aspect, pain. Extreme, agonizing, sometimes maddening pain is apparently the first sign of an encounter, and it can last for as long as twelve hours. There are reports of victims rolling around on the beach screaming and frothing at the mouth. People attempting to help victims have been bitten by them and struck violently.

Writing in *The Medical Journal of Australia*, August 16, 1958, Dr. S.

Wiener says ". . . excruciating pain dominates the clinical picture in the early stages." C. C. Ralph in 1943 *(Victorian Naturalist)* wrote of a patient "screaming and half mad with agony," and morphine did not help the man. Writing in *Copeia* in 1951, Dr. J. L. B. Smith said:

Pain starts almost at once and rapidly becomes intolerable. Within ten to fifteen minutes the victim either collapses or becomes delirious and maniacal, raving and thrashing about in a boat or on the ground. If stabbed whilst wading, it generally takes three or four men to hold him and get him to shore without drowning. The intense agony lasts from 8 to 12 hours, after which it gradually diminishes, but the victim is weak and exhausted.

Those who die generally do so within a time assessed at about six hours. Swelling starts soon after the stab and continues to increase for "some days." Legs may attain elephantine proportions. Some victims are able to walk after 3 weeks, but mostly it is said to be "a long time" before the limb is usable. Often large blisters form and sloughing of large areas of skin occurs. Sometimes the dark pigment is destroyed and the skin of the blistered area remains light pink. Stabs in fingers and toes have led to the loss of those digits which turn black and "fall off." Some persons are still sick as long as a year afterwards.

Six years later, writing in the same journal, Professor Smith told of two rapid fatalities:

In March, 1956 an Indian youth of 15, well-built and athletic, was swimming there [Pont Larus, Mahé, Seychelles] and came towards the rocks. As he trod he felt a stab in the sole of his foot. He pulled himself up, sat on the rock and then saw three punctures. By this time intense pain had developed at the site of the punctures, which spread rapidly up the leg to the body. In a short time he was in agony and showing signs of collapse. Alarmed by his appearance the others managed to find a pirogue in which he was taken to shore. By this time he had turned blue and was frothing at the mouth. He was at once put in a car that set out for the hospital, but he died on the way there.

According to the medical officer who examined the body, this was greatly cyanosed, and the apparent cause of death was a cardiac or respiratory poison that had been injected. His medical attendant reported that he had not suffered from heart trouble.

At Pinda, Mozambique, on the 23rd September, 1956, two men went out in a canoe to the margin of the reef, close on 5 miles from land, and near low tide went wading, hunting for fishes with spears. The elder soon noted that the other had collapsed in the water. Hastening over, he found his companion almost delirious, but able to say that he had been stabbed in the foot by a "sherowa" *(Synanceja)*. Others came to help; the wounded man, now unconscious, was carried to the nearest canoe, and the stonefish was found and killed, cut open and the gall-bladder extracted, for the natives believe this, swallowed, to be an antidote to the poison. The victim was by then unconscious and well within an hour was dead.

I examined the corpse later. There was only one stab in the front of the second toe of the right foot. It was close on ¾" deep and went along the bone. The man must have kicked against the stonefish from behind. There was neither discoloration nor swelling in the toe or foot and from the rapidity with which he succumbed the toxin may well have been injected directly into a blood vessel. The victim was between 30 and 40 years of age and apparently, as well as from enquiry, strong and in good health.

Bulletin no. 159 of the Commonwealth of Australia Council for Scientific and Industrial Research, "Poisonous and Harmful Fishes," says: "This poison is extremely virulent, the Stonefish being the most venomous fish known, and immediately causes fearful pain so that a person may become almost demented . . . he may die."

Fortunately, there is an effective antivenin for the stab of the stonefish. There are, too, chemical agents which reduce or destroy the lethal effects of the venom. Anyone collecting specimens of this fish (they are relatively rare in, and therefore highly prized by, American and European aquaria), or working in waters where they are found, should be advised to (1) know the animal well and (2) go prepared to combat the extremely serious effects of an encounter, should one take place.

If the stonefish is one of the ugliest fish in the sea, the related and dangerously venomous Zebra Fish or Lion Fish (*Pterois* sp.) is one of the most beautiful and bizarre. Once considered rare and highly treasured by aquaria for the spectacular display piece that it is, the zebra fish is now a familiar sight. They have become so common that any good aquarium supply store can obtain one on order. Admittedly, the asking price for this beautiful creature limits its practical appeal to the more advanced home aquarist. The enthusiast who does bring one to the tank in his living room will do well to treat his pet with respect. The zebra fish is a decidedly dangerous animal.

Whether referred to as the lion fish, dragon fish, fire fish, devil fish, zebra fish, turkey fish, feather fish, butterfly cod, or sausaulele, the family Scorpaenidae, or scorpion fishes, are spectacular animals. Hidden in flashy displays of maroon or gray stripes on a creamy silver background and among the peacocklike dorsal, anal, and ventral fins are eighteen venomous spines. Thirteen are in the elegant dorsal fin, three in the anal and one in each ventral. The largest and showiest of its fins, the pectorals, are harmless. Each of the venomous spines has its own venom-producing tissue which is exposed by pressure when the apparatus is brought into play. This tissue is often injected into the

The scorpion fish—genus *Pterois*. There are many related and similar fish with dozens of common names, and all are dangerously venomous and *not* lethargic like the stonefish. These handsome, bizarre animals will meet an intruder midwater and offer their dorsal spines for the encounter.
Courtesy Prof. J. L. B. Smith

The Australian scorpion fish, *Notesthes robusta*, commonly called the bullrout. Spines on each side of the head, in front of the gill covers, can be erected to inject a painful but sublethal venom. Care is suggested when handling these common fish.
Courtesy Australian News and Information Bureau

wound along with the spine. The amount of venom injected, however, is considerably less than that of the stonefish.

Found over pretty much the same range as the stonefish, the zebra fishes have no authenticated human deaths to their credit, but a lot of agonizing injuries. The pain is reportedly severe and can last for a day or more. The deaths reportedly caused by these animals have never been substantiated. It is not possible, of course, to say that none have occurred. It is actually much more likely that some have.

Saunders and Lifton reported a case history in the *U.S. Armed Forces Medical Journal* for February 1960. A thirty-eight-year-old man "in good physical condition" received two spines in the fingers of his right hand while skin-diving off the Marshall Islands. Extreme pain, involving his whole arm, increased in intensity until the patient "was stuporous and in a state of severe shock." The two affected fingers were twice normal size and his entire arm was markedly swollen. His blood pressure dropped dangerously, and only swift medical care enabled him to survive cardiovascular collapse. It is safe to say that had the patient not been attended by physicians, given epinephrine to maintain blood pressure, and treated for shock, he would have succumbed. Such cases apparently indicate that an injury from one of these animals can be fatal.

Like the stonefish, the zebra fishes do not retreat, but hold their ground when threatened. However, unlike the stonefish, they do not wait to be stepped on passively, but constantly maneuver their venomous spines into position, turning rapidly. If the intruder comes too close, an effort is sometimes made to jab at him. While they can hardly be accused of swimming around looking for people to injure, they are much more aggressive than the more virulent stonefish. But, aggressive though they may be, they are relatively easy to avoid. Their appearance is spectacular and they can hardly be confused with other forms. They are not fast swimmers and nature gave them this other defense: Stand pat and dare anything to touch you! Carelessness may result in an occasional agonizing injury, but thoughtful behavior on the part of a man in the sea makes swimming or diving in the shallow waters where the zebra fish abound reasonably safe.

The family Trachinidae is represented by four dangerously venomous species ranging variously through the North Sea, the Mediterranean, and the Eastern Atlantic south along the west coast of Africa. *Trachinus araneus, T. draco, T. radiatus,* and *T. vipera* are all commonly known as Weevers, although dozens of local names are used. The Romans knew them as *tragine*; in England today they are called sea dragons; in Germany, *ragno*; in France, *claquedit*; in Greece, *drakaina*; and so on, throughout their extensive range. They are small fishes, seldom more than eighteen inches long, and are found in shallow bays and coastal waters. Known to be aggressive when approached in their natural habitat, they are also quite dangerous to handle when netted. Even dead specimens can cause extreme pain if improperly handled, and they are almost certainly the most venomous fishes in temperate and northern seas.

The extremely painful venom can be administered by any of the five to seven dorsal spines, or by either of the two opercular spines located on either side of the head. Each spine has its own venom-producing tissue, consisting of large pink cells filled with a finely granular substance. Once again, excruciating agony is reported as a primary symptom and even psychological disorders reportedly can result. It has been recorded that, in at least one case, a fisherman amputed his own finger to gain relief. Other victims have reportedly plunged an affected hand into fire! The central nervous system may become involved, and deaths reportedly have occurred, although none are known to the author at the time of this writing.

Weevers are esteemed as food and many tons are marketed each year. Some countries have enacted legislation requiring the removal of venomous spines before marketing, but the practice is probably not universal.

In addition to the stingrays, weevers, stonefish and zebra fish, there are several other venomous forms reported from most of the tropical, subtropical, and temperate seas of the world. It would be impossible to discuss all of these forms in this book since much of the information is sketchy, often contradictory, and generally unsubstantiated. Table 14 combines reports from most areas, including the forms already discussed.

Reports from all over the world beg for further study. From Teheran comes a report of a diminutive black fish found in the Shatt al Arab River. It reputedly has killed twenty-eight people with a venomous bite. Death is said to be swift. No other information is presently available. (No other fish is known to have a venomous bite, and this report is at least suspect.)

A freshwater, armored catfish of the genus *Cataphractus* is said to have caused a number of deaths in South America. It has a sharp conical spine in its "armpit" behind the base of each of its recurved, bladelike pectoral fins. Although a small creature, it reportedly delivers an extraordinary amount of particularly virulent venom. However, no real research has apparently been done on it.

There are, at the very least, 25,000 species of fishes, and that is a conservative estimate. The total number of species venomous enough

Table 14. Known Venomous Fish of the World

Scientific name	Common name	Range	Remarks
Trachinus araneus	Weever, sea cat, sand eel, sting bull, adderpike, black fin, *Abo*, *Abohor*, plus many more	Portugal, Mediterranean, south along Atlantic coast of Africa	Family Trachinidae—most dangerous temperate forms
T. draco	As above, plus *Foersing*, *Fjärsing*, *Petermänchen*, *Drachenfische*, *Ragno*, *Meerlan*, great weever, plus many more	Norway, British Isles, south to Mediterranean and coasts of Africa	As above
T. radiatus	As above, plus many more	Mediterranean, south along west coast of Africa	As above
T. vipera	As above, plus lesser weever, plus many more	North Sea, Europe, Atlantic coast, Mediterranean	As above
Squalus acanthias and sp.	Spiny dogfish	North Atlantic and North Pacific	Not very dangerous as reported
Seven families: Dasyatidae, Potamotrygonidae, Gymnuridae, Myliobatidae, Rhinopteridae, Mobulidae, Urolophidae	Stingray, whipray, butterfly ray, bat ray, spotted eagle ray, and many more specific to species and area	Worldwide—all tropical, subtropical and coastal regions—specific to species, and in some tropical fresh water	Indeterminate number of species; very large and important group. Some may cause fatal injuries.
Chimaera sp. Hydrolagus sp.	Chimaeras, elephant fish, ray fish, king-of-the-herrings	All temperate, tropical and subtropical Atlantic margins. West coast of U.S.	Painfully venomous. Probably not lethal.
Many and various	Catfish, etc.	Worldwide, fresh water and marine	Over 1,000 species of many genera. Most only mildly venomous. Sting of some tropical forms may be deadly.*

Table 14. Known Venomous Fish of the World—Continued

Scientific name	Common name	Range	Remarks
Family: Scorpaenidae. Genera include: Choridactylus, Emmydrichthys, Erosa, Hypodytes, Inimicus, Leptosynanceja, Minous, Pelor, Pterois, Scorpaena, Scorpaenopsis, Sebasticus, Sebastodes, Snyderina, Synanceja, and others. See below.	Scorpion fishes	Tropical and subtropical seas; particularly Indo-Pacific complex, into eastern Pacific	Large group of most dangerous venomous fish. Include stonefish as below. Some forms are potentially lethal.
Synanceja verrucosa, S. horrida, S. trachynis	Stonefish	Tropical Indo-Pacific—east coast of Africa, Red Sea, Indian Ocean, Australia, Philippines, etc.	One of the Scorpaenidae—most dangerous form known—deadly
Pterois volitans and others	Zebra fish, lion fish, butterfly fish, feather fish, feather fins, dragon fish, fire fish, stingfish, butterfly cod, plus many more	Tropical Indo-Pacific complex.	One of the Scorpaenidae—very dangerous—possibly deadly
Family: Siganidae	Rabbitfish	East Africa to Central Pacific islands	Painful, but not lethal
Family: Batrachoididae. Many genera.	Toadfish, munda, oysterfish, sapo, and others—specific to species and area	Virtually global in tropical, subtropical, and temperate coastal waters. Few freshwater and estuarine forms known	Not lethal as reported
Family: Acanthuridae	Surgeonfish plus many more	Tropical	Not known if venomous. Can inflict painful cuts with retractable lateral spine

Family: Uranoscopidae	Star-gazer plus many more	Indo-Pacific and Atlantic complex	Degree of venomousness not known
Centropogon australis and sp.	Fortescue waspfish	Australian coast	Painful but not believed lethal
Notesthes robusta and sp.	Bullrout sulky	As above	As above
Ruboralga jacksoniensis	Red rock cod	As above	As above
Gymnopistes marmoratus and sp.	Cobbler	As above	As above
Amphacantus sp.	Spinefeet	As above	As above
Halophryne sp.	Frog fish	As above	As above
Pseudobatrachus sp.	Bastard stonefish	As above	As above

*Cataphractus sp., a freshwater, South American armored catfish is reputedly violently venomous, having conical spines under bladelike pectoral fins. Reputedly lethal.

Note: Plus the following families: Plotosidae, Tachysuridae, Siluridae, and others of which little is known. The preceding table is by no means complete, but does offer a cross section of venomous fish distribution.

to be of any possible danger to man is probably less than one hundred. There are undoubtedly many more than that capable of causing some discomfort. These figures are given only to underscore the simple observations that the seas and oceans of the world are not teeming with virulent forms. In a chapter such as this, filled with stonefish, weevers, and the like, it is easy to give, and get, the opposite impression. The majority of fishes in the world are not horrific forms, or dangerous to man. They are shy, retiring, generally very beautiful creatures without either the brains, brawn, or specialized equipment to be dangerous. However, there are those few forms that can be exceedingly dangerous, even deadly, by virtue of highly specialized apparatus and an agonizing neurotoxin. Few, if any, venomous land forms can give so painful an injury. As it is with snakes, most aren't dangerous; some few are. Beware the few.

21 Some Other Fish

The waters of the world, fresh and salt, hold a number of animals not yet discussed in this book which are potentially dangerous to man, at least on occasion. In this chapter, we will discuss some of the more significant of these.

Late in 1941, two native workers in the Brazilian state of Amazonas were walking on a plank stretched across a large cement pool. Nobody seems to know precisely how it happened, but one end of the plank slipped from its mooring and the two men fell into the water. They were killed instantly. The pool contained a number of Electric Eels (*Electrophorus electricus*). These fishes had been collected at the request of Dr. Christopher W. Coates, curator of the New York Aquarium, and Dr. David Nachmansohn, on assignment for the U.S. Army Chemical Corps. The greater part of the research in which they were engaged had to do with finding an antidote for the devastating nerve gas G developed in Germany in the 1930s. (The gas became available to Russia after the war.) The whole episode with the electric eels, and their subsequent transport to the United States, appears to have been in the best tradition of a spy melodrama. Before it was over, at least one other man (an anti-Nazi German working on the project) was killed by the fishes.

The electric eel is not an eel at all. It was, until very recently, included in the family Gymnotidae, but it is now in a family of its own. It grows to a length of ten feet (eight feet is average for a large specimen) and can weigh as much as ninety pounds. It is decidedly eel-like in appearance, and is a fairly common, shallow freshwater fish in Brazil, Colombia, and Peru, at least, and very possibly in surrounding areas as well. It has rudimentary gills that cannot sustain it under water and it will drown if held under; it is strictly an air-breather, and is found only in fresh water. The electric eel releases a massive electrical discharge to compensate for the low conductivity of relatively salt-free waters. Blind at maturity, it undoubtedly uses these discharges for locating prey, as well as for stunning it, and also for protection. All truly electric fishes are believed to use their powers for one or more of four purposes: navigation, locating prey, obtaining prey, and defense.

There is no doubt that the electric eel is the most dangerous electric fish known. This river-dweller can discharge 550 volts at 1 ampere. Average discharges run around 400 volts, although Dr. Coates told the author he personally measured 650. These discharges come with a frequency as high as 400 per second, and, uniquely, the fish can keep it up for days, although the frequency of discharge drops as time passes. The fish is capable of killing a man on contact, and horses attempting to cross streams have been knocked out at a distance of twenty feet. It is probably the only electric fish capable of killing a full-grown man.

The power of the electric eel comes from the fact that it has more special cells for the propagation of electricity than any other fish. More than half its body is given over to this one function. Since, as we have noted, the fish can reach ninety pounds, we have the potential of more than forty-five pounds of electricity-generating apparatus! All vital organs of the fish are contained in the front 20 percent of its body, and that part is strictly nonelectric. The remaining 80 percent of the fish is between 60 and 65 percent electric and nothing else. Each cell in the special tissues produces one-tenth of a volt, no matter what its size. This produces a paradox in that a specimen six inches long, producing 300 volts or more, is at its maximum stage of electrical production per unit of length. As the fish grows, the cells increase in size, but not in number or output. It is at this stage, approximately six inches, that the fish leaves the protection of the parents and goes on its own. At six inches, it is still able to see, but it loses this ability soon after. At no stage is the fish able to control its own voltage; but it can control the bursts of "trains" of its emissions, with ten or eleven discharges constituting a "train." In laboratory tests, these discharges continue eight to nine hours after death. When a specimen is electrically active, the discharge starts at a point 20 percent tailwards from the front end and passes along the length of the animal, running off at the tail tip. As one discharge sequence reaches the end of the tail, another is starting behind the head. This goes on as long as the animal is stimulated. A metal conductor attached to the two ends of the fish's electric tissue

The electric eel *(Electrophorus electricus)*, most potent of all electric fish. The fingers show where the animal's vital organs are located—all of the rest is electricity-producing tissue.
Photograph by Fritz Goro

The potent electric ray *(Torpedo nobiliana)*. Human deaths have probably not occurred, or have been extremely rare. But this fish does provide a serious jolt of short duration.
Courtesy Harvard Museum of Comparative Zoology

The giant manta ray—massive and harmless. Reports of attacks on boats are pure nonsense—these are some of the most inoffensive creatures in the sea. They are often approached and even "ridden" by scuba and skin divers.

mass will cause a short circuit, making the discharges constant and uncontrollable and eventually killing the specimen.

When the electric eel is not stimulated, it gives off a regular pulse of mild discharges used for navigation. When stimulated, the pulse shoots up to a peak and then, by controlling the rate of the discharge, the fish is able to cope with the situation, be it defense or food-getting. Strangely, the electric eel does not kill its prey (amphibians and other fishes, mainly) but stuns them. If they are dead, the eel will not touch them!

Fossil fishes have been found with what appears to have been tissue identical to the electricity-producing tissue of contemporary forms. Probably a very ancient refinement, the ability to generate electricity on demand is one of the most remarkable and bizarre developments in the animal kingdom. Since it is found, as we shall see, in a wide variety of fishes, and since it serves at least four separate functions, it is strange that, today, it is limited to probably no more than forty species. In fact, all animals, from the primitive worms to man, produce some electricity but, in all but the few electric fishes, this is an internal phenomenon— the nervous system. We feel, hear, smell, taste, see, move, and think electrically. Only fishes, because they live in a medium that is a natural conductor (and only a few fishes at that) are capable of transmitting this chemically produced energy to the external world.

There are three separate organs involved: the large electric organ, the bundles of Sachs, and the organs of Hunter. There is no reversal of polarity; the head end is positive, the tail end negative. In marine forms polarity is ventral to dorsal (down to up), dorsal being positive. In the electric eel, the large electric organ is the main battery; the bundles of Sachs are for small single releases, probably for navigation. The chemical production of electricity within the cells and tissues of the fish has been intensively studied.

Africa has an Electric Catfish (*Malopterurus electricus*) that is found in both the Nile and Congo river complexes. The animal grows to a length of four feet and can weigh twenty pounds. The electric output probably doesn't exceed 90 volts, at a tenth of an ampere. It has a relatively small electric organ. The device is apparently defensive, the fish tires easily, and it cannot keep up a sequence of discharges long enough to seriously injure a man. Nevertheless, the form was known for its peculiar talent even to the ancients. Egyptian hieroglyphics dating to 4000 B.C. call it by the name, "He Who Releases Many," the implication being that fishermen hauling in nets in which a specimen was caught would get enough of a jolt to make them drop the nets and lose their catch. The fish is definitely not in the same class as the electric eel, and I know of no human deaths. Contact must, however, be a somewhat startling experience.

The most powerful electric marine fish are undoubtedly the widely distributed Torpedo Rays (*Narcine* and *Torpedo* sp.). They are found all over the world in warm and temperate seas. The torpedo rays grow to a weight of two hundred pounds and can give a discharge of 80 volts at high amperage. The relatively low voltage (when compared with the electric eel) is explained by the high conductivity of saltwater. The device is protective and is strong enough to be dangerous. The danger factor is somewhat mitigated by the fact that the torpedo ray tires very quickly; ten to twenty discharges generally exhaust the animal. I know of no serious accidents with these animals, although 80 volts at high amperage offer good reason to avoid direct contact.

In dealing with the electric fish in general, there is no question of "disposition" or "chances of attack." These fishes do not "attack," they respond to stimulation in a perfectly predictable pattern. There is probably no group of animals in the world more predictable. An expert can draw a graph showing exactly how the fish's response will look on an oscilloscope when a man enters the water near it. To get near one in the water, or to touch one, is to be shocked. The intensity of that shock depends on species more than on size.

Of the world's thirty-five to forty types of electric fishes, only the electric eel and the torpedo rays appear capable of injuring or killing a healthy man. Deaths are known, but no possible means exist for estimating the number that may have actually occurred.

It was a president of the United States who first made the general public aware of the fish we discuss next. It was Theodore Roosevelt, quite naturally, telling stories of "the most ferocious fish in the world" after a South American hunting—exploring trip. The fish was *Serrasalmus nattereri*, one of the piranhas. There are twenty or more closely related species of fishes all known as piranha, piranyas, piris, or pirai, but only four appear to be particularly dangerous. *S. nattereri* grows to a length of nearly eleven inches and travels in immense schools. It is the most widespread species and reportedly is responsible for more human deaths than any other. It is known to range through most of eastern and northern South America, as far south at least as Central Argentina. In the words of Dr. James Atz, "it is prevalent enough to make swimming or wading an extremely risky pastime over about half an entire continent." Dr. Atz says further, "To all intents and purposes, it is *the* Piranha."

The Black Piranha (*S. niger*) is reportedly less savage (a permissible anthropomorphism since it refers not to the fish's attitude but to the effect on the human being), as is the fifteen-inch *Pirambeba (S. rhombeus)*. The São Francisco River in eastern Brazil reportedly has a two-foot piranha or pirai of great ferocity. *S. spilopleura* is often accused of being a confirmed man-eater, but its range, like that of most piranhas, is crossed by that of *S. nattereri,* and it is difficult indeed to get definitive estimates of danger by species.

When President Roosevelt's book, *Through the Brazilian Jungle*, first appeared, the piranha blossomed as the darling of the jungle writers; and little wonder, with this kind of send-off (in Roosevelt's words):

> They belonged to one of the most formidable genera of fish in the world, the Piranha or Cannibal Fish, the fish that eats men when it can get the chance. . . . They are the most ferocious fish in the world. They will snap a finger off a hand incautiously trailed in the water; they mutilate swimmers—in every town in Paraguay there are men who have been thus mutilated; they will rend and devour alive any wounded man or beast; for blood in the water excites them to madness.

The account continues in this vein and, with a few changes in punctuation, has appeared adjective-for-adjective in untold numbers of tales of jungle travel over the past decades.

The late William T. Innes, godfather of the home aquarists, described a movie taken of an attack. A young pig was dipped into a Brazilian stream several times and, as Innes reports, "Each time it was lifted out of the water, it was reduced in size." After two minutes, only the skeleton was left. I have seen two such films, one involving a bullock and the other supposedly a living human being. (In the latter case, a human skeleton did appear in the snapping frenzy caught by the motion picture camera. I suspect a dead human body was used for the episode, although I do not know. Having had some motion picture production experience, I am perhaps a little too suspicious. I rather believe that if a person were in such distressful circumstances, picture taking would be the last concern of his companions. I should like to think so, at least.)

Professor George S. Myers of Stanford described the piranha this way:

> A fish only a foot long with teeth so sharp and jaws so strong that it can chop out a piece of flesh from a man or an alligator as neatly as a razor, or clip off a finger or toe, bone and all, with the dispatch of a meat cleaver. A fish afraid of nothing, which attacks any animal, whatever its size, like lightning! A fish which never attacks singly but always in schools of a hundred or a thousand. A fish which is actually attracted by splashing and commotion in the water! And a fish which, when it smells blood, turns

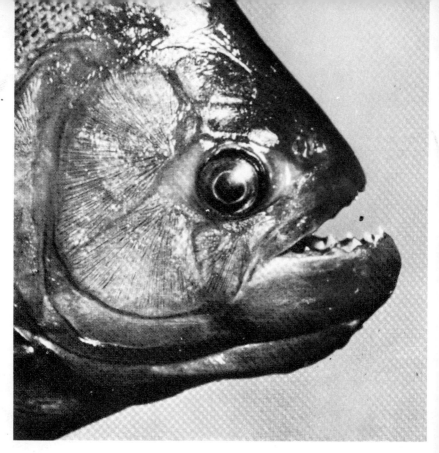

The piranha, a legendary horror since Theodore Roosevelt brought back tales of the fish from a South American journey. Piranhas are voracious in their feeding habits, some species do travel in large schools, and it would probably be better not to swim with them around. As to how many people have been injured or killed, no one will ever know.

The barracuda. There are a number of species of this powerful carnivore. They prowl the sea in search of prey, and accidents have happened, no doubt at times blamed on sharks.
Photograph by Fritz Goro

into a raging demon! This is the piranha, feared as no other animal is feared throughout the whole length of South America.

Until quite recently, piranhas were imported alive into the United States and, although expensive, were sold to home aquarists. The high price was a result of the fishes' cannibalistic nature. A can that would normally be used to ship a hundred smaller fishes had to be used for a single piranha. One to a can was the rule, because that was the count at the end of the trip, if not at the beginning. Now, I am told, there are injunctions against the importation for sale of these creatures. It appears that some were known to have been liberated in our inland waterways and there was a mounting fear that they might become established. Bizarre behavior is known among man, to be sure, but the dumping of piranhas in a local lake certainly would appear to be extreme. It is a kind of fish we can do without, although several species are good eating, if somewhat bony. When it is a toss-up as to whether the angler eats the fish or the fish the angler, few sportsmen would protest being denied their fun. Nevertheless, the various species of piranha are common enough in home aquariums, for a rather large literature has grown up on their care. All such literature advises caution in their handling. More than one aquarist has been bitten, it is reported.

The piranha, or rather the several piranhas, have been so prevalent with popular writers since the days of Theodore Roosevelt that it is impossible to tell where fiction leaves off and fact begins. Everything seems to point toward acceptance of any and all claims. Indeed, while I know of no reason for not accepting them, except that I do not, of course, know them to be true, I do not know the name of a single victim nor a date, a place or a reliable witness to a piranha-caused human death. While there would appear to be no definite reason for discounting the claims so often heard, I bear in mind that when I began these researches there was no reason for discounting the equally horrific tales about the killer whale.

Of course, the piranha has been demonstrated to be a voracious carnivore. So has the killer whale. The piranha is feared throughout its range. So is the killer whale. What, then, is our point? Simply this: the piranha is assumed to be exceedingly dangerous to man. A certain sameness is evident in all the claims made against this fish, so that all look as if they stemmed from a few early accounts by men like Theodore Roosevelt and have simply been repeated again and again. The danger is undoubtedly very great, and, in fact, the piranha may be the most dangerous fish in the world from the point of view of both potential and actual numbers of people injured and killed; but, it would be nice to see some valid eyewitness reports, without the tired old adjectives (five-to-the-line was an actual count in one article). In the meantime, anyone visiting an area where the various species of *Serrasalmus* abound might do well to exercise caution.

The general name barracuda is used for over twenty species of swift, carnivorous fish of the family Sphyraenidae. Many of the species are of little concern to the average swimmer, but one or two at least appear to have been implicated in attacks. The Great Barracuda *(Sphyraena barracuda)* grows to a length of eight feet and is reportedly very aggressive—on occasion. The mouth is huge and filled with particularly sharp teeth. The range of the species is worldwide, from Brazil to Florida, and from the Red Sea to the Hawaiian Islands, and encompasses a number of resort areas.

As for attacks on man, the International Oceanographic Foundation at the University of Miami has records that "show some thirty-one attacks which were either definitely proven to be by barracuda or were thought to be due to barracuda." Dr. Donald P. de Sylva, of the Marine Laboratory at the University of Miami, did his doctoral dissertation at Cornell University on this subject and his paper included "a survey of the literature in which there were authenticated records of barracuda attacking human beings." I have not had an opportunity to study that paper, but Dr. de Sylva wrote to me and said, "I have located about 33 of these which can be for the most part attributed to barracuda." He wrote further, "In general, the likelihood of being attacked by a barracuda is much smaller than that of being attacked by a shark. . . . However, there is always a small possibility that a barracuda will attack a human being. . . ." Since the paper was completed in 1958, Dr. de Sylva has learned of several new cases. One was recently reported from Pompano Beach, Florida.

As is noted in Appendix F, barracuda can be dangerous to eat and severe poisoning is not uncommon. Our concern in his chapter, however, is not barracuda-eating men, but just the opposite. It appears as if this sometimes does occur.

The barracuda is a particularly swift fish and strikes with great force. Its long, narrow jaws leave a wound quite distinct from the jagged u-shaped excavation accomplished by the sharks. A large barracuda, and certainly a five- to eight-foot specimen, could easily do enough damage in one bite to kill a man. Gross damage is generally the case in barracuda attacks, and shock is severe. Reports generally have a question mark attached, and a shark is frequently thought to be the offending animal by many, even when the barracuda is specified.

In 1922 Dorothy McClachie died from shock and loss of blood when she was attacked near the Municipal Pier at St. Petersburg, Florida. A barracuda was blamed for the attack, but the shape of the wound suggested a shark. In July 1953, twenty-six-year-old Mrs. D. F. Gunn was attacked at Juno Beach, Florida, and her left leg was almost severed between the ankle and the knee. She was standing in water only knee-deep at the time and a barracuda was blamed. An attack on Eleanor Nelson at Miami Beach in 1957 was blamed on the barracuda. Again the victim was wading in shallow water.* In a paper in the *Journal of the American Medical Association* in 1928, Gudger and Breder said, "There is little doubt that the barracuda, of all marine fish, is the one most dangerous to man." Total amputations are characteristic of attack by large specimens, according to several researchers.

Bruce Wright made a study of "releasers of attack behavior pattern" in shark and barracuda and reviewed over ten thousand man-hours in the water by divers in close proximity to these animals. His conclusions included the following statements:

1. Blood without movement did not release a feeding pattern in shark or barracuda in the Bahamas.
2. Fish blood and jerky, rapid movements released the attack pattern in both shark and barracuda.
3. Jerky, rapid movement alone released the attack pattern in both shark and barracuda.

He also observed, "A man in the water, alone or in a group, acting quietly and smoothly did not release the attack pattern."

It appears that barracuda respond to stimuli in very much the same way sharks do. There would appear to be steps that can be taken to reduce the likelihood of an attack:

1. Avoid murky water. You are not as apt to spot the fish, and the fish is not as apt to get a clear idea of what you are. A movement in murky water might invite an attack that would not occur in clear water where the fish could get a good estimate of your size.
2. Do not wear flashy metallic swimsuits or gear. A flashing object might appear to the fish to be the silver belly of a food fish. Think in terms of the silver lure you would use if fishing. Don't be a lure yourself.
3. Never tow speared fish along with you. Blood and convulsive

*Pablo Bush Romero, doyen of Mexican skin divers, reports a man had the flesh stripped off one leg while standing in water only a foot deep near the town of Tancah on the Quintana Roo coast of Mexico, in November 1962. A barracuda was seen to be the offending animal. It was the second such incident in that area.

movements will attract predators. Even if fish are dead, their smell and your movements can combine to spell disaster.

4. Don't molest any fish that can obviously be dangerous if aroused. Spearing barracuda is patently dangerous and should never be engaged in without a full awareness of the hazards involved.

5. There are hundreds of reports of swimmers and divers working and playing around barracuda without suffering harm. Don't be misled. Attacks have evidently occurred and will occur again. If you go into the water when barracuda are known to be around, be prepared for trouble. It can occur, and, as in the case with sharks, it is not possible to predict the outcome. The *best* diver in the world is clumsy when compared with a barracuda. When and if the attack does occur, it will not only be at the fish's election, but to its advantage. A man and a barracuda in the water are not equal adversaries.

6. Beware of large solitary specimens. School barracuda (the schools are sometimes vast and dense) are seldom if ever implicated in attacks on man.

The big barracuda, although apparently less prone to attack man than some species of sharks, are dangerous enough when they do attack, and so unfathomable in their response patterns as to justify extreme caution in all dealings with them. Someday, a great deal more will be known about them than is now, and at that time, perhaps some definitive guidelines will be drawn up. In the meantime, anyone exposed to the pikelike barracuda, particularly the large solitary animals (S. *barracuda* and S. *jello*) as opposed to the smaller school fish, should recognize that among the possible eventualities is death or at least mutilation.

Like the barracuda, the moray eels have been responsible for cases of severe poisoning when used for human consumption. Here the similarity stops since unprovoked attacks on man are all but unknown. Members of the family Muraenidae, morays are confined to tropical and subtropical seas, for the most part. There are several species found in temperate waters, but they are seldom involved in incidents with human beings.

Morays can achieve a length of ten feet in some species. There are about forty species worldwide, those in the genera *Muraena* and *Gymnothorax* reaching the greatest size and offering the most threat. They are all bottom-dwellers and are seldom found far from cover. Coral reefs, old wrecks, and similar bottom rubble offer the caves and crevices ideal to their way of life. They remain hidden from view most of the time, waiting for prey to come close enough to be grabbed. Occasionally, one will be spotted undulating along the bottom, snakelike in movement. They are extremely muscular and slippery and grasping one with bare hands is all but impossible. Their jaws are immensely powerful and their teeth sharp, numerous, incurved, and designed for grasping and tearing. They are numerous in some reef areas where they establish territories that they defend vigorously. The threat they offer to man is involved with these territorial claims. Quite simply, anyone intruding on the territory of a moray eel with hand or foot is apt to be severely bitten. Reaching into a crevice or stepping close to a coral cave inhabited by a large moray can result in hospitalization. The bite is deep, crushing, and tenacious.

Contrary to unfounded reports, the moray's bite is not believed to be venomous. It is extremely unlikely that *any* species of moray eel is equipped with venom glands, although the bite can result in infection.

Moray eels are not known to hunt man. They strike out, much as venomous snakes do, in defense of their privacy. Accidents with these animals can be damaging but are undoubtedly always the result of carelessness. I know of no human deaths caused by these animals.

A number of reporters have suggested that the giant groupers or sea bass of the family Serranidae have caused human injuries or worse. They are bold fishes with monumental appetites, are generally quite curious, and they can weigh a quarter of a ton or more. Presumably, someone might get bitten, but I know of very few cases of consequence. The Australian Council for Scientific and Industrial Research uses the word "vicious" to describe huge tropical groupers of the genus *Promicrops*. Some care would seem to be indicated on the part of divers.*

Fish and Cobb quote Whitley as saying of the Australian Black Rock Cod or Giant Sea Bass *(Epinephelus forsythi)*, "[This is] a savage species and several of us were rushed by them as we waded on Middleton Reef and we had to beat them off." Apparently, some large fish, although generally inoffensive, will on occasion see a man as food. Danger would seem to be slight with most species when compared to those other forms known by repeated demonstration to be man-eaters.

In 1930 Dr. R. Biddle, in the *Journal of the Royal Navy Medical*

*The *Sydney Morning Herald* (November 30, 1943) reported salvage divers were repeatedly attacked by groupers attracted by their shiny helmets. One fish engulfed an entire helmet and made off with the diver. The man's rescue came just in time. The magazine *Australian Outdoors* (July 1955) carries accounts of attacks. In their publication, "Know Your Fishes," the Brisbane Department of Harbours and Marine says, "It is thought that the mysterious loss of some native divers of the Torres Strait pearling fleets was due to groupers." There are, perhaps, another half dozen such references.

Service, reported that two species of East Indian Puffers (*Tetraodon fluviatilis* and *Spheroides oblongus*) are not only poisonous to eat but have a particularly disconcerting habit concerning waders and swimmers; they attack and bite the genital organs. Similar reports about one or the other of these species come from the Philippines, Malaya, China, and several other areas. In light of certain known facts about other fishes, this strange accusation may be valid.

Certain minute parasitic catfish of the family Trichomycteridae reportedly have a strange affinity for urine and thus the urogenital openings of both men and women. This truly bizarre behavior constitutes a hazard in many South American rivers and streams. The species *Vandellia cirrhosa,* known as the candiru, is chiefly involved; but others may also be.

These small (2½ inches), scaleless fish, not much thicker than a pencil lead, are equipped with erectile, rear-pointing spines and these they use once they enter the urethra of a bather. The pain, as one might suspect, is agonizing. Bathers in streams where the infamous candiru abound generally wear tight protective clothing over the genitalia, so say the reports.

I have yet to encounter a satisfactory explanation as to why certain Asiatic puffers might attack the genitalia, or why these South American catfish would attempt to take up residence in the urethra. Indeed, the two phenomena may have nothing whatsoever to do with each other, or may be related only on grounds of affinity for urine. The hazard in the latter case is apparently very real, although I do not know of a specific victim. Perhaps, as in our practice in this book, we should say it is *reportedly* real.

John E. Randall of the Marine Laboratory at the University of Miami did considerable research on the bizarre behavior of the various Houndfish or Needlefish (*Strongylura*). He refers to them as "living javelins." These fish are surface-feeders, more active at night, and can achieve a length of nearly five feet and a weight of ten to twelve pounds. When excited, confused, or otherwise overstimulated, they swim at great speeds and leap clear of the water. Clyde Mitchell of Homestead, Florida, received a deep neck wound apparently when struck by a needlefish, although the newspapers reported an attack by a barracuda. In another case a wader had a needlefish ram its beak clear through his neck, and twenty-year-old Lorelei Sullivan was rammed on the side of her nose near the corner of her eye. A piece of the fish's beak was removed surgically at Miami's Mount Sinai Hospital. Capt. William B. Gray of the Miami Seaquarium was pinned to his boat when a needlefish ran him through the leg. *Pacific Islands Monthly,* of June

1958, carried a report of a Papuan killed when his jugular vein was punctured. *Collier's*, a few years earlier, reported two more deaths near Acapulco, Mexico. Randall learned of another death in Tahiti. All of these cases are reported by Dr. Randall in his article "The Living Javelin," in *Sea Frontiers* magazine for November 1960.

The needlefish may be confused by or attracted to light, as most "attacks" occur at night upon fishermen with lanterns. The incidents do not really constitute attacks as much as they do collisions. The danger, however, appears to be real enough and fishing at night, with lights, in an area where needlefish are common would appear to be safer with a protective shield between the fisherman and his lantern.

On November 16, 1962, the Associated Press office in Tokyo reported that two ships were speeding to the rescue of the fifteen-man crew of the thirty-nine-ton *Genyo Maru*. It seems that a swordfish rammed the vessel amidships and she was sinking.

The U.S.N.S. *Mission Capistrano* was conducting acoustical research not far south of Bermuda in 1962 when her instrumental lines were attacked by a 300-pound Swordfish *(Xiphias)*. The animal rammed its spear about a foot into tightly braided line. When the line was pulled aboard, not even the fish's 300 pounds pulled it loose as it hung suspended above the water. The whole performance suggests great force and commendable accuracy on the part of the fish.

There are many more such reports of various billed or beaked fish (black marlin, blue marlin, Pacific blue marlin, silver marlin, striped marlin, white marlin, Atlantic sailfish, Pacific sailfish, and swordfish) becoming involved with human beings or their enterprises. Dories get run through in dozens of reports. Whether or not thirty-nine-ton vessels are really sunk by these animals is somewhat difficult to determine, but they certainly are powerful creatures with a formidable weapon. It is a fact that the crew members on big-game-fish charter boats are careful when handling hooked specimens. More than one man has been badly injured when he misjudged the direction of an infuriated captive's lunge.

The big fish with beaks are in far more danger from man than man is from them. Care is suggested, however, when live specimens are handled or otherwise encountered. They are huge and powerful animals. The Black Marlin *(Makaira)* is known to exceed 1,500 pounds and fourteen feet in length. The Pacific Sailfish *(Istiophorus greyi)* can exceed ten feet and 225 pounds. The International Game Fish Association's record Swordfish *(Xiphias gladius)* is 1,182 pounds, and measures 14 feet, 11¼ inches.

The seas and oceans cover nearly three-fourths of our planet. When the ponds, streams, lakes, rivers, and swamps are added, a vast area is found to be under water. Much of this water teems with life in seemingly endless variety. Some of these forms grow to be very large, many are equipped for self-defense, and some are prone to attack. From time to time, from place to place, there is bound to be a measure of hazard. It is wrong, though, to think of the world of water as a totally hostile environment. It makes good sense to be careful and to know the ways of the forms likely to be encountered. While common sense won't keep a needlefish from jumping out and impaling you, it will go a long, long way toward reducing whatever hazards do exist.

Part V The Invertebrates

22   Insects

The insects of the world outnumber the mammals both in variety and numbers by margins that are absolutely astounding. There are more species of insects than all other animal and plant species combined. Insects outnumber us to a degree that is quite impossible to comprehend; they even *outweigh* man. There are more insects in ten square miles of Arctic tundra than there are mammals in all of North America. There are probably places where one square mile would satisfy this claim.

The insect is the dominant life form on our planet. We need them to pollinate plants on which we depend, but they need us for nothing, although they use us mercilessly. We kill them by the billions but can't make a dent in their strength, while they make human habitation impossible, or at least extremely difficult, in vast areas of badly needed land. In relation to overall world population, they kill more of us than we do of them each year. While it is true the majority of human deaths resulting from insects are due to the diseases they transmit, many insects are capable of causing sickness and death directly.

The earliest known insects appeared more than 275 million years ago; how much more we cannot say because these frail creatures do not fossilize well. Maintaining certain basic characteristics (antennae, six legs, fourteen postcephalic segments, etc.) they diversified and specialized until today there are probably close to a million species. It is only possible to guess at the numbers left to be described but there are, at the very least, tens of thousands. The range of this subphylum is universal;

some insects are marine and live entirely in the sea, no desert is known to be without them, and a wingless, degenerate mosquito is the largest land animal on the six-million-square-mile Antarctic continent. Man knows no natural environment not known better and longer by insects. They utilize every imaginable form of food, reproduce at a rate almost impossible to believe, and are terribly destructive. Indeed, they have inherited the earth!

There is a great temptation to refer to the social structures of many insect forms, but we have to be realistic and refrain from doing so here. In fact, just about all we can do is to pick examples of the particularly dangerous or harmful types and examine their potential threat. We must do this in rather random fashion and the reader must not look on this chapter as being comprehensive. It is indicative only of known troublesome groups, and those which *directly* cause injury or death.

The order Diptera, the fourth largest of the insect orders, contains more than 60,000 species. Best known are the various gnats, flies, and mosquitoes. We need not enlarge on the fact that some hundreds of the species in this order carry disease, often lethally so. *Simulium columbaczense*, a gnat of Central Europe, reportedly has caused death by attacking persistently in swarms and entering body orifices. Death, however, probably followed a generally weakened condition from blood loss.

In some areas, swarms of mosquitoes are so thick that people are blinded by them. Fliers downed in mangrove swamps are believed to have suffered such a fate. Many people are allergic to the "sting" of the mosquito and suffer terribly.

The true flies (Diptera) of the world are carriers of disease as well as suckers of blood. They are found everywhere man is found and constitute an ever present menace. Vast areas in Africa are considered virtually uninhabitable because of the Tsetse Fly (*Glossina*), carrier of the dreaded sleeping sickness. With its permanent damage to the nervous system, the disease is one of the greatest deterrents to progress in some areas in Africa.

There are many species of parasitic and obnoxious biting flies that make areas in South America virtually uninhabitable. Blood poisoning is not an uncommon result of the continued bites of many species.

Some flies are damaging to eyesight and blindness is directly attributable to them in some parts of the world. As for the obnoxious qualities of certain flies, ask any New Englander about the black fly that frequents beach areas. Their bites can all but drive you wild, and infections are common. The no-see-ums of American Indian fame are another group out of hundreds that harass man on every continent except Antarctica. In fact, if I were to choose the group of animals, out of all the animals in the world, that was most consistently dangerous to man, I would choose flies. They bite, they are parasites, and they spread disease—at least forty diseases seriously damaging to man!

The Screwworm Fly (Calligtroga americana) invades the nasal passages of humans, bores into the tissues, and there deposits its eggs. It has been reported by Dr. D. W. Micks and Dr. Victor C. Colma that "The developing larvae inflict serious injury which often results in death in a matter of days." The eyes, ears, and mouth are also attacked. Mortality is reportedly as high as 13 percent. One case will serve to illustrate: An itinerant laborer was hospitalized in Texas with a temperature of 103 degrees. Examination revealed that the patient's nose and throat were infested with mature larvae. Nearly two hundred were removed. This particularly distasteful problem is not as rare as might be thought. In the southwestern United States it is a real health menace, and undoubtedly much more so in tropical parts of the world with other species involved.

Conenose Bugs (Triatoma sp.), also the Kissing Bug, Bellow's Bug, Walpai Tiger, Cross Bug, and others are suckers of blood and will feed on human beings. About 5 percent of the people bitten develop allergic reactions that include symptoms up to and including shock and coma. Other species of the kissing bug group (family Reduviidae) from tropical areas are reported to be much more offensive, and appear to be disease carriers as well. These forms seldom attack people while they are awake but move in to feed after dark. Like scorpions, they often hide in bedding during the day.

In Israel, scientists at Hebrew University in Jerusalem are studying Holotrichius innesi, a true bug and relative to the bedbug. Known only from limited desert areas, this insect is believed to be one of the most venomous animals on earth. One scientist at the university, when questioned by the author during a visit there to photograph the animal, said its bite was to the cobra what the cobra was to the mosquito. The females have large, flat venom glands that take up much of the body cavity. It is believed (but has not yet been proved) that many human fatalities formally attributed to snakes and scorpions can, in fact, be laid at this animal's door. Its Hebrew coloquial name is afrur, which means "dirt." It refers to the animal's habit of kicking sand up over itself when it is come upon in the open. At the same time it secretes a kind of glue that makes the sand adhere to it, giving it nearly perfect camouflage. Desert nomads must have known this bug for millennia but it is only now that we are coming to realize something of its venomous potential. If an insect can escape attention for that long in one of the cradles of Western civilization, what surprising insects await discovery or at least full examination in Amazonia, the Himalayas, or

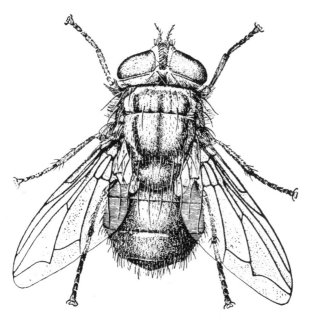

The screwworm fly (*Callitroga americana*) bores into the human nasal passage and deposits its eggs. People so infected can die as a result—possible mortality rate may exceed 13 percent.
Courtesy U.S. Dept. of Agriculture

Holotrichius innesi from the Sinai Desert may be one of the most deadly venomous animals on earth. Its probable potential has only recently been realized at Hebrew University in Jerusalem, where work is still in progress. The more dangerous female is on the right.
Photograph by Roger A. Caras

the middle of the Namib Desert? The story of *afrur*, as it unfolds, is very revealing. When it comes to really understanding the insects we have a long way to go.

There are a number of moths that strangely enough are troublesome to man in the caterpillar stage, if not as adults. In July 1961, the National Safety Council warned in its booklet, "Caterpillar Is Health Menace," that there were 2,130 reported stings in southeastern Texas alone in the summer of 1958. In fifty-four Texas victims in sixteen cities, Dr. Micks found 80 percent had been involved with *Megalopyge opercularis*, the caterpillar of the puss moth or tree asp. Reactions to contact ranged from a slight rash to shock. Fainting, nausea, and vomiting were common. Severe shooting pains were noted in a number of patients. Far from Texas—in Europe, Africa, and Asia—other species of moth and caterpillar cause distress to thousands annually. *Automeris io*, *Euproctis* sp., *Suana concolor*, and *Dendrolimus* sp. are a few of the species known to be involved.

Although I have never heard of a human death from contact with a caterpillar, and although most species are perfectly harmless, some few can variously annoy or disable even healthy adults. Individual sensitivity is the determining factor, whether you get a slight rash or end up in an oxygen tent in a hospital. The venom of the caterpillar is administered by sharp hairlike structures often concealed in its "wool." Each hair has its own venom supply, sometimes from only a single cell, and contact is enough to cause envenomation. The symptoms, as suggested above, run the gamut, as do degrees of sensitivity, which apparently is increased by exposure. The hairs that conduct the venom come in many shapes and sizes.

Writing of the Bushmen of Africa's Kalahari Desert in *National Geographic*, Elizabeth Marshall Thomas captioned a photograph of an arrow, "Crushing a beetle pupa, a hunter rubs its juice behind the arrowhead. One drop kills a man if it enters the bloodstream."

The beetle involved was *Diamphidia simplex* and the pupae are found encased in earth beneath infested Marula trees. So powerful a toxin would suggest further research into the order Coleoptera, the beetles. This is the largest order of insects. Much remains to be learned about this group and if the story of the *Diamphidia* pupa is correct, the investigation may prove to be both exciting and medically worthwhile.

Our discussion of insects dangerous to man has been limited thus far to the minor kinds, but now we must look to the true villains—the order Hymenoptera—the social insects, the ants, wasps, hornets, bees, and their allies.

The ants of the world (superfamily Formicoidea) are among the most amazing creatures known. Their social organizations are as complex as any on earth, their varieties seemingly endless, and their numbers astronomical. The destructive capabilities of ants can be positively cyclonic in effect. The army ants of the New World and the driver ants (subfamily Dorylinae) of Africa are much feared and gruesome, and improbable stories of their forays are endless.

The African forms particularly are reputed to be lethal; literally consuming everything in their path as they emigrate from one breeding ground to another. It is easy to see how humans *could* be consumed if overrun and borne down by thousands of these biting insects but I have been unable to obtain any documented evidence of this having occurred. In South America, the appearance of a column of Army Ants *(Eciton burchelli)* is reputedly welcomed by the natives, who evacuate the area temporarily and then return to homes free of vermin.

The marching—wandering of these ant columns of various species is apparently cyclic, with static periods intervening between nomadic exoduses. The timing is believed to be a matter of ovaries and not of appetite. The ripening of the queen causes the wandering to stop long enough for a cycle of egg-laying and hatching. Once the column is on the move again, everything before it must flee or be consumed. It seems likely that a wounded hunter, an abandoned child, a feeble old-timer (or an enemy staked out for the purpose!) must, from time to time, have fallen victim somewhere along the line. The study of these foraging hordes is fascinating, and not the least interesting aspect of it is the idea that, in special conditions, they are possibly dangerous to man.

Many reports indicate that some South American species split their columns into what amounts to a pincer movement. Caught in the middle of such a maneuver any animal not covered with extremely dense fur would be in serious difficulties. The African driver ants, on the other hand, move on fronts up to two miles wide, according to a number of reports, and the line may be several miles long. These millions upon millions of *Bashukoy,* as they are called in some areas, constitute a formidable problem for humans in their path. Since these movements are usually nocturnal, serious problems to human inhabitants almost certainly arise. Reports from The United Republic of Cameroon are particularly common. The author has seen a lot of ants in Africa, and has been bitten by more than a few, but he has yet to encounter one of these fabled hoards.

A number of ants bite, notably those of the genus *Solenopsis* in the United States. They can be a real handicap to agricultural field workers. Tropical fire ants,* the Australian bulldog ant, and dozens more can give a vicious bite and also sting.

*Stinging Argentine fire ants are now endemic in a dozen states in the South, where they are all but impossible to eradicate.

Dr. D. W. Micks has been conducting a study in Texas of insects and other arthropods of medical importance. A report covering a five-year period (1954–1959) appeared in a 1960 issue of *Texas Reports on Biology and Medicine*. On ants, Dr. Micks reported:

> Twenty-five physicians in twenty-one communities treated a total of seventy-five cases of ant sting. Twenty-seven of these patients were stung by a large red ant, two by Fire Ants and the identity of the remainder is unknown. . . . Twelve (16 per cent) of the . . . cases were characterized by systemic responses to the sting. Anaphylactic shock was the most prominent feature in five . . . and was accompanied in three instances by asthmatic rales, edema of the face, lips and glottis, and a massive generalized urticarial reaction. Fainting and/or vomiting, abdominal cramping . . . were present in the remaining cases. . . .

For *some* people, at least, the sting of ants may be a dangerous matter.

In his *A Texbook of Pathology*, Robert A. Moore commented, "In an occasional person bitten by a bee or a wasp, death results within 30 minutes, frequently within 5 minutes. At autopsy there are edema of the lungs and petechiae in the adrenal and in the serous membranes."

Writing of his adventures in the forests of India, Kenneth Anderson noted in 1961, "Twice more we cross the stream that snakes alongside the track. At the eighth milestone we pass the hamlet of Kundukottai, overshadowed by a rocky hill noted for two things—panthers and the large rock-bee. And remember that of these the bees are far more dangerous when really roused."*

The story can be told in statistics: during the years 1950–1954, seventy-one people in the United States were killed by venomous snakes while eighty-six were killed by hymenopterous insects—one by ants, and eighty-five by bees, wasps, and hornets. Bees alone accounted for fifty-two. Only three of the seventy-one snakebite victims died in the first hour while sixty-six of the eighty-six Hymenoptera victims did. The American Medical Association reports that bees and wasps claim a minimum of seventeen lives a year in the United States alone. One researcher (Dr. Henry M. Parrish) believes many deaths from poisonous stings are erroneously attributed to heart attacks, heat stroke, and other causes. It has been suggested a number of times that otherwise unaccountable automobile accidents, cases where cars traveling normally suddenly go out of control and crash into bridge abut-

---

*At the historical rock fortress of Sigiriya on Sri Lanka the author noted cages along the paths large enough to hold six or more people. A sign on each cage reads "In Case of Bees." It is to these cages people retreat when the great rock bees are on the warpath.

ments, are actually caused by drivers going into shock after being stung by a wasp or bee.

No matter how you approach the subject—medically, statistically, or otherwise—bees, wasps, and hornets can be dangerous to man. Spiders, scorpions, and reptiles combined fail to take as many lives in most years in the United States as these creatures. Many times as many people suffer agonizing pain as actually succumb.

The very large, yellow and black *Geting* of Sweden, a wasp, is reputed to give an extremely painful sting. The giant red bee, found over much of South America, is said to kill even the jaguar. Similar reports come from all over the world, especially tropical regions.

Most people suffer a bee sting sooner or later, and it may be difficult for a person not particularly sensitive to the venom to understand all the fuss over such a seemingly simple occurrence. First of all, it is not a simple matter. A wasp or bee, weighing less than one-one hundredth of an ounce, injects a relatively large dose of dangerous matter. There are inflammatory and stupefying substances, a convulsant factor and various enzymes, and formic acid is sometimes present. This mixture of glandular substances is injected through hollow shafts. The venom alone is powerful enough to account for severe local and general reactions. There is considerable variation between the venoms of different species of Hymenoptera so that some people are sensitive to certain species but not to others. The pharmacological action of some of these hymenopteral venoms is similar to that of cobra venom.

An example of a reaction will illustrate the severity that can be encountered: In 1960 an adult male was stung by two wasps in Baltimore, once on the face and once on the neck. Eight hours later he had a temperature of 105 degrees and had become mentally disoriented. His limbs were twitching by the time he was brought to the hospital. Despite all emergency and follow-up treatment available, it was seven days before his fever could be cracked and before his mentality started to improve. He was one of the *lucky* sensitives—he might have died.

Even for persons not particularly sensitive, the danger can be real. The following medical report is extracted from an article by M. F. Koszalka in the *Bulletin of the U.S. Army Medical Department*:

A patient, a 25-year-old officer, had received innumerable bee stings after he jumped off a ledge during a scout patrol and landed in the midst of a swarm of bees. He tried to scramble away as thousands of bees began to sting him and crawl over his body, into his ears, nose and mouth, but he fell to the ground from exhaustion and lost consciousness. When he came to, he was violently ill, with vomiting and urinary and fecal incontinence. Bees were still swarming over him and he was too weak to move. He was found several hours later . . . on admission his temperature was 101.8 . . .

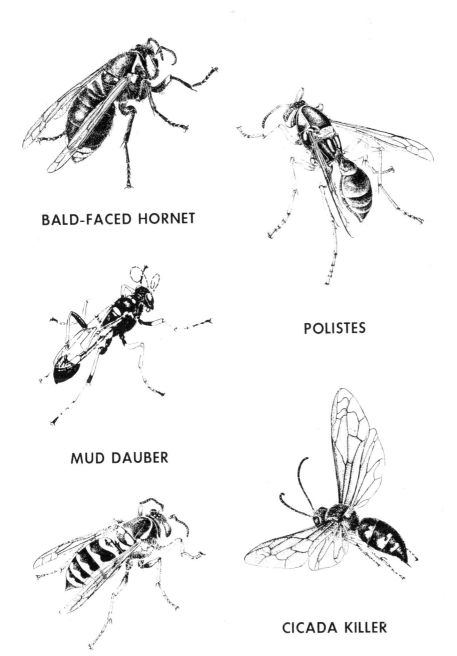

BALD-FACED HORNET

POLISTES

MUD DAUBER

YELLOW JACKET

CICADA KILLER

Garden variety wasps from a U.S. government pamphlet on wasp control. Wasps, unlike bees, do not die after using their envenomating apparatus. Older and more primitive than bees, wasps are predators.
Courtesy U.S. Dept. of Agriculture

all exposed surfaces of his body were inflamed . . . and covered with bee stingers . . . unable to open his eyes, could barely speak, and complained of constricting pain in his throat. His urine was red brown . . . over 300 stingers were extracted from the patient's eyelids, ears, tongue, lips, face, neck and the backs of the hands and wrists; another 300 from the diffusely swollen scalp.

The patient obviously was not sensitive or he could never have survived.

In many parts of the world (Malaya, India, and Africa) there are bees and hornets which are extremely aggressive. It is all but impossible to work in their vicinity without being attacked, and that first, burning stab can be the least important aspect of the sting, as we have seen. In other parts of the world, stings are rare and of little concern to all but the most hypersensitive. It is true that bees, hornets, and wasps, when aroused, will chase and attack a man, singly or in swarms. Pursuit can be relentless and the danger great.

The bees of the world are of enormous importance. Some experts believe that their underground activity in many areas does more to loosen, mix, and aerate soil than the earthworms! Many plants important to man are dependent on bees for pollination. Parasitic wasps are one of the best natural controls of many plant-eating pests. The production of honey and wax and their subsequent uses by man are well known. Life on this planet would be unthinkable without bees and wasps, so here at least is one dangerous animal group we must learn to live with.

We shall always have bees, wasps, and hornets around us. They are important and, for the most part, not particularly harmful. Anyone can be careful in his dealings with wasp nests or beehives. People who suspect that they are sensitive should inquire about the possibility of desensitization.

The billions of insects on this planet (harmless, destructive, and dangerous alike) pose one of the greatest enigmas facing man in his unending effort to control his environment. He may one day (indeed, unfortunately he probably will) kill every bear, wolf, and big cat left in the wild, but at best, man can only strive for a livable balance with the insects. In order to kill them he would have to commit suicide with his own insecticides. Insect generations are so rapid they can develop immunity to our poisons eons before we can.

23 Spiders and Scorpions

Arthropoda, a phylum of the animal kingdom of the utmost importance to man, is a vast network of life, including as it does the insects, arachnids, crustaceans, centipedes, and several other related forms.

The arachnids encompass a wide variety of animals, including the scorpions, the spiders, mites, ticks, harvestmen, and a number of less common types. The mites and ticks are important to man because they are often vectors of disease. Relapsing fever, typhus, scrub typhus, and Rocky Mountain spotted fever are among the known diseases which they carry. The animals themselves, however, are harmless to man. Only the microorganisms they play host to can kill our kind; and so, by the frame of reference we have established for this book, we must pass them by. The spiders and scorpions, on the other hand, can be dangerous on their own.

Arachnidism is defined as poisoning or envenomation by the bite or sting of a venomous arachnid. Only spiders and scorpions, among the arachnids, and only relatively few of them, are dangerously venomous to man. The bites of certain other arachnids may be extremely dangerous to some few persons, but the reactions, however acute, are best described as allergic.

Arachnids lack the insects' paired wings, and are without the antenna system so characteristic of the class Insecta. All are air-breathing, and their distribution falls barely short of universal. The spiders alone range from high altitudes, where they have been caught, windblown, in the scoops attached to the wings of aircraft, to the littoral zones of the sea, into the shallow depths of which they descend, taking captive air down with them in bubbles. They are an ancient, adaptable, rapidly reproducing, and altogether successful animal group.

The true spiders belong to the order Araneae, although the daddy longlegs, or harvestmen (order Phalangida), and the so-called sun spiders (order Solpugida) are popularly thought of as spiders as well; just as spiders in general are popularly and erroneously thought of as insects, or "bugs." The distinction is quite real, however, and no spider, true or otherwise, is an insect in any sense of the word.

Just about all spiders are venomous—that is how they paralyze and kill their prey, which is often very much larger than themselves. Very few spiders, however, have fangs long enough, or venom toxic enough, to endanger the health of man. Very few can administer a bite anywhere near as dangerous or painful as the sting of a wasp or a bee. Some few, as we shall see, can be exceedingly dangerous.

Spiders have the power to give people the *creeps* second only, perhaps, to snakes. They are feared and hated far beyond their power to do harm. As a matter of fact, they are useful animals, doing infinitely more good than harm. They destroy nothing, and in no way compete with man for food. They constitute a valuable natural control on insects. However, those few that are capable of injuring man are well worth avoiding. The pain and rigid muscle cramps that follow their bites contribute to one of the most agonizing experiences a person can undergo.

In the United States, the genus *Latrodectus* contains the species potentially most lethal to man. First and foremost is the Black Widow (*L. mactans*). The female of the species is the deadly one, and the bite while seldom fatal, can be excruciatingly painful. It is rather like getting a charley horse all through the extremities and the abdomen. The species is well distributed throughout the United States, being more common in the rural South than elsewhere, and extends down through Mexico and Central America into South America. It is found in vacant lots in big cities. Many of the islands of the West Indies have them, as does Hawaii. Close relatives give rise to human injury, but rarely death, in areas around the world: *L. tredecimguttatus* in the Mediterranean periphery, *L. hasselti* in Australia, New Zealand, New Caledonia and other South Pacific Islands, and *L. indistinctus* in South Africa are examples of troublesome species.

In their excellent study, *The Black Widow: America's Most Poisonous Spider*, Thorp and Woodson list all of the known cases of injuries and deaths caused by the black widow in the United States between 1726 and 1943. In that 218-year period there were recorded 1,291 bites, 55 of which were known to have proved fatal. The list is almost certainly incomplete. Two subspecies were involved in the cases recorded. There is now an antivenin for black widow envenomation. For the 218 years covered by the Thorp and Woodson study there was not.

There appear to be three subspecies of the black widow in the United States (*L. m. mactans, m. texanus,* and *m. hesperus*) and there may be a difference in toxicity, but the general effect and the mechanism of the bite are the same. The venom is produced in glands in the cephalothorax, and passes by exceedingly slender ducts running through the upper segments of the chelicerae into the two fangs. The venom is introduced by a stab, not a sting or real bite, as no jaw mechanism is involved—the spiders' mouthparts are devised for sucking. It is a small, shiny black creature with a bright red mark, often in the shape of an hourglass, on the underside of the larger segment of the body.

The black widow is essentially (but *not* exclusively) a rural animal and there are bound to be more bites in underdeveloped areas where plumbing is more primitive. The little house with the half-moon cut into the door is a favorite haunt of the shoe-button, as the black widow is often called. (In 1944, as a medical aid man in the Massachusetts National Guard, the author, then sixteen, was called upon to treat a young man who had used a condemned outdoor privy. He had been bitten on the penis by a black widow spider and was in very deep distress by the time an ambulance reached our bivouac area. He survived but at one point was hoping not to.)

The black widow is not a deliberate foe of man. In fact, it is shy and retiring like most spiders. If trapped in your shoe by your foot it will, of course, attempt to defend itself. The relatively large number of cases reported from outdoor privies have occurred because of the creature's poor eyesight. Like all web-spinners, it responds automatically to vibrations set up by prey in collision with its net. It attacks at the place where the disturbance occurs. Privies generally boast a large insect population, and it is quite natural that there the black widow builds its webs. Humans are painfully vulnerable in this domain.

There are five other species found in the United States which have serious effects on man. All are second to the black widow, although two are closely related:

L. geometricus—the brown widow or gray widow, found in southern Florida and *perhaps* in southern California. Resembles the black widow in size and markings, although the characteristic hourglass is orange rather than red. Abdominal markings are bold and colorful. It ranges into Central and South America, the West Indies, Pacific Islands, Afric, Australia, and India. It is apparently much less likely to bite than its cousin, and the effects of its venom, while marked, are not known to be fatal to man.

L. bishopi—believed to be limited to the southern half of Florida. It resembles the brown widow and was once thought to be a variety or subspecies of the black widow. Bites are rare and milder than those of the black widow, although generally similar.

Loxosceles reclusa—a long-legged, medium-sized, brownish creature. Common in Missouri, the brown recluse or fiddleback spider is now known to be spreading all across the country—inside clothing and furniture on moving vans! It is a "house spider." The bite feels rather like the sting of a bee, but the effects are much more pronounced. While fever and chills testify to a systemic effect, the main cause of concern is the local damage. Necrotic tissue forms despite medication and infections are common. It is a nasty affair at best, and seven human deaths have been recorded.

Chiracanthium inclusum—a very small spider (about one-third of an inch long) with a neurotoxic bite. The male is venomous as well as the female, although neither is apt to bite except under most unusual circumstances. Reports of incidents are very rare. This greenish-white spider occurs over much of the United States.

C. diversum—common in Hawaii, is apparently more prone to bite than its near-relative *inclusum*. The bite of this diminutive creature is painful but not known to be deadly. The case widely reported in 1956 of a woman who died after being bitten was an unfortunate coincidence. An autopsy revealed another cause of death not associated with the bite.

As a boy working in a grocery store, I heard many tales about the fearful, hairy tarantula. Every banana delivery occasioned stories of stowaway spiders leaping out of the great stalks of yellow-and-green fruit to administer an immediately lethal bite. Such stories persist today and appear to be generally accepted. In fact, the tarantulas (family Aviculariidae—the "bird-eating spiders") are calm, docile, mildly venomous animals of no appreciable menace to man. A bee sting is at least as painful and frequently more dangerous than the rare bite of one of these interesting creatures.

The family Aviculariidae is comprised of approximately 600 species, about 300 of which are now customarily called tarantulas. About 10 percent of these 300 live in the southwestern part of the United States. The other 270 species find homes in Central and South America, many Caribbean islands, several large areas of Africa, Australia, India, and on Madagascar, New Guinea, and Sri Lanka.

The real tarantulas (family Tarantulidae) are not even spiders but

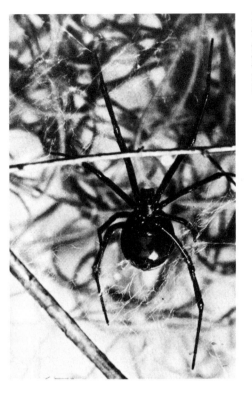

Latrodectus mactans, the black widow, is truly the most seriously venomous spider in the world. The dangerous female is shown here with the typical red-to-orange hourglass marking on the underside of her abdomen.
Photograph from The Lower Animals

The dangerous brown recluse or fiddleback spider whose range in the United States is being extended by the activities of man. Usually offering a sublethal bite, this species is believed to have caused human deaths in seven cases.
Courtesy U.S. Dept. of Agriculture

constitute a separate order of arachnids known as the Pedipalpi or (one of the) whip scorpions. They are short-bodied, flat, and have exceedingly long limbs, the first pair of which are carried like those of a praying mantis, but horizontally, and are grasping devices, while the second pair form long whip-shaped feelers. They are the worldwide distribution in the tropics, subtropics, and some warmer temperate areas. They are in no way a menace to man.

However, this is not all there is to this confusion of terms, for there is also a true spider popularly known as the tarantula to a considerable segment of humanity since long before animals were first named and classified in the modern scientific manner. This is a southern European spider named *Lycosa narbonensis*, whose bite has been known since Roman times to be toxic. However, these effects were greatly exaggerated in the Middle Ages, resulting in the most extraordinary outbreaks of mass hysteria. This took the form of wild and furious dancing, ultimately to specially composed music, which was called the *Tarantella*. The name derived from the south Italian city of Taranto where, in ancient times, continuous dancing was advocated as the only cure for the bite of a tarantula spider and which, if not kept up till the symptoms had subsided, would result in death. This dancing however became infectious, resulting in the strange hysteria called tarantism. How much the spider eventually had to do with all this nonsense is moot.

The French entomologist Fabre conducted studies on this spider and found that its bite was instantaneously fatal to insects but that a young sparrow took three days to die, while a large mole succumbed in thirty-six hours. His conclusion was that a human being bitten by this species would be seriously affected and should take all measures possible, be they traditional or scientific, to counteract them. The *Lycosa* are the long-legged spiders usually called wolf spiders or house spiders. How the name first became transferred to the much-less-dangerous hairy spiders (Aviculariidae) is not known; however, it is now firmly established.

The avicularid tarantula spiders are long-lived and cannibalistic. They may live close to each other in some areas, but not in colonies. Each reigns over a separate domain that may range from a nest in a tall tree, for some species, to a hole in the ground two feet deep for others.

When attacked, a tarantula rises on its four hind legs and offers its fangs to the intruder. The venom is very mild. Professor William J. Baerg, who spent more than thirty years studying these animals, tested the venom of twenty-six species, twelve of the tests on himself. He states in his book, *The Tarantula*, that, "All the species in the United States, as far as I have been able to determine, are harmless to man."

Some from the tropics can cause painful local reactions, but none are known to be deadly to man except, perhaps, in cases of massive anaphylactic shock.*

Australia has three spiders known to be at least harmful to man: the relative of the black widow, the Red Back (*L. hasselti*), and the Funnel-Web Spiders (*Atrax robustus* and *A. formidabilis*). The red back has been known to cause death, particularly in small children. It is, however, a shy animal, most frequently involved in human injuries in outdoor privies. Worth avoiding, it is seldom a menace. There have been enough bites, though, to justify the development and production of an antivenene** by the Commonwealth Serum Laboratories.

South Africa reports injuries, and a few deaths, from *Latrodectus indistinctus* and *L. geometricus*. A species of the genus *Harpactirella* (probably *lightfotti*) is also reportedly troublesome. It is difficult to tell which species caused the few reported deaths, although the natives fear the so-called *Knoppiespinnekop*, or button spider. It is the common name for the female of *L. indistinctus*.

It is not necessary or even possible to catalog the spiders of the world, but the same general rules seem to apply nearly everywhere that venomous forms are to be found. Spiders are useful destroyers of insects, seldom aggressive toward man unless interfered with (and not even always then), are rarely dangerous and seldom deadly. Very few species can possibly kill a human. Unfortunately, fatal cases generally involve small children. If you are to be in an area where venomous spiders exist, learn to know them and then to avoid them. Be careful about using primitive toilet facilities and other areas with a thick concentration of insect life. You stand very little chance of becoming the victim of a spider if you observe these rules. British scientists have calculated that an acre of pastureland may have a spider population of 2.25 million. The number of "exposures" a person must realize in a lifetime must be astronomical, yet even minor injury is extremely rare. If it ever happens, the chances are you will be thankful it wasn't a wasp or bee!

The scorpions, order Scorpionida, are of great antiquity and were almost surely the first terrestrial arachnids. They are venomous, nocturnal, solitary creatures found in all the warm regions of the world. They are particularly abundant in deserts, but are sparsely represented in the temperate zones. They are extremely adaptable and can stand fierce,

---

*Anaphylactic shock is an exceedingly dangerous reaction to a foreign substance due to individual sensitivity. It is an ultimate allergic reaction and can prove fatal in seconds.
**Antivenene is the British (and Australian) spelling of antivenin.

A large West African scorpion of undetermined species, showing perfect scorpion "conformation." The final series of segments so often referred to as the tail actually belong to the abdomen. This is a typical "at ready" stance.
Photograph by Chris and Barbara Hansen

The dangerously venomous Indian scorpion, *Palamneus gravimanus*, eating a cockroach. Note the length of the stinger at the tip of the last abdominal segment.

An animal that *looks* as if it must be dangerous, but isn't—a wolf spider, only mildly venomous and not at all harmful to man. The nightmarish aspects of these animals when seen close up create an altogether false impression.

burning heat. There are about 650 species in 6 families. Some are very dangerous to man.

The venom apparatus of the scorpion is situated at the tip of its five-segmented "tail," actually part of its abdomen. There is a single sharp stinger at the end with two exceedingly small orifices. Two relatively large venom glands feed these openings. In animals like the seven-inch African scorpion *Pandinus imperator*, the sting is huge and the venom plentiful. The lobster scorpion of Sumatra is even larger but, being a shy denizen of the deep forest, has never, to my knowledge, been indicted for stinging a human. The pincers, or pedipalps, are harmless. The real danger represented by these animals is their practice of entering human habitations. The scorpion-in-the-boot-in-the-morning is an old tale for most adventure story readers. It is often quite true.

The scorpion, from the human point of view, is far more insidious than the spider. The scorpion regularly establishes itself in beds, closets, bureaus, shoes, under carpets, in furniture—in short, just about everywhere in and around human dwellings. In the open, they are found under bark, leaves, and rocks. They crawl in the open at night, and turn up with startling and dangerous regularity in houses and even vehicles. Living in an area where they are common can be hazardous for the careless and unobservant. Insecticides are generally effective against all species and are often used with excellent results in limited enclosed areas. It is a useful practice to keep children's beds and cribs away from walls, with the legs of nursery furniture standing in cans of kerosene. Children, of course, are much more vulnerable to a venomous sting.

The United States has about 40 of the nearly 650 known species. These forty range from harmless, to pain-producing, to deadly. Only two North American species generally fall into the last category: *Centruroides sculpturatus* and *C. gertschi*, both found in the extreme Southwest. Dr. Herbert L. Stahnke, former director of the Poisonous Animals Research Laboratory at Arizona State University, reports that Arizona alone suffered sixty-four human deaths from these two animals in one twenty-year period. The peak month was July, indicating, perhaps, the peak month for outdoor activities.

Scorpions, like spiders, are found around the world, but most commonly in the tropics. More species of scorpions than spiders, however, are dangerous to man and the problem is very much greater. While the stab of a dangerous spider is rare, the sting of a deadly scorpion is rather more common. In North America, principally in the United States and Mexico, many more people are killed by scorpions than by snakes.

Belo Horizonte is the capital of Minas Gerais State in Brazil. At an altitude of over 3,000 feet, it has a population of about 1.5 million. In 1954 alone, more than 171 people received emergency medical treatment after being stung by scorpions. Algerians suffer more from scorpions than snakes, and the Sudanese species *Leiurus cinquestriatus* is worse than many dangerous reptiles. Several Indian species are decidedly dangerous, as are a number of other African forms. New Zealand and Oceania are uniquely free of this problem.

Frequently, the scorpion population is very dense around human habitations. One catch, which was described by Dr. P. J. Deoras of the Haffkine Institute in Bombay as "casual," turned up 14,903 specimens, in an area with only 13,000 human inhabitants. A thorough search would have undoubtedly turned up many times that number. While camping in the Mocamedes and Namib deserts in Angola, the author and his wife frequently found themselves in areas heavily infested with scorpions. At night they would be encountered every few feet and often closer than that. The author had to treat a teen-ager who sat on one with a bare bottom, resulting in a stiff leg for twenty-four hours but no other serious effect. Not just a little showmanship was expected in the treatment, and provided. After "dosing" the young man with antihistaminics the author attached an aspirin to the site of the wound with a Band-Aid. This visible "treatment" was much appreciated.

It may be of value to review a case of scorpion sting. Dr. Deoras reported the following medical history in *Probe*, in 1961. The incident occurred in Ichalkaranji, India, two years earlier. The offending animal was *Palamneus* sp. The report below is condensed to some degree:

A girl aged 15 years was admitted . . . about 1½ hours after a scorpion bite. She was . . . in a collapsed condition, pulseless, perspiring profusely, skin cold and clammy, and having chills. She had vomited 4–5 times soon after the bite, and was complaining of burning sensation in the abdomen. Immediately an injection of coramine, glucose 25% 100 cc, and calcium gluconate 10% 10 cc was given. She felt a little better and the pulse was felt at the wrist. Soon after she began to shiver again and her pulse became imperceptible. . . . Then, adrenaline 0.5 cc was given . . . in addition . . . an antihistaminic, but the perspiration and shivering continued . . . sweating so profuse that clothes had to be changed every ½ hour. When her shivering became less, hypertonic saline was started. Since admission, oxygen was given . . . and it was observed that the patient was mentally quite clear and answered all the questions. Perspiration continued and she began to get difficulty in breathing . . . went into respiratory distress, was restless and finally succumbed (15 hours after bite) with profuse frothy fluid coming out of the mouth and nostrils.

Certain centipedes (which are *not* arachnids but of the class Chilopoda) grow to large size, and some are dangerous to man. The southwestern deserts of the United States have *Scolopendra heros* which achieves six to eight inches and which gives a painful bite (not sting). It is not known to have caused fatalities. Venom produced in glands at the base of the jaw is introduced by a bite only.

Tropical Asiatic species grow to be nearly a foot in length and the bite is reportedly very severe. Cases in India and Burma have kept victims bedridden for as much as three months. A Malayan species (identity not known to the author) is said to be particularly dangerous, with symptoms more spectacular than from the bite of indigenous vipers.

Relatively little is known about many of the tropical centipedes, and caution is advised in dealing with them. Many are apparently harmless, some few administer a damaging bite, and some few may be far more dangerous yet. Some species of this class (Chilopoda) from Sri Lanka may similarly be particularly dangerous. Reports are confusing, often contradictory, but care is advisable in all cases where the species is not known to be harmless. Since more than 1,500 different kinds have been identified, all centipedes are best left alone by anyone not expert in their identification.

The 6,500 known millipedes of the world (class Diplopoda) differ from centipedes in several obvious ways. They are essentially vegetarians (centipedes are all believed to be carnivorous), and they have two pairs of legs on each body segment—about 200 legs in all (while centipedes have one pair of legs per body segment). They are not known to have a venomous bite and are generally safe to handle. They can secrete hydrocyanic acid which can cause a rash. Small animals are reportedly blinded by this acid. A species of the genus *Spirostreptus* found in the Sunda Islands, and a species of *Julus*, on Amboina Island, have been reported as venomous, although this seems doubtful at best. One or two species are feared in Malaya, but apparently without reason. Here again, reports are contradictory and information is lacking. It does appear, however, that most, if not all, of the world's many millipedes are harmless to man.

The so-called whip scorpions (not scorpions at all) are believed by many to be dangerous. However, they are not venomous and not dangerous to man. One of the *Uropygi*, the *Ecrebiche Bois* ("Crayfish of the Woods") found in Haiti, is feared because of its reputed habit of squirting acid. Also known as vinegaroons, these whip scorpions smell acidic and do secrete a noxious substance. Any real danger is to the eyes and is likely to occur only to woodcutters. Logwood once was

Haiti's principal export, and it was then that these animals obtained their reputation.

Certain "false spiders" (order Solpugida) *may* be troublesome, according to some reports. One large desert-dweller from North Africa is reported quite painful to encounter, and is commonly seen rearing its front parts off the sand in a fighting posture. Once again, unfortunately, specific information is lacking.

It has not been possible in this chapter to review all of the forms of the arachnids. The group is vast, worldwide, and not yet by any means completely known. Most are harmless, some are capable of a painful or even harmful bite, and a very few are really dangerous. Certain of the scorpions, as we have seen, kill more people than snakes in several parts of the world. Anyone visiting areas where venomous forms are found, and who anticipates field work, is urged to obtain as much information about them as possible. In many places, the sting or stab of an arachnid is the one dangerous animal eventuality worth considering.

24 Venomous Cones

In all the shapes in which you would expect to find an animal deadly to man, a delicate, beautifully colored seashell would seem to be the least likely. Nevertheless, there is such a danger. It is a lesson a few people, at least, have died learning.

The phylum Mollusca, a major division of the animal kingdom containing all of the so-called shellfish, is divided into six great classes: the Gastropoda (the whelks, snails, etc.—single-shelled animals); the Pelecypoda (clams, oysters, etc.—bivalves, or two-shelled animals); the Cephalopoda (nautilus, squid, cuttlefish, octopus—shell-less, or nearly so, for the most part); the Amphineura (the chitons or hinged shells); the Scaphopoda (tusk shells); and the Monoplacophora, only discovered in 1956. Most of these classes contain animals that are dangerous for man—*to eat*. But that is not our concern here. We are here interested in one class in this chapter containing animals that actually sting with a venom strong enough to kill a man.

The class Gastropoda (the snails and allies) contains thousands of species, many of the most interesting being in the order Prosobranchiata, and the family Conidae. There are between 400 and 500 species of Cone Shells (genus *Conus*), and all of them have a highly developed venom apparatus. These seashells are among the most beautiful and most sought after in the world. Collectors have paid highly for them at auction and one—the "Glory-of-the-Seas"—is worth up to $600 for a single good specimen. The cones are found in many of the world's tropical and subtropical waters, and are commonly found under coral

Two of the most deadly cone shells, side by side. The textile cone (*Conus textile*), top, and the geographer's cone (*Conus geographus*), bottom, are among the most seriously venomous of the approximately five hundred known species in this genus.

and rocks, or crawling about on or under sandy bottoms. The animals that construct and live in these delicately beautiful shells are shy and generally retire into their shell when disturbed. Handling live specimens can, however, cause a violent and shocking reaction.

The device used by the cone to administer its venom is unique. A fleshy snout, or proboscis, of surprising length is extended and pushed, suddenly, against the skin of the assailant. This snout contains a number of rigid, hollow, harpoonlike devices that are actually modified radula teeth—normally used by the snail for rasping its food. The dart—for that is what it most resembles—is thrust into the skin of the victim. Each dart or harpoon carries its own venom supply, having been previously "charged" by a complex of venom-producing tissues inside the animal deep inside the shell. It is a sophisticated, complicated system. The effects range from pain similar to that from a bee sting to death within four or five hours. The entire stinging process is rapid and usually takes place before the victim knows what has happened.

A person is unlikely to suffer the sting of a cone shell unless he actually picks one up and handles it without regard for the animal's soft parts, the shell itself, of course, being harmless. One can suppose that it would be possible to step on one and get stung, but in almost all of the cases reported the victim was a shell collector handling a live specimen. An occasional specimen brought up in a net could cause problems.

The U.S. Navy Diving Manual gives these animals a danger rating of 2 plus, putting them on a par with the octopus, groupers, and tiger, porbeagle, sand, Lake Nicaragua, and lemon sharks. Kohn, Saunders, and Wiener open their paper, "Preliminary Studies on the Venom of the Marine Snail Conus," with the statement, "One of the most virulent, but least studied of animal venoms is that produced by marine snails belonging to the genus Conus." Most contemporary literature in this field refers to the animal's deadly qualities, and there can be little doubt as to the danger inherent in handling living specimens. The venom is apparently a neurotoxin.

Dr. Alan J. Kohn reports ("Recent Cases of Human Injury Due to Venomous Marine Snails of the Genus Conus") that "twenty-five humans are known to have been stung as a result of handling cone-shells—and five have died!" A 20 percent mortality rate exceeds that of the common cobra and the rattlesnakes! Indeed, very few venomous animals cause such a high rate of death.

Hirataka Yasiro gave a detailed report of a fatal cone-shell bite that was translated by Dr. Joe Niiya of the U.S. Army's 406th Medical General Hospital:

Mr. Kamekichi Fujisato, age 32, eldest son of Kamato Fujisato, residing at 1126 Hechichiya, Katsuren-mura, Nakagami-gun was collecting seashells on the beach . . . when he was bitten. He was attended by a doctor, but died the same day. Mr. Kiyokage Asato was asked to obtain data from the local police box, town office, and physician concerning the accident. The shell was obtained from the town office, and forwarded to the author by Mr. Asato. This shell was damaged badly, but was clearly identifiable as *Conus geographus*. The length of the shell was 13.5 cm, rather large for the species in that district. On the day of the accident, Mr. Fujisato went to the beach to swim and collect seashells. He was collecting shells on the southeast beach, which faces Nakagusuku Bay, when the accident occurred at about 10 o'clock in the morning. Mr. Fujisato had picked up the shell, not realizing it was venomous. His friend, who did recognize the shell, shouted a warning, but Mr. Fujisato was stung on the thumb before he could drop the shell. He did not feel any pain at first, but when pain commenced, he began to walk towards the road which bordered the shore. This was about 15 chos distant [1 cho is about 119 yards]. Mr. Fujisato finally reached the road, but was not able to walk any further, and rolled into the potato field near the road. When the physician arrived the patient was still conscious, but was having difficulty in breathing. The pulse was slow, and the temperature was low, 36.7 degrees C. Soon after the arrival of the physician, the patient lost consciousness, and his extremities became purple-violet in color. He expired between 1400 and 1500 hours, about three or four hours after he had been stung. There was no swelling around the puncture mark on the thumb. The site of the sting appeared to have been scraped.

Dr. Kohn reports cases from the Moluccas, Melanesia, New Hebrides, New Caledonia, Tuamotu Islands, New Britain, Fiji, Japan, Australia, Seychelles, New Guinea, Hawaii, Marshall Islands, and Guam in the Marianas. Although Hawaii is in the central Pacific, and the Seychelles are far to the west in the Indian Ocean, most of the trouble has occurred in the western Pacific from Japan to Australia.

Dr. Halstead gives the symptoms of a cone's bite as: localized numbness, lack of blood supply, and bluish coloration of the skin. A sharp stinging or burning sensation may be experienced. Numbness and tingling, starting at the site of the wound, may spread rapidly and affect the entire body. It is particularly severe about the lips and mouth. Paralysis may set in with coma and eventual death, probably due to cardiac failure. The symptoms can, of course, be very much less severe and pass in a matter of minutes or hours.

Which of the four hundred cones are most dangerous to man? There is not too much latitude in the opinions of the experts whose findings appear in Table 15.

Kohn, in the summary of the paper cited above, notes, "All species of

Table 15. The Most Dangerous Cones

Scientific name	Common name	Range	Listed by[a]				
			Halstead	Kohn	Hiyama	Hermitte	Fish & Cobb
Conus aulicus	Court cone	Polynesia to Indian Ocean	*	*	*	*	*
C. geographus	Geographer cone	Indo-Pacific: Polynesia to East Africa	*	*[b]	*	*	*
C. marmoreus	Marbled cone	Polynesia to Indian Ocean	*	*		*	*
C. striatus	Striated cone	Indo-Pacific: Australia to East Africa	*		*[c]		*
C. textile	Textile cone	Polynesia to Red Sea	*	*[b]	*	*	*
C. tulipa	Tulip cone	Polynesia to Red Sea	*	*	*	*	*
C. obscurus		Hawaii		*			
C. lividus		Marianas,		*			
C. imperialis		Seychelles,		*			
C. omaria		New Guinea, and		*			
C. catus	Cat cone	Indo-Pacific		*			
C. quercinus	Oak cone	Indo-Pacific		*			
C. sponsolis		Indo-Pacific		*			
C. pulicarius	Flea cone	Indo-Pacific		*			
C. litteratus	Lettered cone	Indo-Pacific		*			

[a]This list is probably complete: fourteen, and perhaps fifteen, appear to be most harmful to man.
[b]Kohn states that all known fatalities were caused by either C. geographus or C. textile.
[c]No reported cases; listed by Hiyama, however, so not included here.

Conus are potentially dangerous to man, but certain species are particularly venomous." There can be no serious doubt that these beautiful animals are dangerous and, in some instances, deadly. However, snakes kill more people in a three-hour period than all the known Conus deaths in history combined. How, then, are these animals important enough for discussion in our context?

It is certain that at least ten people have been killed by these molluscs. The range of these deaths covers some of the most remote human outposts on our planet—the Pacific and Indian Ocean islands. Most of these smaller islands are seldom visted by outsiders, and, since most cone shells prefer shallow water, they are often found in isolated bays and inlets. There is no way of knowing how many victims there actually have been.

Another factor is that the collecting of seashells is not only a science but a hobby with many thousands of enthusiastic adherents. With the advent of skin-diving and scuba equipment, tens of thousands of people have been diving in the littoral zones of the sea. More people, too, have taken to traveling to distant lands in recent years. With some cone shells bringing high prices from collectors, live animals of the genus Conus will be picked up and handled as never before. With office workers, doctors, lawyers and enthusiastic teen-agers entering the sea with a kind of freedom never before available, shell collecting will move from the beach where it has usually stayed, and become a matter of hunting rather than finding. A lot of people are going to be hurt, and some will die, unless it becomes common knowledge that some pretty seashells also can be pretty dangerous.

25 The Giant Clam

Everything about the pearl is romantic and mysterious. The secrets of the sea glimmer in its rich luster, and the fantastic designs of the misshapen baroque pearls seem to picture gods and demons. The very fact of the pearl's origin, the birth of a treasure in the bowels of a lowly oyster, is in itself magical. Men have died for pearls, killed for pearls, and kings' ransoms have been spent for them.

A complex of legends that could fill many volumes has grown up around these coveted prizes. The dangers experienced by the natives who dive in search of these treasures are often quite real. Reality, however, hasn't been enough. Fabled hazards have been compiled with real ones to fill out the vision of these romantic figures. The fictionalizers of fact have had a field day with the realm of the pearl and the pearl diver.

No legend of the pearl diver has been more often repeated, more apparently based on fact, nor more readily accepted than the story of the giant man-eating clam. In 1962, the first year in which men circled the earth in spaceships, a gentleman from Minneapolis wrote to the editors of *Sea Secrets* magazine, a question-and-answer publication of the International Oceanographic Foundation, and asked: "What is the giant man-eating clam? Is there such a thing?" Those are perfectly legitimate questions in the light of what has been put into print on the subject. We shall examine them in this chapter.

Tridacna gigas, T. derasa, and perhaps a few other forms are all variously known as the tridacna clam, giant clam, killer clam, or man-

The giant clam, *Tridacna gigas*, subject of many legends, has never been known actually to drown a man. A true giant, it is harmless unless involved in the most bizarre of accidents.
Photograph by Fritz Goro

eating clam. In fact, these clams *are* giants, the soft parts of the largest (*T. gigas*) weighing as much as twenty pounds, and the shells as much as a quarter of a ton. The shells exceed four feet in length. They are common animals in much of the Indo–Pacific region, and abound off many South Pacific island groups. They are well known off the east coast of Africa. These animals are the largest known shelled molluscs in the world. Without its shell the tridacna clam is small when compared to the great cephalopods—molluscs with which we deal in Chapter 26.

That is the answer to one question: The giant clam does exist. It is a well-known living animal whose shell is often used in interior decorating. Polynesian restaurants in many American cities use them as lighting fixtures. The giant is not at all rare over much of its range, and, strangely enough, it is as big as they say. The question then remains: Is it dangerous to man?

C. M. Yonge, in his volume, *A Year on the Great Barrier Reef*, reports that men have been killed by the tridacna clam. C. J. Fish and M. C. Cobb repeat the claim, crediting it to Yonge, in their *Noxious Marine Animals of the Central and Western Pacific Ocean*. Dr. Halstead makes the claim in his worthwhile *Dangerous Marine Animals*, and gives instructions for releasing yourself by severing the great adductor muscles with which the animal controls its massive valves, or shells. The *U.S. Navy Diving Manual* gives it a 2 plus (out of a possible 4 plus) danger rating, with the comment, "Traps legs and arms between shells." It is not possible to estimate how many other times the claim has been repeated, although generally on less authority than the sources cited above.

If you examine one of these great shells, it is difficult to see how they could fail to be a trap for man. Muscles that can control such weights must be immensely powerful. The serrated edges of the shell fit together like giant teeth, and the fit is a tight one. Are the stories then true?

The first examination of this question offered one peculiar problem. Nowhere were there recorded names, dates, and places of such incidents. It has apparently been assumed by most people (specialists and nonspecialists alike) that men have been killed by these animals. There have been no witnesses; or at least none who have cared to go on record. What descriptions do exist are all too obviously fiction and cannot be relied upon. As in the case of the killer whale a survey of the specialists was the only solution. The following are some authoritative opinions.

Donald P. de Sylva, of the Marine Laboratory, University of Miami, reports:

... There are many tales attributing people being drowned or killed by these. Dr. Gilbert Voss, Chairman of our Biology Division, believes that it is unlikely that a person would accidentally step in one of these because of the large, brightly colored mantle ... which would tend to make them very conspicuous. There are rumors that occasionally divers do make a false step and are held down by these until they drown, but these clam shells close so slowly that it is unlikely that one would snap shut quickly enough to grab a man's foot.

S. Wiener, South Caulfield, Victoria, Australia, writes:

The evidence which incriminates the giant clam in causing injury to man is circumstantial and largely hearsay. However, it must be remembered that whenever such injury may have occurred, the chances of having it recorded by a competent observer would be remote. I do not know of any authentic record of injury or death. . . .

Harold A. Rehder, curator of the Division of Mollusks at the Smithsonian Institution, states: "We here feel ... that such an occurrence could happen only by accident, through a person not looking where he was putting his foot, because the mantle of these clams are of such a vivid color that they act as conspicuous danger signals."

R. S. Irwin, Glen Innes, New South Wales, Australia, reports:

The late Hugo Flecker of Cairns was, I think, the best authority in Australia on Marine Zoology in the tropics and he told me personally that this giant clam was, in fact, practically harmless, and that reports of its clamping the leg of a victim only occurred in fiction and in the movies. He said that the jaws approximated so slowly that there was plenty of time for a possible victim to get his leg out of danger and that he had heard of no authentic case where any harm had been done.

John E. Randall, professor of zoology, University of Puerto Rico, Mayaguez, notes, "I know of no injuries or deaths resulting from man's contact with ... tridacna. One biologist told me that the giant clam does not close its valves rapidly and even if it did, he doubted that it could hold a man's leg."

Gilbert Voss, chairman of the Biological Sciences Division, the Marine Laboratory, University of Miami, writes, "As far as the giant clam is concerned ... I have been unable to unearth a single case history of an attack. Mr. Roughly in his book on the Great Barrier Reef states that several cases occur each year in that area. However, he too fails to cite a single case. I am afraid [these] are myths."

J. L. B. Smith, professor of ichthyology, Rhodes University, Grahamstown, South Africa:

. . . we worked over a great area of tropical East Africa where it occurs, and while we did not ourselves encounter any case of fatality, native divers were extremely wary of this creature and told us that divers had been caught and drowned. However, our experience of the natives of East Africa . . . will invariably tell you what they think you would like to hear. What I do know is that we ourselves treated them with great respect and on one occasion when a net handle was pushed into a moderate clam that was open, it closed on this with great force.

R. V. Southcott, honorary zoologist, South Australian Museum, Hyde Park, South Australia, reports:

. . . as far as I know there is no authentic story on record; I have made as exhaustive a search as possible for this, without success. Halstead (1959) gives the traditional view, which is stated in Whitley and Boardman (1929), also by Yonge (1936, on the advice of Iredale). MacGillivary (in Cleland 1942) disputed these earlier statements, which have never been authenticated by case histories. Roughly (1940) also was dubious, and Flecker (1957) also declared that there was no authentic case of a diver being trapped. In view of these challenges, which have never been met, it must be concluded there has been no real evidence of human injuries.

Sea Secrets answered the gentleman from Minneapolis to the effect that there were no known records. Paul A. Zahl did an article for the *National Geographic Magazine* (January 1957) entitled "On Australia's Coral Ramparts." On page twenty is a picture of Dr. Zahl holding a large specimen out of the water. He had introduced a stout pole between the valves and had been able to haul the animal out by its grip on the piece of wood. No conclusion is drawn, but the caption on the photograph does point out that "firsthand evidence is scarce," and "The subject is a favorite with fiction writers." The photograph is impressive nonetheless. G. H. Gunter in *Adventures of a Trepang Fisher* reports on seeing an octopus held fast by a tridacna off the coast of North Australia. And so it goes. References occur in great numbers. What are the facts? What conclusions can be drawn?

Despite its immense size, the tridacna clam feeds much the same way other bivalves do. It opens its valves, spreads its mantle and filters food from algae raised within its own shell, at least as an adult. It does not clamp down on large animals in order to eat. The mantle, as so often recorded, is boldly marked. It is not something one is apt to miss. Most of the stories of this animal clamping down on men are fairly logical on all but one point. When these reports refer to the "bear trap" snapping shut, they may give themselves away. When a tridacna clam closes, it must not only move two ponderous dead weights toward each other, it must also displace a great quantity of water. No matter how powerful the adductor muscles, the shell could not be snapped shut, no bear-trap effect would be likely.

Here, then, is what we have. A diver is not *likely* to miss a giant clam if it is open, the only time it could be dangerous. If a diver did put his foot in between the valves, the valves would close slowly, but close they most certainly would. There is no known record of anyone ever being caught. Does, then, the tridacna clam trap men? This author does not know, and doubts very much that anyone else does. Frankly, I doubt that the animal ever has, but that is not evidence. In seeking a definite answer, this author's doubts and other people's beliefs are not admissible evidence. What is evidence in the context of this book is this: until an animal has been demonstrated to be dangerous, we ought to vote it not guilty. No one seems equipped to demonstrate that the "giant man-eating clam" has caused human death or injury. It should be pointed out that the seemingly serious claims which do exist do not accuse the tridacna of eating man. The trapping of man is described as a defensive reflex action. Even this, however, remains for the moment in the realm of fiction, or at least speculation.

26 Octopus and Squid

If anyone is really intent on creating an animal horror story, and wishes to launch his tale from a familiar point, he can do no better than the octopus and squid, molluscs without external shells. Wonderfully morbid tales have been drifting around for centuries. Because these incredible stories have often been offered as personal narratives, legends have grown to absolutely monstrous proportions. This ancient race of animals has inspired an almost impenetrable fog of ignorance and misinformation which rivals even that concerning venomous snakes.

Considering the amount of attention the cephalopods have received, it is confounding to discover how little *accurate* information is common knowledge. Even well-educated people don't seem to realize that these animals are invertebrates. If the facts of their physical structure are not known, how much more confusion must there be about their behavior? Since these animals are remote from the lives of most people, this ignorance is perhaps understandable. However, since many cephalopods—from the Greek, meaning "head-footed"—are accused of appalling crimes against man, the purpose of this book will be served by a general clearing of the air.

The cephalopods are broken down into three subclasses, a number of orders and suborders, and seemingly endless families. It is obviously a large and diverse group, but we will concern ourselves here with only two groups: the octopuses (order Octopoda), and the squids (suborder Teuthoidea of the Decapoda). We shall limit our inquiry for two reasons: the other cephalopods (cuttlefish, the nautilus, etc.) are rarely accused, and quite probably never involved, in human injuries and deaths; and the state of cephalopodan systematics looms like a giant crossword puzzle, in a combination of Braille and Sanskrit.

Octopuses (that is a correct plural form), the best known of the cephalopods, are represented by approximately 150 living species. A number of these species are apparently exceedingly rare, no more than a single example being known in some cases. Since many species are believed to live at extreme depths, there is no telling to what extent the list may be expanded as abyssal oceanography develops in the coming decades. Everything we have to say about the group in this chapter will apply to shallow-water forms that are well known. We don't know much about the nature of the truly deep-sea species.

Perhaps no single aspect of the octopus' appearance gives rise to more conversation than size. People always ask, when the subject of the animal is raised, "How big *do* they grow?" The size ranges from approximately two inches *(Octopus arborescens)* to thirty-five feet *(Octopus hong–kongensis)*; that is, by measuring the diameter of its eight arms stretched equally in all directions to form a circle like the spokes of a wheel. The latter form, the presently known giant of the group, seems to reach maximum size in Alaskan waters and in waters off Washington State. It must be pointed out that even a thirty-five-foot specimen, and that is being generous, is about $^{16}/_{17}$ arms. (By the way, those are arms, *not* tentacles. Octopuses do not have tentacles; these are found in the decapods, which include the squid.)

Octopus, like squid, are active hunting animals. Specimens establish territories, and either chase away or eat intruders. They can move with considerable speed by jetting water from an adjustable siphon, cloud the water around them with their ink, change color to a degree and with a speed that puts the legendary chameleon to shame, and hold on with a tenacity that is nothing short of astounding, once they take hold with their suckers—adjustable discs that line the inner surface of their arms. These devices consist of a muscular membrane with a thick rim. The center acts somewhat like a piston and is controlled by the animal with delicate precision.

Octopuses can squeeze themselves through any hole or crevice large enough to admit their hard, parrotlike beak, walk on their arms, hang suspended in midwater, jet around with fine control, or lie patiently for hours waiting for their prey. They are stubborn, tenacious, efficiently predatory animals of considerable economic importance to man. In many parts of the world they are fished for as food along with other cephalopods. Squids are more significant as a food source, however. The range of the various octopus species is global. The author has seen them in coral formations astride the equator, and once sat watching a newly caught specimen acclimate itself to an aquarium in a biology laboratory 840 miles from the South Pole. It had been taken only hours before through a hole in sea ice several feet thick, a few hundred yards off frigid Ross Island. They range into Arctic waters as well.

Is any octopus dangerous to man? Only under special circumstances. A man in a boat is almost assuredly safe from them as long as he leaves the octopus in the water. Attacks on boats by cephalopods appear to have been made by squid, not octopus, even though the latter animal, being better known, has been accused. A man in the water, *if* attacked, *could* be placed at considerable disadvantage, particularly if the attack occurred near a solid anchor point. In midwater, the octopus might have a great deal of trouble overcoming a well-set up, well-organized man. Skin divers from Washington regularly catch the largest known octopuses with their bare hands, as a kind of sport! Frank W. Lane, in *Kingdom of the Octopus,* gives these figures: a man weighing 200 pounds can be held below the surface by a pull of about 10 pounds, if he doesn't struggle. A medium-sized octopus can exceed that pull several times over. If a man were grabbed firmly by an octopus that was anchored equally firmly to a solid foundation, he might be held down long enough to drown. Certainly, if the man was inexperienced in the water and panicked, the octopus might very well have an advantage. It is a reasonable assumption—but only that—that this has happened on rare occasions. It is certainly not a common occurrence, and must be looked upon as a freak accident involving a very large and particularly determined animal, and a very weak and inept person. A diver inadvertently intruding into a cave lair might trigger an attack, particularly with a sexually excited animal that could mistake an arm or leg for a potential mate's member.

Once engaged, an octopus frequently, but not always, tends to hang on. As capable a predator as the octopus is, however, its energy is expended on practical prey like crustacea and molluscs. The octopus has many enemies in the sea—even the larger octopuses are regularly attacked by moray eels, sharks, and some of the toothed whales—and are wary of large animals approaching them. Faced with anything as formidable as a man, the octopus is generally shy and retiring. To characterize it as an enemy of man (at least any of the species presently known) is absurd. Man is certainly an enemy of the octopus (he collects millions every year for food), but the converse is rarely true.

Frank Lane researched a number of cases of attack and came to the conclusion that there is occasional danger to man. In 1940, in Poverty Bay, New Zealand, a Maori lad was grabbed by a thirty-six-inch specimen, and was unable to free himself. Friends saved him in time. During

World War I, a parson was taking a group of boys on an outing along the Victoria coast of Australia. An octopus *left the water* and attacked the parson, rapidly encircling him with its arms. It was apparently a good-sized animal and it took the combined efforts of several teen-age boys to rescue the man. Since octopuses are occasionally reported leaving the water to attack shore-dwelling rats, this may not be as strange as it sounds. Just how far from the water they will go, or how long they will stay out, is not clear. There are other accounts, as well, of attacks on men that would appear to be reliable, but they are few in number, and the circumstances under which they allegedly took place are generally open to question. So much obvious nonsense has been written—and believed, and repeated, and believed again—that there is the equally unscientific temptation to ignore all stories one encounters.

Under no circumstances does any octopus strangle or crush anything to death with its arms. Its arms are for holding things. When hunting, it holds victims while it eats, or first administers a venomous bite. Some octopuses, at least, are venomous. Their posterior salivary gland produces a glycoprotein of immense complexity. This substance paralyzes their prey and enables their chitinous beaks to dismember and devour their meal without struggle. The venom apparently inhibits respiration. Tests on laboratory animals reveal it to be quite potent. It is known that it can affect man.

The bite of the octopus usually consists of two small puncture wounds. The beak is not particularly dangerous, although a good-sized animal is capable of giving a pretty good bite. When venom is involved, a local burning sensation will be the first symptom. There may be an anticoagulant constituent in the venom, since profuse bleeding has been reported a number of times. Octopus bites are relatively rare, and reactions to the venom beyond that of purely local discomfort, rarer still. But there are cases that do demand our attention.

On September 18, 1954, twenty-one-year-old Kirke Dyson–Holland, an Australian skin diver, was killed by the bite of a *six-inch octopus*. He and his diving companion, John Baylis, were coming ashore near Port Darwin when Baylis saw the little blue creature. He caught it, played with it, allowing it to crawl over his arms and torso, and tossed it to Dyson–Holland, a perfectly natural thing for a diver to do. Octopuses, it seems, are rarely left in peace by energetic young enthusiasts out for a day in coastal waters. The animal evidently hung on to Dyson–Holland's arm or shoulder for a moment, then crawled across to the middle of his back before dropping off into the water. The men came ashore without further regard for the creature which made off in typical fashion the moment it hit the water.

No sooner had the two men come up on the beach when Dyson–

A large octopus looks formidable, but is all but harmless to man. Many scuba divers routinely "play" with octopuses when they encounter them.
Photograph by Franz Thorbecke

The exceedingly dangerous little blue-ringed octopus (probably *Hapalochlaena maculosa*) can be deadly to man. Its venom acts with startling swiftness— death can take less than an hour. Found off Australia, the animal need be no more than six inches long to be deadly.
Courtesy Australian News and Information Bureau

Holland complained of a dry sensation in his mouth, and difficulty in swallowing. Baylis said he noticed a small puncture wound and trickle of blood on his companion's back where the octopus had lodged briefly. The afflicted man rapidly became violently ill. He vomited, began to lose muscular coordination, and finally collapsed. He was carried to a car and rushed four miles to a Darwin hospital muttering, "It was the little octopus." He lost consciousness during the brief but frantic run for medical help. By the time they got to town he had turned blue (cyanosis), and his breathing could no longer be detected. Adrenalin and an iron lung failed to help. Without rallying, he died fifteen minutes after being placed in the respirator. Less than two hours after handling a six-inch octopus. Dyson–Holland was dead. The species has not been positively identified. It was probably an animal variously known as *Octopus maculosa* or *Hapalochleana maculosa*—the little blue-ringed octopus.

How was Kirke Dyson–Holland killed? It first appeared as if he might have been particularly susceptible to foreign proteins, since he did have a history of asthma and one allergy can indicate the presence of others. Subsequent to his death three other young men were made very seriously ill by the bite of what was then and is now believed to be the same species. Then, on June 21, 1967, Pvt. James Arthur Ward became the second verified death from the bite of the little blue-ringed octopus. We know young Ward was in good condition since he had been inducted into the Australian Army two days earlier. On the day of his death he was exploring some rock pools in the Camp Cove area near Sydney. According to the two other soldiers who were with Ward, the animal who bit him was less than four inches across. Ward died of respiratory failure in less than ninety minutes.

The octopus is equipped with venom as a food-getting device, and any use in defense would be secondary. The animal is not equipped to inject the venom but rather bites with its beak and then spits venom down into the wound. They are separate actions and one need not follow the other. The same venom, it is believed, can be discharged into the water near potential prey and is said to cause convulsions and total loss of motor control in crabs and similar animals. As far as is known, the little blue-ringed octopus is the only species seriously venomous enough to be of danger to man. It is not an uncommon animal in shallow coastal waters around Australia and warrants a great deal of care when being handled, if it must be handled at all.

Although the octopus is the cephalopod with the reputation for mayhem, it is the squid which might answer to some of the seemingly fantastic tales that are told. If there are sea monsters, certain squids are the most likely suspects. They are the most varied and colorful of the class, the most numerous, and among them are numbered the largest of the cephalopods. Lane says they are the most ferocious of all inverte-brates. Aside from the giant *Cyanea* jellyfish with their endless stream of tentacles, these giant squid are the largest invertebrates known to exist. They *might* even exceed the *Cyanea's* length of 120 feet!

There are over 350 species of living squid recognized today. The smallest known is probably *Sandalops pathopsis*, measuring under one inch at maturity. The giant is *Architeuthis* sp., whose maximum length is a matter of great debate with 60 feet at one end of the spectrum, and 300 at the other! Squids are widely distributed in the seas and oceans, both vertically and horizontally. In addition to eight arms, squids have two tentacles which they shoot out with considera-ble speed to capture prey and draw it toward their beaks.

Since before the birth of Christ, writers had been recording tales of monster cephalopods. The conservatives in the sciences tended to pooh-pooh the whole thing right up to the end of the last century, when it finally became eminently clear that they *did* exist. *Architeuthis* came into being officially, and is the genus now used to define the animals popularly known by the old Norse name of *kraken*. Giant squid, true giants, do exist, and are to the everyday squid what the 110-foot blue whale is to the common dolphin. Thirty- to sixty-foot specimens have been taken, and the maximum size they may reach is not known. They appear to be nocturnal creatures of the deep coastal shelves. The fact that they have been occasionally troublesome when encountered dur-ing the day may indicate that only sick and disoriented specimens come up to the surface when the sun is high. Nothing like a definitive answer exists.

Carl C. Cutler of West Mystic, Connecticut, a gentleman long inter-ested in and connected with marine matters, kindly supplied a quote from the *Mystic Press*, dated July 31, 1874:

SCHOONER SUNK BY A SQUID

Schooner *Pearl*, 150 tons, James Floyd, master, with a crew of six, was reported sunk by a giant squid in Lat. 8.50 N., Long. 84.05 E. on May 10th, 1874. The sinking was witnessed and reported by passenger steamer *Strathowen* bound from Columbo to Madras. Passengers first noted a large brownish mass lying on the surface between the steamer and the schooner, which was becalmed two or three miles away. Someone on the schooner fired a rifle at the object and it began to move toward the schooner and squeezed on board between the fore and mainmast, pulling the vessel over and sinking it. Its body was as thick as the schooner and about half as long, with a train that appeared to be 100 feet long. The steamer put out boats

A very large squid hooked at night off the west coast of South America. These large predators often travel in dense schools and there is some question as to a person's safety should they go overboard into their midst.
Photograph by Michael Lerner

The *kraken* or giant squid does exist. No one knows what real role this animal has played in the sea-serpent legends that still persist into modern times, nor what the maximum size of these invertebrates might really be. There is evidence that the largest have yet to be seen by man.
Photograph by Erling Sivertsen

and picked up five of the crew swimming in the water. The other members of the crew was crushed between the mast and one of the creature's tentacles, which were as thick as a barrel.

The remarkable thing about this century-old account is its matter-of-factness. "Of course there are squids big enough to sink a schooner," it seems to say. One can't help but wonder how a contemporary tabloid would treat a similar report from Latitude 8.50 N! How many adjectives would be used?

This story of the disaster of the *Pearl* has been quoted innumerable times. It has been a favorite of the sea-monster set. Any attempt to really evaluate it is virtually hopeless. Witnesses swore it was true, and we are stuck with what they had to say. Either we accept the notion that squids exceed 100 feet in length, or we don't. Since the burden of the *Pearl* is known to have been 150 tons, there are calculations of a sort that might be made to determine what pull would have been necessary to roll her over. However, unknown factors like the weight and distribution of cargo, skill of the skipper, direction of sail in relation to the prevailing wind, velocity of that that wind (slight, at best, since the *Pearl* was reportedly becalmed), amount of ballast being carried, and amount of water in the bilges would tend to make these calculations about as speculative as your own good guess! What it boils down to is this—it may have happened—we just don't know.

The *Pearl* wasn't the only vessel reputed or reported to have encountered these giants of the cephalopod tribe. Captain Haley, a harpooner on the last of the old wooden whalers, the *Charles W. Morgan*, wrote in his *Whale Hunt* of seeing a squid 300 feet long! He judged its length by comparing it to the vessel on which he was sailing. Cutler, the gentleman who kindly supplied the report on the *Pearl*, is a relative of Captain Haley's and refers to him as a sober and trustworthy man. Captain Haley reported that the monster was accompanied by two smaller squids, each about 150 feet long. Cutler, as a boy in the nineties, knew a good many old whalemen. He reports there was a general acceptance among them of the existence of these giants. The French steam dispatch boat *Alecton* met and unsuccessfully attempted to capture one in 1861. This latter reported incident, however, involved a specimen very much smaller than 150 feet.

In the 1870s, for reasons not known, kraken considerably larger than the ones known as good bait to European fishermen, began to appear off Newfoundland. A large specimen, inadvertently prodded with a boat-hook, attacked a fishing dory off Portugal Cove, Newfoundland, on October 26, 1873. Quick action with a hatchet by the twelve-year-old son of one of the two fishermen aboard saved the three occupants from drowning. The severed tentacle of the beast was presented to an amateur biologist, Rev. Moses Harvey, of St. John's. It was Harvey who subsequently purchased the carcass of a thirty-two-foot specimen taken in the same general waters in November 1873.

It is known that the Sperm Whale (*Physeter catodon*) feeds on giant squids. Captured sperms almost always are heavily scarred by sucker marks. The suckers of the giant squid are tooth-rimmed, and, once affixed to a whale's hide, cannot be ripped free without the squid's cooperation except by colossal effort, and not without leaving scars. Sucker marks have been found on sperm whales' heads measuring three inches across. Whalers reported harpooned sperm whales vomiting up hunks of squid arms as thick as barrels while in their death throes. The battle between a sperm whale and a giant squid must be a sight to behold!

There is a Humboldt Current Squid (*Ommastrephes gigas*) taken regularly by fishermen off the west coast of South America. These animals are very aggressive and may weigh three hundred pounds and stretch twelve feet in length. It is said that their beaks can do more damage to a steel boathook than the bite of a big shark. Native fishermen allegedly fear these animals more than any other in the sea.

Are squids dangerous to man? Aside from a sailor who was reputedly pulled under as he clung to a raft following the sinking of the troopship *Britannia* in the mid-Atlantic, on March 25, 1941, there are few if any authentic reports of men in the water being injured or killed by these creatures. Certainly, anyone in the water when a thirty- to sixty-foot *Architeuthis* is around had better get out. Similarly, a swim in the Humboldt Current at night when masses of feeding squids are on the prowl would be unwise. These animals are probably dangerous under the right set of circumstances. Large squids are almost always nocturnal animals and lie off in deeper water during the day, making an encounter with one by a man in the water an exceptional case. Serious injuries could result from carelessness with freshly caught specimens, however.

As for the giants who attack vessels: it is pretty much a case of what you want to believe. All manner of logic can be applied, but logic isn't the answer when the number of unknowns surpasses the number of established facts. The answers are reliable eyewitnesses, photography, and calm evaluation. The eyewitnesses of these recounted tragedies of course aren't around any longer, no pictures are known to exist, and calm evaluation of something that may have occurred scores of years ago isn't too profitable. Time will no doubt yield further information.

27 Jellyfish

The opening comment of an article in the *U.S. Naval Medical Bulletin* for March 1943 reads: "Contrary to popular belief, the sting of a jellyfish can be extremely dangerous, *even fatal.*" That statement, with the author's italics added, is, unfortunately, quite true.

New York papers, on Tuesday, August 7, 1962, carried an AP release datelined Newport, Rhode Island. It read, in part, "Second Beach here was closed to bathers yesterday when ten persons—nine of them children—were stung by Portuguese Men-of-War."

The *Cairns Post*, a Queensland, Australia, newspaper carried this account in the issue for January 21, 1937 (only the first paragraph is quoted):

> Within eight minutes of being stung by the deadly Portuguese man-o'-war while bathing at Bramston Beach (40 miles south of Cairns), 12 miles from Mirriwinni, this morning, D.W.T. (19) collapsed and died. Young T., who had been holidaying with his aunt at Mirriwinni, was in the water with a friend. They waded out waist deep and almost instantly the man-o'-war tentacles became wrapped around the victim's abdomen. His companion helped to free him and assisted him to the shore. T. staggered about 50 yards and collapsed. He was dead within eight minutes. . . .

What is the nature of the animal involved, and to what extent is it a danger to man? The answers to these questions are not as well known as they should be. We will discuss what has, in fact, been established.

The jellyfish belong to the phylum Coelenterata, or group of animals known as coelenterates, which is a general term embracing several related types of animals such as the hydroids, corals, and sea anemones. They are found, in one form or another, in all of the world's seas and oceans. They are simple animals composed of many highly specialized cells. Many of them are venomous to man, on contact, and what we have to say about the true jellyfish will apply to these related forms as well. A major difference between the jellyfish per se and these other forms is that the former are free to drift or float for much of their life, while the others are generally fixed and stationary during that part of their lives when they are dangerous to man. Of course, to the man who rubs against "fire coral" and thus suffers the agony of coelenterate envenomation, the jellyfish are not the most dangerous forms. In fact, however, they are. The free-floating characteristic of the jellyfish greatly increases the likelihood of an encounter between them and man. Also, it now appears that the most virulent coelenterate venom is produced in this group. Anyone who dives in waters where any venomous coelenterates—such as hydroids, anemones, and corals— abound would do well to learn to recognize the dangerous forms.

A major exception to our division of coelenterates into sessile and mobile are the siphonophores, which include the much-feared Portuguese Man-of-War *(Physalia physalis).* This is not a true jellyfish, but a free-swimming colonial hydroid: a collection of specialized hydroid animals living together in a kind of grand cooperative, each with a special job to do, and each benefitting from the actions of the whole colony. It must be pointed out that, once again, common names let us down. The Portuguese man-of-war, or bluebottle, is properly any animal in the genus *Physalia,* but the names are used in various places for animals of at least a half dozen other genera. Here, we refer only to *Physalia.* But we must deal with the true jellyfish or *Scyphozoa* first.

These vary in size from the almost microscopic to the giant *Cyanea capillata,* which ranges northward to Arctic waters, and may reach a body diameter of over 7 feet, with 100-foot tentacles. Deep-water work now in progress may yet reveal even larger forms. All known coelenterates employ a similar stinging mechanism, and all are to a degree venomous. Some are harmless to man, some can cause mild discomfort, some inflict agonizing pain, and a very few can cause death. The difference apparently lies in the venom and not in the size of the animal or the method of stinging. Dr. R. V. Southcott, a scholar who has written extensively on the subject, states in the *Australian Medical Society Review* for May 1962: "At present, about two dozen species of jellyfish are known to have some medical effect. This number is growing rapidly."

Jellyfish characteristically have tentacles hanging from their globe, the jellylike umbrella by which they are usually recognized. The outer layers of these tentacles contain highly specialized, microscopic stinging mechanisms (specialized intracellular structures or organelles) known as nematocysts, which in turn are contained in cells called cnidoblasts. A hairlike trigger, the cnidocil, projects out of these and it is when the victim touches or is touched by this trigger that the mechanism is released. (There may also be a central releasing mechanism that is at least in part chemical.) A lid on the nematocyst springs open (it is called the operculum), and a pointed and barbed, threadlike tube flies out of the nematocyst like a coiled spring, carrying venom with it. This whole device is exceedingly small, and the man who encounters one of these animals does not trigger one cnidocil, but many thousands, in some cases hundreds of thousands. So powerful are these devices that they have been able to penetrate laboratory gloves in experimental encounters. In effect, the victim is shot with thousands of tiny, sinuous, venomous darts. Most jellyfish stings cause nothing more than a slight burning or itching sensation—if that. Unfortunately, this is not always the case. The most feared of all "jellyfish" (as was pointed out, not a true jellyfish at all) is the Portuguese man-of-war. The tentacles of this animal can run to many feet in length, and a man who unknowingly dives into their midst is in for a bad time.

On July 14, 1942, a twenty-year-old soldier encountered a Portuguese man-of-war while swimming off Puerto Rico. He was stung across the back and left shoulder, and "his appearance was as though he were recovering from an epileptic convulsion." Stuart and Slagle's report in the *U.S. Naval Medical Bulletin* goes on to say:

> ... the skin of the whole body was flushed ... expression of marked anxiety ... he breathed with great difficulty ... coughing expirations ... complained of severe oppression of the chest ... pain in the abdomen and lumbar regions ... board-like rigidity of the lumbar and abdominal muscles ... muscle cramps in the extremities ... skin was raised in an urticarial rash. ...

A twenty-seven-year-old sailor was involved in the same kind of accident on the same day and, as reported, "Four weeks later the marks of the tentacles were still plainly visible." Klein and Bradshaw, in the *U.S. Armed Forces Medical Journal*, report a case off North Miami Beach in April 1950. The last of the victim's lesions disappeared twenty-four days after the encounter, but white hairlike scars remained, perhaps permanently. There have been untold thousands of such cases, both reported and unrecorded, but seldom, if ever, are they fatal where the Portuguese man-of-war—that is, an animal of the genus *Physalia*—is involved.

Although the author cannot pin down the actual point at which it started, some time back a fiction writer apparently made the statement that the Portuguese man-of-war was the only deadly jellyfish. I clearly recall being raised on this bromide and never really thought to question it until research for this book was begun, and I read the medical reports. Doubtless this belief still has worldwide currency and so strongly is it believed that cases of death and injury by coelenterates are credited to the man-of-war—without the offending species ever being seen. Among others, H. Flecker of Queensland, a specialist in marine biology, doubted the validity of these assignments and attributed many recorded accidents to "*Irukandji* sting," unidentified animal stings. In actual fact, although the Portuguese man-of-war is a dangerous creature to encounter physically, it is probably only deadly, if ever, in rare cases. The author knows of no case where a death was finally attributed to this animal after proper identification by a qualified person, although the report from the *Cairns Post* cited earlier does blame the death of a nineteen-year-old boy on this animal.* The report may not be accepted on face value because there is simply too much evidence to suggest an altogether different culprit was involved.

In 1941, a seven-and-a-half-year-old boy died rapidly after being stung in shallow water. His mother identified the attacking animal as a Portuguese man-of-war from strands of tentacles she saw sticking to the boy's legs when he ran ashore in agony. This identification cannot be accepted when we take into account the evidence used, and the mental condition of the woman as she bent over her dying son.

And so it goes: a ten-year-old boy at North Mission Beach in 1949; a fourteen-year-old girl at Kissing Point Baths, Australia; and a number of other incidents from the Philippine Islands. Time after time, someone yelled, "Portuguese man-of-war," and the legend was intensified. More than likely, all of these cases, or certainly the vast majority, were victims of the various "sea wasps" or "box jellies." The genera involved could have been *Chiropsalmus*, *Chironex*, or *Carybdea*. The first-named is common in Philippine waters; the second around Australia; the third, although having a wider range, is probably the least virulent of the group.

The sea wasps or box jellies are decidedly dangerous** to man as witness this 1938 report:

> ... A boy aged 12 years, was bathing in the local swimming baths [Darwin, Australia]. He dived into the water and when he came to the

*Since the above was written, a 73-year-old man died in Miami after being stung by a Portuguese man-of-war. An autopsy revealed that he died of heart failure.

**There is no longer any doubt that jellyfish of the genus *Chironex* are the most seriously venomous in the world by an extremely wide margin.

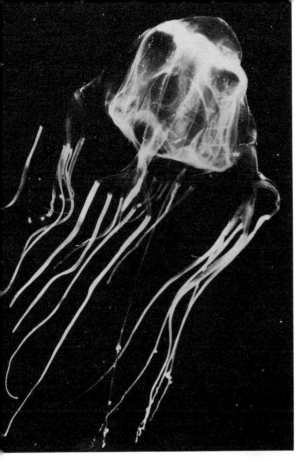

One of the most seriously venomous animals in the world, and the most deadly of all jellyfish—the sea wasp or box jelly, *Chironex fleckeri*. Common from the Philippines to Australia, it has caused scores of human deaths, many of them in less than ten minutes. Truly one of the world's deadliest animals.
Courtesy Australian News and Information Bureau

The most maligned of sea creatures: the Portuguese man-of-war. This colonial hydroid is related to the jellyfish but actually is not one itself. It offers a very painful sting but is not lethal despite scores of claims of human deaths.
Courtesy University of Miami

surface was distressed and just able to reach the beach. He said that he had been stung by a jellyfish. He died shortly afterwards . . . witnesses stated that the jellyfish was still sticking to the boy when he staggered to the beach. This specimen was submitted to the Australian Museum and identified as *Chiropsalmus quadrigatus* Haeckel, commonly known as the "Sea Wasp."

That account was given to Dr. H. Flecker by Professor E. Ford, director of the School of Public Health and Tropical Medicine, Sydney.

Although the sea wasps have relatives as far away from Australia as the Atlantic coast of South America, most, if not all, deaths have been reported from the southwest Pacific and the Indian oceans. So swift is the onslaught of violently painful symptoms that anyone in deep water would probably simply sink and drown without a trace. More than forty cases, however, are reported in scientific literature, and a far greater hazard evidently exists here than has been generally realized.

At certain times of the year, single jellyfish will be encountered floating free. At other times, the water will be cluttered with them. Entering the water at such a time is a hazardous practice. These swarms that occur in harbors and bays may result from offshore weather and sea conditions. There is no known way of controlling these invasions of the surface waters. Man has no choice but to avoid contact. In the case of the Portuguese man-of-war, such assemblages are generally produced at interfaces or boundaries between water masses offshore, or by the continued action of onshore winds.

The venom of the coelenterates appears to be essentially neurotoxic. It causes violent local symptoms up to and including permanent scarification, and it can result in dangerous systemic reactions. Since jellyfish frequently infest areas by the hundreds of thousands during specific seasons, and since man hasn't yet devised a means of ridding himself of this dangerous pest, he had best use his powers of observation and common sense. Jellyfish don't swim around attacking men, they pulse and float along their own stupid, blind way waiting patiently to bump into something they can eat. They sting anything they encounter. They are never in a hurry and have been floating around this way for untold years. It is obviously a successful way of life since billions of them are still around. While they can't very well make a meal of a man, they don't know it. They just bump and sting, bump and sting. To avoid the sting, man has only to avoid the bump. While he may be able to depend on the fear, quiet good nature, or the escape "reflexes" of other potentially dangerous animals, he cannot do this with jellyfish. He must learn to keep out of the way.

Part VI Epilogue

28 Other Potential Dangers

In the preceding twenty-seven chapters we have reviewed some facts about a varied number of "unpleasant" but interesting creatures. If it has appeared that I have been trying to construct a collection of horror stories, I have failed to make a basic point. What I have, in fact, been attempting to do is simply shed some light on a very cloudy subject— the story of animals potentially hazardous to man. Biology is an interpretive science. We do not yet fully understand life; we cannot simulate it; and we still know comparatively little about animal behavior— human as well as other animals. To draw what I think is a reasonable parallel we need only look at the record of human crime.

A shocking number of crimes of violence are committed by men and women who have been paroled from prison or released from mental institutions. If human beings under restraint and under searching psychiatric care do not provide valid clues to their future behavior, how then do we dare say what a lion, a shark, or a bear will do? These "lower" creatures, some will say, have less complex minds and therefore are more fathomable. Less complex perhaps, but therefore automatically less known or understood. In fact, categoric statements as to what any animal will, or will not, do are worthless.

It is quite possible for an experienced game ranger to approach a pride of lions in full view in relative safety. He knows his cats and the risk is minimal for the expert. However, we must never forget that it is the exceptions, the miscalculations that provide the statistics with which we have been dealing in this book.

By a very wide margin, most people injured or killed by wild animals are victims of circumstances rather than of intent on the part of the creatures themselves. While some elephants may indeed suffer a kind of insanity, and some cats may take to man-eating and actually hunt man as prey, most accidents are caused by a misunderstanding on the part of an animal as to man's intentions, and even more so a misunderstanding on the part of the man as to the animal's reactions. Snakes and spiders strike in defense, big carnivores if wounded or in defense of young, and animals in general in reaction to territorial incursion.

In this book I have tried to determine what, if any, facts exist to substantiate the most oft-heard claims. In many cases, this has not been possible, and the best we could do was attempt a logical examination of what the facts probably are. There are many more marginal cases left that cry out for study. Some examples follow.

Some time ago, a men's magazine told of foot-long crabs called Robber, Birgus, or Coconut Crabs (probably referring to a species known as *Birgus latro*) found on the shores and islands of the South Pacific, the Indian Ocean, and adjacent seas. The statement that they grow to be a foot long is not an exaggeration. It is also true that these huge creatures climb trees, cut down coconuts with their pincers, and tear the extremely tough covering apart to get at the meat. But what of the article's contention that twenty-six people were killed by these crabs, when they attacked thirty marooned Moslem pilgrims on an island in the Red Sea, and punctured the skulls of those too weak to escape or defend themselves? This reputedly happened in 1951. The "facts" were revealed in a court case in Massawa, Ethiopia. Since island people regularly hunt the giant *Birgus latro* for food, and not vice versa, the case, if true, is exceptional, to say the least.

Many stories exist about a Platyhelminthine (flatworm)—a Planarian of biology-class fame in this case—in Central America that "slimes" about in and on rotten logs exuding a perfectly dreadful poison. The results of contact with it are variously described as raising everything from a rash to a gravestone. The story is not surprising if geography be taken into consideration, for just about everything in Central America has been accused of being venomous by some "explorer" or another, a surprisingly large number of whom have operated exclusively from the area lying between 39th and 67th Streets on Manhattan Island! Nevertheless, as long ago as 1860, some of the brightly colored land planarians were reported to be "disagreeable to the taste of man and some birds."

Many of the corals and anemones are venomous and sting with a device very similar to that of the jellyfish. None are known to cause death, although the discomfort may be acute. Accidents with these forms occur by the thousands and perhaps tens of thousands annually. In some areas, the phenomenon of dermatitis resulting from contact with them can be a health problem.

A number of leeches (class Hirundinea) feed on man and, although they do not transmit disease, they can be debilitating. Large, tropical, aquatic leeches are said to be capable of taking from a man as much as 10 cc of blood in as many minutes. Troops working their way through tropical swamps are said to have picked up as many as a hundred leeches a day per man. Stories abound about men being killed by swarms of leeches at night, although I know of no documents that bear this out. Widely distributed throughout Southeast Asia is *Dinobdella ferox*, a nasopharyngeal leech that works its way into the throat and nasal passages of mammals (including man) who drink from streams. Although not deadly, leeches are a horrible nuisance and terribly disturbing to even the slightly sensitive.

Many sea urchins (Echinodermata) can cause serious injuries when trodden upon by swimmers and waders. Some are actually venomous, and some have spines up to a foot in length which are acutely pointed and very brittle. Reputedly, too many of these broken off in a man's body can cause death. Certainly, being impaled on one or more spines ten to twelve inches long (that are bound to break off in the wound) is a serious matter.

Some segmented worms, notably the marine bristle worms (Annelids), can bite and cause painful rashes. Deaths are not known to have occurred, but injuries are very common in a number of areas.

The list of animal forms that can and do cause injuries to man is, at this stage of our knowledge, endless, and an examination of the new claims made each year would fill many volumes. Professional medical and scientific literature of Australia, India, many parts of South America, and Africa contain numerous case histories, reports, and suggestions, and even postmortem findings. The literature is quite overwhelming. Taken on the surface, this mass of material would make it seem that life anywhere except in your own living room is hazardous in the extreme. Such is not the case.

If you had the time and the energy, you could walk completely around the world in any latitude you might select (at least across the land surfaces in any given latitude) and never fall victim to more than an occasional insect bite. In point of fact, it would be extremely rare for you to suffer any ill at all from contact with wildlife. When you take into account the numbers of people in daily contact with or at least in proximity to wild animals, attacks upon and injuries to man are really very rare.

There are, however, some forms of animal life that are really dangerous to man, and some that are deadly. Although contact even with these is extremely rare, from a statistical point of view, these forms are well worth knowing when travel or residence in the places where they live is anticipated.

Part VII Appendixes

Appendix A Treatment of Injuries Caused by Wild Animals

As has been stated a number of times in this book, an injury resulting from a traumatic encounter with a wild animal frequently constitutes a medical emergency. The size of the injury may vary from a slight pinprick, to gross amputations and extensive mutilations. While some injuries will more obviously demand immediate professional care than others, even the smallest injury may require the help of medical specialists. A nip from a small bat that barely draws blood can mean that the rabies virus has been transmitted. A sting from a scorpion's tail is hardly represented by gross tissue damage, yet a lethal substance may have been injected.

For our purposes, there are three considerations in the evaluation, care, and treatment of an animal-caused injury:

1. Introduction of microorganisms: bacteria, viruses, protozoans, etc.
2. Tissue damage: bleeding, shock, and other gross local or systemic effects.
3. Venoms: the introduction of noxious substances, and resultant complications.

Each of these considerations indicates a separate health problem and a separate course of treatment.

The Introduction of Microorganisms

Animal bites, gorings, and clawings are inevitably dirty wounds. The puncturing effect of a bite, the raking of claws, and goring of horns and antlers will almost always introduce microorganisms into the victim's tissues and bloodstream. Rarely would an injury of any of these types heal uneventfully if left untreated. Even in cases where normal body defenses are able to engulf and destroy invading hosts, dangerous chemicals are liberated and the body will suffer. In two very special cases, the natural, unaided body defenses are totally incapable of any effective defense.

In the case of rabies, as we shall see, the human body is defenseless. The viruses involved will destroy the nerve and brain tissue of the new host and bring inevitable death. The human body has been unable to "learn" how to meet this threat; an antibody must be stimulated or the victim will die. The utter helplessness of man's natural defenses in the face of newly incubated rabies virus cannot be overestimated.

Tetanus, or "lockjaw," is caused by an anaerobic bacterium, *Clostridium tetani*. Anaerobic bacteria are microorganisms that can grow and reproduce only where atmospheric oxygen is lacking, or severely reduced. Once deposited deep in human tissue, as in an animal bite, and particularly in wounds that scab over and start to heal, they grow rapidly and begin to secrete poisonous substances that bring on the characteristic disease. *C. tetani* is inevitably introduced in animal injuries. This microorganism is present in stools, on the body, and in the saliva of most animals—including man. It is a natural inhabitant there. Specific medical treatment can prevent the uncontrolled growth of these organisms and can head off the deadly disease. Introduction of the tetanus organism into a wound is almost impossible to avoid. If the wound closes quickly, or is at all deep, it will then permit these bacteria to reproduce. *Virtually all animal injuries indicate tetanus prophylactic measures.*

A catalog of the other microorganisms that can be introduced by animal injuries would be far too extensive to present here, both by virtue of the number of organisms involved and the qualifying statements required for each. Suffice it to repeat the statement above, *animal bites, gorings, and clawings are inevitably dirty wounds.* The wounds themselves require careful cleansing, and the body needs help in preventing the uncontrolled growth of dangerous microorganisms. Help, such as rabies vaccine, tetanus shots, or a broad-spectrum antibiotic course are invariably indicated. But the decision is for the doctor to make. The speed with which the victim is put under a doctor's care will, in many cases, be a major factor in determining the speed with which he will recover. Of course, some microorganisms allow a more flexible time factor than others.

Recapitulating briefly, nonvenomous animal wounds, from the point of view of microorganisms, require (1) the same first aid indicated by any filthy injury; and (2) professional medical consultation and care.

Tissue Damage

Of immediate concern—even more immediate than the problem of microorganisms—can be the matter of tissue damage and the loss of body fluids. In the majority of animal injuries, such as bites and stings by small venomous and nonvenomous reptiles, fishes, insects, and arachnids, tissue damage is not primarily a first aid problem. The concern for the safety of the victim will center around, in order of urgency, (1) venoms and (2) microorganisms. Only in the minority of cases will tissue damage be the primary concern.

On the other hand, shark attacks, injuries inflicted by big cats, bears, and other carnivores, and gorings by hoofed animals can result in appalling damage. Rule number one in such gross injuries is *stop the bleeding.* Nothing you or a doctor can do for a patient will have much value if he bleeds to death. In the really massive traumas, such as those characteristically inflicted by sharks, the prevention of run-away hemorrhage is just about all a bystander can do—except to treat for shock and try to obtain professional help. Any first aid manual will outline the three ways to control bleeding: pressure point, tourniquet, and pressure bandage. Anyone exposed to wildlife should know basic first aid, and basic first aid includes the control of blood loss at the top of the list. The *environments,* the surroundings in which you will find wildlife, are more apt to do you injury than the wildlife itself, but first aid is still the first and most essential knowledge for everyone in the field. A knowledge of artificial respiration, mouth-to-mouth resuscitation, basic bandaging techniques, and the immobilization of injured limbs are also essential information for everyone to have. The interested reader is referred to any good first aid manual, and is urged to take a comprehensive first aid course.

Shock is always attendant upon gross injury. It can have a wide range of effects and manifestations, from a slight giddy feeling, or weakness in the knees, to nausea, cold sweat, coma, and death. *Anyone injured by a wild animal will suffer from shock. Shock can, and does, kill.*

More often than not, shock is more severe than the victim realizes.

The number of injured people who have said, "I'm O.K. now," or "I'm all right," seconds before passing out are legion. In an injury of any size, or where much pain or particularly disturbing circumstances have been involved, *treat for shock*. Try to make the patient remain calm, sitting or lying down. Keep him warm, avoid artificial stimulants, discourage the examination of the wound by the victim, and, as much as possible, avoid fuss and confusion. The patient's mind and body will be struggling to offset and overcome the trauma that has been forced upon him. Help him in that struggle with calm, firm control, warmth, pain relief (other than depressant drugs), immobilization, comfort, bandaging, quiet, and reassurance.

In most injuries, particularly gross traumas, the conscious patient will be in a dangerous state of mind. The horror of what has happened can help increase the disposition to shock; stark terror can impede first aid measures; and an inability to accept a true evaluation of the situation can reduce the victim's ability to cope with his problem. Calm, quiet, isolation from crowds of the morbidly curious, and assertive reassurance are all part of effective first aid. There will always be loads of "experts" around. Above all, keep them from getting at the victim with their shouted advice, ghoulish admiration of the extent of the injuries, and generally appalling lack of appreciation of how the victim feels. Categorically, anyone who knows he cannot help but runs to look is an enemy of the patient. Keep them away even if you make enemies; but don't let the victim see or hear you rushing them off. That will only add to the horror of the moment.

Animal injuries inevitably come as a shock. Seldom does the victim even see the creature, except perhaps at the very last moment. It is a rare individual who is emotionally prepared for an assault by a wild animal. A skier shouldn't be too surprised if he breaks an arm or a leg and anyone working with sharp instruments is at least subconsciously aware of the hazards to which he is exposed. A hiker, on the other hand, is literally stunned when a venomous snake lashes out from a pile of dead leaves; a swimmer is utterly horror-stricken when suddenly grabbed from below; and a black widow spider under a toilet seat can transfix almost anyone. Take this into consideration when dealing with the victim of an animal injury. The state of mind resulting from this kind of accident is highly conducive to shock.

Venomous Bites and Stings

While there are rare but nonetheless notable exceptions (the bite of a sea snake, for one), an injury caused by a venomous animal is generally accompanied by excruciating pain. The pain may be immediate (venomous fishes), quick in coming (many venomous snakes), or relatively slow in developing a peak (spiders), but pain is invariably a major factor in an encounter of this kind. The agony of a stonefish sting (immediate), or the overall charley horse resulting from the bite of certain spiders can make a victim difficult to help. Restraint may sometimes be necessary.

The author was called upon to perform first aid on a young man bitten by a cottonmouth snake in a Louisiana swamp and required the assistance of three strong men to hold the victim down. The pain, coupled with the horror of the moment, not only makes first aid at times difficult but contributes to shock. Pain, agonizing pain, is usually a major problem in venomous bites and stings.

The best-known method for the treatment of venomous stings and bites is the so-called T-C-S technique, the initials standing for Tourni-quet-Cut-Suction. This method has been the standard first aid system for years, and relatively few laymen realize that it is held in disfavor by many doctors today. This technique simply involves the placing of a tourniquet, when possible, between the wound and the body, making small cross cuts over the punctures, and applying suction. Regular "snakebite kits" containing a tourniquet, a sterile scalpel encased in wax, a suction pump, iodine, and a capsule of ammonia are sold in drugstores, by mail-order houses, and issued by the armed forces to units in the field. The American Red Cross First Aid Book, and most others on the subject, seem almost automatically to set forth this method with each new printing. But, is it the best method to use?

A great deal of damage can be done by anxious administrators of first aid. Whenever possible one should get the victim to a doctor and avoid incisions and other possible causes of trauma. The proper treatment of a venomous injury requires medical attention (viz., antivenin, where you combat chemical with chemical) and not first aid. There are occasions, of course, when medical help is hours away and the usually prescribed first aid measures are essential. But, by no means should you start slashing and hacking at a snakebite victim unless there is no other course open to you.

Antivenin (not *antivenom*) kits can be purchased in a drugstore by any layman and, with due attention to the instructions enclosed, can be used in an emergency. It is always better to have the administration of such materials done by a professional but that is not always possible.

A note of caution: Antivenin can kill. It is usually made from horse serum. Some people are violently allergic to this serum and can die from its use, whereas they might not succumb to the venom itself. Antivenin kits include materials and instructions for testing for horse sensitivity. *Do not panic* and start plunging needles into people. Read those instructions and test for sensitivity. The victim of a venomous bite or sting has enough trouble without your putting him into anaphylactic shock, or even into a severe hyperallergic state.

Antivenins are happily now available for a wide variety of venomous bites and stings. Hospitals, and frequently doctors, in areas where venomous species are found, generally stock fresh supplies. All of the common venomous animals in North America are now covered by available antivenins, many of them broad-spectrum polyvalents. However, exotic species may pose an altogether different problem, and field work in new areas where venomous forms may offer a problem should be preceded by a check on antivenin availability, as a matter of course. Anyone importing, working with, or otherwise exposed to foreign forms should certainly bring in supplies to hold in readiness. There is seldom an excuse for a fatal accident with venomous forms for which antivenin is readily available. *The antivenin should be imported before the venom!*

There are many bites and stings for which no antivenins are available. This is particularly true of marine forms, and the reader is referred to Dr. Bruce W. Halstead's *Dangerous Marine Animals* for specific details of treatment for these forms. (The bibliography will further guide the interested reader to researchers in the various specialized fields.)

Most of the people in this world will never be called upon to aid someone who has been attacked by a wild animal. Despite the astounding statistics we hear, these injuries are rare. However, a camper who is mauled by a bear, bitten by a venomous snake, or stung by a scorpion is in serious trouble. Knowledgeable first aid and prompt, professional medical attention will keep the death rate low. It has not been high since the advent of sophisticated medicine and surgery, but could be lower yet. Except in the extremely rare cases of massive trauma (big cats and sharks being the principal offenders), many of those who do succumb could be saved with the proper attention. Don't go into the field without first aid equipment, and don't take equipment you haven't really learned to use. You will probably never use it on an animal-attack victim, but the saving of a human life is a motive grand enough to warrant all of the preparation and investment each of us can afford. What is more, it could be *your* life.

Appendix B   Rabies

This book is about reputedly dangerous animals that can be seen with the naked eye. In it we avoid discussion of bacteria and viruses. Not only does there have to be a limit to the size of any book, the matter of "disease" resulting from microorganisms constitutes quite a separate subject, and would require a whole new frame of reference. Two exceptions are, however, required; the subject of the disease commonly called *rabies;* and, as discussed in Appendix F, poisoning caused by eating certain fishes.

Rabies, hydrophobia, or lyssa is an acute, infectious disease of mammals, and particularly carnivores, that is *always fatal** to man once it takes hold; viz., passes the incubation period. A person exposed to the saliva of an infected animal by reason of a bite and who receives the causative neurotropic virus in his tissues is doomed to a particularly horrible death unless immediate and extensive counteractive measures are carried out. Anywhere from ten days to two years after the bite (fifty to sixty days is average) the symptoms will start.** Restlessness and depression will be followed by gradually increasing anxiety. Fear will grow into terror, periods of violent, uncontrollable rage will alternate with sudden listless calm, as the brain tissues are first irritated

*There have apparently been one or two rabies cases where the people survived, but with uncounted thousands of fatalities as recorded facts the disease is still generally considered fatal.

**Among those working on bat-transmitted rabies, forty-eight hours is held to be the limit before professional medical countermeasures are instituted.

and eventually injured beyond control or repair. A ringing telephone, a draft from a small electric fan, or the light from a cigarette lighter will induce convulsions. Spastic contractions of the pharynx and larynx will cause pain when an attempt is made to swallow. Extreme thirst, coupled with a dread of strangling, will turn the victim into a raging maniac on the sight, or even mention of, water. Mercifully, death from cardiac or respiratory failure will usually come within three to five days after the onset of symptoms. There is a second form of rabies generally referred to as the "dumb form"* where the violent, convulsive symptoms are lacking, and paralysis precedes death.

In 1884 Pasteur developed the counteractive vaccine used today. A person who has been bitten by a suspected carrier *must* receive repeated doses of this vaccine (prepared from the brain tissue of an infected animal) *before* the symptoms appear. Since fourteen days are required for the human body to produce rabies antibodies, this serum is used to cover this dangerous gap. Pure carbolic acid on the wound may prolong the incubation period, but it cannot be relied upon to kill all the viruses and its use has fallen into general disfavor among most doctors. *No first aid measure can defer the absolute necessity of a vaccine course.*

The incidence of rabies in nature is peculiar and complex. It infects the central nervous system and finally concentrates in the brain in an area called Ammon's horn where it forms minute black clots called Negri or inclusion bodies. These are readily identifiable on autopsy.

Rabies seems to be a universally distributed malady, and used to be before the discovery of its cause, a constant menace. Even the ancients recognized that it followed animal bites, and long before Pasteur's work, pariah and other feral dogs were slaughtered whenever it broke out in epidemic form. It must be stressed that it still probably remains all over the world in endemic form; that is to say, there are "reservoirs" of it, in a latent form, in some species of animals in almost all countries. It appears to become increasingly common as one approaches the equatorial regions.

The disease occurs in the two distinct forms already referred to (these are *not* different strains or "kinds," they differ only in symptoms) and may alternate, in that carnivorous animals usually display the furious while their vegetarian victims display the paralytic. However, there is usually a comatose period in the former and often a furious phase in the latter. All animals—including man—infected with this disease will, or may, bite uncontrollably, but the worst are perhaps (naturally) the meat-eaters. Some animals, like man, may go into coma before they

*That is, *paralytic* as opposed to *furious.*

reach this stage. Herbivores may simply become paralyzed; and this paralysis may involve the jaw muscles at an early stage, thus preventing them from biting.

The true vampire bats (several other kinds of bats are called vampire bats in various areas but are either fruit-or insect-eaters) are inhabitants of South and Central America and, it seems, have been slowly extending their range into North America. They live in caves and other retreats along with other kinds of bats and are just about the only animals that are likely to infect these other bats. Many of our common bats migrate in winter to the far south and become infected there, then fly north again to infect other bats that then start biting other animals they would normally avoid.

A further and added menace of *Desmodus* is that it apparently can carry rabies for very long periods, if not indefinitely, without displaying symptoms of the disease. In fact, much of the *Desmodus* population may even be immune to it, though still housing Negri bodies.

Strangely enough, it wasn't until 1953 that clinical data substantiated the long-suspected fact that bats were transmitting rabies in the United States, for *Desmodus* is not found much north of the Mexican border. On the morning of June 23 in that year, the seven-year-old son of a Florida ranch employee ran into some bushes after a ball. A bat flew at him and bit him on the chest, maintaining a firm hold. It was knocked to the ground and killed. The ranch owner, recalling that vampire bats were known to be infected with rabies in Mexico, sent the bat to a laboratory in Tampa, where Negri bodies were found in the brain. Further tests were conducted at Jacksonville and Montgomery. The boy was put into an immunization course and recovery was uneventful. Had the rancher not remembered a piece he had read about Mexican bats, the boy would probably have died.

Of the world's estimated two thousand species and subspecies of bats, sixty-five are regularly found in the United States. How many of these are reservoirs of rabies is not known, but presumably all can be, since all mammals, it is believed, can be infected.

After the 1953 Florida attack, a careful study was made of bat bites. It turned out that a woman was bitten by a bat in Texas in 1951, and died in less than a month. An autopsy revealed Negri bodies in her brain. An insectivorous bat bit a Pennsylvania woman in 1953, and was found to be rabid. A man was bitten in Harrisburg, Pennsylvania, in April 1957, by a bat that proved to have been infected.

Although it is now clear that any bat that bites a human must be immediately suspect, these small flying mammals are not the only wild creatures involved in the spread of this disease. At the end of the Civil War, it is reported, skunks were infected throughout the western states. Campers were attacked in their tents at night, and reportedly many died. Skunks were dreaded by everyone and killed on sight. Foxes, and more particularly coyotes, are known to be carriers, and probably help to spread the disease among domestic dogs.

Rabies is not only of concern to man because he can contract it and be killed by it but because it is also deadly to domestic stock and causes "mad" (or dumb) and unpredictable behavior among wild animals. There can be little doubt that some attacks on humans by species not normally prone to attack—mountain lion and deer included—are caused by this disease. How many attacks can be accounted for in this way is not known. Household pets become savage beasts as they approach the terminal stages of the infection. Livestock must be destroyed once the symptoms become apparent, and many otherwise inexplicable accidents with farm animals can probably be traced to rabies.

How do you avoid becoming a victim? Here are a few ground rules:

1. *Do not be a hero* if an oddly behaving dog shows up in the neighborhood. Get your family, your pets, *and yourself* indoors and call the police. If you even suspect a pet animal of having gotten near a "mad dog," get it to a veterinarian immediately. If you are driving along and an animal suddenly dashes in front of your car and is knocked down, control your natural instincts and don't pick the injured animal up in your exposed hands. By all means, try to help the creature, but throw a blanket or rug around it and don't let its head near your face when you carry it. The animal may have been reacting to a rabies infection when it dashed under your wheels in the first place.

2. If a pet suddenly displays a change in temperament, get it to a vet. If it is unusually cranky, if it reacts too violently to light or noise, don't take chances.

3. If you come across a small wild creature that seems to be sick or dying, or unusually "tame" or lacking fear of you *do not handle it*. This is particularly true of bats, foxes, and skunks. If a wild animal enters your campsite and acts viciously, avoid any personal contact. Destroy it without exposing yourself to a possible bite, or trap it without handling it. Turn it over to the nearest health authorities. Most important of all, don't touch a wild animal that shows no fear of you, or is wandering about by day and lets you approach it. It is probably diseased, and the disease may be rabies.

4. Be careful in caves, hollow trees, and barns. Do not pick up any

bat that seems unable to fly. Avoid *any* area where you note bats crawling around on the floor or ground.

5. If bitten by any wild mammal, *secure the animal*—killing it is the safest course—and take it *at once* to the nearest health authority, hospital, or game warden.

6. If you have reason to suspect a dog that has bitten you or anyone you know, do everything you can to secure or identify the animal, and go to a doctor immediately. (By *secure* is meant trap it in a garage or by some similar technique—do *not* attempt to handle it.) Do not let stories of how unpleasant a course of rabies vaccine is deter you from seeking treatment. It is nothing like the disease itself. Rabies is *not* like most other viral infections that can be treated at home or that will pass in time. *If you are exposed to the disease and do not receive professional help, you will die!*

7. Do not go crawling around in bat dung on cave floors. Dry dung rising up as dust can infect you with the rabies virus if rabid bats have been using the cave, a fact not generally appreciated.

At the beginning of this book we said we would discuss only wild animals, not domestic ones. This chapter is an exception to that rule, for any animal, even a human being, may be a "carrier" of this dread disease—even your lovable dog if it has been so much as scratched by an infected animal. A rabid animal, however small, is the most dangerous animal alive. Unlike snakes, scorpions, spiders, and all other venomous forms, untreated bites of a rabid mammal are *100 percent fatal.*

Appendix C   The Rattlesnakes

Because of the special interest in this group of reptiles among residents of the Western Hemisphere, the following tables are provided. Information was obtained from Laurence M. Klauber's two-volume work, *Rattlesnakes: Their Habits, Life Histories, and Influence on Mankind*.

Table C-1.   The Rattlesnakes

Species and subspecies	Popular name	Range (words "parts of" implied
Crotalus adamanteus	Eastern diamondback rattlesnake*	Lowland coastal plains: North Carolina, South Carolina, Georgia, Florida (and some adjacent keys), Alabama, Mississippi, Louisiana
C. atrox	Western diamondback	Arkansas, Oklahoma, Missouri (?), Kansas, Oklahoma, Texas (and coastal islands), New Mexico, Arizona, Nevada, California, Baja California, Mexico, and islands in Gulf of California
C. basiliscus basiliscus	Mexican west coast	Mexico
C. basiliscus oaxacus	Oaxacan	Mexico—limited range

Species and subspecies	Popular name	Range (words "parts of" implied)
C. catalinensis	Santa Catalina Island	Mexican Santa Catalina Island—not the California island of that name
C. cerastes cerastes	Mojave Desert sidewinder**	California, Nevada, Utah, Arizona
C. cerastes cercobombus	Sonoran Desert sidewinder**	Arizona, Mexico, Tiburon Island
C. cerastes laterorepens	Colorado Desert sidewinder**	California, Arizona, Baja California, Mexico
C. durissus durissus	Central American	Mexico, Guatemala, Honduras, El Salvador, Nicaragua, Costa Rica, British Honduras (?)
C. durissus culminatus	Northwestern neotropical	Mexico
C. durissus terrificus	South American	Colombia, Venezuela, British Guiana, Surinam, French Guiana, Brazil, Peru, Bolivia, Paraguay, Uruguay, Argentina, Ecuador (?)
C. durissus totonacus	Totonacan	Mexico
C. durissus tzabcan	Yucatan neotropical	Mexico, Guatemala (?), British Honduras (?)
C. durissus vegrandis	Urucoan	Venezuela
C. enyo enyo	Lower California	Baja California and west coast Mexican islands
C. enyo cerralvensis	Cerralvo Island	Cerralvo Island, Mexico, Gulf of California
C. enyo furvus	Rosario	Baja California
C. exsul	Cedros Island diamondback	Cedros Island, Baja California
C. horridus horridus	Timber	Vermont, New Hampshire, Virginia, West Virginia, Ohio, Kentucky, North and South Carolina, Georgia, Tennessee, Alabama, Indiana, Illinois, Wisconsin, Minnesota, Iowa, Missouri, Nebraska, Kansas, Arkansas, Oklahoma, Texas, New York, Massachusetts, Connecticut, New Jersey, Rhode Island,

Table C-1. The Rattlesnakes—Continued

Species and subspecies	Popular name	Range (words "parts of" implied)
		Pennsylvania; formerly also Maine and Delaware; Canada (Ontario)
C. horridus atricaudatus	Canebrake	Virginia, North and South Carolina, Georgia, Florida, Alabama, Mississippi, Kentucky, Tennessee, Louisiana, Arkansas, Missouri, Illinois, Texas
C. intermedius intermedius	Totalcan small-headed	Mexico
C. intermedius omiltemanus	Omilteman small-headed	Mexico
C. lepidus lepidus	Mottled rock	New Mexico, Texas, Mexico
C. lepidus klauberi	Banded rock	Arizona, New Mexico, Texas, Mexico
C. lepidus morulus	Tamaulipan rock	Mexico—limited range
C. mitchelli mitchelli	San Lucan speckled	Baja California, Mexico, Gulf and Pacific coast Mexican islands
C. mitchelli muertensis	El Muerto Island speckled	El Muerto Island only, off Baja California
C. mitchelli pyrrhus	Southwestern speckled	California, Nevada, Arizona, Utah, Baja California, Pacific coast Mexican islands
C. mitchelli stephensi	Panamint	California, Nevada
C. molossus molossus	Northern black-tailed	Texas, Arizona, New Mexico, Mexico, Gulf of California, Mexican islands
C. molossus estebanensis	San Esteban Island	San Esteban Island, Gulf of California
C. molossus nigrescens	Mexican black-tailed	Mexico
C. polystictus	Mexican lance-headed	Mexico
C. pricei pricei	Arizona twin-spotted	Arizona, Mexico
C. pricei miquihuanus	Miquihuanan twin-spotted	Mexico
C. pusillus	Tancitaran dusky	Mexico
C. ruber ruber	Red diamondback	California, Baja California, Mexico, Gulf of California islands

Species and subspecies	Popular name	Range (words "parts of" implied)
C. ruber lucasensis	San Lucan diamondback	Baja California, Gulf of California islands
C. scutulatus scutulatus	Mojave	California, Nevada, Utah, Arizona, New Mexico, Texas, Mexico
C. scutulatus salvini	Huamantlan	Mexico
C. stejnegeri	Long-tailed	Arizona, Mexico
C. tigris	Tiger	Arizona, Mexico
C. tortugensis	Tortuga Island diamondback	Tortuga Island, Gulf of California
C. transversus	Cross-banded mountain	Mexico
C. triseriatus triseriatus	Central-plateau dusky	Mexico
C. triseriatus aquilus	Queretaran dusky	Mexico
C. unicolor	Aruba Island	Aruba Island (coast of Venezuela)
C. viridis viridis	Prairie	Canada (Alberta, Saskatchewan), Mexico, Montana, Idaho, Wyoming, Colorado, Utah, Arizona, New Mexico, North and South Dakota, Iowa, Nebraska, Kansas, Oklahoma, Texas
C. viridis abyssus	Grand Canyon	Arizona
C. viridis caliginis	Coronado Island	South Coronado Island, off Baja California
C. viridis cerberus	Arizona black	Arizona, New Mexico
C. viridis decolor	Midget faded	Wyoming, Utah, Colorado
C. viridis helleri	Southern Pacific	California, Baja California, Santa Catalina Island
C. viridis lutosus	Great Basin	Idaho, Utah, Arizona, Nevada, California, Oregon
C. viridis nuntius	Arizona prairie	Arizona, New Mexico
C. viridis oreganus	Northern Pacific	Canada (British Columbia), California, Washington, Oregon, Idaho
C. willardi amabilis		Mexico
C. willardi willardi	Arizona ridge-nosed	Arizona, Mexico
C. willardi meridionalis	Southern ridge-nosed	Mexico
C. willardi silus	Chihuahuan ridge-nosed	Mexico, New Mexico

Table C-1. The Rattlesnakes—Continued

Species and subspecies	Popular name	Range (words "parts of" implied)
Sistrurus catenatus catenatus	Eastern Massasauga**	New York, Canada (Ontario), Pennsylvania, Michigan, Ohio, Indiana, Illinois, Wisconsin, Minnesota, Iowa, Missouri, Nebraska, Kansas
S. catenatus tergeminus	Western Massasauga**	Nebraska, Kansas, Colorado, Oklahoma, New Mexico, Arizona, Texas, Mexico
S. miliarius miliarius	Carolina pygmy	North and South Carolina, Georgia, Alabama
S. miliarius barbouri	Southeastern pygmy	South Carolina, Georgia, Florida, Alabama, Mississippi
S. miliarius streckeri	Western pygmy	Mississippi, Louisiana, Tennessee, Missouri, Arkansas, Oklahoma, Texas, Alabama (?)
S. ravus	Mexican pygmy	Mexico

*Unless otherwise noted, the word *rattlesnake* is part of the preferred popular name.
**Word *rattlesnake* not included in common or preferred popular name.

Working from Table C-1, it is worth noting statistically where the rattlesnake is encountered and in what variety. Once again, these figures are not to be taken as an indication of actual population. Some areas are literally infested and others rarely offer even a single specimen. In some cases, only a small corner or pocket of the geographic area indicated has any rattlesnake population at all. A state line or a national boundary is a man-made thing and a rattlesnake in pursuit of prey or shelter is not apt to take much note of an artificial barrier.

Table C-2. Rattlesnake Distribution

Canada			
Alberta (1)	British Columbia (1)	Ontario (2)	Saskatchewan (1)

United States			
Alabama (5, possibly 6)	Alaska (none)	Arizona (17)	Arkansas (4)
California (10)	Colorado (3)	Connecticut (1)	Delaware (unlikely, but possibly 1)

'lorida (3)	Georgia (5)	Hawaii (none)	Idaho (3)
Illinois (3)	Indiana (2)	Iowa (3)	Kansas (5)
Kentucky (2)	Louisiana (3)	Maine (unlikely, but possibly 1)	Maryland (1)
Massachusetts (1)	Michigan (1)	Minnesota (2)	Mississippi (4)
Missouri (4, possibly 5)	Montana (1)	Nebraska (4)	Nevada (6)
New Hampshire (1)	New Jersey (1)	New Mexico (9)	New York (2)
North Carolina (4)	North Dakota (1)	Ohio (2)	Oklahoma (5)
Oregon (2)	Pennsylvania (2)	Rhode Island (1)	South Carolina (5)
South Dakota (1)	Tennessee (3)	Texas (10)	Utah (6)
Vermont (1)	Virginia (2)	Washington (1)	West Virginia (1)
Wisconsin (2)	Wyoming (2)	District of Columbia (unlikely, but possibly 1)	

Mexico

Exclusive of Baja California and adjacent islands—35;
Baja California and adjacent islands—18

Central America

British Honduras (1)	Guatemala (1)	El Salvador (1)	Honduras (1)
Nicaragua (1)	Costa Rica (1)	Panama (probably none)	Canal Zone (probably none)

South America

Colombia (1)	Venezuela (2)	Guyana (1)	Surinam (1)
French Guiana (1)	Brazil (1)	Ecuador (possibly 1)	Peru (1)
Bolivia (1)	Paraguay (1)	Uruguay (1)	Argentina (1)
Chile (none)	Aruba Island (1)		

Note: Numbers indicate number of presently recognized species and subspecies known to inhabit
the area indicated.

Appendix D   The Reptile "Hall of Infamy"

The author initially had every intention of compiling a "Reptile Hall of Infamy" to round out this work. The original intention was to prepare this table from statistics and reports of "snakebites" gathered from all over the world. After several abortive attempts, it became obvious that no one man could possibly prepare such a table and expect any single expert to agree with his conclusions.

A second effort was made along different lines. A set of criteria was prepared and dispatched to a number of authorities with the request that they use it to prepare individual lists. This too was hopeless. No set of criteria would fit all of the opinions.

Finally, the authorities were asked to prepare a list along any lines they thought best. From these different lists, with these different criteria, a master table (Table D-1) has been prepared. The remarks and observations of the experts are as revealing as their lists. (Reference to these remarks in the table are noted as numbers in parentheses.) The other numbers under the experts' names, and opposite the species listed on the left, refer to the place in the "most dangerous" list assigned to the species by the expert. Number 1 refers to most dangerous, etc. An asterisk under an expert's name (and opposite a species) means that the expert included the snake as belonging on the most dangerous list but that a position on the list was not indicated. The positions and species listed for each expert are meaningless without the footnotes which contain the criteria used. After studying this unique table, the reader is free to decide for himself which is the most dangerous snake in the world.

Table D-1. The Reptile Hall of Infamy

Reptile	Carl Kauffeld (1)	Laurence Klauber (2)	Robert Inger (3)	Clifford Pope (4)	Sherman Minton (5)
King cobra (Ophiophagus hannah) (6)	*	1–1	*	*	1–1
Taipan (Oxyuranus scutellatus)	*	1–2	*		1–2
Mambas (Dendroaspis sp.) (7)	*	1–3		*	1–3 2–8
Common cobra (Naja naja) (8)	*	1–6		*	1–9 2–1
Javan krait (Bungarus javanicus) (9)	*				
Tiger snake (Notechis scutatus)		1–5	*	*	1–7
Bushmaster (Lachesis muta)		*			1–4
Western diamondback rattlesnake (10) (Crotalus atrox)		*		*	1–5 (10)
Fer-de-lance (Bothrops atrox)		*		*	1–6 2–2
Tropical rattlesnake (Crotalus durissus)		1–7		*	1–8 2–7
Jararacussu (Bothrops jararacussu)					1–10
Saw-scaled viper (Echis carinatus)		1–10			2–3
Russell's viper (Vipera russelli)		1–9		*	2–4
Puff adder (Bitis arietans)		1–8			2–5
Egyptian cobra (Naja haje) (8)		*			2–6
Jararaca (Bothrops jararaca)				*	2–9
Indian krait (11) (Bungarus caeruleus)		*		* (12)	2–10
Death adder (Acanthophis antarcticus)		1–4			
Australian blacksnake (Pseudechis porphyiacus)		*			

Table D-1.   The Reptile Hall of Infamy—Continued

Reptile	Carl Kauffeld (1)	Laurence Klauber (2)	Robert Inger (3)	Clifford Pope (4)	Sherman Minton (5)
Australian copperhead (*Denisonia superba*)		*			
Gaboon viper (*Bitis gabonica*)		*			
Eastern diamondback rattlesnake (*Crotalus adamanteus*) (10)		*			
Ringhals (*Hemachatus haemachatus*)		*			

Notes:

(1) As a single criterion, the late Carl Kauffeld, former curator of reptiles at New York's Staten Island Zoo, used *"chances for survival,"* what snake you would have the *least* chance of surviving if bitten. He lists five snakes, but did not indicate that they were in order; they are indicated on the chart with an asterisk (*).

(2) Speaking of his two lists, the late Dr. Laurence M. Klauber said:

. . . based almost exclusively on the literature of herpetology . . . in making selections I have been guided more by the characteristics of the snakes themselves, rather than by the human factors involved. . . . I have given the greatest weight to such criteria as venom quantity, venom toxicity, physiological effects of venom, length of fangs, length and weight of adult snakes, aggressiveness or disposition, abundance of the species, extent of territorial range, etc., all of which are natural characteristics inherent in the snakes themselves. . . . In compiling my list, I have considered all snakes at the species level and have introduced no subspecific distinctions. From the standpoint of the human hazard, subspecific differences are usually technical and minor in character.

Speaking of his first list (indicated on the table as 1–), Dr. Klauber says, "Necessarily it is highly subjective; tomorrow it might be quite different, both in content and order." Speaking of his second list (indicated on the table as *), "Among the candidates that were given consideration but have been relegated to the second ten are these, not here given in any order of relative danger."

(3) Robert F. Inger, curator of reptiles at the Chicago Natural History Museum, says of his list:

Your request for an opinion is difficult to comply with because we just don't have enough information. . . . I am willing to give you my impression of the three most dangerous poisonous snakes. By all accounts the three are: . . . This rating is based not upon the number of human fatalities each species is responsible for, or upon the potency of the venom drop by drop. Instead it is based upon an estimate of the chances for survival following a bite.

No order was indicated and his three choices are indicated on the table by an asterisk (*).

(4) Clifford H. Pope says of his list, "Applied to snakes the word dangerous may mean potentially a menace or actually destructive. I assume that you mean the latter and would list the following species:. . . They are not listed in order of dangerousness."

The snakes on his list are indicated on the table by an asterisk (*).

(5) Speaking of his list, Dr. Minton says:

List one is the snakes I consider intrinsically most dangerous—that is, the species I would least care to be locked up in a phone booth with. All are large snakes with a reputation for having an uncertain temper at best. All have large fangs and a good supply of moderately to highly potent venom. Quite a few of them, however, contribute very little to the world mortality for snake bite. . . . List two is the snakes that I estimate, on very inadequate data, are the species that kill the most people. These must obviously have a lethal venom and some inclination to use it, but more importantly they are snakes that have adapted to life with relatively dense human populations living and working under conditions that make snakebite a real hazard. Nearly every one of these snakes has a big geographic range and is plentiful over the greater part of it.

Dr. Minton's two lists are indicated on the table by the respective prefixes, 1– , 2– .

(6) The King cobra is listed by specific *hannah* but is put into two genera by different experts, *Naja* and *Ophiophagus*. The specialists represented on this chart preferred: *Ophiophagus*—Minton, Kauffeld, Klauber; *Naja*—Inger, Pope.

(7) Speaking of the mambas, Minton says, "The four or more species of mambas confuse even herpetologists, so it is hard to say which one any given account refers to. Those who know the genus best seem agreed that *D. polylepis* is the worst of the lot." However, Dr. Minton refers to *Dendroaspis* sp. on his list. Clifford Pope refers to *D. polylepis* on his; Kauffeld says, "Mambas, *Dendroaspis* any species, but *angusticeps* and *polylepis* probably tops. . . ."; Klauber says, "Black and/or Green Mamba *Dendroaspis polylepis* and/or *D. angusticeps*."

(8) The names common cobra and Indian cobra are apparently both applied to the species *Naja naja*. Dr. Minton, when speaking of the appearance of the species on his list, says: "I suspect there would be very little choice between this species and any of the big African cobras, for example, N. haje or N. nigricollis."

(9) Speaking of the Javan krait, Carl Kauffeld says: " . . . This is an obscure species described by Dr. Felix Kopstein on the basis of a specimen which was responsible for the death of three natives, bitten in succession by the same snake. I am unaware that any specimens of the type have come to light, but it must be a heller!"

(10) Dr. Klauber puts both the western and the eastern diamondback rattlesnakes on his second list; Pope puts just the western species on his, and Minton says of the western species holding down fifth position on his first list: "Strictly speaking, I'd put the Eastern Diamondback (*C. adamanteus*) in number 6 or 7 slot. In this list I haven't distinguished between these two closely related rattlesnakes."

(11) Minton refers to the Indian Krait (*B. caeruleus*) on his second list; Pope refers to *B. fasciatus* on his; Klauber refers to *caeruleus* on his. The author has taken the liberty of combining the two on the table as *caeruleus* with this explanation. Kauffeld's *B. javanicus* is apparently a different animal altogether.

What then is the deadliest snake in the world? All five experts named the king cobra—no other snake was so honored. The two experts who listed their choices in the order they considered most dangerous put the king cobra in first position. I must concur—the king cobra, the largest venomous snake in the world, probably by several feet, is the animal I would least like to step on, or, as Dr. Minton put it, "I would least care to be locked up in a phone booth with." It must be remembered, however, that the king cobra is not necessarily a major contributor to world snakebite mortality. This apparent contradiction arises from the fact that the king cobra prefers heavily forested and generally remote regions. It does not invade agricultural areas as regularly as do the other cobras, and so many other truly dangerous serpents the world over. If it did, the bite/death ratio would shoot up even higher than it already has. The bite of the king, evidently, is not easy to survive.

Appendix E   Snakebite Case Histories

Thousands of venomous injuries have reached the medical literature over the decades, and nothing better characterizes the nature of these emergencies than the verbatim quotes in such recorded case histories. The following are the report of Dr. Romulus Whitaker of the Madras Snake Park Trust in Madras, India, and are reprinted in their entirety from the February 15, 1974, *Journal of the Bombay Natural History Society*, by permission of Dr. Whitaker.

1. May 24th, 1971. Medavakkam, near Madras.
   Girl, 18, suspected krait bite, fatal. Sleeping on a mat on the floor of the hut when bitten on leg. Snake was killed and described as being long, thin and black. Girl was given "country" remedies but died before daybreak.
2. August 25th, 1971. Tambaram, near Madras.
   Gurkha, Nepali night watchman, about 40 years old, suspected krait or cobra bite. At 7 A.M. men came rushing to me to say that this man had been bitten and died but could I somehow help anyway!? (This has happened several times). Watchman stepped on and was bitten at 1 A.M. by an unknown, "large" snake. His wife and he then sat around. By 3 A.M. the man succumbed. No help was sought, till morning.
3. January, 1972. Boy, 10 years, died possibly as a result of complications from bite of *Echis carinatus* (see case 9, *Echis* bites).

4. May 26th, 1972. Madavakkam, near Madras. Friday morning—rainy, windy. 8 A.M. two men arrive with news of snake bite at Medavakkam (4 miles away on Velachery Rd.). I reached the hut 8.15 A.M. A crowd of people, mostly women were crying and yelling and beating themselves on the breast in anguish. The young man, of about 22, lay flat on back, arms folded, flower petals on eyelids, only light in the room was an oil lamp. No pupil response, no pulse, heartbeat or breath. The left lower leg quite swollen, with two obvious punctures below ankle bone. An Irla (tribal snake catcher) was digging around the hut trying to find the snake which was supposed to have been called cobra by the bitten man—he saw it crawl away in the moonlight. Possibly krait. It was as likely or more so that it was a krait since it is a common nocturnal prowler and seems less wary than a cobra; these "bites while sleeping" are common. The sleeping man may have felt the snake brushing against him and in his sleep pressed the snake with his foot (perhaps rolled over it). He woke up, saw the snake which seemed to go into a hole in the hut. Many people woke and carried him to a village 2 miles away for "country medicine", a plaster of green paste supposed to contain the remedy. He came back and sat and was slowly paralyzed to death by the neurotoxins in the venom. Had trouble breathing at 6 A.M. and collapsed at 7 A.M. Just 4 miles away is a dispensary and my home; it is well known that we have antivenom serum. We treated or supplied serum for about 2 dozen bites in the last year (mostly *Echis*). If the use of antivenom was publicized, there would be very few fatal snakebites in India and the public attitude towards snakes could gradually become realistically tolerant. At present a supernatural fear of snakes prevails and no wonder when the venom can kill so surely in spite of all the "remedies" tried out.

5. 17th August, 1972, Madras City.
Lady, 58 years, suspected krait bite, fatal. At 6 A.M. went into bathroom to take a bath, stepped on "small black snake about 2 feet". Local symptoms absent, small single wound, little bleeding, slight oozing. In the first 6 hours the blood pressure rose, complained of trouble in swallowing, breathing, 6 hours after bite she went into a coma. 2 vials antivenin given, supportive therapy, antihistamines, blood pressure drugs, haemodialysis. Lady succumbed without coming out of coma next day at 11:30 A.M. (about 36 hours later).

6. June 2, 1972—Chinnappa—18 year old Irula tribal snake-catcher of Sotalapakkam village near Tambaram, Madras 44, cobra bite, recovered.

The day after a heavy shower Chinnappa was hunting snakes with his uncle. They were hunting in separate farm areas near rocky hills about 18 miles from Madras City. Chinnappa, searching carefully for tracks, made out the fresh track of a large snake (he thought cobra) going into a rat hole. Rat holes are everywhere in the earthen and rock mounds and bunds near paddy fields. He dug with a small crow bar and poked with a thin stick down the various branches of the hole. In one the stick moved. He dug forward carefully; he was only about 2 feet deep into the mound when he gradually uncovered a very fine healthy cobra just under 5 feet long. Quickly he pressed the flat side of the little crowbar on the snake's head and grabbed a secure hold on the neck with his left hand. He had a small cloth shopping bag with handles to tie the open end shut. Then he did an odd thing for an experienced snake catcher, "not thinking for a moment": holding the bag open with thumb and forefinger encircled, he pushed the cobra's head into the resultant hole. The cobra partly entered the bag then very quickly turned and bit Chinnappa through the cloth on the fleshy part of the left hand below the little finger with both fangs. He immediately threw the snake down (which was caught in the same mound the next day!) and clutched his left wrist. He walked a little and called to his uncle about half a mile away. His uncle tied a piece of cloth tightly on the upper arm, the hand had already begun swelling. 3½ hours later (4 P.M.) he had walked and ridden on the back of a cycle the 6 or 7 miles to Madras Snake Park. The swelling was halfway up the arm and he complained of much burning pain throughout the arm below the tourniquet. Antivenin was ready and we removed the tourniquet to relieve the pressure on his arm. Until 8 P.M. there was little change except the steadily increasing swelling now above the elbow. At 8.30 P.M. Chinnappa started having the symptoms of drooping eyelids and puffed lips called ptosis, the first sign of systemic neurotoxic poisoning. We immediately drove him to the clinic nearby where the lab tech, supervised by Dr. Sarangapani gave 10 cc Haffkine polyvalent antivenin with 5 mg cortisone IV. Shortly afterwards, Chinnappa vomited but looked more lively. We waited at the clinic for an hour and then returned home where Chinnappa, with his old mother watching over, started a fitful night. His arm was less painful, most of the pain was at the site of the bite. At about 11 P.M. he started shivering violently, so he was covered with blankets and rubbed by mother and cousin. The shivering went away in 20 minutes (maybe allergic reaction to antivenom). Gave two aspirins and he slept well till morning. His arm swelling reached a painful peak and then subsided except for the hand within 12 hours. A ten day supply of multivitamins given. Twelve days later hand is still very swollen, site of bite appears as some skin will slough. Advised daily dressing changes. Thirty days later, bit of skin loss took place but except for stiffness hand and arm are OK, advised exercises for hand.

BITES OF *ECHIS CARINATUS*

1. Panvel, near Bombay, October, 1967. An adult male Adivasi aged about 35 was bitten in the evening just behind big toe on top of right foot by an *Echis* about 10 inches long. Came next day 2 P.M. for treatment. Dorsum of foot edemal, slight discoloration of site of bite. Blood pressure 100/60, complains of pain, didn't sleep. Slight bleeding from gums. Treated with tetanus toxoid and antibiotics. Next evening (48 hours post bite) gum-bleeding stopped, foot seems more swollen, complains of pain and discomfort. Aspirin and sulfa tablets given. Adivasi plastered jungle medicine that looks like cow dung all over bitten foot. Six days later Iodex applied to bitten limb and patient said swelling went down soon after application. Eight days later foot appears normal, no necrosis or swelling.

2. Deogad, Ratnagiri District, Maharashtra, September, 1969, 7 A.M. N. Gate, a male worker, aged 30 walking to work through a field near Deogad town, stepped on a 300 mm long *Echis* and was bitten on right lateral side of ankle joint on the right foot. The victim walked two miles to the dispensary with a friend's help. Snake was killed and brought in at 8.30 A.M. When the patient reached the doctor there was swelling and tenderness around the site of bite; dark bluish discoloration about 2 inches in diameter. Shooting pain in calf muscle, adenitis behind knee and in lower inguinal glands. Swelling of ankle and foot increasing.

   9 A.M. as patient did not exhibit any alarming or systematic symptoms, 10 cc of Haffkine serum was injected intramuscularly. Procaine-penicillin injected, aspirin given and patient sent home.

   Next day, 8 A.M. patient reported to doctor that he had recovered; only slight signs remained at the site of bite.

3. Jamsande, Ratnagiri Dist., 15 January, 1963, A.M. S. S. Bhadsabe, a male worker age 25 years was moving stones and got a toe bite from an *Echis*. Within one hour he came to dispensary with severe local bite symptoms. Urine cloudy and bloody. 15 cc Haffkine antivenom given intravenously which provoked immediate allergic reaction including: urticaria, severe itching, heat, headache, asthmatic breathing. Administered .5 cc adrenalin and treated patient for shock for half an hour. Additional 5 ml antivenom given. Calcium lactate given. Next day local symptoms diminished, urine trace blood; calcium gluconate and cal-

cium lactate given. Third day patient seemed completely recovered, calcium lactate given.

4. Deogad, Ratnagiri Dist., 27 January, 1965 A.M. A. G. Kawale, a 1½ year old male child was playing in the garden and picked up an *Echis* which he mistook for a rope. He was bitten on the right palm and there was swelling at site of bite and whole of palm within half an hour. The child's crying attracted attention and he was brought to the doctor within 45 minutes after the bite. 10 cc Haffkine antivenom injected intramuscularly in the buttocks one hour after bite. 20 grains calcium gluconate given. Local symptoms subsided by evening of the same day, recovery complete.

5. Deogad, Ratnagiri Dist., August, 1964 A.M. Female age 65 was bitten on the instep of left foot by an *Echis* and came to dispensary within one hour. 10 cc Haffkine antivenom was given intramuscularly as local symptoms of swelling and pain were apparent. After five hours there was bleeding from gums and evidence of blood in stools. An additional 10 cc serum was injected intravenously. The patient had moderate allergic reaction which was treated and patient recovered but weak after 6 hours. Second day recovery complete.

6. Sembakkam, near Madras, October 20, 1970. A male child about 10 years, was bitten the evening before by an *Echis* on the big toe while going out to the bathroom. When he came at 10 A.M. foot was moderately swollen and slight swelling of the lower leg. Little pain, weakness and discomfort evident. Taken to a nearby doctor where he was observed for a few hours treated locally and sent home with instructions to parents to look for bleeding gums etc. Swelling subsided within 2 days and there were no after effects.

7. Sembakkam, near Madras, November 17, 1970. A woman about 40 years old was bitten by an *Echis* while cutting branches from a low thorn tree. Finger was tied tightly with a string and was tautly swollen. I released the string. The patient exhibited great pain and anxiety. Took her to doctor where she was kept for observation that afternoon then sent home. In two days there was a little tissue loss and dressings were applied. Swelling and sloughing persisted a week.

8. Tambaram, near Madras, December 15, 1970. An Irula snake-catcher, was bitten by an *Echis* on the right thumb while catching it. Didn't suffer on the first day. Second day had swollen hand and for 2 days had difficulty using hand. Untreated and no more symptoms.

9. Tambaram, near Madras, November 25, 1970. Natesan, an Irula snake catcher about 40 bitten on base of left index finger while catching. Swelling slight, stiff hand for two days, pain only for first hour or so. No other symptoms, complete recovery without treatment.

10. Sembakkam, near Madras, September, 1971. Boy about 10 years bitten on foot in evening near home by *Echis*. Two hours later when he arrived at my house leg was greatly swollen and boy very frightened, near collapse. No evidence of systemic poisoning. Gave local treatment, observed for a few hours then told them to go home unless something like bleeding gums occurred. One month later the father came to say that the swelling still hadn't gone down though they had seen doctors. In January, four months later, the boy died, cause unknown but the father feels it's the same snake bite. (?)

11. Sembakkam, near Madras, July, 1971. Adult male 35 years bitten by *Echis* on right foot at night while walking on road. Arrived at our house 8 A.M. foot and lower leg greatly swollen and bleeding profusely from gums. Otherwise he was feeling all right and normal. I gave him 2 vials of serum to take to the nearby doctor and asked him to check with me later. Few days later he came back with still swollen leg and asked what to do. I advised soaking in salts and seeing a doctor. In April 1972, 8 months later, this man came obviously in great discomfort with his foot still swollen. It seems that the lymphatic and general circulatory congestion so common in viper bites can persist for a long time and cause permanent defects.

I am most grateful to Dr. Nene, Deogad for cases 2–5 and to my sister, Nina Chattopadhyaya for helping with most of the other cases.

The following notes were given to me in an interview by Dr. B. Bapiraju, presently working at King Institute, Guindy, Madras.

During the years 1963 to 1965 Dr. Bapiraju practiced medicine at the medical station in the town of Panjapatti, 30 miles from Trichy. During this two year period 40 to 50 cases of snake bite came to hospital for treatment. 60 to 70 per cent occurred at night and over 95 per cent were on the feet, a small per cent on legs, hands and arms. Most bites appeared to be from *Echis carinatus* which abounds in that area.

Patients arrived usually within a few hours of the bite; in this area the villagers are aware of the effectiveness of antivenom due to the work of the doctors. There was swelling of the limb and pain, often severe, at the site of bite. Some cases complained of severe pain in pharyngeal region. Bleeding gums not noticed. Blood in vomit in a few cases, bloody urine in 70 per cent of cases.

Treatment was by Haffkine polyvalent antivenom serum, intravenously when serious, intramuscularly when not severe. Antivenom preceded by adrenalin and cortisone. Two or three cases of anaphylaxis from sensitivity to serum. Most patients vomit within 15 minutes after receiving serum intravenously. There were no fatalities or after effects like necrosis or prolonged swelling or permanent stiffness.

The south Indian *Echis carinatus* only average 10 or 12 inches in length thus making it too small to be of great medical significance for which the big northern race is notorious.

R. WHITAKER
MADRAS SNAKE PARK,
GUINDY DEER SANCTUARY,
MADRAS 600 022,
November, 1972.

Appendix F   Ciguatera—"Fish Poisoning"

For most of the people on this planet, fish is not a luxury food. Fishes are the sole source of animal protein for many millions; and, as earth's population expands, the importance of food from the sea increases each year. Unfortunately, some fish can be dangerously poisonous; but where, and why, are mysteries of significant concern in some parts of the world.

From ancient times, up to the present, whole families or even villages have been suddenly stricken with a debilitating sickness caused by eating poisonous fish. Many lives have been lost. The cause of the ailment has often been traced to fish species which only days before were perfectly safe to eat. On the next island, or in the next village down the coast, the same species may have been eaten on the same fateful day without harm to anyone.

The mysterious workings of fish poisoning still, to a very large degree, elude us. The disease, or rather diseases, are properly labeled (generically) as *ichthyosarcotoxism*—as opposed to *ichthyoacanthotoxism*, which is the subject of Chapter 20 and means "injurious injection of venom" by fish specially equipped for the purpose. Specifically, the ailment is variously referred to as *ciguatera*, tetraodon poisoning, elasmobranch poisoning, gymnothorax poisoning, clupeoid poisoning, scombroid poisoning, or "hallucinatory" mullet poisoning, according to the fish involved. The word *ciguatera*, the most commonly heard name for fish poisoning, comes from the American–Spanish word *cigua*, the name of a certain kind of poisonous sea snail, *Livona pica*. Molluscs, as well as fishes, can be responsible for the condition. It is commonly called, simply, "fish poisoning," but it is not to be confused with "ptomaine poisoning."

An attack of *ciguatera* can be likened, symptomatically, to poisoning by curare, muscarine, or aconitine. A definite poisonous substance is involved, and a number of these substances have been isolated. Only in scombroid poisoning are bacteria involved, the other forms being caused solely by the noxious substance found in the animal's tissues.

Before discussing where fish poisoning occurs and which animals are responsible, it is necessary to have a general impression of what it is like when it strikes. An actual case history can best serve this purpose. *The Indian Journal of Medical Research*, in April 1956, carried the following case report in an article by S. Jones of the Central Marine Fisheries Research Substation, Calicut, Malabar:

> Early morning on 11th February, 1954, one Muthukumaran, a fisherman of about 65 years of age belonging to Pattimacherry brought home the roes of a large sized "Plachee" fish [Tetraodontid] out of which a curry was prepared. His wife, Kuppamma, aged about 50, and an adopted daughter of about 8 years took this curry along with rice at 8 A.M. After taking the food both of them felt drowsy. Muthukumaran, who in the meanwhile was away at work returned at 10 A.M. and took rice with a very small quantity of this roe curry. His wife and child had a second meal at this time and soon after both became unconscious. In the case of the woman it was gradual and it is reported that during the semi-conscious state she told her husband that she was feeling giddy and could not see the house or anything around and that she was feeling as if she was going to Kailas [the sacred mountain peak in the Himalayas, believed to be the abode of Lord Shiva]. The girl became completely unconscious and died at about 12 noon. In the meanwhile Muthukumaran showed different symptoms. He felt quite restless and vomited several times. Some of the neighbors removed the ailing old couple to the Local Fund Hospital, Porayar. The woman died at 5 P.M. just as she was being carried into the hospital. The Medical Officer observed that the death was due to "respiratory failure." Muthukumaran was admitted to the hospital for "weakness, giddiness and inability to walk." The diagnosis was "fish poisoning" and the condition on admission was given as follows: "A well-built man of 65 years. Not anaemic. Strong. Able to talk. Cannot walk. Slightly restless and thirsty. Pupils dilated. Heart—nil abnormal. Respiration—19. Pulse—80." The temperature was normal and nothing except coffee was given to the patient on the day of admission. On the next day [12-2-54] he was feeling better and on the third day he appeared normal and was discharged at his own request in the evening.

The report goes on to say that a few years previously, five members of another family were killed in the village of Negapatam by the roe of a *Plachee*. Actually, Muthukumaran and his family were stricken with tetraodon poisoning. The disease is caused by puffer fishes of the family Tetraodontidae, and it kills many people, particularly in Japan, each year. There is a saying in Japan: "Great is the temptation to eat 'Fugo' [puffer] but greater is the dread of losing life."

The puffers are tetraodonts, but not all members of the family are poisonous and not all parts of the poisonous specimens are necessarily dangerous. It is generally accepted that the ovaries, gonads, skin, bile, and liver are most apt to be dangerous. The flesh is sometimes safe to eat, at other times deadly. Certain other fishes of the order Tetraodontiformes (but not of the family Tetraodontidae) may be similarly hazardous as food.

Table F-1 gives a breakdown of fishes of *all* orders known to be directly and edibly poisonous to man—at least part of the time.

Table F-1. Fishes Known to Have Been Dangerously Poisonous on Occasion

Type of poisoning	Representative fishes (by genera) known to be involved	Remarks
Ciguatera or tropical marine fish poisoning	Snappers: Monotaxis. Gnathodentex, Aprion, Lethrinus, Lutjanus Parrot fish: Scarus, Callyodon Wrasse: Coris, Epibulus Groupers: Variola, Julis, Cepthalopholis, Epinephelus, Plectopomus Barracuda: Sphyraena, plus others Jacks: Caranx Surgeonfish: Acanthurus, Ctenochaetus Zebrasoma Ladyfish: Albula Herring: Clupanodon (only) Surmullet: Parupeneus, Upeneus Sea bass: Myceteroperca (see groupers above) Trunkfish: Lactoria. Lactophrvs Porgy: Pagellus, Pagrus Squaretails: Tetragonurus Chinamanfish: Paradicichthys Filefish: Aleutera Triggerfish: Balistoides, Rhineacanthus, Baliates, Pseudobalistes Anchovy: Engraulis (only) Squirrelfish: Myripristis, plus others Bonito: Katsuwonus	Limited to tropics: reef fishes involved, particularly larger carnivorous species and specimens. Neurological damage and death can result. Recovery can take years.
Tetraodon	Puffers: Arothron, Sphaeroides, Canthigaster Triggerfish: Balistoides, Balistes, Rhineacanthus, Pseudobalistes Filefish: Aleutera	Not limited to tropics

Table F-1.   Fishes Known to Have Been Dangerously Poisonous on Occasion—Continued

Type of poisoning	Representative fishes (by genera) known to be involved	Remarks
	Boxfish: Ost··:cion Ocean sunfish: (types uncertain) Porcupine fish: *Diodon*	
Elasmobranch	Sand sharks: *Carcharhinus* White shark: *Carcharodon* Hammerheads: *Sphyrna* (only) Seven-gilled: *Heptranchus* Six-gilled: *Hexanchus* Greenland: *Somniosus* Plus some rays	Liver particularly dangerous. May be caused by sharks eating poisonous fishes. May be closely related to *ciguatera*. Most common in tropics, but known far to the north. "Intoxicating." be fatal.
Gymnothorax	Moray eels: *(Gymnothorax)*	Resembles *ciguatera,* but can be even more severe. Reportedly *at least* 10 percent fatal. *Moray eels should not be eaten.*
Scombroid	Tuna, skipjack, bonito, and all other mackerellike fishes—all of the numerous genera	*Bacterial:* Strains of *Proteus morganii* involved. Caused by improperly stored fish. Violent allergylike reactions. Histamine and other substances produced in tissues by bacteria.
"Hallucinatory" mullet	Mullet: *Mugil, Neomyxus* Goatfish: *Mulloidichthys, Upeneus, Parauoeneus* Surgeonfish (Tang): *Acanthurus, Ctenochaetus, Zebrasoma* Rudderfish: *Kyphosus* (plus)	Seasonal: Pacific islands—limited range—generally mild. *Not fatal.*
Clupeoid	Herringlike fishes: *(Clupea, Melleta)* Possibly *Sardinella*	Very little known. Can be extremely serious. Known to be fatal. May be connected with the swarming of non-poisonous marine worm Palolo (?)

Table F-1 is certainly not complete. Indeed, even if it were desirable to give a complete listing here, it would not be possible. Fish and Cobb—in *Noxious Marine Animals of the Central and Western Pacific Ocean*—list eighty-three species of nineteen families as poisonous from that region alone. Of these eighty-three, they list eleven as moderate, twenty-five as strong, four as variable, one as a "?," one as *deadly*, and sixteen as nonspecifically *poisonous*. A great deal of research and statistical analysis stands between the cross section given in this chapter and full knowledge.

It is believed by many investigators that fish poisoning is a result of a food chain. Presumably, a fish eats a poisonous plant, mollusc, or other marine form, and is then eaten by man, or by a larger fish which is eventually caught by man, and consumed. *Ciguatera*, particularly, appears to be caused by larger predatory fish. It is quite possible that the original organism that triggers this unfortunate chain reaction is harmless to man, but induces a chemical reaction within the tissues of the *ciguatera*-causing fish that *is* harmful. It is frequently pointed out that the occurrence of clupeoid poisoning, occasionally with high mortality, *always* coincides with the swarming of the palolo worm. The worm itself has been shown to be harmless to man.

Marine biologist Philip Helfrich prepared a report on the study of the possible relationship between radioactivity and toxicity in fishes. The report, published by the U.S. Atomic Energy Commission, concluded as follows: "The accumulated data show an absence of any correlation between radioactivity (gross beta and gamma activity) and *Ciguatera*-type toxicity in samples of muscle, liver, and gonads from Lutjanid fishes from the Marshall and Line Islands."

As indicated earlier, fishes are not the only poisonous marine forms. A marine annelid *Lumbriconereis heteropoda* produces a poison commonly called nereistoxin. This may contribute to the poisoning of man in a food chain. Gastropods of the genus *Neptunes* are toxic, perhaps on a seasonal basis. A number of mussels and clams can produce paralytic intoxication, and can be deadly. Respiratory arrest and cardiovascular collapse are the causes of death in fatal cases. Shellfish poisoning has been frequently connected with "red tides," the swarming of a motile, photosynthetic dinoflagellate, *Gonyaulax catenella*. Certain sea cucumbers are quite dangerously poisonous, and a number of cockles can cause serious disturbances. Shellfish poisoning is generally divided into three self-explanatory types: (1) *gastrointestinal* which *may* be bacterial in origin; (2) *allergic*, probably the result of individual sensitivity; and (3) *paralytic*, frequently regarded as the most serious type, and the form generally associated with dinoflagellates ingested by shellfish.

Halstead reports that certain sea turtles taken in the vicinity of the Philippines, Sri Lanka, and Indonesia can be dangerously poisonous. He implicates the Green Sea Turtle *(Chelonia mydas)*, the Hawksbill Turtle *(Eretmochelys imbricata)* and the Leatherback Turtle *(Dermochelys coriacea)*, all of which are eaten in vast numbers each year. Here, too, a food chain may be involved. Halstead points out that the liver is particularly dangerous.

Polar Bear *(Thalarctos maritimus)* liver and kidneys can cause a serious but seldom fatal poisoning, possibly due to a dangerous level of vitamin A concentration. Some of the seals and sea lions are reportedly dangerous to eat, as are certain whales and dolphins.

Unlike the other health hazards discussed in this book, poisoning by marine forms requires a specific action on the part of man. Nothing happens to man at the will, discretion, or choice of another creature. It is the positive act of eating that causes the distress. To avoid the distress, man need only avoid the action. It is not really that simple, however, since man can hardly give up eating the abundant food made available to him by the sea. He must utilize seafood, and increasingly so, and extensive research is called for to eliminate the present guesswork.

It is doubtful that these forms of poisoning will ever be completely eliminated. If you, an individual, are in unfamiliar surroundings, particularly in the tropics, the only safeguard, aside from totally avoiding seafood, is a check with local inhabitants as to what is considered safe food and what is not. If you fish and eat your catch, there will always be a measure of hazard, but this can be substantially reduced by the advice of the locals. For the time being, at least, poisoning by marine forms, including fish, is a distinct hazard, and a cause of not infrequent medical emergencies.

[Note: Subsequent to the completion of this appendix a note was received about *ciguatera* research in Cuba about 1930. A list was maintained of all species ever implicated. After ten years, just about every commercial species was on the list, and the list was dropped!]

It has been suggested that this appendix include advice on the treatment of "fish poisoning." Since the treatment involves taking medicines and other substances, I would hesitate to give such advice. Anyone interested is referred to the bibliography. The Halstead book is valuable, as are others listed therein. Researchers interested in the problem can be found in the listing and should be approached directly. Travel in tropical areas should be preceded by some careful study of this problem.

Subsequent to writing the above, the author visited a southern Asian country and was dining at the home of the Prime Minister's brother.

Noting that the other people present (all natives of the country) were eating some particularly large and beautiful shrimp, the author followed suit. Within three hours he was stricken with a form of paralytic poisoning and was desperately ill for about eight hours. The doctor attending to the case warned the author that local people can have an immunity to forms of seafood poisoning that foreigners may not have. It is a matter to be investigated. From personal experience, at least, the form of poisoning experienced by the author is a very debilitating disease.

Bibliography

The following bibliography covers *most* of the references used in the preparation of this book. Since a great many references were cited from second and third recountings, some original references are missing. In every case, an effort was made to go to the original source, but it was not always possible to do so.

In a bibliography as large as this must be, it may be difficult for the average reader to find suggested reading for himself should he desire further information. In an effort to make this bibliography serve as a suggested reading list as well, I have made notations in the left-hand margin that reflect my own personal opinion. The notations do not necessarily indicate an evaluation of literary quality—indeed they don't. The books are marked which will be of most interest to the group involved:

*	of more than average interest
**	of great interest
***	essential reading in the field
G	for general readers
S	for specialists

**GS   Abbott, R. Tucker (1954). *American Seashells*. D. Van Nostrand Co., New York.

Adamson, Joy (1960). *Born Free*. Pantheon Books, New York.

———(1962). *Forever Free*. Harcourt, Brace & World, New York.

Allen, Durward L., & L. David Mech (1963). "Wolves Versus Moose on Isle Royale." *National Geographic*, vol. 123, no. 2.

*G   Allen, E. Ross, & Wilfred T. Neill (1961). *Alligators and Crocodiles in Florida*. Florida Game & Freshwater Fish Comm., Tallahassee.

*GS   Allen, Glover M. (1939). *Bats*. Harvard Univ. Press, Cambridge, Mass.

Allington, Herman V., & R. R. Allington (1954). "Insect Bites." *Jour. Amer. Med. Assoc.*, vol. 155, no. 3, pp. 240–247.

*G   Alpers, Antony (1960). *Dolphins: The Myth and the Mammal*. Houghton Mifflin Co., Boston.

**S   Altamirano, Mario, C. W. Coates, H. Grundfest, & D. Nachmansohn (1953). "Mechanisms of Bioelectric Activity in Electric Tissue." *Jour. Genl. Physiology*, vol. 37, no. 1, p. 91.

Altamirano, Mario, & C. W. Coates (1957). "Effect of Potassium on Electroplax of Electrophorus Electricity." *Jour. Cellular & Comparative Physiol.*, vol. 49, no. 1.

Amaral, Afranio Do (1963). "Snake Venoms and Their Antidotes," in *Practice of Pediatrics*, vol. 1, ed. Brennemann–Kelly, D. Chap. 19N.

American Medical Association (1961a). "Insects and Man." *Jour. Amer. Med. Assoc.*, vol. 177, no. 7, pp. 505 ff.

Anderson, Kenneth (1961). *The Call of the Man-Eater*. Chilton Books, Philadelphia.

Anderson, Louis (1957). "This Happened to Me! Killer Foiled!" *Outdoor Life Magazine*, vol. 119, no. 4.

Andrews, Carl E., et al. (1968). "Venomous Snakebite in Florida." *Jour. Florida Med. Assoc.*, vol. 55, no. 4.

*GS   Arcisz, W. (1950). "Ciguatera: Tropical Fish Poisoning." U.S. Fish & Wildlife Service Special Scientific Report, Fisheries 27, Washington, D.C.

Arno, Stephen F. (1969). "Interpreting the Rattlesnake," *National Parks Magazine*, vol. 43, no. 267.

Asano, Motokazu, & Mosoo Itah (1960). "Salivary Poison of a Marine Gastropod *Neptunea arthritica bernardi* and the Seasonal Variation of Its Toxicity." *Annals of the N.Y. Acad. of Science*, vol. 90, art. 3.

**GS   Ash, Christopher (1962). *Whaler's Eye*. Macmillan Co., New York.

Ashe, James (1967). "Some Facts about Snake Fangs." *Africana*, vol. 3, no. 4.

Attenborough, David (1958). *Zoo Quest to Guiana*. The Reprint Society, Ltd. (England) by arrangement with Lutterworth Press.

Atz, James W. (1954). "Most Dangerous to Man? (Piranha)." *Animal Kingdom*, vol. 57, no. 3.

*GS   ———(1960). "Stonefishes: The World's Most Venomous Fishes." *Animal Kingdom,* vol. 63, no. 5.

*GS   ———(1962). "The Flamboyant Zebra Fish." *Animal Kingdom,* vol. 65, no. 2.

Austin, Oliver L., Jr. (1961). *Birds of the World.* Golden Press, New York.

Aymar, Brandt (ed.) (1956). *Treasury of Snake Lore.* Greenberg, New York.

Backus, Richard H., S. Springer, & E. L. Arnold, Jr. (1956). "A Contribution to the Natural History of the White-Tip Shark." *Deep-Sea Research,* vol. 3. Pergamon Press, London.

Baerg, W. J. (1933). "The Effects of the Bite of *Latrodectus mactans.*" *Jour. Parasitology,* vol. 9, no. 3, pp. 161–169.

**GS   ———(1958). *The Tarantula.* Univ. of Kansas Press, Lawrence.

**GS   ———(1959). "The Black Widow and Five Other Venomous Spiders in the United States." Agric. Experiment Sta. Bull. no. 608. Univ. of Arkansas, Fayetteville.

———(1961). "Scorpions: Biology and Effect of Their Venom." Agric. Experiment Sta. Bull. no. 649, Univ. of Arkansas, Fayetteville.

Ballering, R. B., et al. (1972). "Octopus Envenomation Through a Plastic Bag Via a Salivary Proboscis." *Toxicon,* vol. 10, no. 3.

Banner, Albert H., & H. Boroughs (1957). "Observations on Toxins of Poisonous Fishes." *Proc. Soc. Experimental Biol. Med.,* vol. 98, pp. 776–778.

Banner, Albert H., et al. (1960). "Observations on Ciguatera-Type Toxin in Fish." *Annals N.Y. Acad. Science,* vol. 90, art. 3.

Banner, Albert H., S. Satoshi, Philip Helfrich, Charles B. Alender, & Paul J. Schener (1961). "Bioassay of Ciguatera Toxin." *Nature,* vol. 189, no. 4760, pp. 229–230.

Barber, Carolyn (1971). *Animals At War.* Harper & Row, New York.

Barnes, J. H. (1963). "Stingings by Jelly-Fish." *Suppl. Bull. Post Grad. Comm. Med.,* vol. 18, no. 12. Univ. of Sydney, Australia.

———(1966). "Studies on Three Venomous Cubomedusae," in *The Cnidaria and Their Evolution,* ed. W. J. Rees. Academic Press, New York.

Bartlett, Norman (1954). *The Pearl Seekers.* Coward-McCann, New York.

Bartsch, Paul (1934). *Mollusks,* vol. 10 (Series). Smithsonian Institution, Washington, D.C.

"Bat Rabies" (1957). *What's New,* no. 202.

Baughman, J. L. (1947*a*). "Sharks, Sawfishes and Rays." *Texas Game & Fish,* Oct.

———(1947*b*). "Sharks." *Texas Game & Fish,* Apr.

Baughman, J. L., & S. Springer (1950). "Biological and Economic Notes on the Sharks of the Gulf of Mexico." *Amer. Midland Naturalist,* vol. 44, no. 1.

Beebe, B. F. (1963). *American Lions and Cats.* David McKay Co. New York.

*G Beebe, William (1918). *Jungle Peace.* Henry Holt & Co., New York.

*G ———(1924). *Galapagos: World's End.* G. P. Putnam's Sons, New York.

*G ———(1925). *Jungle Days.* G. P. Putnam's Sons, New York.

*G ———(1926). *The Arcturus Adventure.* G. P. Putnam's Sons, New York.

*G ———(1928). *Beneath Tropic Seas.* G. P. Putnam's Sons, New York

*G ———(1932). *Nonesuch Land of Water.* Harcourt, Brace & Co., New York.

**GS ———(1934). *Half Mile Down.* Harcourt, Brace & Co., New York.

*G ———(1938). *Zaca Venture.* Harcourt, Brace & Co., New York.

Bell, Thomas (1839). *A History of British Reptiles.* John Van Voorst London.

Bennetts, J. A. W. (1956). "The King of the Mambas." *African Wild Life,* vol. 10, no. 1.

Bent, William H. (1952). *A Field Guide to the Mammals.* Houghton Mifflin Co., Boston.

Benton, Allen W., et al. (1963). "Bioassay and Standardization of Venom of the Honey Bee." *Nature,* vol. 198, no. 4877.

Benton, Allen W. (1963). "Venom Collection from Honey Bees." *Science,* vol. 142, no. 3589.

Benton, Allen W., & R. L. Patton (1965). "A Qualitative Analysis of the Proteins in the Venom of Honey Bees." *Jour. Insect Physiology,* vol. 2.

Benton, Allen W., & R. A. Morse (1966). "Collection of the Liquid Fraction of Bee Venom." *Nature,* vol. 210, no. 5036.

Benton, Allen W. (1967). "Esteras and Phosphotases of Honeybees Venom." *Jour. Apicultural Res.,* vol. 6, no. 2.

Benton, Allen W., et al. (1969). "Bee Venom Tolerance in White Mice in Relation to Diet." *Science,* vol. 145, no. 3639.

Best, E. A. (1961). "Occurrence of the Round Stingray *Uroloplus halleri* Cooper in Humboldt Bay, California." *California Fish & Game,* vol. 47, no. 4.

*G Bishop, Sherman C. (1943). *Handbook of Salamanders.* Comstock Publishing Co., Ithaca, N.Y.

———(1947). *Handbook of Salamanders.* Comstock Publishing Co., Ithaca, N.Y.

Blackwelder, Richard E. (1963). *Classification of the Animal Kingdom.* Southern Illinois Univ. Press, Carbondale.

"Black Widow Spiders May Be Dangerous" (1958). *Home Safety Review,* vol. 15, no. 2, Feb.

Blair, W. F., et al. (1957). *Vertebrates of the United States*. McGraw-Hill, New York.

Blanquet, Richard (1972). "A Toxic Protein from the Nematocysts of the Scyphozoan Medusa *Chrysaora quinquecirrha*." *Toxicon*, vol. 10, no. 2.

Blomberg, Rolf (1956). "Giant Snake Hunt." *Natural History*, vol. 65, no. 4.

Bogen, Emil (1932). "Poisonous Spider Bites." *Jour. Amer. Med. Assoc.*, vol. 99, no. 24.

Bogert, Charles M. (1943). "Dentitional Phenomena in Cobras and Other Elapids with Notes on Adaptive Modification of Fangs." *Bull. Amer. Mus. Nat. Hist.*, vol. 81, art. 3.

———(1954). "Snakes That Spit Their Venom." *Animal Kingdom*, vol. 57, no. 3.

***GS Bogert, Charles M., & Rafael Martin Del Campo (1956). "The Gila Monster and Its Allies—The Relationships. Habits and Behavior of the Lizards of the Family Helodermatidae." *Bull. Amer. Mus. Nat. Hist.*, vol. 109, art. 1.

Bolin, Rolf L. (1954). "Report on a Fatal Attack by a Shark." *Pacific Science*, vol. 8, no. 1.

Bonta, I. L., et al. (1970). "Method for Study of Snake Venom-Induced Hemorrhages." *Toxicon*, vol. 8, no. 1.

Bourlière, François (1954). *The Natural History of Mammals*, H. M. Parshley translation. Alfred A. Knopf, New York.

*G Boys, Floyd, & H. M. Smith (1959). *Poisonous Amphibians and Reptiles: Recognition and Bite Treatment*. Charles C Thomas, Springfield, Ill.

Brand, J. M., et al. (1972). "Fire Ant Venoms: Comparative Analysis of Alkaloidal Components." *Toxicon*, vol. 10, no. 3.

Brattstrom, Bayard H. (1954). "The Fossil Pit-Vipers (Reptilia: Crotalidae) of North America." *Trans. San Diego Soc. Nat. Hist.*, vol. 12, no. 3.

———(1964). "Evolution of the Pit-Vipers." *Trans. San Diego Soc. Nat. Hist.*, vol. 13, no. 11.

Brodie, Edmund D., Jr. (1969). "Investigations of the Skin Toxin of the Red-Spotted Newt, *Notophthalmus viridescens viridescens*." *Amer. Midland Naturalist*, vol. 80, no. 1.

**GS Brown, G. W., Jr. (ed.) (1968). *Desert Biology*, vol. 1. Academic Press, New York.

Brown, Margaret E. (ed.) (1957). *The Physiology of Fishes*, vol. 2, *Behavior*. Academic Press, New York.

Brown, M. V., & C. W. Coates (1952). "Further Comparisons of Length and Voltage in the Electric Eel *Electrophorus electricus* (Linnaeus)." *Zoologica*, vol. 37, part 4.

*G Brunner, Josef (1941). *Tracks and Tracking*. Macmillan Co., New York.

Bryson, Kenneth B. (1954). "The Treatment of Chronic Arthritis with a Combination of Cobra Venom, Formic Acid, and Silicic Acid." *Amer. Surg.*, vol. 20, no. 7.

***S Bücherl, Wolfgang, & Eleanor E. Buckley (eds.) (1968). *Venomous Animals and Their Venoms*, vol. 1. Academic Press, New York.

***S ———(1970). *Venomous Animals and Their Venoms*, vol. 2. Academic Press, New York.

***S ———(1971). *Venomous Animals and Their Venoms*, vol. 3. Academic Press, New York.

Buchsbaum, Ralph, & Lorus J. Milne (1960). *The Lower Animals.* Doubleday & Co., New York.

***GS Buckley, Eleanor E., & Nandor Porges (eds.) (1956). *Venoms.* American Association for the Advancement of Science, Washington, D.C.

Bue, Gerald T., & M. H. Stenlund (1953). "Recent Records of the Mountain Lion *Felis concolor* in Minnesota." *Jour. Mammalogy*, vol. 34, no. 3.

Bullen, Frank T. (1904). *Denizens of the Deep.* Fleming H. Revell Co., New York.

Burden, W. D. (1945). "Development of a Shark Deterrent." *Air Surg. Bull.*, vol. 2, no. 10.

**GS Burnet, MacFarlane (1962). *Natural History of Infectious Diseases.* 3d ed. The University Press, Cambridge, Mass.

Burnett, J. W., & R. Goldner (1970). "Effect of *Chrysaora quinquelcirrha* (Sea Nettle) Toxin on Rat Nerve and Muscle." *Toxicon*, vol. 8, no. 2.

Burnett, J. W. (1971). "Some Immunological Aspects of Sea Nettle Toxins." *Toxicon*, vol. 9, no. 3.

*G Burrell, H. (1927). *The Platypus.* Angus & Robertson, Sydney, Australia.

Burton, E. Milby (1935). "Shark Attacks Along the South Carolina Coast." *Scientific Monthly*, vol. 40, pp. 279–283.

Burton, Maurice (1956). *Living Fossils.* Readers Union, Thames & Hudson, London.

———(1960). *In Their Element: the Story of Water Mammals.* Abelard-Schuman, London.

Byers, Robert D. (1940). "The California Shark Fishery." *California Fish & Game*, vol. 26, no. 1.

Cameron, Ann M., & R. Endean (1971). "Venom Glands in Scatophagid Fish." *Toxicon*, vol. 8, no. 2.

Cameron, Ann M. (1971). "The Axillary Glands of the Plotosid Catfish *Cnidoglanis macrocephalus*." *Toxicon*, vol. 9, no. 4.

Caras, Roger A. (1962). *Antarctica: Land of Frozen Time.* Chilton Books, Philadelphia.

————(1967). *North American Mammals*. Meredith, New York.

————(1974). *Venomous Animals of the World*. Prentice-Hall, New York.

Carithers, Hugh A. (1958). "Mammalian Bites of Children." *Jour. Amer. Med. Assoc. Diseases Child.*, vol. 95, no. 2.

Carlson, Fred A. (1946). *Geography of Latin America*. Prentice-Hall, New York.

Carlson, R. W., et al. (1971). "Some Pharmacological Properties of the Venom of the Scorpionfish *Scorpaena guttata*—I." *Toxicon*, vol. 9, no. 4.

Carper, Jean (1960). "Snakes Are Safe (but Stick to Cats and Dogs)." *Natl. Safety Council Education*, Apr.

Carr, Archie, & the Editors of *Life* (1963). *The Reptiles*. Time Inc., New York.

***G   Carrington, Richard (1959). *Elephants: A Short Account of Their Natural History, Evolution, and Influence on Mankind*. Basic Books, New York.

**G   Carson, Rachel L. (1954). *The Sea Around Us*. Oxford Univ. Press, New York.

Cheesman, Evelyn (1949). *Six-Legged Snakes in New Guinea*. George G. Harrap & Co., London.

Chen, K. K., & Alena Kovarikova (1967). "Pharmacology and Toxicology of Toad Venom."*Jour. Pharm. Sci.*, vol. 56, no. 12.

**S   Christensen, Poul Agerhohn (1955). *South African Snake Venoms and Antivenoms*. South African Institute of Medical Research, Johannesburg.

————(1969). "The Treatment of Snakebite." *South African Med. Jour.*, vol. 43.

Clark, Eugenie (1959). "Instrumental Conditioning of Lemon Sharks." *Science*, vol. 130, no. 3369.

Clark, Leonard (1953). *The Rivers Ran East*. Funk & Wagnalls Co., New York.

Clarke, Arthur C. (1955). *The Coast of Coral*. Harper & Row, New York.

Cleland, J. B. (1924). "Injuries and Diseases in Australia Attributable to Animals." *Med. Jour. Austral.*, vol. 2, p. 339.

Cleland, John B., & R. V. Southcott (1965). *Injuries to Man from Marine Invertebrates in the Australian Region*. Commonwealth of Australia, National Health and Medical Research Council, Special Report Series no. 12, Canberra.

Clench, W. J., & Y. Kondo (1943). "The Poison Cone Shell." *Amer. Jour. Trop. Med. & Hyg.*, vol. 23, pp. 105–121.

*GS   Cloudsley–Thompson, J. L. (1968). *Spiders, Scorpions, Centipedes and Mites*. Pergamon Press, London.

**GS   ————(1969). *The Zoology of Tropical Africa*. W. W. Norton, New York.

***GS Coates, C. W., R. T. Cox, & L. P. Granath (1937). "The Electric Discharge of the Electric Eel *Electrophorus electricus* (Linnaeus)." *Zoologica*, vol. 22 (part 1).

Coates, C. W., R. T. Cox, W. A. Rosenblith, & M. V. Brown (1940). "Propagation of the Electric Impulse along the Organs of the Electric Eel *Electrophorus electricus* (Linnaeus)." *Zoologica*, vol. 25 (part 2).

Coates, C. W. (1955). "Three More Gymnotid Eels Found to Be Electrogenic." *Zoologica*, vol. 40 (part 4).

Cochran, D. M. (1943). "Poisonous Reptiles of the World: A Wartime Handbook." Smithsonian Institution. War Background Studies, no. 10. Washington, D.C.

———(1954). "Our Snake Friends and Foes." *National Geographic*, vol. 106, no. 3.

*G Cochran, Doris M. (1962). *Living Amphibians of the World*. Doubleday, Garden City, N.Y.

Cochran, Doris, & Coleman J. Goin (1970). *Frogs of Colombia*. Smithsonian Institution Bull. no. 288. Washington, D.C.

Cogger, Harold G. (1963). "Sea-Snakes." *Suppl. Bull. Post Grad. Comm. Med.*, vol. 18, no. 12. Univ. of Sydney, Australia.

**G Colby, C. B. (1963). *Fur and Fury*. Duell, Sloan & Pearce, New York.

Cole, Robert A. (1960). *Bat Rabies, A New Health and Safety Challenge*. Natl. Safety Council, Chicago.

Collins, Henry Hill, Jr. (1959). *Complete Field Guide to American Wildlife*. Harper & Row, New York.

Colman, John S. (1950). *The Sea and Its Mysteries*. W. W. Norton & Co., New York.

Commonwealth Serum Laboratories (1961). *Treatment of Snakebite in Australia*. Melbourne, Australia.

———(1966). *Red-Black Spider Antivenene* (instruction leaflet). Melbourne, Australia.

———(1967). *Stone-Fish Antivenene*. Melbourne, Australia.

———(1967). *Treatment of Snakebite in Australia and New Guinea Using Antivenene*. Melbourne, Australia.

*GS Comstock, John Henry (1940). *The Spider Book*. Cornell Univ. Press, Ithaca, N.Y.

Conant, Roger (1958). *A Field Guide to Reptiles and Amphibians*. Houghton Mifflin Co., Boston.

Constance, Arthur (1958). *The Impenetrable Sea*. Citadel Press, New York.

***GS Coon, Carleton S. (1962). *The Origin of Races*. Alfred A. Knopf, New York.

***GS *Copeia, The Quarterly of the American Society of Ichthyologists and Herpetologists*. Philadelphia.

***GS Coppleson, V. M. (1962). *Shark Attack*. Angus & Robertson, Sydney and Melbourne, Australia.

———(1963). "Distribution and Pattern of Australian Shark Attacks," "Biting and Attack Mechanisms of Sharks." *Suppl. Bull. Post Grad. Comm. Med.*, vol. 18, no. 12. Univ. of Sydney, Australia.

***GS Corbett, Jim (1946). *Man-Eaters of Kumaon.* Oxford Univ. Press, Oxford.

***GS ———(1948). *The Man-Eating Leopard of Rudraprayag.* Oxford Univ. Press, Oxford.

***GS ———(1954). *The Temple Tiger and More Man-Eaters of Kumaon.* Oxford Univ. Press, Oxford.

Cott, Hugh B. (1938). "Wonder Island of the Amazon Delta." *National Geographic*, vol. 74, no. 5.

**G Cousteau, Jacques-Yves (1953). *The Silent World.* Harper & Row, New York.

———(1952). "Fish Men Explore a New World Undersea." *National Geographic*, vol. 52, no. 4.

**G Cousteau, Jacques-Yves (with James Dugan) (1959). *Captain Cousteau's Underwater Treasury.* Harper & Row, New York.

**G ———(1963). *The Living Sea.* Harper & Row, New York.

Cox, R. T., & C. W. Coates (1937). "Electrical Characteristics of the Electric Eel *Electrophorus electricus.*" *Zoologica*, vol. 22 (part 8), no. 1.

Cox, R. T., & C. W. Coates (with M. V. Brown) (1946). "Electrical Characteristics of Electric Tissue." *Annals N.Y. Acad. Science*, vol. 47, art. 4.

Craig, John D. (1941). *Danger Is My Business.* Garden City Pub. Co., Garden City, N.Y.

***GS Crisler, Lois (1958). *Arctic Wild.* Harper & Row, New York.

Cromie, William J. (1963). "Killer Whale!" *Reader's Digest*, Mar.

Crompton, John (1963). *The Snake.* Faber & Faber, London.

Crone, H. D., & T. E. B. Keen (1971). "Further Studies in the Biochemistry of the Toxins from the Sea Wasp *Chironex fleckeri.*" *Toxicon*, vol. 9, no. 2.

Cropp, Ben (1970). "Sea Snakes." *Oceans*, vol. 3, no. 2.

Dack, G. M. (1965). *Food Poisoning* (3rd ed.). Univ. of Chicago Press, Chicago.

Daly, J. W., et al. (1965). "Batracotoxin: The Active Principle of the Colombian Arrow Poison Frog, *Phylobates bicolor.*" *Jour. Amer. Chem. Soc.*, vol. 87, no. 124.

Daniel, J. F. (1934). *The Elasmobranch Fishes.* Univ. of California Press, Berkeley.

Davis, Harry T. (n.d.). *Poisonous Snakes of the Eastern United States with First Aid Guide.* North Carolina State Museum, Raleigh.

"Deadly Octopus Plague," (1969). *Science News*, vol. 96, no. 4.

Dear, L. S. (1955). "Cougar or Mountain Lion Reported in Northwest Ontario." *Canadian Field–Naturalist*, vol. 69, no. 1.

Dearborn, Ned (1927). "An Old Record of the Mountain Lion in New Hampshire." *Jour. Mammalogy*, vol. 8, no. 4.

Deas, Walter (1970). "Venomous Octopus." *Sea Frontiers*, vol. 16, no. 6.

Dees, John (1963). "Florida Snake Bite Data—1963." *Jour. Florida Med. Assoc.*, vol. 49, no. 12.

Denson, K. W. E., & W. E. Rousseau (1970). "Separation of the Coagulant Components of *Bothrops jararaca* Venom." *Toxicon*, vol. 8, no. 1.

Deoras, P. J. (1959). "Snakes: How to Know Them." The Directorate of Publicity, Govt. of Bombay, Bombay, India.

——(1965). *Snakes of India*. National Book Trust, New Delhi.

Department of the Navy, Bureau of Medicine & Surgery (1965, rev.). *Poisonous Snakes of the World*. Government Printing Office, Washington, D.C.

de Sylva, Donald P. (1967). "Stingers, Biters—and Divers." *Sea Frontiers*, vol. 13, no. 6.

Diniz, Carlos R., & A. P. Corrado (1971). "Venoms of Insects and Arachnids," in *Pharmacology and Toxicology of Naturally Occurring Toxins*, vol. 2, ed. H. Raskova. Pergamon Press, Oxford, England.

**GS Dobie, J. Frank, Jr. (1947). *The Voice of the Coyote*. Curtis Publishing Co., New York.

 **G ——(1965). *Rattlesnakes*. Little, Brown, Boston.

  *G Dodge, Natt N. (1961). *Poisonous Dwellers of the Desert*. Southwestern Monuments Assoc., Globe, Ariz.

Doery, Hazel M. (1956). "Purine Compounds in Snake Venoms," *Nature*, vol. 177, Feb. 25.

——(1957). "Additional Purine Compounds in the Venom of the Tiger Snake *(Notechis scutatus)*." *Nature*, vol. 180, Oct. 19.

——(1958). "The Separation and Properties of the Neurotoxins from the Venom of the Tiger Snake *Notechis scutatus scutatus*." *Biochemical Jour.*, vol. 70, no. 4.

Doery, Hazel M., & Joan E. Pearson (1961). "Haemolysins in Venoms of Australian Snakes." *Biochemical Jour.*, vol. 78.

Doukan, Gilbert (1957). *The World Beneath the Waves*. George Allen & Unwin, London.

Doyle, Adrian Conan (1953). *Heaven Has Claws*. Random House, New York.

Duhig, J. V., & G. Jones (1928). "The Venom Apparatus of the Stone Fish *(Synanceja horrida)*." *Memoirs Queensland Museum*, vol. 9, p. 136.

Dunson, William A. (1971). "The Sea Snakes Are Coming." *Natural History*, vol. 80, no. 9.

Dykstra, Philip (1961). "Is the Bite of the Black Widow Spider

Deadly?" *Natl. Safety Council Home Safety Review*, summer.

**GS Dyson, James L. (1962). *The World of Ice*. Alfred A. Knopf, New York.

Eadie, R. (1935). *The Life and Habits of the Platypus*. Stilwell & Stephens, Melbourne, Australia.

Edery, H., et al. (1972). "Pharmacological Activity of Oriental Hornet *(Vespa orientalis)* Venom." *Toxicon*, vol. 10, no. 1.

El Asmar, M. F., et al. (1972). "Fractionation of Scorpion *(Leiurus quinquestriatus h.* and *e.)* Venom." *Toxicon*, vol. 10, no. 1.

Ellison, Norman (1932). "Shark Fishing—An Australian Industry." *National Geographic*, vol. 62, no. 3.

Emerton, James H. (1902). *The Common Spiders of the United States*. Ginn & Co., Boston.

Endean, R. "A Study of the Distribution, Habitat, Behavior, Venom Apparatus, and Venom of the Stonefish." *Austral. Jour. Marine & Freshwater Res.*, vol. 12, no. 2.

———(1962). "Stonefish." *Austral. Nat. Hist.*, vol. 14, no. 1.

Endean, R., & Mary Noble (1971). "Toxic Material from the Tentacles of the Cubomedusan *Chironex fleckeri.*" *Toxicon*, vol. 9, no. 3.

Engel, Leonard, & the Editors of *Life* (1961). *The Sea*. Time Inc., New York.

Essex, H. E. (1945). "Animal Venoms and Their Actions." *Physiol. Rev.*, vol. 45, p. 148.

Evans, Howard E., & Mary Jane West Eberhard (1970). *The Wasps*. Univ. of Michigan Press, Ann Arbor.

Evans, H. M. (1921). "The Poison Organs and Venoms of Venomous Fish." *Brit. Med. Jour.*, vol. 2, p. 690.

———(1943). *Sting-fish and Seafarers*. Faber & Faber, Ltd., London.

***GS Ewer, R. F. (1973). *The Carnivores*. Cornell Univ. Press, Ithaca, N.Y.

Ewers, B. (1963). "Swimmer's Itch *(Schistosome dermatitis).*" *Suppl. Bull. Post Grad. Comm. Med.*, vol. 18, no. 12. Univ. of Sydney, Australia.

Explorers Newsletter. New York Explorers Club, New York.

Fairley, N. H., & Beryl Splott (1929). "Venom Yields in Australian Poisonous Snakes." *Med. Jour. Austral.*, vol. 1, no. 11.

Fänge, Ragnar (1960). "The Salivary Gland of *Neptunea antiqua*," in *Biochemistry and Pharmacology of Compounds Derived from Marine Organisms. Annals N.Y. Acad. Science*, vol. 90, art. 3.

Fansler, Thomas (1958). "Are Dog Bites a Home Safety Problem?" *Home Safety Review*, vol. 15, no. 6.

***GS Fish, Charles J., & Mary Curtis Cobb (1954). *Noxious Marine Animals of the Central and Western Pacific Ocean*. U.S. Dept.

of the Interior, Fish & Wildlife Service, Research Report no. 36. Government Printing Office, Washington, D.C.

Fitch, John E. (1949). "The Great White Shark *Carcharodon carcharias* (Linnaeus) in California Waters During 1948." *California Fish & Game*, vol. 35, no. 2.

Fitzsimons, D. C. (n.d.). *A Guide to the Durban Snake Park*. Durban, South Africa.

***GS Fitzsimons, Vivian F. M. (1962). *Snakes of Southern Africa*. Purnell & Sons, Cape Town.

*GS Flecher, Hugo (1945). "Injuries by Unknown Agents to Bathers in North Queensland. *Med. Jour. Austral.*, Jan. 27.

*GS ——(1952). "Fatal Stings to North Queensland Bathers." *Med. Jour. Austral.*, Jan. 12.

*GS ——(1952). "Irukandji Sting to North Queensland Bathers Without Production of Weals but with Severe General Symptoms." *Med. Jour. Austral.*, July 19.

——(1955). "Injuries Produced by Marine Animals in Tropical Australia." Unpublished.

**GS Flecker, H., & Bernard C. Cotton (1955). "Fatal Bite from Octopus." *Med. Jour. Austral.*, vol. 2, p. 429.

Flecker, H. "Injuries Produced by Marine Animals in Tropical Australia." Unpublished remarks made available by Dr. R. S. Irwin of Glen Innes, N.S.W. (Private communication.)

Floyd, Jim (1960). "Snakes Can Kill." Florida Game & Freshwater Fish Comm., Tallahassee.

Fluno, John A. (1961). "Wasps as Enemies of Man." *Bull. Entomological Soc. Amer.*, vol. 7, no. 3.

Fogelberg, J. M., & F. E. Brinnock (1944). "First Partial Report on the Uses of Chemical Materials as Shark Repellents." Naval Res. Lab. Rep. no. P2230, Feb.

——(1944). "Final Report on the Use of Chemical Materials as Shark Repellents." Naval Res. Lab. Rep. no. P2373.

Ford, W. J. A. (1957). "The Treatment of Dog Bites and the Rabies Problem." *Amer. Jour. Surg.*, vol. 93, no. 4.

Foucher-Creteau, Jean (1957). *My Adventures Under the Sea*. Frederick Muller, Ltd., London.

Fowler, H. W. (1908). "Notes on Sharks." *Proc. Acad. Nat. Sci. Phila.*, Apr.

*GS Fox, M. W. (ed.) (1968). *Abnormal Behavior in Animals*. W. B. Saunders, Philadelphia.

Frachtman, H. J., & W. T. McCollum (1945). "Portuguese Man-of-War Stings: A Case Report." *Amer. Jour. Trop. Med.*, vol. 25, no. 4.

G Fraser-Brunner, Alec (1973). *Danger in the Sea*. Hamlyn, New York.

Free, John B., & Colin G. Butler (1959). *Bumblebees*. Collins, London.

Freeman, Shirley E., & R. J. Turner (1972). "Cardiovascular Effects of

Cnidarian Toxins: A Comparison of Toxins Extracted from *Chiropsalmus quadrigatus* and *Chironex fleckeri*." *Toxicon*, vol. 10, no. 1.

Friere-Maia, L., et al. (1970). "Effects of Purified Scorpion Toxin on Respiratory Movements in the Rat." *Toxicon*, vol. 8, no. 4.

Friese, U. Erich (1972). "Death in a Small Package: The Blue-Ringed Octopus." *Animal Kingdom*, vol. 75, no. 2.

Froom, Barbara (n.d.). *The Massasauga Rattlesnake*. Federation of Ontario Naturalists, Special Publication no. 2. Don Mills, Ontario.

Frye, O. E., & Bill and Les Piper (1952). *The Disappearing Panther*. Florida Game & Freshwater Fish Comm., Tallahassee.

Fuhrman, Frederick A. (1967). "Tetrodotoxin." *Scientific American*, vol. 217, no. 2.

Funk, Ben (1958). "Keeper of the Cobras." *Coronet*, Apr.

***S Gans, Carl, et al. (eds.) (1969). *Biology of Reptilia*, vol. 1. Academic Press, New York.

***S Gans, Carl, & Thomas S. Parsons (eds.) (1970). *Biology of Reptilia*, vol. 2. Academic Press, New York.

***S Gans, Carl (ed.) (1970). *Biology of Reptilia*, vol. 3. Academic Press, New York.

Ganthavorn, S. (1971). "A Case of Cobra Bite." *Toxicon*, vol. 9, no. 3.

Gennaro, Joseph F., Jr. (1959). "Studies on Snake Venom Toxicity." Address to the Thirty-fifth Annual Meeting of the Florida State Veterinary Medicine Association, Oct. 6.

**GS Gertsch, Willis J. (1949). *American Spiders*. D. Van Nostrand Co., Princeton, N.J.

Gheerbrant, Alain (1953). *The Impossible Adventure*. Victor Gollancz Ltd., London.

Ghiretti, F. (1960). "Toxicity of Octopus Saliva Against Crustacea," in *Biochemistry & Pharmacology of Compounds Derived from Marine Organisms. Annals N.Y. Acad. Science*, vol. 90, art. 3.

Gilbert, Perry W. (1958). "Conference on Shark Repellents." *Bull. Amer. Inst. Biol. Sci.*, vol. 8, no. 3.

Gilbert, Perry W. (with Henry Kritzler) (1960). "Experimental Shark Pens at the Lerner Marine Laboratory." *Science*, vol. 132, no. 3424.

**GS Gilbert, Perry W. (with Leonard P. Schultz & Stewart Springer) (1960). "Shark Attacks During 1959." *Science*, vol. 132, no. 3423.

Gilbert, Perry W. (1960). "The Shark Research Panel." *AIBS Bull.*, Feb.

———(1962). "About Sharks." *The New York Times Magazine*, Aug. 5.

**GS ———(1962). "The Behavior of Sharks." *Scientific American*, vol. 207, no. 1.

Gilbo, Catherine M., & N. W. Coles (1964). "An Investigation of Certain Components of the Venom of the Female Sydney Funnel-Web Spider, *Atrax robustus* Cambr." *Austral. Jour. Biol. Sci.*, vol. 17.

Gillis, R. G. (1961). "Some Observations on Stonefish." *North Queensland Naturalist,* vol. 29, no. 130.

Gilluly, Richard H. (1971). "Consequences of a Sea-Level Canal: A New Study of Sea Snakes Reinforces Ecologists' Concerns about the Proposed Canal." *Science News,* vol. 99.

Gilmore, C. W. (1938). "Fossil Snakes of North America." Geological Society of America, Special Paper no. 9.

Ginsburg, Isaac (1953). "Western Atlantic Scorpionfish." *Smithsonian Misc. Coll.,* vol. 121, no. 8.

Gitter, S., Chaya Moroz, et al. (1961). *Pathogenesis of Snake Venom Intoxication.* (Part I, Neurotoxins; Part II, Coagulation Factors and Hemorrhagins; Part III, Hemolysins). Beilinson Hospital Suppl. no. 10. Tel Aviv.

Gladney, William J. (1972). *Controlling the Brown Recluse Spider.* U.S. Dept. of Agriculture, Leaflet no. 556. Government Printing Office, Washington, D.C.

Goe, D. R., & B. W. Halstead (1955). "A Case of Fish Poisoning from *Caranx Ignobilis* Forskal from Palmyra Island with Comments on the Sensitivity of the Mouse-Injection Technique for Screening of Toxic Fishes." *Copeia,* vol. 3, pp. 238–240.

Gordon, Bernard L. (1956). "The Amazing Angel Shark." *Sea Frontiers,* vol. 2, no. 2.

Gorshenin, N. (1963). "Shark Meshing in New South Wales." *Suppl. Bull. Post Grad. Comm. Med.,* vol. 18, no. 12. Univ. of Sydney, Australia.

Gorsky, Bernard (1954). *Mediterranean Hunter.* Souvenir Press, Ltd., London.

*G Gowanloch, James Nelson, & Clair A. Brown (1943). *Poisonous Snakes, Plants and Black Widow Spider of Louisiana.* Louisiana Dept. of Conservation, New Orleans.

Graham, D. H. (1954). *A Treasury of New Zealand Fishes.* A. H. & A. W. Reed, Wellington.

Greathouse, Tedford L. (1960). "Killer Whale." *Skin Diver,* vol. 9, no. 1.

Gregor, Paul (1962). *Amazon Fortune Hunter.* Souvenir Press, Ltd., London.

*SG Griffiths, Mervyn (1968). *Echidnas.* Pergamon Press, London.

Grimble, Arthur (1952). *We Chase the Islands, a Six-Year Adventure in the Gilberts.* Wm. Morrow & Co., New York.

Grocott, Robert G., & Glendy G. Sadler (1958). *The Poisonous Snakes of Panama.* Mount Hope, Canal Zone.

Gruber, Michael (1971). "Lancers of the Reef." *Sea Frontiers*, vol. 17, no. 1.

Gudger, E. W. (1915). "Natural History of the Whale Shark." *Zoologica*, vol. 1, no. 19.

———(1930). "Poisonous Fishes and Fish Poisonings with Special Reference to. Ciguatera in the West Indies." *Amer. Jour. Trop. Med.*, vol. 10, no. 1.

———(1932). "Cannibalism Among the Sharks and Rays." *Scientific Monthly*, vol. 34, no. 5.

———(1936). "Open Ocean and Coastal Sharks: Do They Attack Man?" *The Collecting Net*, vol. 40, no. 6.

———(1937). "Will Sharks Attack Human Beings?" *Natural History*, vol. 40, no. 1.

———(1940). "The alleged pugnacity of the swordfish and the spearfishes as shown by their attacks on vessels." *Memoir Royal Asiatic Soc. Bengal*, vol. 12, no. 2.

———(1943). "Is the Sting Ray's Sting Poisonous? A Historical Resume Showing the Development of Our Knowledge That It Is Poisonous." *Bull. Hist. Med.*, vol. 14, no. 4.

———(1950). "A Boy Attacked by a Shark, July 25, 1936, in Buzzard's Bay, Massachusetts, with Notes on Attacks by Another Shark Along the New Jersey Coast in 1916." *Amer. Midland Naturalist*, vol. 44, no. 3.

***GS Guggisberg, C. A. W. (1961). *Simba: The Life of the Lion*. Bailey Bros. and Swinfen, Ltd., London; Chilton Books, Philadelphia (1963).

Gunter, G. H. (1937). *Adventures of a Trepang Fisher*. Hurst and Blackett, London.

Haast, William E., & Melvin L. Winer (1955). "Complete and Spontaneous Recovery from the Bite of a Blue Krait *(Bungarus caeruleus)*." *Amer. Jour. Trop. Med. Hyg.*, vol. 4, no. 6.

Haley, N. C. (1948). *Whale Hunt*. Washburn, New York.

Halford, George Britton (1894). *Thoughts, Observations, and Experiments on the Action of Snake Venom on the Blood*. Stillwell & Co., Melbourne, Australia.

Halstead, B. W., et al. (1956). "Stonefish Stings and the Venom Apparatus of *Synanceja horrida* (Linnaeus)." *Trans. Amer. Microsc. Soc.*, vol. 75, no. 4.

Halstead, B. W. (1957). "Weever Stings and Their Medical Management." *U.S. Armed Forces Med. Jour.*, vol. 8, pp. 1441–1451.

***GS ———(1959). *Dangerous Marine Animals*. Cornell Maritime Press, Cambridge, Md.

***GS Halstead, B. W., & D. A. Courville (1965–70). *Poisonous and Venomous Marine Animals of the World*, 3 vols. Government Printing Office, Washington, D.C.

Halstead, B. W., & D. D. Danielson (1970). "Death from the Depths." *Oceans Magazine*, vol. 3, no. 6.

Hansen, T. J. (1963). "Sea-Wasp Syndrome or Acute Nematocyst Poisoning." *Suppl. Bull. Post Grad. Comm. Med.*, vol. 18, no. 12. Univ. of Sydney, Australia.

***GS Hardy, Alister (1959). *The Open Sea—Its Natural History*. Part II, *Fish and Fisheries*. Collins, London.

***S Harmon, R. W., & C. B. Pollard (1948). *Bibliography of Animal Venoms*. Univ. of Florida Press, Gainesville.

Hartman, William J., et al. (1960). "Pharmacologically Active Amines and Their Biogenesis in the Octopus." *Annals N.Y. Acad. Science*, vol. 90, art. 3.

Hashimato, Y. (1956). "A Note on the Poison of a Barracuda *Sphyraena picuda*." *Bull. Japan. Soc. Sci. Fisheries*, vol. 21, no. 11.

**GS Haskins, Caryl P. (1943). *The Amazon: The Life History of a Mighty River*. Doubleday & Co., New York.

Hass, Hans (1952). *Manta, Under the Red Sea with Spear and Camera*. Rand McNally & Co., Chicago.

———(1959). *We Come from the Sea*. Doubleday & Co., New York.

Hawkey, Christine, & C. Symons (1966). "Coagulation of Primate Blood by Russell's Viper Venom." *Nature*, vol. 210, no. 5032.

Helfrich, Philip (1960). "A Study of the Possible Relationship Between Radioactivity and Toxicity in Fishes from the Central Pacific." U.S. Atomic Energy Comm., Tech. Info. Serv. TID–5748, May.

———(1961). *Fish Poisoning in the Tropical Pacific*. Pamphlet prepared in conjunction with survey by the U.S. Natl. Inst. Health, Honolulu.

Hemingway, L., & J. C. Devlin (1961). "Watch Out for Sharks." *Reader's Digest*, July.

Henriques, S. B., & Olga B. Henriques (1971). "Pharmacology and Toxicology of Snake Venoms," in *Pharmacology and Toxicology of Naturally Occurring Toxins*, vol. 1, ed. H. Raskova. Pergamon Press, Oxford.

Herald, Earl S. (1951). "The Relative Abundance of Sharks and Bat Stingrays in San Francisco Bay." *California Fish & Game*, vol. 37, no. 3.

———(1961). *Living Fishes of the World*. Doubleday & Co., Garden City, N.Y.

Hermitte, L. C. P. (1946). "Venomous Marine Mollusks of the Genus Conus." *Trans. Royal Society Trop. Med. Hyg.*, vol. 39, pp. 485–512.

Hesse, Donald W., et al. (1960). "Marine Biotoxins. I, Ciguatera Poison: Some Biological and Chemical Aspects," in *Bio-*

chemistry and Pharmacology of Compounds Derived from Marine Organisms. *Annals N.Y. Acad. Science*, vol. 90, art. 3.

**G Heuvelmans, Bernard (1955). *On the Track of Unknown Animals.* Hill and Wang, New York.

*G Heyerdahl, Thor (1950). *Kon-Tiki.* Rand McNally & Co., Chicago.

Hibbern, Frank C. (1948). *Hunting American Lions.* Thomas Y. Crowell Co., New York.

Hill, Ralph N. (1956). *Window in the Sea.* Holt, Rinehart & Winston, New York.

———(1956)."Victory Over the Shark."*Natural History*, vol. 65, no. 7.

Hills, Ralph G., & Warfield M. Firor (1952). "The Use of More Potent Venom for Intractable Pain." *Amer. Surg.*, vol. 18, no. 9.

Hiyama, Y. (1943). "Report of an Investigation of Poisonous Fishes of the South Seas." U.S. Fish & Wildlife Service Special Science Report no. 25 (Van Campen translation).

**GS Holzworth, John M. (1930). *The Wild Grizzlies of Alaska.* G. P. Putnam's Sons, New York.

*G Hornaday, W. T. (1904). *The American Natural History.* Charles Scribner's Sons, New York.

**GS Horsfall, William R. (1962). *Medical Entomology: Arthropods and Human Disease.* Ronald Press, New York.

Hoyt, Murray (1965). *The World of Bees.* Bonanza Books, New York.

Humbert, Arthur C. (1898). "Photographing a Wounded African Buffalo." *Harper's New Monthly Magazine*, Apr.

***GS Hutton, Robert F. (1959). *The Florida Shark Story.* Educational Series no. 13, State of Florida Board of Conservation. Tallahassee.

Ikehara, Isaac (1959). Progress Report: Shark Research Control Program Apr. 1 to Aug. 27, 1959. State of Hawaii Board of Comm. of Agric. & Forestry, Div. of Fish & Game.

**G Innes, William T. (1954). *Exotic Aquarium Fishes* (7th ed.). Innes Publishing Co., Philadelphia.

Irwin, Richard L., et al. (1970). "Toxicity of Elapidae Venoms and an Observation in Relation to Geographical Location." *Toxicon*, vol. 8, no. 1.

Irwin, R. S. (1952). "Funnel-Web Spider Bite." *Med. Jour. Austral.*, Sept., p. 342.

* Isemonger, R. M. (1962). *Snakes of Africa.* Thomas Nelson & Sons, Johannesburg, South Africa.

Jaeger, Ellsworth (1948). *Tracks and Trailcraft.* Macmillan Co., New York.

Jaeger, Robert G. (1971). "Toxic Reaction to Skin Secretions of the Frog *Phrynomerus bifasciatus.*" *Copeia*, no. 1.

Jackman, A. I. (1954). "Cobra Venom Therapy in the Neuroses." *Diseases of the Nervous System*, vol. 15, no. 4.

Jacobs, Werner (1962). "Floaters of the Sea." *Natural History*, vol. 71, no. 7.

Jacques, H. E. (1964). *How to Know the Insects*. Wm. C. Brown Co., Dubuque, Iowa.

Jobin, F., & M. P. Esnouf (1966). "Coagulant Activity of Tiger Snake *(Notechis scutatus)* Venoms." *Nature*, vol. 211, no. 5051.

Johnson, Bob Duel (1967). "Some Interrelationships of Selected *Crotalus* and *Agkistrodon* Venom Properties and Their Relative Lethalities." Dissertation, Arizona State Univ.

Johnson, Murray, L., & L. K. Couch (1954). "Determination of the Abundance of Cougar." *Jour. Mammalogy*, vol. 35, no. 2.

Kaire, G. H. (1964). "The Sydney Funnel-Web Spider *(Atrax robustus)* in Captivity." *Victoria Naturalist*, vol. 81, June.

Karlsson, E., & D. Eaker (1972). "Isolation of the Principal Neurotoxins of *Naja naja* Subspecies from the Asian Mainland." *Toxicon*, vol. 10, no. 3.

**G   Kaston, B. J. (1937). The Black Widow Spider. New England Museum of Natural History, Museum Leaflet no. 5, Boston.

Kaston, B. J. & Elizabeth (1953). *How to Know the Spiders*. Wm. C. Brown Co., Dubuque, Iowa.

Kathan, R. H., G. S. Huber, & R. S. Leopold (1956). "Evolution of the Tourniquet-Incision and Suction Treatment of Snake Bite." Naval Med. Field Res. Lab., NM 005 052.08, Spec. Rep. vol. 7.

Katz, N. L., & C. Edwards (1972). "The Effect of Scorpion Venom on the Neuromuscular Junction of the Frog." *Toxicon*, vol. 10, no. 2.

**GS   Keegan, Hugh L. (1960). "Some Venomous and Noxious Animals of the Far East." Med. Gen. Lab. (406) U.S. Army Med. Command, Japan.

***GS   Keegan, Hugh L. (with W. V. Macfarlane) (1963). *Venomous and Poisonous Animals and Noxious Plants of the Pacific Region*. Pergamon Press, New York.

Keen, T. E. B. (1971). "Comparison of Tentacle Extracts from *Chiropsalmus quadrigatus* and *Chironex fleckeri*." *Toxicon*, vol. 9, no. 3.

Keith, Elmer (1948). *Big Game Hunting*. Little, Brown & Co., Boston.

Kent, Melvin, & H. L. Stahnke (1939). "Effect and Treatment of Arizona Scorpion Stings." *Southwestern Med.*, vol. 4, no. 39.

Kenyon, Karl W. (1959). "A 15-foot Maneater from San Miguel Island, California." *California Fish & Game*, vol. 45, no. 1.

*GS   Kinloch, Alexander A. A. (1892). *Large Game Shooting in Thibet, the Himalayas, Northern and Central India*. Thacker, Spink & Co., Calcutta.

Klauber, Laurence M. (1939). *A Statistical Study of the Rattlesnakes.* San Diego Society of Natural History, Occasional Paper no. 5 (Aug. 30).

***GS ——(1956). *Rattlesnakes: Their Habits, Life Histories, and Influence on Mankind.* 2 vols. Univ. of California Press, Berkeley.

Klots, Alexander B. & Elsie B. (1959). *Living Insects of the World.* Doubleday & Co., Garden City, N.Y.

*G Kobler, John (1957). "The Terrible Threat of Nerve Gas." *Saturday Evening Post,* vol. 230, no. 4.

Kocholaty, W. F., et al. (1971). "Toxicity and Some Enzymatic Properties and Activities in the Venoms of Crotalidae, Elapidae, and Viperidae." *Toxicon,* vol. 9, no. 2.

**GS Kohn, Alan J. (1958). "Recent Cases of Human Injury Due to Venomous Marine Snails of the Genus *Conus.*" *Hawaii Med. Jour.,* vol. 17, July–Aug.

**GS Kohn, Alan J., et al. (1960). "Preliminary Studies on the Venom of the Marine Snail *Conus,*" in *Biochemistry & Pharmacology of Compounds Derived from Marine Organisms. Annals N.Y. Acad. Science,* vol. 90, art. 3.

Koszalka, M. F. (1949). "A Case of Hemoglobineuria in Bee Sting." *Bull. U.S. Army Med. Dept.,* 9.212, 3/49. As abstracted by National Safety Council, Chicago.

Kroeber, Theodora (1961). *Ishi in Two Worlds: a Biography of the Last Wild Indian in North America.* Univ. of California Press, Berkeley.

LaFarge, Oliver (1956). *A Picture History of the American Indian.* Crown Publishers, New York.

Lane, Charles E. (1960). "The Toxin of *Physalia* Nematocysts." *Annals N.Y. Acad. Science,* vol. 90, art. 3.

——(1963). "The Deadly Fisher." *National Geographic,* vol. 123, no. 3.

**G Lane, Frank W. (1960). *Kingdom of the Octopus.* Sheridan House, New York.

Lanham, Url (1964). *The Insects.* Columbia Univ. Press, New York.

Larsen, J. B., & Charles E. Lane (1970). "Direct Action of *Physalia* Toxin on Frog Nerve and Muscle." *Toxicon,* vol. 8, no. 1.

de Latil, Pierre (1954). *The Underwater Naturalist.* Jarrolds Ltd., London.

Lee, Chen-Yuan, et al. (1971). "Mode of Neuromuscular Blocking Action of the Desert Black Snake Venom." *Toxicon,* vol. 9, no. 4.

Lee, R. K. C., & H. Q. Pang (1945). "An Outbreak of Fish Poisoning in Honolulu, Hawaii." *Hawaii Med. Jour.,* vol. 4, no. 1.

——(1945). "Ichthyotoxism—Fish Poisoning." *Amer. Jour. Trop. Med.,* vol. 25, no. 3.

Leopold, A. Starker. *The Desert* ("Life Nature Library"). Time Inc., New York.

Lett, William P. (1890). *The Wolf. (The Big Game of North America,* ed. G. O. Shields.) Rand McNally & Co., Chicago.

Linaweaver, Paul G. (1968). "Toxic Marine Life." *U.S. Navy Medical News Letter,* vol. 51, no. 5.

Llano, G. A. (1957). "Sharks vs. Men." *Scientific American,* vol. 196, no. 6.

———(1957). "Airmen Against the Sea." Arctic, Desert, Tropic Information Center Research Study Inst.

Lockhard, William E. (1965). "Treatment of Snakebite." *Jour. Amer. Med. Assoc.,* vol. 193, no. 5.

Lockwood, R. A. (1963). "Fatal Case of Sting by Box Jellyfish." *Suppl. Bull. Post Grad. Comm. Med.,* vol. 18, no. 12. Univ. of Sydney, Australia.

Loeb, L., et al. (1913). *The Venom of Heloderma.* Carnegie Institute Publication no. 177. Washington, D.C.

Loosanoff, Victor L. (1962). *Jellyfishes and Related Animals.* U.S. Dept. of the Interior, Fishery Leaflet no. 535.

Loveridge, Arthur (1931). "On Two Amphibious Snakes of the Central African Lake Region." *Bull. Antivenin Inst. of America,* vol. 5.

Lowe, Charles H. (1968). "Appraisal of Research on Fauna of Desert Environments," in *Deserts of the World,* ed. William G. McGinnies, et al. Univ. of Arizona Press, Tucson.

Ludwig, Emil (1937). *The Nile: The Life-Story of a River.* The Viking Press, New York.

Lumiere, Cornel (1956). *Beneath the Seven Seas.* Hutchinson & Co., London.

Lumpkin, William R., & Warfield M. Firor (1954). "Evaluation of the Bryson Treatment of Arthritis." *Amer. Surgeon,* vol. 20, no. 7.

Lydekker, R. (1894). *Marsupials.* John F. Shaw & Co., London.

Macfarlane, R. G. (1967). "Russell's Viper Venom, 1934–64." *Br. Jour. Haematology,* vol. 13.

Macht, David I. (1940). "New Developments in the Pharmacology and Therapeutics of Cobra Venom." *Trans. Amer. Therapeutic Soc.,* vol. 40.

Madon, Minoo B., & Ronald E. Hall (1970). "First Record of *Loxosceles rufescens* (Dufour) in California." *Toxicon,* vol. 8, no. 1.

**GS Marais, Eugene N. (1939). *My Friends the Baboons.* Methuen & Co., London.

Marden, Luis (1944). "A Land of Lakes and Volcanoes." *National Geographic,* vol. 86, no. 2.

Märki, F., & B. Witkop (1963). "The Venom of the Colombian Arrow Poison Frog *Phyllobates bicolor.*" *Separatum Experientia*, vol. 19.

Marr, A. G. M., & E. H. Baxter (1971). "Effect of Proteolytic Enzymes on the Venom of the Sea Wasp *Chironex fleckeri.*" *Toxicon*, vol. 9, no. 4.

**GS Marsh, J. A. (1964). *Cone Shells of the World.* Jacaranda Press, Brisbane, Australia.

Marsh, Helene (1970). "Preliminary Studies of the Venoms of Some Vermivorous Conidae." *Toxicon*, vol. 8, no. 4.

———(1971). "The Caseinase Activity of Some Vermivorous Cone Shell Venoms." *Toxicon*, vol. 9, no. 1.

Martin, W. B. (1946). "Clinical Experience with Snake Bites on Okinawa." *Bull. U.S. Army Med. Dept.*, vol. 5, no. 1.

Master, R. W. P., & S. Spinwaso Raio (1961). "Identification of Enzymes and Toxins in Venoms of Indian Cobra and Russell's Viper After Starch Gel Electrophoresis." *Jour. Biol. Chem.*, vol. 236, no. 7.

GS Matthews, L. Harrison (1969). *The Life of Mammals.* 2 vols. Weidenfeld & Nicolson, London.

***GS Matthiessen, Peter (1959). *Wildlife in America.* The Viking Press, New York.

———(1961). *The Cloud Forest.* The Viking Press, New York.

Maxwell, Gavin (1952). *Harpoon at a Venture.* Rupert Hart-Davis, London.

Mayer, A. G. (1910). *Medusae of the World.* 3 vols. Carnegie Inst., Publ. no. 109, Washington, D.C.

Mayer, Charles (1921). *Trapping Wild Animals in Malay Jungles.* Duffield & Co., New York.

McCollough, Newton C. (1963). "Venomous Snake Bite." *Jour. Florida Med. Assoc.*, vol. 49, no. 12.

McCollough, Newton C., & Joseph F. Gennaro (1963). "Coral Snake Bites in the United States." *Jour. Florida Med. Assoc.*, vol. 49, no. 12.

———(1963). "Evaluation of Venomous Snake Bite in the Southern United States." *Jour. Florida Med. Assoc.*, vol. 49, no. 12.

———(1963). "Summary of Snake Bite Treatment." *Jour. Florida Med. Assoc.*, vol. 49, no. 12.

McCollough, Newton C. (1968). "Emergency Room Treatment of Venomous Snakebite." *Jour. Florida Med. Assoc.*, vol. 55, no. 4.

McCollough, Newton C., & Joseph F. Gennaro (1968). "Diagnosis, Symptoms, Treatment, and Sequelae of Envenomation by *Crotalus adamanteus* and Genus *Ancistrodon.*" *Jour. Florida Med. Assoc.*, vol. 55, no. 4.

***GS McCormick, Harold W., Tom Allen, & William Young (1963). *Shadows in the Sea*. Chilton Books, Philadelphia.

**GS McGinnies, William G., et al. (eds.) (1968). *Deserts of the World*. Univ. of Arizona Press, Tucson.

McMichael, Donald F. (1963). "Dangerous Marine Molluscs." *Suppl. Bull. Post Grad. Comm. Med.*, vol. 18, no. 12. Univ. of Sidney, Australia.

———(1963). "Slides of Dangerous Molluscs." *Suppl. Bull. Post Grad. Comm. Med.*, vol. 18, no. 12. Univ. of Sydney, Australia.

McNeil, F. A., & E. C. Pope (1943). "A Venomous Medusa from Australian Waters." *Austral. Jour. of Sci.*, vol. 5.

McNeil, F. A. (1963). "Stinging Coral and So-called Stinging Seaweed." *Suppl. Bull. Post Grad. Comm. Med.*, vol. 18, no. 12.

Meadows, Paul E., & Findlay E. Russell (1970). "Milking of Arthropods." *Toxicon*, vol. 8, no. 4.

Medway, Lord (1969). *The Wild Mammals of Malaya*. Oxford Univ. Press, London.

Merck, Sharp & Dohme (1965). *Lyovac Antivenin (Latrodectus mactans)*. Direction circular.

Merriam, T. W., Jr. (1962). "Snake Bite Survey." Abstracted in *Naval Res. Rev.*, from *Naval Med. Field Res. Lab. Rep.*, Camp Lejeune, N.C.

Micks, Don W. (1952). "Clinical Effects of the Sting of the 'Puss Caterpillar' (*Megalopyge opercularis* S and A) on Man." *Tex. Rep. Biol. Med.*, vol. 10, no. 2.

Micks, Don W. (with Victor C. Colma) (1952). "Nasal Myiasis of Man Due to the Screwworm Fly (*Caitroga americana* C and P)." *Tex. Rep. Biol. Med.*, vol. 10, no. 4.

**GS Micks, Don W. (1960). "Insects and Other Arthropods of Medical Importance in Texas." *Tex. Rep. Biol. Med.*, vol. 18, no. 4.

———(1962). "An Outbreak of Dermatitis Due to the Grain Itch Mite *Pyemotes ventricosus* Newport." *Tex. Rep. Biol. Med.*, vol. 20, no. 2.

Middelbrook, R. E., et al. (1971). "Isolation and Purification of Toxin from *Millepora dichotoma*." *Toxicon*, vol. 9, no. 4.

Miller, Charles (1950). *Cannibal Caravan*. Museum Press Ltd., London.

*G Miller, Wilford L. (1959). *Wildlife in North Dakota*. Bismarck Tribune Co., Bismarck, N.D.

Mills, Ernest M. (1959). "Rats—Let's Get Rid of Them." U.S. Dept. of the Interior, Fish & Wildlife Service, Bureau of Sport Fisheries & Wildlife, Circ. no. 22.

Milne, Louis J. & Margery (1962). *The Mountains*. ("Life Nature Library.") Time Inc., New York.

**GS Minton, Sherman A., Jr. (1957). "Snakebite." *Scientific American,* vol. 196, no. 1.

———(1968). "Venoms of Desert Animals," in *Desert Biology,* vol. 1, ed. G. W. Brown, Jr. Academic Press, New York.

———(1969). "The Feeding Strike of The Timber Rattlesnake." *Jour. Herpetology,* vol. 3.

***GS Minton, Sherman A., Jr. & Madge R. (1969). *Venomous Reptiles.* Charles Scribner's Sons, New York.

**GS Minton, Sherman A., Jr. (ed.) (1971). *Snake Venom and Envenomation.* Marcel Dekker, New York.

*G ———(1973). *Giant Reptiles.* Charles Scribner's Sons, New York.

*S ———(1974). *Venom Disease.* Charles C Thomas, Springfield, Ill.

Mohamed, A. H., et al. (1971). "Effects of *Naja nigricollis* Venom on Blood and Tissue Histamine" and "The Effects of *Naja nigricollis* Venom on Blood Clotting." *Toxicon,* vol. 9, no. 2.

Monkman, Noel (1958). *From Queensland to the Great Barrier Reef.* Doubleday & Co., Garden City, N.Y.

Moore, Robert Allan (1945). *A Textbook of Pathology.* W. B. Saunders Co., Philadelphia.

Moore, Richard E., & Paul J. Scheuer (1971). "Palytonin: A New Marine Toxin from a Coelenterate." *Science,* vol. 172, no. 11.

Moreton, Ann (1971). "Spiders—Feared, Revered, and Loathed the World Over." *Smithsonian Magazine,* vol. 2, no. 5.

Morgan, Robert (1956). *World Sea Fisheries.* Methuen & Co., London.

Morris, Ramona, & Desmond Morris. *Men and Snakes.* McGraw-Hill, New York.

Morse, Roger A., & Allen W. Benton (1964). "Notes on Venom Collection from Honeybees." *Bee World,* vol. 45, no. 4.

Mueller, Harry Louis (1960). "Yellow Jacket Sting." *Jour. Amer. Med. Assoc.,* vol. 173, no. 10.

Munjal, D., & W. B. Elliott (1971). "Studies of Antigenic Fractions in Honey-Bee *(Apis mellifera)* Venom." *Toxicon,* vol. 9, no. 3.

Murphey, R. C., & J. T. Nichols (1916). "The Shark Situation in the Waters About New York." *Brooklyn Museum Quart.,* vol. 3, no. 4.

Murtha, Edmund F. (1960). "Pharmacological Study of Poisons from Shellfish and Puffer Fish." *Annals N.Y. Acad. Science,* vol. 90, art. 3.

Nachmansohn, David (1950). "Electric Currents in Nerve Tissue and Electric Organs." *Electrical Engineering,* Mar.

National Geographic Magazine (1917). "Our Flag Number," vol. 32, no. 4.

National Geographic Society (1960). *Wild Animals of North America.*

National Safety Council (1948). "Domestic Animals." Safety Educ. Data Sheet no. 26.

———(1949). "Poisonous Reptiles." Safety Educ. Data Sheet no. 35.

———(1949). "Animals in the Classroom." Safety Educ. Data Sheet no. 37.

———(1958). "Black Widow Spiders May Be Dangerous." *Home Safety Review,* vol. 15, no. 2.

———(1958). "Tick Bites." NSC Data Sheet D-228.

———(1958). "If You Can't Avoid Snakes." *Natl. Safety News,* May.

———(1959). "Fight Flies—Safely." *Safety Newsletter.*

———(1959). "Wild Pets." *Home Safety Review,* winter.

———(1960). "Bites and Stings." *NSC Natl. Safety News,* Apr. *Safety Newsletter,* Aug. (Textile Section).

———(1960). "Bee-ware of Wasps." *NSC Bulletin Board,* May.

———(1960). "Bites and Stings." *NSC Natl. Safety News,* Apr.

———(1960). "Beware: Rabies in the Wild." *Home Safety Review,* fall.

———(1961). "Don't Invite Snakebite." *NSC Home Safety Review,* spring.

———(1961). "Caterpillar Is Health Menace." *Safety Newsletter* (Occupational Health Section).

———(1961). "Bats Can Carry Rabies." *NSC Newsletter,* June (Occupational Health Nursing Section).

———(1962). "Poisonous Snakes." *NSC Natl. Safety News,* Mar.

———(n.d.) "Black Widow Spiders." NSC Data Sheet no. 258 (Revised).

*G Neumann, Arthur H. (1966). *Elephant Hunting in East Equatorial Africa.* Abercrombie & Fitch, New York.

New York Zoological Society (1966). *Emergency Snakebite Procedures.* Reptile Dept. Leaflet no. 9. Rev., May 16.

Nichols, John T. (1921). "What Sharks Really Eat." *Natural History,* vol. 21, no. 3.

Nichols, John T. (with Paul Bartsch) (1946). *Fishes and Shells of the Pacific World.* Macmillan Co., New York.

Norman, J. R. (1948). *A History of Fishes.* Frederick A. Stokes Co., New York.

O'Connor, P. Fitzgerald (1953). *Shark-O!* Secker & Warburg, London.

"Octopus Venom Isolated" (1968). *Science News,* vol. 93, June 29.

Old, E. H. (1908). "A Report of Several Cases with Unusual Symptoms Caused by Contact with Some Unknown Variety of Jellyfish *(Scyphozoa)*." *Philippine Jour. Sci.,* vol. 3.

*G Oliver, James A. (1952). *The Prevention and Teatment of Snakebite.* N.Y. Zoological Soc., New York.

**G   ——(1955). *North American Amphibians and Reptiles*. D. Van Nostrand Co., New York.

**G   ——(1958). *Snakes in Fact and Fiction*. Macmillan Co., New York.

  G   Olsen, Jack (1969). *Night of the Grizzlies*. G. P. Putnam's Sons, New York.

Ouyang, Chaoho, & Shoei-Yn Shiau (1970). "Relationship Between Pharmacological Actions and Enzymatic Activities of the Venom of *Trimeresurus gramineus*." *Toxicon*, vol. 8, no. 2.

Packard, Vance (1950). *Animal I.Q.* The Dial Press, New York.

Pacy, J. R. (1963). "Stingray, Blackfish and Catfish Injuries." *Suppl. Bull. Post Grad. Comm. Med.*, vol. 18, no. 12. Univ. of Sydney, Australia.

Parke-Davis (1962). "Camp Medicine." *Therapeutic Notes*, vol. 69.

Parrish, Henry M., et al. (1957). "Human Allergy Resulting from North American Snake Venoms." *Jour. Florida Med. Assoc.*, vol. 43, May.

Parrish, Henry M. (1957). "Mortality from Snakebites, United States, 1950–1954." *Public Health Reports*, vol. 72, no. 11.

Parrish, Henry M. (with F. B. Clark, D. Brobst, & J. F. Mock) (1959). "Epidemiology of Dog Bites." *Public Health Reports*, vol. 74, no. 10.

Parrish, Henry M. (1959). "Deaths from Bites and Stings of Venomous Animals and Insects in the United States." *A.M.A. Arch. Internat. Med.*, vol. 104, Aug.

——(1960). "Treatment of Poisonous Snakebites: Present Status of Incision and Excision." *Jour. Indiana State Med. Assoc.*, vol. 53, no. 10.

——(1963). "Analysis of 460 Fatalities from Venomous Animals in the United States." *Amer. Jour. Med. Sci.*, vol. 245, no. 2.

——(1963). "Intravenous Antivenin in Clinical Snake Venom Poisoning." *Missouri Med.*, vol. 60, no. 3.

——(1964). "Poisonous Snakebites in North Carolina." *North Carolina Med. Jour.*, vol. 25, no. 3.

——(1964). "Texas Snakebite Statistics." *Texas State Jour. Med.*, vol. 60, July.

——(1964). "Pit Viper Bites in Pennsylvania." *Pennsylvania Med. Jour.*, vol. 67, Aug.

——(1964). "Characteristics of Snakebites in Missouri." *Missouri Med.*, Oct.

Parrish, Henry M., et al. (1964). "Counting California's Snakebites." *California Med.*, vol. 101, Nov.

——(1965). "Snakebite: A Pediatric Problem." *Clinical Pediatrics*, vol. 4, no. 4.

Parrish, Henry M. (1965). "Comments on Snakebites in New Jersey." *Jour. Med. Soc. New Jersey*, vol. 62, no. 6.

———(1965). "Comparison between Snakebites in Children and Adults." *Pediatrics,* vol. 36, no. 2.

———(1965). "Nature of Poisonous Snakebites in New York." *New York State Jour. Med.,* vol. 65, no. 17.

Parrish, Henry M., & M. S. Khan (1966). "Bites by Foreign Venomous Snakes in the United States." *Amer. Jour. Med. Sci.,* vol. 251, no. 2.

Parrish, Henry M., et al. (1966). "Poisonous Snakebites Causing No Envenomation." *Postgraduate Med.,* vol. 39, no. 3.

Parrish, Henry M. (1966). "Incidence of Treated Snakebites in the United States." *Public Health Reports,* vol. 81, no. 3.

———(1967). "Bites by Cottonmouths *(Ancistrodon piscivorus)* in the United States." *Southern Med. Jour.,* vol. 60, no. 4.

Parrish, Henry M., & M. S. Khan (1967). "Bites by Coral Snakes: Reports of 11 Representative Cases." *Amer. Jour. Med. Sci.,* vol. 253, no. 5.

Parrish, Henry M. (1967). "Pitfalls in Treating Pit Viper Bites." *Medical Times,* vol. 95, no. 8.

Parrish, Henry M., & Carole A. Carr (1967). "Bites by Copperheads *(Ancistrodon contortrix)* in the United States." *Jour. Amer. Med. Assoc.,* vol. 201, Sept. 18.

Parrish, Henry M. (1968). "Current Concepts of Snakebite Treatment." *U.S. Navy Medical News Letter,* Dec. 20.

Parrott, Arthur W. (1958). *Big Game Fishes and Sharks of New Zealand.* Hodder & Stoughton Ltd., London.

***GS Patterson, J. H. (1926). *The Man Eaters of Tsavo.* Macmillan Co., London.

Patton, Walter Scott (1929–31). "Insects, Ticks, Mites, and Venomous Animals of Medical and Veterinary Importance," Parts I and II, in *Medical and Public Health.* H. R. Grubb, Ltd., Croyden.

Percival, Arthur Blayney (1924). *A Game Ranger's Note Book.* Geo. H. Doran Co., New York.

Perlmutter, Alfred (1961). *Guide to Marine Fishes.* N.Y. Univ. Press, New York.

Perry, Richard (1970). *The World of the Jaguar.* Taplinger, New York.

———(1973). *The Polar Worlds.* Taplinger, New York.

Perry, W. A. (1890). "The Cougar," in *The Big Game of North America,* ed. G. O. Shields. Rand McNally & Co., Chicago.

*GS Peters, James A. (1964). *Dictionary of Herpetology.* Hafner Pub., New York.

Phillips, Craig, & W. H. Brady (1953). "Sea Pests: Poisonous and Harmful Sea Life of Florida and the West Indies." Spec. Public. Marine Lab., Univ. of Miami.

Phelps, R. (1963). "Experiences with Stonefish Stingings in New Guinea." *Suppl. Bull. Post Grad. Comm. Med.,* vol. 18, no. 12. Univ. of Sydney, Australia.

Picken, L. E. R., & R. J. Skaer (1966). "A Review of Researches on Nematocysts," in *Cnidaria and Their Evolution,* ed. W. J. Rees. Zoological Society of London, Academic Press, London.

Pickwell, Gayle (1947). *Amphibians and Reptiles of the Pacific States.* Stanford Univ. Press, Palo Alto, Calif.

Pike, Gordon C. (1954). "The Killer Whale." *Western Fisheries,* vol. 48, no. 1.

Pillsbury, R. W. (1957). "Avoidance of Poisonous Eggs of the Marine Fish *Scorpaenichthys marmoratus* by Predators." *Copeia,* no. 3, Aug.

Pincher, Chapman (1948). *A Study of Fish.* Duell, Sloan & Pearce, New York.

Pinney, Roy (n.d.). "Poisonous Snake-Bite Therapy." Unpublished manuscript.

Platt, Rutherford (1949). "Shells Take You Over World Horizons." *National Geographic,* vol. 96, no. 1.

Pope, Clifford H. (1946). *Snakes of the Northeastern United States.* New York Zoological Soc., New York.

**GS ———(1961). *The Giant Snakes.* Alfred A. Knopf, New York.

———(1962). "The Six Giants." *Natural History,* vol. 71, no. 6.

**G ———(1966). *The Reptile World: A Natural History of the Snakes, Lizards, Turtles, and Crocodilians.* Alfred A. Knopf, New York.

Pope, Elizabeth C. (1963). "Some Noxious Marine Invertebrates from Australian Seas." *Suppl. Bull. Post Grad. Comm. Med.,* vol. 18, no. 12. Univ. of Sydney, Australia.

Porter, J. Hampden (1894). *Wild Beasts.* Charles Scribner's Sons, New York.

"Rabies—Animal Bites in Small Children" (1958). *Vet. Pub. Health Newsletter,* Apr. 15.

"Rabies—a Present-Day Problem" (1961). *School Health,* May.

Radcliffe, Lewis (1914). "The Sharks and Rays of Beaufort, North Carolina." *Bull. U.S. Bur. Fisheries,* pp. 239–284.

Ramsey, H. W., et al. (1972). "Fractionation of Coral Snake Venom. Preliminary Studies on the Separation and Characterization of the Protein Fractions." *Toxicon,* vol. 10, no. 1.

**GS Randall, John E. (1958). "Review of Ciguatera (Fish Poisoning)." *Bull. Marine Science Gulf & Caribbean,* vol. 8, no. 3.

———(1960). "The Living Javelin." *Sea Frontiers,* vol. 6, no. 4.

———(1961). "Let a Sleeping Shark Lie" and "Ciguatera: Tropical Fish Poisoning." *Sea Frontiers,* vol. 7, no. 3.

**S Raskova, H. (ed.) (1971). *Pharmacology and Toxicology of Naturally Occurring Toxins*. 2 vols. Section 71: *International Encyclopedia of Pharmacology and Therapeutics*. Pergamon Press, Oxford.

Ratcliff, J. D. (1943). "Sharks." *Collier's*, vol. 112, no. 6.

Reed, Allen C. (1953). "Arizona's Venom Man." *Arizona Highways*, vol. 24, no. 2.

Rees, W. J. (ed.) (1966). *The Cnidaria and Their Evolution*. Zoological Society of London, Academic Press, London.

**GS Reid, H. A. (1959). "Sea-Snake Bite and Poisoning." *The Practitioner*, vol. 183, p. 530.

Reid, H. A. (with P. C. Thean, K. E. Chan, & A. R. Baharom) (1963). "Clinical Effects of Bites by Malayan Viper *(Ancistrodon rhodostoma)*." *The Lancet*, Mar. 23.

Reid, H. A. (1969). "Snakebite in the Tropics." *U.S. Navy Medical News Letter*, vol. 53, no. 2.

Resources Agency of California–Department of Fish & Game (1962). "Skin Divers Hitch Ride with Sharks." *Outdoor California*, vol. 23, no. 5.

Rhoten, William, & Joseph F. Gennaro, Jr. (1968). "Treatment of the Bite of a Mojave Rattlesnake." *Jour. Florida Med. Assoc.*, vol. 55, no. 4.

Riegel, B., et al. (1949). "Paralytic Shellfish Poison." *Jour. Biol. Chem.*, vol. 177, no. 7.

Robertson, Phyllis L. (1968). "A Morphological and Functional Study of the Venom Apparatus in Representatives of Some Major Groups of Hymenoptera." *Austral. Jour. Zoology*, vol. 16, no. 1.

Rodahl, Kaare (1953). *North: The Nature and Drama of the Polar World*. Harper & Row, New York.

Roedel, Phil M., & W. E. Ripley (1950). "California Sharks and Rays." State of Calif. Dept. of Nat. Res., Div. of Fish & Game, Bur. of Mar. Fish, Fish Bull. no. 75.

Roosevelt, Theodore (1893). *The Wilderness Hunter*. G. P. Putnam's Sons, New York.

——(1905)."A Colorado Bear Hunt."*Scribner's Magazine*, vol. 38, no. 4.

——(1905). "A Wolf Hunt in Oklahoma." *Scribner's Magazine*, vol. 38, no. 5.

——(1910). *African Game Trails*. Charles Scribner's Sons, New York.

——(1914). *Through the Brazilian Jungle*. G. P. Putnam's Sons, New York.

Rothschild, Lord (1965). *A Classification of Living Animals*. Longmans, London.

Rosenblatt, Richard H., & W. J. Baldwin (1958). "A Review of the Eastern Pacific Sharks of the Genus *Cardrarkinus* with a Redescription of *C. malpeloensis* (Fowler) and California Records of *C. remotus* (Dumeril)." *California Fish & Game*, vol. 44, no. 2.

Roughly, T. C. (1954). *Wonders of the Great Barrier Reef*. Angus & Robertson, London.

Roule, Louis (1953). *Fishes, Their Ways of Life*. George Routledge & Sons, London.

Russell, Findlay E. (1953). "Stingray Injuries." *Amer. Jour. Med. Sci.*, vol. 226, p. 611.

Russell, Findlay E. (with W. C. Barritt & M. D. Fairchild) (1957). "Electrocardiographic Patterns Evoked by Venom of the Stingray." *Proc. Soc. Exper. Biol. Med.*, vol. 96, p. 634.

Russell, Findlay E. (with T. C. Powers, L. W. Kang, A. M. Warner, & T. C. Colket, III) (1958). "Studies on the Mechanism of Death from Stingray Venom." *Amer. Jour. Med. Sci.*, vol. 235, p. 566.

Russell, Findlay E. (1959). "Stingray Injuries." *Public Health Reports*, vol. 74, no. 10.

Russell, Findlay E. (with J. A. Emery) (1960). "Venom of the Weevers *Trachinus draco* and *T. vipera*." *Annals N.Y. Acad. Science*, vol. 90, art. 3.

Russell, Findlay E. (1960). "Rattlesnake Bites in Southern California." *Amer. Jour. Med. Sci.*, vol. 239, p. 51.

———(1962). "Muscle Relaxants in Black Widow Spider *(Lactrodectus mactans)* Poisoning," *Amer. Jour. Med. Sci.*, vol. 243, p. 2.

Russell, Findlay E., & R. S. Scharffenberg (1964). *Bibliography of Snake Venoms and Venomous Snakes*. Bibliography Assoc., West Covina.

Russell, Findlay E. (1965). "Toxic Marine Animals." Excerpts from a paper presented to the First Inter-American Naval Research Conference, San Juan, July.

Russell, Findlay E., & L. Lauritzen (1966). "Antivenins." *Trans. Royal Soc. Trop. Med. Hygiene*, vol. 60, no. 6.

Russell, Findlay E., & Paul R. Saunders (eds.) (1967). *Animal Toxins*. Pergamon Press, New York.

Russell, Findlay E., et al. (1970). "Clinical Use of Antivenin Prepared from Goat Serum." *Toxicon*, vol. 8, no. 1.

Russell, Findlay E. (1970). "Bite by the Spider *Phidippus formosus*: Case History." *Toxicon*, vol. 8, no. 2.

———(1971). "Pharmacology of Toxins of Marine Organisms," in *Pharmacology and Toxicology of Naturally Occurring Toxins*, ed. H. Raskova. Pergamon Press, Oxford.

St. Clair, Gordon P. (1956). "Snake Bite Manual." National Safety Council, Chicago.

Sanderson, G. P. (1896). *Thirteen Years Among the Wild Beasts of India.* W. H. Allen & Co., London.

**G Sanderson, Ivan T. (1955). *Living Mammals of the World.* Hanover House, Garden City, N.Y.

**G ———(1956). *Follow the Whale.* Cassell & Co., London.

*G ———(1957). *The Monkey Kingdom.* Hanover House, Garden City, N.Y.

***G ———(1962). *The Dynasty of Abu: a History and Natural History of the Elephants and Their Relatives, Past and Present.* Alfred A. Knopf, New York.

Saunders, Paul R. (1959). "Venom of the Stonefish *Synanceja verrucosa.*" *Science,* vol. 129, no. 3344.

———(1959). "Venom of the Stonefish *Synanceja horrida* (Linnaeus)." *Arch. Int. Pharmacodyn.,* vol. 123, nos. 1–2.

*S Saunders, Paul R. (with P. B. Taylor) (1959). "Venom of the Lionfish *Pterois volitans.*" *Amer. Jour. Physiol.,* vol. 197, pp. 437 ff.

*S Saunders, Paul R. (1959). "Venom of the Scorpionfishes." *Proc. of Western Pharm. Soc.,* vol. 2, no. 4.

Saunders, Paul R. (with Solomon E. Lifton) (1960). "Sting by a Venomous Lionfish." *U.S. Armed Forces Med. Jour.,* vol. 11, no. 2.

Saunders, Paul R. (1960). "Pharmacological and Chemical Studies of the Venom of the Stonefish (Genus *Synanceja*) and Other Scorpionfishes." *Annals N.Y. Acad. Science,* vol. 90, art. 3.

Saunders, Paul R. (with L. Tokes) (1961). "Purification and Properties of the Lethal Fraction of the Venom of the Stonefish *Synanceja horrida* (Linnaeus)." *Biochem. Biophys. Acta,* vol. 52, pp. 527 ff.

Schaeffer, R. C., Jr., et al. (1971). "Some Chemical Properties of the Venom of the Scorpionfish *Scorpaena guttata.*" *Toxicon,* vol. 9, no. 1.

Schall, Joseph (1969). "Sea Snakes—Mysterious Mariners." *Frontiers,* vol. 33, no. 3.

***GS Schaller, George B. (1963). *The Mountain Gorilla: Ecology and Behavior.* Univ. of Chicago Press, Chicago.

**GS ———(1972). *The Serengeti Lion.* Univ. of Chicago Press, Chicago.

Schantz, Edward J. (1960). "Biochemical Studies on Paralytic Shellfish Poisons." *Annals N.Y. Acad. Science,* vol. 90, art. 3.

***GS Scheffer, Victor B. (1958). *Seals, Sea Lions and Walruses.* Stanford Univ. Press, Stanford, Calif.

*G Schmidt, Karl P. (with Robert F. Inger) (1957). *Living Reptiles of the World.* Hanover House, Garden City, N.Y.

Schnurrenberger, Paul R., & Jack H. Russell (1961). "A Rabies Control Program in Ohio." *Public Health Reports,* vol. 76, no. 4.

Schultz, Leonard P. (with E. M. Stern) (1948). *The Ways of Fishes.* D. Van Nostrand Co., New York.

**GS Schultz, Leonard P. (with Perry W. Gilbert & Stewart Springer) (1961). "Shark Attacks." *Science,* vol. 134, no. 3472.

"Scorpion Stings and Heart Diseases," (1969). *Science News,* vol. 95, no. 4.

Scott, Jack Denton (1962). "Prince of Cats—the Lethal Leopard." *Reader's Digest,* July. (Condensed from *Rod and Gun,* June 1962.)

* Scott, Robert Falcon (1913). *Scott's Last Expedition.* Smith, Elder & Co., London.

*GS Scullard, H. H. (1974). *The Elephant in the Greek and Roman World.* Cornell Univ. Press, Ithaca, N.Y.

Sea Secrets. International Oceanographic Foundation. Various issues of this monthly question-and-answer bulletin.

Seton, Ernest Thompson (1904). "The Whitetailed (Virginia) Deer and Its Kin." *Scribner's Monthly,* vol. 40.

**G ———(1929). *Lives of Game Animals,* vol. 2, part 1, *Bears,* etc. Charles Scribner's Sons, New York.

———(1937). *Great Historic Animals—Mainly about Wolves.* Charles Scribner's Sons, New York.

Severin, Jurt (1953). "The Land-Locked Man-Eaters." *True Magazine,* July.

Shields, G. O. (ed.) (1890). *The Big Game of North America.* Rand McNally & Co., Chicago.

Siemel, Sasha (1952). "The Jungle Was My Home." *National Geographic,* vol. 102, no. 5.

**GS Sikes, Sylvia (1971). *The Natural History of the African Elephant.* Weidenfeld & Nicolson, London.

Slaughter, Scott G. (as told to Wm. M. Stephens) (1962). "My War with Sharks." *Saturday Evening Post,* vol. 235, no. 26.

***GS Slijper, E. J. (1962). *Whales: the Biology of the Cetaceans.* Basic Books, New York.

**S Smart, John, et al. (1965). *A Handbook for the Identification of Insects of Medical Importance.* British Museum (Natural History), London.

Smith, Emil J., Jr. (1960). "Seals and Sea Lions." *Skin Diver,* vol. 9, no. 1.

Smith, F. G. Walton (1961). "Sea Monsters in the Telling." *Sea Frontiers,* vol. 7, no. 2.

Smith, Hugh M. (1916). "Sharks—Man-Eaters and Others." *Amer. Mus. Jour.,* vol. 16, no. 6.

Smith, J. L. B. (1953). *The Sea Fishes of Southern Africa*. Central News Agency, Cape Town.

**GS ———(1957). "Two Rapid Fatalities from Stonefish Stabs." *Copeia*, no. 3, Aug. 26.

———(1957). "The Fishes of the Family *Scorpaenidae* in the Western Indian Ocean." Part II. *Ichth. Bull.*, no. 5, Rhodes Univ., Grahamstown, South Africa.

———(1960). "Are Whales a Serious Danger to Small Boats?" *Skin Diver*, vol. 9, no. 1.

Smythe, R. H. (1961). *Animal Vision, What Animals See*. Herbert Jenkins, London.

Snakebite (n.d.). Bilingual pamphlet. Siamese Red Cross Society, Bangkok.

**G Snow, Keith R. (1970). *The Arachnids: An Introduction*. Columbia Univ. Press, New York.

Sommer, H., R. P. Monmer, B. Riegel, et al. (1948). "Paralytic Shellfish Poison." *Jour. Amer. Chem. Soc.*, vol. 70, no. 1015.

Songdahl, J. H., & C. E. Lane (1970). "Some Pharmacological Characteristics of the Alphabet Cone, *Conus spurius atlanticus*." *Toxicon*, vol. 8, no. 4.

Sonneborn, Duane G. (1946). "Poisonous Snake (Habu) Bites." *U.S. Naval Med. Bull.*, vol. 46, no. 1.

Southcott, R. V. (1956). "Studies on Australian Cubomedusae, Including a New Genus and Species Apparently Harmful to Man." *Austral. Jour. Mar. & Freshwater Res.*, vol. 7, no. 2.

**S ———(1959). "Tropical Jellyfish and Other Marine Stingings." *Military Med.*, vol. 124, no. 8.

———(1960). "Venomous Jellyfish." *Good Health*, Jan.

———(1963). "Fatal and Other Stingings by Sea-Wasps." *Suppl. Bull. Post Grad. Comm. Med.*, vol. 18, no. 12. Univ. of Sydney, Australia.

———(1969). "Injuries to Man from Marine Invertebrates in the Australian Seas." *Documenta Geigy, Nautilus*, Oct.

Sowder, Wilson T., & George W. Gehres (1963). "Snakebites in Florida." *Jour. Florida Med. Assoc.*, vol. 49, no. 12.

———(1968). "Snakebite Myths and Misinformation." *Jour. Florida Med. Assoc.*, vol. 55, no. 4.

Sparger, Charles Forrest (1969). "Problems in the Management of Rattlesnake Bites." *Arch. Surgery*, vol. 98, Jan.

**S Spector, William S. (1955). *Handbook of Toxicology*. W. B. Saunders Co., Philadelphia.

Springer, Stewart (1943). "Sharks and Their Behavior." *Coord. Res. & Devel.*, *U.S.N. Emerg. Rescue Equip. Sect.*, Oct.

*G Stackhouse, John (1970). *Australia's Venomous Wildlife*. Paul Hamlyn, London.

Stackpole, Edouard A. (1953). *The Sea-Hunters: the Great Age of Whaling.* J. B. Lippincott Co., Philadelphia.

**GS   Stahnke, Herbert L. (1953). "The L–C Treatment of Venomous Bites or Stings." *Arizona Highways,* vol. 29, no. 2.

——(1956). "Scorpions." Poisonous Animals Research Laboratory, Tempe, Ariz.

***GS   ——(1958). "The Treatment of Venomous Bites and Stings." Poisonous Animals Research Laboratory, Tempe, Ariz.

Stankik, V. J. (1960). *Introducing Poisonous Snakes.* Spring Books, London.

Stebbins, R. C. (1954). *Amphibians and Reptiles of Western North America.* McGraw-Hill, New York.

**GS   Stefansson, Vilhjalmur (1925). *The Friendly Arctic: the Story of Five Years in Polar Regions.* Macmillan Co., New York.

Stejneger, Leonhard (1897). "The Poisonous Snakes of North America." U.S. National Museum, Washington, D.C.

Steward, J. W. (1970). *The Tailed Amphibians of Europe.* Taplinger, New York.

Stickel, William H. (1952). *Veromous Snakes of the United States and Treatment of Their Bites.* U.S. Dept. of the Interior, Fish and Wildlife Service, Wildlife Leaflet no. 339, Washington, D.C.

Stigand, C. H. (1913). *Hunting the Elephant in Africa.* Macmillan Co., New York.

Stillway, L. W., & C. T. Lane (1971). "Phospholipase in the Nematocyst Toxin of *Physalia physalis.*" *Toxicon,* vol. 9, no. 3.

Stokoe, W. J. (compiler) (1938). *The Observer's Book of Wild Animals of the British Isles.* (Revised by Maurice Burton, 1958.) Frederick Warne & Co., London.

"The Stone Fish" (1956). *African Wildlife,* vol. 10, no. 1.

"Stone-Fish and Other Antivenenes" (1959). *Med. Jour. Austral.,* vol. 1, no. 19.

Street, Philip (1971). *Animal Weapons.* Taplinger, New York.

Strydon, D. J., & D. P. Bates (1970). "I. Preliminary Studies on the Separation of Toxins of Elapidae Venoms." *Toxicon,* vol. 8, no. 3.

Stuart, Montgomery A., & T. D. Slagle (1943). "Jellyfish Stings, Suggested Treatment, and Report on Two Cases." *U.S. Naval Med. Bull.,* vol. 41, no. 2.

Suarez, G., et al. (1971). "*Loxosceles laeta* Venom—Partial Purification." *Toxicon,* vol. 9, no. 3.

Sutherland, Struan (1967). "The Ringed Octopus Bite: A Unique Medical Emergency." *Med. Jour. Austral.,* Sept. 2.

——(1969). "Toxins and Mode of Envenomation of the Common Ringed or Blue-banded Octopus." *Med. Jour. Austral.,* May 3.

Sutherland, Struan, et al. (1970). "Octopus Neurotoxins: Low Molecular Weight Non-Immunologic Toxins Present in the Saliva of the Blue-ringed Octopus." *Toxicon*, vol. 8, no. 3.

**GS Swaroop, C. C., & B. Grab (1954). "Snakebite Mortality in the World." *Bull. World Health Organization*, vol. 10, no. 1.

Syder, C. C., et al. (1968). "A Definitive Study of Snakebite." *Jour. Florida Med. Assoc.*, vol. 55, no. 4.

Taboada, Oscar (1967). *Medical Entomology*. National Naval Medical Center, Bethesda, Md.

Talliez, Philippe (1954). *To Hidden Depths*. William Kimber, London.

***S Taylor, F. H., & R. E. Murray (1946). "Spiders, Ticks and Mites Including the Species Harmful to Man in Australia and New Guinea." Commonwealth of Australia, Dept. of Health, School of Pub. Health & Trop. Med., Serv. Publication no. 6.

**GS Thompson, J. R., & Stewart Springer (1961). "Sharks, Skates, Rays and Chimaeras." U.S. Dept. of the Interior, Fish & Wildlife, Circ. no. 119.

***GS Thorp, R. W., & W. D. Woodson (1945). *The Black Widow: America's Most Poisonous Spider*. Univ. of North Carolina Press, Chapel Hill.

Thorpe, W. H. (1974). *Animal Nature and Human Nature*. Doubleday & Co., New York.

Thorton, Thomas (1806). *A Sporting Tour Through Various Parts of France in the Year 1802*. Series of letters published in London.

Tidswell, F. (1906). *Australian Venoms*. Dept. of Public Health, Sydney.

Tokuyama, T., et al. (1968). "The Structure of Batrachotoxinin A, a Novel Steroidal Alkaloid from the Colombian Arrow Poison Frog, *Phyllobates aurotaenia*." *Jour. Amer. Chem. Soc.*, vol. 90, no. 1917.

Townsend, Charles H. (1919). "Making Use of the Shark." *Bull. N.Y. Zoological Soc.*, vol. 23, no. 6.

———(1930). "Twentieth Century Whaling." *Bull. N.Y. Zoological Soc.*, vol. 24, no. 6.

Travis, William (1961). *Shark for Sale*. George Allen & Unwin, London.

Trinca, John C., & Peter Schiff (1970). "Deadly Sea Wasp." *Sea Frontiers*, vol. 16, no. 1.

**GS Troughton, Ellis (1947). *Furred Animals of Australia*. Charles Scribner's Sons, New York.

Truitt, J. O. (1968). *A Guide to the Snakes of South Florida*. Hurricane House, Miami.

Tucker, Denys W., & C. T. Neenham (1957). "The Blue Shark *Prionace glauca* (L) Breeds in British Seas." *Ann. & Mag. Nat. Hist.*, ser. 12, vol. 10.

*G   Turnbull–Kemp, Peter (1967). *The Leopard.* Bailey Bros. & Swinfen, London.

Tuve, Richard L. (1947). "The Technology of the U.S. Navy 'Shark Chaser.'" *U.S. Naval Inst. Proc.*, vol. 73, no. 5.

**GS   Tweedie, M. W. F. (1941). *Poisonous Animals of Malaya.* Malaya Pub. House, Singapore.

U.S. Government, Department of the Air Force (1952). *Survival,* Air Force Manual no. 64–5.

U.S. Government, Department of the Army (1957). *Military Sanitation,* FM 21–10 AF, 160–46.

————(1957). *Survival,* FM 21–76.

————(1960). *Jungle Operations,* FM 31–30.

U.S. Department of Health, Education & Welfare (1955). "Practical Problems in Rabies Control." *Public Health Reports,* vol. 70, no. 6.

U.S. Government, Department of the Interior, Fish & Wildlife Service (Various years). Annual reports for the Bur. Comm. Fisheries; Bur. Sport Fish & Wildlife; Branch of Wildlife Res.

————(1961). *Hints on Bobcat Trapping.* Fish & Wildlife Circ. no. 1.

U.S. Government (1944). "Final Report on the Use of Chemical Materials as Shark Repellents." NRL Rep. No. P–2379, Naval Res. Lab. Anacostia Station, Washington, D.C.

————(1958). *U.S. Navy Diving Manual.* Navships 25–253 (part 3) Change no. 1.

————(1959). *Shark Sense.* Aviation Training Div., Off. Ch. Nav. Op. (NAVAER OO–80Q–14).

————(1961). *U.S. Navy Diving Manual.* Navships 250–538.

Van Densen, Hobart M., & R. F. Peterson (1958). "Chiroptera of New Guinea." *Natural History,* Oct.

Venters, H. D., et al. (1954). "Rabies in Bats in Florida." *Amer. Jour. Pub. Health,* vol. 44, no. 1.

Verrill, A. H. (1948). *Strange Fish and Their Stories.* L. C. Page & Co., Boston.

*G   Vesey–Fitzgerald, Brian (1966). *The Worlds of Ants, Bees, and Wasps.* Pelham Books, London.

Vick, James A., & James Lipp (1970). "Effect of Cobra and Rattlesnake Venoms on the Central Nervous System of the Primate." *Toxicon,* vol. 8, no. 1.

Viosca, Percy Jr. (n.d.). *Poisonous Snakes of Louisiana.* Louisiana Wild Life and Fisheries Comm., New Orleans.

*GS   Visser, John (1966). *Poisonous Snakes of Southern Africa.* Howard Timmins, Cape Town.

Vogt, W. (1970). "What Is Toxin?" *Toxicon,* vol. 8, no. 3.

Von Fraenkel, P. H., & E. S. Krick (1945). "Fish Poisoning by Barracuda in the Marianas." *U.S. Naval Med. Bull.,* vol. 44, p. 430.

Voss, Gilbert L. (1959). "Hunting Sea Monsters." *Sea Frontiers,* vol. 5, no. 3.

Wade, H. W. (1928). "Post Mortem Findings in Acute Jellyfish Poisoning." *Amer. Jour. Trop. Med.,* vol. 8.

Waknis, Vijaya N., R. W. P. Master, & S. S. Rao (1961). "Use of Ion-Exchangers in the Separation of Proteins of Cobra Venoms." *Proc. Symposium on Proteins,* Aug. C.F.T.T.I., Mysore, India.

Walford, L. A. (1944). "Observations on the Shark Fishery in the Central Part of the Gulf of Calif." *Fishery Market News,* vol. 6, no. 6.

Waterman, Stanton A. (1962). "Dr. Gilbert vs. the Shark." *Skin Diver,* vol. 11, no. 7.

Webster, David K. (1963). *Myth and Maneater.* W. W. Norton & Co. New York.

Webster, Dwight A. (1960). "Toxicity of the Spotted Newt, *Notophthalmus viridescens,* to Trout." *Copeia,* no. 1, Mar. 25.

Wehrle, L. P. (1939). "Observations on Three Species of Triatoma." *Bull. Brooklyn Ento. Soc.,* vol. 24, no. 3.

Weis, R., & R. J. McIsaac (1971). "Cardiovascular and Muscular Effects of Venom from Coral Snake, *Micrurur fulvius.*" *Toxicon,* vol. 9, no. 3.

Wells, A. L. (1958). *The Observer's Book of Sea Fishes.* Frederick Warne & Co., London.

Wendt, Herbert (1959). *Out of Noah's Ark.* (Bullock trans.) Houghton Mifflin Co., Boston.

Werler, John E. (1963, rev.). *Poisonous Snakes of Texas.* Texas Fish & Game Comm., Bulletin no. 31, Austin.

Wheeler, William Morton (1910, 1965). *Ants: Their Structure, Development, and Behavior.* Columbia Univ. Press, New York.

Wheeling, C. H., & Hugh L. Keegan (1972). "Effects of Scorpion Venom on the Tarantula." *Toxicon,* vol. 10, no. 3.

**GS Whitley, G. P. (1940). *The Fishes of Australia:* part I, *The Sharks, Rays, Devil-Fish, and Other Primitive Fishes of Australia and New Zealand.* Sydney & Melbourne Pub. Co., Sydney & Melbourne.

**GS ———(1943). *Poisonous and Harmful Fishes.* Commonwealth of Australia, Coun. for Sci. & Ind. Res., Bull. no. 159, Melbourne.

Whitley, G. P. (with G. H. Payne) (1947). "Testing a Shark Repellent." *Austral. Zool.,* vol. 2, no. 2.

Whitley, G. P. (1950). "Butterfly Cod." *Austral. Mus. Mag.,* vol. 10.

———(1951). "Shark Attacks in Western Australia." *West. Austral. Naturalist,* vol. 2, no. 8.

———(1963). "The Identity of Man-Killing Sharks," "Stonefish," and "Dangerous Australian Fishes." *Suppl. Bull. Post Grad. Comm. Med.,* vol. 18, no. 12. Univ. of Sydney, Australia.

Whittaker, V. P. (1960). "Pharmacologically Active Choline Esters in Marine Gastropods." *Annals N.Y. Acad. Science,* vol. 90, art. 3.

Wieman, H. L. (1938). *General Zoology.* McGraw-Hill, New York.

Wiener, Saul (1957). "The Sydney Funnel-Web Spider *(Atrax polustus),* I, Collection of Venom and Its Toxicity." *Med. Jour. Austral.,* Sept.

———(1958). "Stone-Fish Sting and Its Treatment." *Med. Jour. Austral.,* Aug.

———(1959). "Observations on the Venom of the Stone-fish *(Synanceja trachynis)."* *Med. Jour. Austral.,* May.

———(1959). "The Sydney Funnel-Web Spider *(Atrax robustus):* II. Venom Yield and Other Characteristics of the Spider in Captivity." *Med. Jour. Austral.,* Nov.

———(1959). "The Production and Assay of Stone-fish Antivenene." *Med. Jour. Austral.,* Nov.

———(1960). "Venoms Yields and Toxicity of the Venoms of Male and Female Tiger Snakes." *Med. Jour. Austral.,* Nov. 5.

———(1960). "Active Immunization of Man Against the Venom of the Australian Tiger Snake *(Notechis scutatus)."* *Amer. Jour. Trop. Med. Hygiene,* vol. 9, no. 3.

———(1961). "The Sydney Funnel-Web Spider *(Atrax robustus):* III. The Neutralization of Venom by Haemolymph." *Med. Jour. Austral.,* Mar. 25.

**S ———(1963). "Stone-fish Venom" and "Stonefish Stingings: Venom and Treatment." *Suppl. Bull. Post Grad. Comm. Med.,* vol. 18, no. 12. Univ. of Sydney, Australia.

Wiles, James (1962). "Wanted: Shark Hunters." *Sea Frontiers,* vol. 8, no. 2.

Wilson, Edward O., & Fred E. Regnier, Jr. (1971). "The Evolution of the Alarm-Defense System in the Formicine Ants." *Amer. Naturalist,* vol. 105, no. 943.

Wilson, G. S., & A. A. Miles (1946). *Topley and Wilson's Principles of Bacteriology and Immunity.* Williams & Wilkins Co., Baltimore.

Wise, H. D. (1937). *Tigers of the Sea.* Derrydale Press, New York.

Witkop, Bernhard (1965). "Poisonous Animals and Their Venoms." *Jour. Washington Acad. Science,* vol. 55.

Wittle, L. W., et al. (1971). "Isolation and Partial Purification of a Toxin from *Millepora alcicornis."* *Toxicon,* vol. 9, no. 4.

Wolf, Bill (1953). "The Most Vicious Animal." *Sports Afield,* Dec.

Woollen, Arthur (1953). "Trapping the Cougar." *Amer. Woodsman,* Feb.

Works Projects Administration Writers Program (1940). *American Wild Life.* Wm. H. Wise & Co., New York.

*G   Worrell, Eric (1963). *Reptiles of Australia.* Angus & Robertson, Sydney.

*G   ———(1963). *Dangerous Snakes of Australia and New Guinea* (5th ed.). Angus & Robertson, Sydney.

Wright, Bruce S. (1948). "Releasers of Attack Behavior Pattern in Shark and Barracuda." *Jour. Wildlife Management,* vol. 12, no. 2.

———(1948). "Survival of the Northeastern Panther *(Felis concolor)." Jour. Mammalogy,* vol. 29, no. 3.

———(1953). "Further Notes on the Panther of the Northeast." *Canadian Field–Naturalist,* vol. 67, no. 1.

***GS   ———(1959). *The Ghost of North America: The Story of the Eastern Panther.* Vantage Press, New York.

———(1961). "The Latest Specimen of the Eastern Puma." *Jour. Mammalogy,* vol. 42, no. 2.

**GS   ———(1962). *Wildlife Sketches, Near and Far.* Brunswick Press, Fredericton, N.B., Canada.

———(1962). "Notes on North Atlantic Whales." *Canadian Field– Naturalist,* vol. 76, no. 1.

*G   Wyeth Laboratories (1961). "Antivenin *(Crotalidae)* Polyvalent." Wyeth Laboratories, New York.

*G   Wykes, Alan (1961). *Snake Man.* Simon & Schuster, New York.

Wylie, Evan McLeod (1959). "Caution—Stingers at Work!" *Reader's Digest,* June.

Yarom, Rena, & Karl Braun (1970). "Cardiovascular Effects of Scorpion Venom Morphological Changes in the Myocardium." *Toxicon,* vol. 8, no. 1.

Ylla (1958). *Animals in India.* Hamish Hamilton, New York.

Ylla (n.d.). *Animals in Africa.* Harper & Row, New York.

Yonge, C. M. (1931). *A Year on the Great Barrier Reef.* G. P. Putnam's Sons, New York.

Young, Stanley P. (1941, rev. 1955). *Hints on Coyote and Wolf Trapping.* U.S. Department of the Interior, Fish & Wildlife Service, Circ. no. 2.

———(1945). *Mountain Lion Trapping.* U.S. Department of the Interior, Fish & Wildlife Service, Circ. no. 6.

**GS   ———(1946). *The Wolf in North American History.* Caxton Printers, Caldwell, Ida.

***GS   Young, Stanley P. (with Edward A. Goldman) (1944). *The Wolves of North America.* American Wildlife Management Inst. Washington, D.C.

***GS   ———(1946). *The Puma—Mysterious American Cat.* American Wildlife Management Inst., Washington, D.C.

**GS Young, William E., & H. S. Mazet (1934). *Shark! Shark! The Thirty-Year Odyssey of a Pioneer Shark Hunter.* Gotham House, New York.

Zahl, Paul A. (1957). "On Australia's Coral Ramparts." *National Geographic,* vol. 3, no. 1.

Zaki, Omer, et al. (1970). "Black Mamba Venom and Its Fractions." *Arch. Pathol.,* vol. 89.

Zern, E. (ed.) (1952). *Zane Grey's Adventures in Fishing.* Harper & Row, New York.

Zim, Herbert S., & Hobart M. Smith (1953). *Reptiles and Amphibians.* Simon & Schuster, New York.

Zim, Herbert S., & Donald F. Hoffmeister (1955). *Mammals.* Simon & Schuster, New York.

Zim, Herbert S., & Hurst H. Shoemaker (1956). *Fishes.* Simon & Schuster, New York.

Zlotkin, E., et al. (1971). "A New Toxic Protein in the Venom of the Scorpion *Androctonus australis* Hector," and "The Effect of Scorpion Venom on Blowfly Larvae—A New Method for the Evaluation of Scorpion Venom's Potency." *Toxicon,* vol. 9, no. 1.

Zlotkin, E. (1972). "Proteins in Scorpion Venoms Toxic to Mammals and Insects." *Toxicon,* vol. 10, no. 3.

Index

Acalyptophis peroni, 186
Acanthophis antarticus, 174
Acanthuridae, 248
Acinonyx jubatus, 22
Adamson, Joy, *illus.* 38
  Born Free, 38
Adder, *see* Viper
African Wild Life, 182
Afrur, 271-273, *illus.* 272
Agkistrodon, 141, 186
  bilineatus, 153
  contortrix contortrix, 153
  c. laticinctus, 153
  c. mokasen, 153, 155
  c. pictigaster, 153
  halys, 154, 165
  himalayanus, 190
  North American genera and range
    (table), 153
  Old World species, 154
  piscivorus leucostoma, 153
  p. piscivorus, 153, 156
Ahuja and Singh
  "Snakebite in India," 190
Akeley, Carl, 81

Alces, 106
Alligator, *illus.* 203
  American, 196, 198, 206
  Chinese, 197
  general characteristics, 198, 205
  range, 196-197
  size, 196-197
Alligator, 195
  mississippiensis, 196
  sinensis, 197
Alopias vulpinus, 217
Alpers, Antony
  *Dolphins: The Myth and The
    Mammal,* 71
Amphacantus, 249
Amphibia
  general characteristics, 209-210
  range, 209, 210
  see also Frog; Toad; Salamander
Amphineura, 291
Anaconda, 129
  length, 130, 132
  range, 130
Anderson, Kenneth, 275
Anemone, 322

Aniliidae, 139
Annelids, 323
Anteater, spiny, 87, 88-90
Antelope, 100, 109;
    see also Gazelle
Anthropoids, see Chimpanzee; Gib-
    bon; Gorilla; Orangutan; Sia-
    mang
Antivenin, 144, 285, 331-332
Ants, 273-275
    army ants, 274
    Australian bulldog ants, 274
    driver ants, 274
    fire ants, 274
Apes, see Chimpanzee; Gibbon;
    Gorilla; Orangutan; Siamang
Arachnidism, 279
Arachnids, 279-290
    general characteristics, 279-280
    see also Scorpion; Spider
Architeuthis, 309, 312
Arthropoda, 279
Artiodactyla, 100
Asp, Egyptian, see Cobra: Egyptian
Ass, 100
Atelopodidae, 212
Atelopus boulengeri, 213
    planispina, 213
    zateki, 213
Atractaspis, 166, 193
Atrax formidabilis, 285
    robustus, 285
Atz, James W.
    Animal Kingdom, 239
Austin, Oliver L.
    on cassowary, 116
Australian black rock cod, see Sea
    bass
Australian Outdoors, 263n
Automeris io, 273
Aviculariidae, 282, 284

Baboon, 91
Badger, 94
Baerg, William J.
    The Tarantula, 284
Balaenoptera musculus, 67

Ballantyne, R. M.
    Hudson's Bay, 214
Barracuda, 260-262, illus. 258
    great, 260
    safety precautions toward, 261-
    262
Bass, see Sea bass
Bat
    attacks on man, 99-100
    as disease-carrier, 99
    usefulness to man, 100
    vampire bat, 99, 335, illus. 102
Batrachoididae, 248
Bear family (Ursidae), 100
    American black bear, 43, illus. 49
        attacks on man, 48
        general characteristics, 47-48
        glacier bear (blue phase), 47
        range, 43, 47
    Asiatic black bear, 43
    brown bear, 43, see also Bear:
        grizzly; Kodiak
    general characteristics, 42-43, 44,
        52-53
    glacier bear, see Bear family:
        American black bear
    grizzly bear, 43, illus. 49
        attacks on man 44-47
        general characteristics, 44
        in National Park areas, 46-47
        range, 43
    Himalayan black bear, 51
    human behavior toward bears in
        National and Provincial Parks,
        46-47
    Kodiak bear, 43-44
        range, 43
    polar bear, 43, 360, illus. 50
        attacks on man, 48-51
        general characteristics, 51
    range, 42-43
    sloth bear, 43, 51, 52, illus. 49
    snow bear, 51
    spectacled bear, 43
    sun bear, 43, 52
    Taxonomy, 43
Bedbug, 271

Bees, 273, 275-278
  giant red bee, 276
  rock bee, 275n
Beetles, 273
Benchley, Peter
  Jaws, 221
Bennetts, J. A. W., 182
Biddle, Dr. R., 263
Birgus latro, 322
Bison, 40, 100, 107
Bitis, 143
  arietans, 161, 164
  atropos, 161-162
  caudalis, 161
  cornuta, 161
  gabonica, 143, 161
  nasicornis, 161
Black panther, see Leopard:
  melanism
Blarina brevicauda, 86, 89
Bluebottle, see Portuguese man-o'-
  war
Boa constrictor, 130, 139
  constrictor technique, 130
  length, 130
  range, 130
Boar, wild, 105
Bobcat, 30
Bogert, Charles, and Martin Del
  Campo, Rafael, 127
  The Gila Monster and Its Allies,
  125
Boicininga, see Rattlesnake: South
  American
Boidae, 130, 139
Boiguira, see Rattlesnake: South
  American
Boomslang, see Snake
Bos gaurus, 108
Bothrops, 141, 154, 157, 159, 186
  jararaca, 158
  jararacussu, 158
  lanceolatus, 154
  nummifer, 158
  schlegeli, 163
Boulengerina, 181
Bubalus, 12, 109

Buffalo, 100
  cape (African) buffalo, 107-108
  water buffalo, 12, 109
Bufo, 212
Bugs, blood-sucking, 271
Bullen, Frank T.
  Denizens of the Deep, 60
Bungarus caeruleus, 177, 190
  candidus, 181
  fasciatus, 179, 181
  flaviceps, 188
Bureau of Sport Fisheries and
  Wildlife
  Hints on Bobcat Trapping, 30
Bushmaster, see Pit viper

Caiman, 205-206
  black, 196, 201, illus. 203
  broad-nosed, 196
  Central American, 196
  dwarf, 196
  Paraguayan, 196
  range, 196
  size, 196
  smooth-fronted, 196
  spectacled, 196
Caiman, 195
  crocodilus crocodilus, 196
  c. fuscus, 196
  latirostris, 196
  yacare, 196
Cairns Post, 313, 316
Call-Bulletin (San Francisco)
  killer whale story, 62-64
Calligtroga americana, 271, 272
Callophis beddomei, 190
Camel, 100
Candiru, 264
Canidae, see Dog family
Canis lupus, 32
  niger, 33
Cantil (Mexican moccasin), illus.
  156
  danger to man from, 154
  range, 153
Cape (African) hunting dog, 32n,
  94, illus. 97

Caras, Roger
  Antarctica: Land of Frozen Time,
    59
Carcharhinidae, 228
Carcharhinus (leucas) nicaraguen-
    sis, 219, 229
  maculipinnis, 229
  obscurus, 229
  zambezensis, 229
Carcharias arenarius, 229
  gangeticus, 229
  taurus, 229
Carchariidae, 228
Carcharodon carcharias, 65, 215,
    216, 225, 229
Carnivores
  confusion of man with natural
    prey by, 69
  families in order Carnivora, 94
  food chain and, 40-41
  general characteristics, 98
  see also animals by name
Carybdea, 316
Cascabel, *see Rattlesnake:* South
    American
Cascavela, *see* Rattlesnake: South
    American
Casuariidae, 116
Casuarius, 116
Cassowary, 115
  Schlater's cassowary, *illus.* 117
Cat family (Felidae), 94
  general characteristics, 7-8, 30-31
  intelligence of, 7
  man and, 30-31
  see also Bobcat; Cheetah; Euro-
    pean wildcat; Jaguar; Leopard;
    Lion; Lynx; Mountain lion;
    Tiger
Catamount, *see* Mountain lion
Cataphractus, 246
Caterpillars, 273
Catfish, 246
  parasite, 264
Catharacta skua, 119
Causus, 166, 193

rhombeatus, 161
Centipedes, 289
Centropogon australis, 249
Centruroides gertschi, 287
  sculpturatus, 287
Cephalopods, 303, 304, 308, 309
Ceratophrys, 210
  calcarata, 210
  ornata, 210
  varia, 212
Cerastes cerastes, 166
  vipera, 162
Cervus, 107
Cetacea, 60
Cetorhinus maximus, 216
Cheesman, Evelyn
  *Six-Legged Snakes in New
    Guinea*, 200
Cheetah, *illus.* 24
  general characteristics, 22-23
  range, 23
Chelonia mydas, 360
Chevrotain, 100
Chilopoda, 289
Chimaera, 216
Chimaira, 247
Chimpanzee, 92-93
Chiracanthium diversum, 282
  inclusum, 282
Chironex, 316
  fleckeri, 317
Chiropsalmus, 316
  quadrigatus, 318
Chiroptera, 99; *see also* Bat
Choeropis, 105
Ciconiidae, 119
Ciguatera poisoning, 355-361
  poisonous fish (table), 357-358
Civet, 94
Clam, tridacna ("giant man-eating")
    illus. 298
  man and, 297-302
  names known by, 297-299
Clark, Leonard
  The Rivers Ran East, 152
Clostridium tetani, 236, 328

Coates, Dr. Christopher W., 251, 252
Coati, 94
Cobra, 140, 190
  black, 181
  Burmese (monocellate), 189
  cape, 181
  Egyptian, 181, *illus.* 180
  hood of, 193n
  Indian cobra, 145, 181, *illus.* 179
  king, 188, 190, 347
  spectacled, 189
  spitting, 181
  tree, 181
  venom of, 145
  water, 181
Coelenterata, 313
Coleoptera, 273
Collier's, 265
Colma, Victor C., 271
Colubridae, 139, 182
Cone shells, 291-296
  geographer's 294, *illus.* 292
  most dangerous cones (table), 295
  textile, *illus.* 292
  venom of, 291, 293
Conidae, 291
Conus aulicus, 295
  catus, 295
  geographus, 292, 294, 295
  imperialis, 295
  litteratus, 295
  lividus, 295
  marmoreus, 295
  obscurus, 295
  omaria, 295
  pulicarius, 295
  quercinus, 295
  sponsolis, 295
  striatus, 295
  textile, 292, 295
  tulipa, 295
Copeia journal, 152, 242
Copperhead
  Australian "copperhead," 141, 174, 175
  broad-banded, 153
  danger to man from, 154
  northern, *illus.* 155
  range, 153
  range, 141
  southern
    range, 153
  Trans-Pecos
    range, 153
Coral, 322
Coralitos, 177
Corbett, Col. Jim, 10
  The Man-Eating Leopard of Rudraprayag, 9
  on man-eating tigers, 13, 15, 16
  Man-Eaters of Kumaon, 15
  The Temple Tiger, 15
Cottonmouth
  danger to man from, 154
  eastern, *illus.* 156
  range, 153
  range, 141
  venom, 147
  western
    range, 153
Cougar, *see* Mountain lion
Cousteau, Capt. Jacques-Yves
  on killer whale, 71
Coyote, 33, 34
  rabies and, 40
Crab, 322
Craig, John D.
  Danger Is My Business, 59
  on killer whale, 59-60
Crisler, Lois, 32
Crocodilia, *see* Alligator; Caiman; Crocodile; Gavial
Crocodile, *illus.*, 203
  African slender-snouted, 197
  American, 196, 205, 206
  Australian, 197
  Congo dwarf, 197
  Cuban, 196
  of eastern hemisphere (table), 197
  general characteristics, 198
  man and, 195, 198-205

Crocodile (continued)
mugger (marsh), 197, *illus.* 202
New Guinea, 197
Nile (African), 197, 198-199, 205, 206, *illus.* 204
Orinoco, 196
Philippine, 197
range, 196-197
saltwater, 197, 199-201, 206, *illus.* 204
Siamese, 197
size, 196-197
West African dwarf, 197
of western hemisphere (table), 196
Crocodylus, 195, 206
acutus, 196, 205
cataphractus, 197
intermeditus, 196
johnstoni, 197
mindorensis, 197
moreleti, 196
niloticus, 197, 205
novae-guineae, 197
palustris, 197
porosus, 197, 199
rhombifer, 196
siamensis, 197
Crotalidae, 140-141, 144
genera in (table), 141
Crotalinae, 140
Crotalus, 140, 141, 186
adamanteus, 134, 144, 146
atrox, 134, 144, 146, 149
catalinensis, 141
durissus, 145
d. terrificus, 149
d. vegrandis, 149
horridus horridus, 134, 149
scutulatus, 145
unicolor, 149
viridis oreganus, 135, 149
v. viridis, 135, 149
Cryptobranchidae, 210
Cutler, Carl C., 309
Cyanea, 309

capillata, 314
Cygnus, 116

Dasyatidae, 234, 236, 247
Dasyotis brevicaudata, 234
centroura, 235
Decapoda, 303
Deer, 100
general characteristics, 106, 107
mule deer, 106
in North America, 40
white-tailed (Viriginia) deer, 106-107
see also Antelope; Elk; Gazelle; Moose; Okapi; Reindeer
Demansia textilis, 174
Dendroaspis angusticeps, 180
Dendrobates auratus, 213
flavopictus, 213
trivittatus, 213
Dendrobatidae, 212
Dendrolimus, 273
Denisonia superba, 174
Deoras, Dr. P. J., 190
on scorpion sting, 288
Dermochelys coriacea, 360
Desmodus, 99, 102, 335
Dhole (wild dog), 32n
Diaemus, 99
Diamondback, *see* Rattlesnake
Diamphidia simplex, 273
Dingo, *illus.* 97
Dinobdella ferox, 323
Diphylla, 99
Diplopoda, 289
Diptera, 270
Dispholidus typus, 180, 182
Dog family (Canidae)
feral dogs, 34, *illus.* 97 (Dingo)
see also Cape (African) hunting dog; Coyote; Dhole; Dingo; Fennec; Fox; Jackal; Wolf
Doliophis bilineatus, 188
philippinus, 188
Dolphin, 60, 71, 72
Dorylinae, 274

Eagle, 115, 118, 119
  bald eagle, *illus.* 117
Echidnas, 87, 88-90
Echinodermata, 323
Echis carinatus, 162, 165, 189, 190,
  348, 351
  coloratus, 165
Eciton burchelli, 274
Eel, *see* Electric fish; Moray eel
Elapidae, 140, 173-182
Electric fish, 251-256
  electric catfish, 255-256
  electric eel, 251-255, *illus.* 253
  manta ray, *illus.* 254
  torpedo ray, 256, *illus.* 253
Electrophorus electricus, 251
Elephant
  African elephant, *illus.* 78
    range, 75
  age, 76
  assessment of, 84-85
  charge by, 76, 83-84
  diet, 79
  Indian (Asiatic) elephant, *illus.*
    77
    range, 75
  legendary graveyard of, 75-76
  locomotion, 76
  man and, 73-74, 75, 79-85
  memory span, 76
  "rogue" elephant behavior, 82-83
  size and appearance, 76-79
  systematic control of (cropping),
    80
Elephas maximus, 75
Elk
  Wapiti (American Elk), 107
  see also Moose
Elsa Wild Animal Appeal, 38
Enhydrina schistoma, 190
Epinephelus forsythi, 263
Eretmochelys imbricata, 360
Escorpion, *see* Gila monster
Euarctos americanus, 47
Eunectes murinis, 130
Euproctis, 273

European wildcat, 30
Eyelash viper, *see* Pit viper

Falcon, 118
Fawcett, Maj. Percy
  on anaconda, 132
Felidae, *see* Cat family
Felis concolor, 26
  sylvestris, 30
Fennec, 94
Fer-de-lance, *see* Pit viper
Field magazine, 116
Field and Stream, 107
Fish
  poisonous, 355-361
    listed (table), 357-358
  poisonous vs. venomous, 238
  venomous, 238-250
    listed (table), 247-249
  see also names of fish
Fish and Cobb
  Noxious Marine Animals of the
    Central and Western Pacific
    Ocean, 263, 299, 359
Flatworm, 322
Fleay, David
  on platypus, 88
Flecker, H., 316
Flies, 270-271
  black fly, 270
  no-see-ums, 270
  screwworm fly, 271, *illus.* 272
  tsetse fly, 270
Formi coidea, 273
Fox, 32, 94
Frog, 210-213
  arrow-poison, 212
  Colombian horned, 210
  North American pickerel, 212
  poisonous South and Central
    American (table), 213
Frye, O. Earle, and Piper, B. and L.
  "The Disappearing Panther," 28

Galeocerdo, 214
  cuvieri, 216, 229

Galeolamna macrurus, 229
Gaor, see Gaur
Gastropoda, 291
Gaur, 108
Gavial, 197, 205, 206
  false, 197
  range, 197
  size, 197
Gavialis, 195
  gangeticus, 197
Gazelle, 100
  Thompson's, 23
  see also Antelope
Gibbon, 92
  siamang gibbon, 92, illus. 96
Gila monster, illus. 126
  assessment of, 127-128
  banded Gila monster, 124, 125
  general characteristics, 124-127
  range, 124
  reticulated Gila monster, 124, 125
Gilbert, Dr. Perry, 224
Gilliard, Dr. Thomas
  on crocodiles, 199-200
Gilmore, C. W., 141
Gilmore, Raymond, M., 65
Ginglymostoma cirratum, 227, 229
Giraffe, 100
Glossina, 270
Gnats, 270
Goat, 100
  mountain goat, 40
Gonyaulax catenella, 359
Goose, 119
Gorilla, 92
  general characteristics, 93-94
  lowland gorilla, 93, illus. 96
  mountain gorilla, 93
  range, 93
Gorilla, 92
Grab, B., 174, 175
Graham, Alistair
  Eyelids of the Morning, 199
Greathouse, Dr. Tedford L.
  on killer whale, 60, 64
Grouper, 263

Guggisberg, C. A. W.
  on lions, 18, 21
  Simba, 18
Gunter, G. A.
  Adventures of a Trepang Fisher, 301
Gymnopistes marmoratus, 249
Gymnothorax, 262
Gymnotidae, 251
Gymnuridae, 234, 236, 247

Habu, see Pit viper
Haitian solenodon, see Shrew
Halophryne, 249
Halstead, Bruce W., 233
  on cone-shell bite, 294
  Dangerous Marine Animals, 234, 299, 332, 360
Hansen, Paul
  on killer whale, 70-71
Hapalochlaena maculosa, 307, 308
Harper's New Monthly Magazine, 108
Hawk, 118
Helarctos, 43
Helfrich, Philip, 359
Heloderma horridum alvarezi, 124
  h. exasperatum, 124
  h. horridum, 124
  matthewi, 123
  suspectum cinctum, 124
  s. suspectum, 124
Helodermatidae, 123, 124
Hemachatus haemachates, 181, 192
Heuvelmans, Bernard
  On the Track of Unknown Animals, 132
Hexanchus, 216
Hippopotamus, 100, illus. 103
  general characteristics, 105
Hippopotamus, 105
Hirundinea, 322
Hog
  feral razorback, 105
  red forest hog, 105
  wild hog, 104

Holmes, Sherlock
"Speckled Band," 167
Holotrichius innesi, 271-273
Holzworth, John M.
on grizzly bear, 44, 45
Hoofed animals, *see* Ungulates
Hornaday, William T.
on collared peccary, 104
on crocodile, 205
on grizzly bear, 44
on wolves, 34
Hornets, 273, 275-278
Horse, 100
Houndfish, *see* Needlefish
Houston, A. S.
on killer whale, 71
Humbert, Arthur C.
on cape (African) buffalo, 108
Hyaena
attacks on man, 95, 98
brown hyaena, 97
general characteristics, 95
range, 94
spotted (laughing) hyaena, 97
striped hyaena, 97
taxonomy, 94-95
Hyaenidae, 94
Hydrolagus, 247
Hydrophiidae, 139, 168, 169, 170
Hydrophinae, 169
Hydrophis cyanocinctus, 171, 186
semperi, 169
spiralis, 190
Hydrophobia, *see* Rabies
Hydrurga leptonyx, 55
Hylobates, 92
Hymenoptera, 273, 275, 276

Ichthyoacanthotoxism, 355
Ichthyosarcotoxism, 355
Inger, Robert F.
on snakes, 345, 346
Injuries caused by wild animals
treatment of, 327-332
Innes, William T.
on piranha, 258

Insects, 269-278
afrur, 271-273, *illus.* 272
ants, 273-275
bedbug, 271
bees, 273, 275-278
beetles, 273
caterpillar, 273
flies, 270-271
screwworm fly, *illus.* 272
gnats, 270
hornets, 273, 275-280
kissing bugs, 271
mosquitoes, 270
moths, 273
suckers of blood, 271
wasps, 273, 275-278, *illus.* 277
Irwin, R. S.
on giant clam, 300
Istiophorus greyi, 265
Isuridae, 228
Isurus, 221, 228
oxyrinchus, 229

Jackal, 32, 94
Jaguar, 8, 9, *illus.* 24
general characteristics, 23-25
man and, 25-26
range, 23, 24, 25
Jararaca, *see* Pit viper
Jararacussu, *see* Pit viper
Javelina, *see* Peccary: collared peccary
Jellyfish, 313-318
attacks on man, 316-318
box jelly, 316-318, *illus.* 317
general characteristics, 314-315
lethal effects of, 313
sea wasp, 316, 317, 318
venom of, 314, 315, 318
Jones, S.
on fish poisoning, 356
Julus, 289
Jumping viper, *see* Pit viper
Jungle Operations (U.S. Army manual), 194

Kangaroo, 110
Kauffeld, Carl, 188, 195
  on snakes, 345, 346
Keith, Elmer
  Big Game Hunting, 28
  on wolves, 36-37
Kinkajou, 94
Kinloch, Brig. Gen. A.A.A.
  on bears of India, 51-52
  on elephants, 81-82
  on gaur, 108
  Large Game Shooting in Thibet,
    the Himalayas, Northern and
    Central India, 81
  on wolves, 32, 36
Klauber, Laurence M., 143, 145, 146,
  147, 149
  Rattlesnakes, 338
  on snakes, 345, 346
Koala, 53
Kohn, Alan J.
  on cone shell, 293, 294
Kopstein, Felix
  on reptiles, 129
Koszalka, M. F., 276
Krait, 140, 177, 181, 190
  banded, 181, *illus.* 179
  Malayan (blue), 181
Kraken, *see* Squid
Kufa, *see* Pit viper

Lachesis, 141
  muta, 151, 155
Lamna nasus, 229
Lampropeltis doliata, 176
Lane, Frank W.
  Kingdom of the Octopus, 305
Lanthanotidae, 123
Lanthanotus borneensis, 123
Laticauda colubrina, 171
  crockeri, 160
Laticaudinae, 169
Latrodectus bishopi, 282
  geometricus, 285
  hasselti, 280, 285
  indistinctus, 280, 285

mactans, 280, 283
  m. hesperus, 281
  m. mactans, 281
  m. texanus, 281
Law, Philip
  on leopard seal, 58
Leech, 323
Leiurus cinquestriatus, 288
Leopard, 40, *illus.* 19
  albinism, 9
  clouded leopard, 30
  general characteristics, 8-11
  man-eating, 9-10
  melanism, 8
  Palestinian race, *illus.* 19
  "panther" terminology, 8
  predatory skill, 8
  range, 8n, 10
  snow leopard, 10-11
Leopard seal, 54, *illus.* 57
  general characteristics, 55-56
  man and, 56-58
  range, 55
Leptomicrurus, 177
Leptotyphlopidae, 139
Lewis and Clark
  on grizzly bear, 44
"Liger," 16
Lion, 30, *illus.* 20
  general characteristics, 16-17
  man-eating, 18-22
    Tsavo man-eaters, 21-22
  predatory habits, 17
  range, 16
  speed of, 7
  see also Mountain lion
Lion fish, 243
Livona pica, 356
Lizard
  black (chiapan) beaded lizard
    range, 124
  Mexican beaded lizard, *illus.* 126
    range, 124, 125
  monitor lizard, 123
  Rio Fuerte beaded lizard
    range, 124

Lizard *(continued)*
  venomous lizards
    general characteristics, 124-127
  venomous lizards
    range, 123, 124
    venom apparatus, 123-124
    see also Gila monster
Llama, 100
Lobodontinae subfamily, 55
Lockjaw
  treatment for, 328
Loveridge, Arthur, 136
Loxodonta africana, 75
Loxosceles reclusa, 282
Lumbriconereis heteropoda, 359
Lycaon, 32n, 94
Lycosa narbonensis, 284
Lynx, 30
Lyssa, see Rabies

Macaca, 92
Mack, George
  on killer whale, 70
Mail (Madras), 95
Makaira, 265
Malopterurus electricus, 255
Mamba, 181-182
  green, *illus.* 180
Mammals, venomous, *see* Anteater, spiny; Platypus, duck-billed; Shrew
Mamushi, *see* Pit viper
Maracaboia, *see* Rattlesnake: South American
Marais, Eugene
  My Friends the Baboons, 91
Marlin, 265
  black, 265
Marsupials, 110
  see also Kangaroo; Koala; Tasmanian devil; Thylacine
Marten, 94
Massasauga, *see* Rattlesnake
Maticoar, 177

Mayer, Charles
  Trapping Wild Animals in Malay Jungles, 130
Medical Journal of Australia, 241
Megalobatrachus japonicus, 210, 211
Megalopyge opercularis, 273
Melanism
  defined, 8
Melanosuchus, 195
  niger, 196, 201
Melursus, 43
Merriam
  on deer, 107
Mexican moccasin, *see* Cantil
Micks, D. W., 271, 273, 275
Micruroides, 186
  euryxanthus, 176
Micrurus, 177, 178, 186
  fulvius barbouri, 176
  f. fulvius, 176
  f. tenere, 176
  spixi, 177
Millipedes, 289
Mink, 94
Minton, Sherman
  on snakes, 345, 346, 347
  on vipers, 162, 166
Mobulidae, 234, 247
Moccasin, *see* Cottonmouth
Mollusca, 291
Mongoose, 94
Monkey
  dog-faced, 91
  rhesus, 92
Monoplacophora, 291
Monotremata, 86, 87-90
Moore, Robert A.
  A Textbook of Pathology, 275
Moose, 106
  in North America, 40
Moray eel, 262-263
Morgan, F. G., 174
Morgan, Capt.
  Whale Hunt, 311
Mosquitoes, 270

Moths, 273
  puss moth, 273
  tree asp, 273
Mountain lion, 8
  man and, 26-30
  range, 26
Muraena, 262
Muraenidae, 262
Mustelidae, 94
Myers, George S.
  on piranha, 258
Myliobatidae, 234, 236, 247
Mystic (Conn.) *Press*, 309
Mysticeti, 60

Naja haje, 180, 181
  Melanoleuca, 181
  naja, 179, 181, 190
  nicricollis, 181
  nivea, 181
Narcine, 256
National Audubon Society, 46
National Observer, 48
Naucrates, 226
Needlefish, 264-265
Negaprion, 215
  brevirostris, 229
Neomys fodiens bicolor, 87
  f. fodiens, 87
Neptunes, 359
News-Call Bulletin (San
  Francisco), 65
Night adder, *see* Viper
Noble, Col. William A., 177
Notechis scutatus, 174, 178
Notesthes, 244
  robusta, 249

Octopoda, 303
Octopus, *illus.*, 307
  blue-ringed, 308, *illus.* 307
  general characteristics, 304-305
  man and, 305-308
  venom of, 307, 308
Octopus arborescens, 304
  hong-kongensis, 304
  maculosa, 308

Odobenus rosmarus divergens, 54
  r. rosmanus, 54
Odocoileus hemionus, 106
  virginianus, 106
Okapi, 100
Oliver, James A.
  "The Prevention and
    Treatment of Snakebite,"
    142, 144
Olsen, Jack
  Night of the Grizzlies, 46
Ommastrephes gigas, 312
Ophiophagus hannah, 190
Orangutan, 92
Orcinas orca, 59
Ornithorhynchidae, 87
Orinthorhynchus amatinus, 87
Osteolaemus, 195, 197
Ostrich, 115, 116, 119
Otter, 94
Outdoor Life magazine
  on killer whale attack, 64, 65
Ox, *see* Gaur
Oxyuranus scutellatus, 174

Pacific Islands Monthly, 264
"Painter," *see* Leopard: "panther"
Palamneus, 288
  gravimanus, 286
Paleosuchus, 195
  palpebrosus, 196
  trigonatus, 196
Pan, 92
Panda, giant, 53
Pandinus imperator, 287
Panther
  definition of term, 8
  see also Leopard; Mountain lion
Panthera leo, 16
  onca, 23
  pardus, 0
  tigris, 11
  uncia, 10
Papio, 91
Parrish, Henry M., 275
Parrot, 119
Pasteur, Louis, 334

Patterson, Lt.-Col. J. H.
  on Tsavo man-eating lions, 21-22
Pavo, 118
Peacock, 115, 118
Pearson, Oscar ("Ed"), 80
Peccary, 100, *illus.* 102
  collared peccary (javelina), 104-105; *illus.* 102
  white-lipped peccary, 104
Pelamis platurus, 168, 169, 192
Pelecypoda, 291
Penguin
  emperor penguin, 69
  killer whale and, 69
Percival, A. Blayney
  A Game Ranger's Note Book, 82
Perissodactyla, 100
Perry, W. A., 29
  The Big Game of North America, 28
Phobosuchus, 198
Phocidae, 55
Phyllobates bicolor, 213
Physalia physalis, 314
Physeter catodon, 109, 312
Pig, 100
  wild pig, 104
Pilot fish, 226
Pinnipedae, 54, 58; see *also* Leopard seal; Walrus
Piper, Bill and Les, 28
Piranha, 256-260, *illus.* 258
  black, 256
  pirambeba, 257
Pit viper
  arboreal, 157
  bamboo, 190
  bushmaster, *illus.* 155
    common names for, 151
  general characteristics, 151-152
    man and, 152-153
    range, 141-151
  danger to man, 157-158
  eyelash (Schlegel's) viper, 159, *illus.* 163
  fer-de-lance, 154, 157
  general characteristics, 140
  green, 190
  ground-dwelling, 157-158
  habu, 159, 160
  Himalayan, 190
  jararaca, 158
  jararacussu, 158, *illus.* 162
  jumping viper (Tommygoff), 158
  kufa, 160
  Old World pit viper, 141
  Pallas's pit viper (mamushi), 154, *illus.* 165
  range, 141
  venom, 144
  Wagler's viper, 160
Platyhelminthine, 322
Platypus, duck-billed, 87-88; *illus.* 89
Pongo, 92
Pope, Clifford H.
  The Giant Snakes, 130
  on snakes, 345, 346
Porpoise, 60
Portuguese man-o'-war, 313, 314, 315, 316, 318, *illus.* 317
Potamotrygon motoro, 237
Potamochoerus, 105
Potamotrygonidae, 234, 247
Pretoria News (South Africa), 137
Prionace, 228
  glauca, 229
Proboscidae, 75
Procyonidae, 94
Profelis nebulosa, 30
Pronghorn, 40
Prosobranchiata, 291
Pseudechis prophyriacus, 174
Pseudobatrachus, 249
Pseudocerastes persicus, 190
Pseudohaje, 181
Psittaciformes, 119
Pterois, 243, 244
  volitans, 248
Pterolaminops longimanus, 229
Puff adder, see Viper
Puffer, East Indian, 264
Puma, see Mountain lion

Python, 137, 139
  African rock python
    attacks on man, 136
    length, 132
    range, 132
  amethystine python
    length, 132
    range, 132
  Australian carpet python, *illus.*
    131
  Indian python
    range, 132
    size, 132
  reticulated python
    attacks on man, 129
    length, 132
    range, 132
Python amethystinus, 132
  molurus, 132
  reticulatus, 129, 132
  sebae, 132, 136
Pythonidae, 130

Rabies
  treatment for, 328, 333-337
Raccoon, 94
Ralph, C. C., 242
Rana palustris, 212
Randall, John E.
  on giant clam, 300
  on killer whale, 70
  on needlefish, 264-265
Rat
  attacks on man, 98-99
  black rat, 98n
  brown rat, 98n
  as disease-carrier, 98
  rat control, 99
Rattlesnake
  Aruba Island rattlesnake, 149
  assessment of, 148-150
  danger to man from, 146-148
  eastern (Florida) diamondback,
    144, 145, 146, 147, 148, *illus.*
    134
  fang and venom apparatus, 142-
    146, 147-148

  massasauga, 146
    range, 141, 149
  Mohave rattlesnake
    venom, 145
  mortality rate from bite of, 146
  Northern Pacific rattlesnake,
    illus. 135
    range, 149
  origins, 141
  prairie rattlesnake, *illus.* 135
    range, 149
  pygmy rattlesnake
    range, 141
  range data (tables), 338-343
  rattle, 140-141, *illus.* 135
  "rattlesnake flag," 150
  Santa Catalina Island rattle-
    snake, 141
  South American rattlesnake, 149
    venom, 145
  timber rattlesnake, *illus.* 134
    range, 149
  western (Texas) diamondback,
    144, 145, 146, 147, 148, *illus.*
    134
    range, 149
Rattus norvegicus, 98n
  rattus, 98n
Ray, 216, 219, 233-237
Reduviidae, 271
Rehder, Harold A.
  on giant clam, 300
Reid, Dr. H. A., 170, 173
Reindeer, 100
Requa, A. G.
  on collared peccary, 105
Rhincodon typus, 216, 217
Rhinoceros, 100
  black rhinoceros, *illus.* 101
  charges by, 104
  general characteristics, 101, 104
  white rhinoceros, *illus.* 101
Rhinopteridae, 234, 247
Robertson, Douglas
  Survive the Savage Sea, 68
Rodahl, Kaare
  on polar bear, 48

Rodentia
   destructiveness of, 98
   range, 98
   see also Rat
Romine, Aden F.
   on killer whale, 60, 61, 64, 65, 67,
      72
Roosevelt, Theodore
   African Game Trails, 81
   on cape (African) buffalo, 108
   on grizzly bear, 44
   on hyaena, 95
   Through the Brazilian Jungle, 258
   The Wilderness Hunter, 28
Ruboralga jacksoniensis, 249
Russell, Findlay E., 233, 236
Ryhiner, Peter
   on ostrich, 116

Sailfish, 265
   Pacific, 265
Salamander
   giant, 210, illus. 211
Sandalops pathopsis, 309
Sanderson, G. P.
   on man-eating tigers, 14-15
   Thirteen Years Among the Wild
      Beasts of India, 82
Sanderson, Ivan
   on lions, 18
   Living Mammals of the World, 17
Sarcophilus harrisii, 110
Sauria, 123
Sawfish, 216, 219
Scaphopoda, 291
Schaller, George B., 94
   The Mountain Gorilla, 93
Scheffer, Victor B., 58
   on killer whale attack stories, 64-
      65, 70
   Seals, Sea Lions and Walruses,
      54, 64
Schlegel's viper, see Pit viper
Schmidt, Karl P., 152, 153
Schmidt & Inger
   on crocodiles, 195, 198

Schmidt and Inger
   Living Reptiles of the World, 136
   on pit vipers, 160
Scolopendra heros, 289
Scorpaenidae, 248
Scorpions, 125, 285-288
   African, 287
   Indian, illus. 286
   lobster, 287
   West African, illus. 286
Scorpion fish, 243-245, illus. 244
Scorpionida, 285
Scott, Capt. Robert, 56
   and killer whales, 59, 62, 68
Scyphozoa, 314
Sea bass, 263
Sea dragon, 245
Sea Frontiers, 265
Sea Secrets, 297, 301
Sea urchin, 323
Sea wasp, see Jellyfish
Seal, 60, 61
   killer whale and, 69
Seal leopard, see Leopard seal
Seashells, see Cone shells
Selenarctos, 43
Serranidae, 263
Serrasalmus, 260
   nattereri, 256, 257
   niger, 256
   rhombeus, 257
   spilopleura, 257
Seton, Ernest Thompson
   on grizzly bear, 45
   on polar bear, 51
   on white-tailed deer, 107
Shackleton, Sir Ernest
   on leopard seal, 56-57
Shark, 58
   attacks on man, 64, 65, 214-215,
      221-222, 225-232
   basking, 216
   blue, 221, 225, 228, 229, illus. 224
   species known as, 228
   bull, 229
   confusion in common names, 228
   dangerous to man (table), 229

Shark *(continued)*
  dusky, 229
  fishing industry, 221
  Ganges River, 229
  general characteristics, 215-221, 223
  gray nurse, 229
  great black-tipped, 229
  great white, 65, 215, 216, 219, 225, 229
  Greenland, 216, 219
  hammerhead, 216, 219, 229, *illus.* 218
  Lake Nicaragua, 219, 229
  lemon, 229
  leopard, 215
  mackerel, 228
  mako 221, 228, 229
  nurse, 227, 229
  Pacific sleeper, 219
  porbeagle, 229
  "rogue" shark, 225-226
  safety precautions toward, 230-232
  sand, 229
  shark cage, *illus.* 218
  sixgill, 216
  size (table), 216
  tooth marks on boat attacked by, 65, *illus.* 66
  teeth of, *illus.* 224
  thresher, 216
  tiger, 214, 216, 219, 229
  whale, 216, *illus.* 217
  whaler, 229
  white-tipped, 229
  Zambezi, 229
Sheep, 100
  wild sheep, 40
Shrew
  British bicolored water shrew, 87
  European water shrew, 87
  Haitian solenodon, 87
  masked shrew, 87
  short-tailed, 86-87, *illus.* 89
  venom of, 87

Siamang, *see* Gibbon
Siganidae, 248
Simpson, Maj. C. H.
  on elephant attacks on man, 73-74
  on snakebite, 190-191
  on tigers, 13
Simulium columbaczense, 270
Siphonophores, 314
Sistrurus, 140, 141, 186
  catenatus catenatus, 149
Skate, 216
Skin Diver magazine
  on killer whale attacks, 60, 65
Skua, 119
Skunk, 94
Slijper, E. J.
  Whales, 109
Smith, Dr. J. L. B., 242
  on giant clam, 300-301
  on whale attacks on man, 66-67
Snake
  bird snake, 182
  blindsnake, 139
  boomslang, 182, *illus.* 180
  common brown, 174, 175
  constrictor attacks, 129-137
    assessment of, 137-138
  coral snake, 140, *illus.* 178
    Indian, 190
    North American (table), 176
  fang apparatus, 142-144
  India's dangerous snakes (table), 190
  pipesnake, 139
  in pre-history, 141
  red-bellied black, 174
  reptile "hall of infamy" (table), 344-347
  scarlet king, 176-177
  sea snake, 139, 149, 154, 168-173, 188, 190
    banded, *illus.* 171
    blue-ringed, *illus.* 171
    yellow-bellied, 168
  sensory perception by, 133-136

Snake (continued)
  shieldtailed snake, 139
  slender blindsnake, 139
  taxonomy, 139-140
  tiger, snake, 174, illus. 178
  venom production and storage
    system, 144-145
  venomous snakes of Europe
    (table), 162
  see also Anaconda; Boa constric-
    tor; Cantil; Cobra; Copper-
    head; Cottonmouth; Krait;
    Mamba; Pit viper; Python;
    Rattlesnake; Taipan; Viper
Snakebite, 160
  case histories, 349-354
  mortality statistics, 158-159
  reptile "hall of infamy" (table),
    344-347
  treatment for, 330-332
  worldwide data on, 183-194
"Snorkel Snooper" (Long Island
    Dolphins)
  on killer whale, 71
Solenodon paradoxus, 87
Solenopsis, 274
Solpugida, 290
Somniosus, 219
  microcephalus, 216
Sorex cinereus, 87
Soricids, 86-87
South African Scope, 119n
Southcott, R. V.
  on giant clam, 301
  on jellyfish, 314
Spheroides oblongus, 264
Sphyraena barracuda, 260
Sphyraenidae, 260
Sphyrnidae, 228
Sphyrna, 229
  tubes, 216
Spiders, 280-285
  black widow, 280-281, illus. 283
  brown recluse, 282, illus. 283
  brown widow, 281-282
  button spider, 285

false spiders, 282-285, 290
fiddleback spider, 282, illus. 283
funnel-web spider, 285
gray widow, 281-282
hairy spider, 284
house spider, 284
red back spider, 285
tarantula, 284
wolf spider, 284, illus. 286
see also Tarantulas (false spiders)
Spirostreptus, 289
Squalus acanthias, 247
Squid, 308-312, illus. 310
  giant squid, 309
  Humboldt Current squid, 312
  man and, 309-312
Squamata, 123
Squirrel, flying, 99
Stadelman, Raymond E., 152
Stahnke, Dr. Herbert L.
  on scorpions, 287
  "The Treatment of Venomous
    Bites and Stings," 144, 148
Stingray, illus. 235
  attacks on man, 233-237
  Australian giant, 234
  dangerous to man (table), 234
  range, 233
  round, illus. 235
  South American freshwater, 237
  venom apparatus, 236
Stonefish, 239-243, illus. 240
  attacks on man, 241-243
  general characteristics, 239-241
Stork
  jabiru stork, 119
  maribou stork, 119
Strongylura, 264
Struthio, 116
Suana concolor, 273
Sus, 104
  scrota, 105
Swan, 115, 119
  mute swan, 116-118
Swaroop, C. C., 174, 175

Swaroop and Grab
  "Snakebite Mortality in the
    World," 158
Swine, wild
  general characteristics, 104, 105
  see also Boar; Hog; Peccary; Pig
Swordfish, 60, 265
Sydney Morning Herald, 263n
de Sylva, Dr. Donald
  on barracuda, 260
  on giant clam, 299-300
  on killer whale, 69
Symphalangus, 92
Synanceja, 240
  horrida, 239, 248
  trachynis, 239, 248
  verrucosa, 239, 248

Tachyglossidae, 87
Taipan, 174, 175
Tapir, 100
Tarantulas (false spiders), 282-285
Tarantulidae, 282
Tasmanian devil, 110
Tasmanian wolf, see Thylacine
Tayassu pecari, 104
Tayassuidae, 104
Tetanus, 236
  treatment for, 328
Tetraodon fluviatilis, 264
Teuthoidea, 303
Thalarctos, 43, 48
  maritimus, 360
Thelotornis kirtlandi, 182
Thomas, Elizabeth Marshall, 273
Thorp and Woodson
  The Black Widow, 280
Thylacine (Tasmanian wolf), 110
Thylacinus cynocephalus, 110
Tiger
  albinism, 11
  Bengal tiger, illus. 20
  general characteristics, 11-12
  man-eating, 12-16
  range, 11
  Siberian tiger, 7, 11, 16
"Tiglon," 16

Tigre, el, see Jaguar
Tissue damage in man, through animal injuries
  treatment for, 329-330
Toad, 210-213
Tomistoma, 195
  schlegeli, 196
Tommygoff, see Pit viper
Torpedo, 256
  nobiliana, 253
Toxicity in fish, 238-250, 355-361
Trachinidae, 245
Trachinus arameus, 245, 247
  draco 245, 247
  radiatus, 245, 247
  vipera, 245, 247
Tremarctos, 43
Triatoma, 271
Trichomycteridae, 264
Tridacna derasa, 297
  gigas, 297, 298
Trimeresurus, 141, 154
  albolabris, 188
  flavoviridis, 159
  gramineus, 190
  malabaricus, 190
  okinavensis, 160
  wagleri, 160, 188
Typhlopidae, 139

Ungulates (hoofed animals)
  general characteristics, 100-104
  significance of, to man, 100
  see also Antelope; Ass; Bison;
    Boar; Buffalo; Camel; Chevro-
    tain; Deer; Elk; Gazelle; Gi-
    raffe; Goat; Hippopotamus;
    Hog; Horse; Llama; Moose;
    Okapi; Peccary; Pig; Prong-
    horn; Reindeer; Rhinoceros;
    Sheep; Tapir; Zebra
U.S. Antarctic Research Program,
  64
U.S. Fish and Wildlife Service
  Mountain Lion Trapping, 27
  wolf-control program, 39
Uranoscopidae, 249

Urolophidae, 234, 236, 247
Urolophus jamaicensis, 235
Uropeltidae, 139
Uropygi, 289
Ursidae, see Bear family
Ursus, 43
  horribilis, 43
  middendorffi, 43

Vandellia cirrhosa, 264
Venom
  of centipede, 289
  of cobra, 145
  of cone shells, 291, 293
  of copperhead, 154
  of fer-de-lance, 154
  of fish, 238-250
  of insects, 271, 273, 276
  of jellyfish, 314, 315, 318
  of lizard, 123-124
  in mammals, 86-90
  of octopus, 307, 308
  of pit viper, 144
  of scorpion, 287
  of snakes, 123, 144-145, 147-148
  of spiders, 280, 281, 285
  of stingray, 236
  venomous stings and bites, treatment for, 330-332
Victorian Naturalist, 242
Vinegaroon, see Whip scorpion
Viper, 140
  berg adder, 161-162
  common viper, 161
  common European, illus. 164
  death adder, 174, 175
  fangs of, 143
  gaboon viper, 143, 161
  horned adder, 161, 166, 167
  Levantine, 166
  night adder, 161
  Old World species, 160-167
  puff adder, 161, 166, illus. 164
  range, 166-167
  rhinoceros viper, 161
  Russell's (Daboia), 166, 190
  sand viper, 162

saw-scaled, 162, 166, 167, 190, illus. 165
tree, 188
triangular-headed horned viper, 190
  see also Pit viper
Vipera ammodytes, 161, 162
  a. meridionalis, 162
  aspis, 162
  berus, 161, 162, 164
  latasti, 162
  lebetina, 166
  renardi, 162
  russelli, 166, 190
Viperidae, 140
Viverridae, 94
Voss, Gilbert
  on giant clam, 300
  on killer whale, 69-70
Vulture, 118-119

Wagler's viper, see Pit viper
Walker, Ernest P.
  on echidnas, 90
Walrus, illus. 57
  Eskimo economy and, 55
  general characteristics, 54-55
  range, 54
Wapiti, see Elk
Wasps, 273, 275-278, illus. 277
  bald-faced hornet, 277
  cicada killer, 277
  geting, 276
  mud dauber, 277
  polistes, 277
  yellow jacket, 277
Water moccasin, see Cottonmouth
Weasel, 94
Weever fish, 245-246
Whale, 109-110
  baleen whale, 60, 61
  beaching of, 61
  blue whale, 61
  gray whale, 110
  killer whale, 56, 58, illus. 66
    analysis of whale attack story (Calif. 1952), 62-67

Whale (continued)
    assessment of, 71-72
    diet, 60-61
    general characteristics, 60-61, 72
    as man-eater, 69-72
    range, 61
    reported attacks on man, 59-72
    sperm whale, 68, 109, 312
        attacks on man, 109-110
        rogue male, 109
    Taxonomy, 60
Whip scorpion, 289
Whitaker, Rr. Romulus, 348
Wiener, Dr. S., 241-242
    on giant clam, 300
Wilson, Edward A.
    on leopard seal, 56
Wolf, *illus.* 35, 38
    Custer wolf, 34, 36, 41
    extermination of, in eastern America, 34
    food supply-reproduction cycle 39-40
    gray wolf, 33
    general characteristics, 33
    Indian wolf, 33
    livestock damage, 36
    man and, 33-41
    rabies and, 40, 41
    range, 33
    red wolf, 32-33
    taxonomy, 32-33

    timber wolf, *illus.* 35
Wolf, Tasmanian, *see* Thylacine
Wolverine, 94
World Wildlife Fund
    on grizzly bear, 45
Worm
    marine bristle, 323
Wright, Bruce, 29, 261
    on crocodiles, 200-201
    on killer whale, 70
    on polar bear, 48
    Wildlife Sketches—Near and Far, 28, 200

Xiphias, 60
    gladius, 265

Yasiro, Hirataka
    on cone-shell bite, 293-294
Yonge, C. M.
    A Year on the Barrier Reef, 299
Young, Stanley P.
    on monotreme venom, 90
Young and Goldman, 39
    The Wolves of North America, 37

Zahl, Dr. Paul
    on crocodile, 200
    and giant clam, 301
Zebra, 100
Zebra fish, 243, 245